The Theaetetus
of Plato

MYLES BURNYEAT

The Theaetetus
of Plato

with a translation of
PLATO'S *Theaetetus* by
M. J. LEVETT
revised by
Myles Burnyeat

Hackett Publishing Company

Indianapolis / Cambridge

Copyright © 1990 by Hackett Publishing Company
Printed in the United States of America

99 98 97 96 95 94 93 92   2 3 4 5 6 7 8 9 10

Design by Dan Kirklin

For further information, please address
Hackett Publishing Company
P.O. Box 44937
Indianapolis, Indiana 46244-0937

Library of Congress Cataloging in Publication Data
Burnyeat, Myles.

The Theaetetus of Plato/Myles Burnyeat; with a translation of
Plato's Theaetetus by M. J. Levett, revised by Myles Burnyeat.
    p.   cm.
Includes bibliographical references.
ISBN 0-915144-82-4: ISBN 0-915144-81-6 (pbk.)
1. Plato. Theaetetus. 2. Knowledge, Theory of. I. Levett, M. J.
II. Plato. Theaetetus. English. 1990. III. Title.
B386.B87   1990
121—dc20   89-26936
                                                                      CIP

The paper used in this publication meets the minimum requirements
of American National Standard for Information Sciences—Permanence of
Paper for Printed Library Materials, ANSI Z39.48-1984.

CONTENTS

For Ruth

MEMOIR

The following brief account of the translator may be of interest.

Youngest of the five children of a yeoman farmer, Florence Margaret Jane Levett was born at Bodiam, near the border between Kent and Sussex, and retained throughout her life an affection for that part of England. A leading influence on her intellectual development was her elder sister, Ada Elizabeth, who (somewhat to her own surprise, in view of the mainly practical and out-door interests of the male members of the family) became successively Tutor in Modern History and Vice-Principal at St. Hilda's College, Oxford, and Professor of History at Westfield College, University of London.

With the active encouragement of this distinguished sister, some thirteen years her senior, Jane Levett studied Classics at Queen Anne's School, Caversham, and Clapham High School, and in 1913 went up to Lady Margaret Hall, Oxford. At Oxford she read Classical Moderations and *Literae Humaniores*, or 'Greats', a course in which ancient history and philosophy are studied in the original Greek and Latin, and philosophy, taught by the 'tutorial method', is treated as a living subject of current debate in the light of modern writings. Among her mentors were Cyril Bailey, editor of Lucretius, and J. A. Smith, the influence of whose scholarship and remarkable gifts as a philosophy tutor was much greater than might be supposed from his very limited output of published work.

At Oxford she met women whose friendship meant much to her and whose deaths (for she survived most of them) brought her many griefs, none more deeply felt than that arising from the too early death of the dearly loved sister to whom she owed so much.

After three years as a Lecturer at Cardiff, Miss Levett took up the appointment in the Department of Logic in the University of Glasgow which she retained until her retirement in 1958. It was for the benefit of the large Ordinary Class in this Department that she made her translation of Plato's *Theaetetus*, providing in lectures the comments and explanations of which raw students stood much in need. Other teaching which she undertook included Formal Logic, in a pre-Russellian tradition based on the syllogism and so-called 'immediate inference' and leading, it was hoped, to the detection and avoidance of fallacies with names like 'Amphiboly', 'Composition', 'Division', *'Ignoratio Elenchi'*, and *'Petitio Principii'*. She lectured on the history of modern philosophy, understood as comprising British Empiricism and continental Rationalism, and took her full share in tutorial and administrative work, in examining, and in deliberations about the curriculum and other student affairs. The rigorous standards which she strenuously upheld led a colleague in the Department to describe her as the keeper of its academic conscience.

Apart from the present translation and a short article on the alleged fallacy in the argument of Descartes's *Meditations*, she did not publish, and it may have been this lack of publication which deprived her of promotion to which, at least in the opinion of her friends, she would otherwise have been entitled. Her lectures were always carefully prepared, and the leisure of retirement was occupied in writing in her book-lined study under the discipline of intended publication.

A countrywoman by birth and upbringing, Miss Levett never became reconciled to the gloomy streets of a Scottish industrial city. Saturdays and Sundays, indeed, she spent among the heathery hills, the lochs and streams which lie within easy reach of Glasgow. But the end of each term saw her in her little car making for her home territory in Sussex or latterly for the cottage near Tenterden, in Kent, where eventually she spent the sixteen years of her retirement. Her large garden, with its apple trees and hedges, its vegetable patch and flower borders, its beloved birds and hated cats; walks among the lanes and on footpaths through the woods; the herons fishing in the flooded water-meadows and the sheep scattered over the Romney Marsh—these were to her the breath of life.

By nature a very private person, she was capable of deep friendship and to her friends was known as a person of outstanding intelligence, wit, and charm. She was also combative, as befits her family nickname of 'Lion'. Stupidity, vulgarity, or injustice aroused her contempt, expressed with vigour but also with some of the elegance of her admired Jane Austen. In keeping with her character was her fastidious and legible handwriting. It would be wrong to omit the very geninue humility which characterised not only her scholarship but also her personal relations.

She died in 1974, in her eightieth year.

July 1980   D.R.C.

PREFACE

The Translation

M. J. Levett's translation of the *Theaetetus*, first published in 1928, may claim to be the finest translation of any Platonic dialogue into English. No-one has equalled the skill, tact, and grace with which Miss Levett reproduces the imagery and idiomatic speech, the natural flow of conversation, the subtle shifts of tone, that make a Platonic dialogue so enchanting to read in the original and so hard to bring alive in a modern language.

A translation of such quality deserves to be more widely known. To this end I have tried to bring the text up to contemporary standards of accuracy without spoiling the style. The changes I have made are very numerous, and almost always very small: a word here, a phrase there, occasionally a sentence or two, but seldom fewer than six changes a page. This close scrutiny of Miss Levett's work, over a period of years, has confirmed and strengthened my respect for her achievement as a translator of Plato.

In revising Parts I and II of the dialogue, I was able to submit proposed changes to the late Professor D. R. Cousin for discussion and improvement. I am grateful to him both for the careful consideration he gave to approving them on Miss Levett's behalf and for the memoir of her which he wrote for this volume. The revisions to Part III and the final version of the whole are my responsibility.

The notes to the translation are my responsibility also. Some are her work, some mine, some a combination of the two. But it seemed appropriate to leave unchanged the Analysis of the dialogue added when the translation was reissued in 1977. 'Originally prepared by the translator, this was slimmed down in consultation with her and has long been in use in the University of Glasgow in practically its present form' (D. R. Cousin, Preface to 1977 edition). It is a record of her understanding of the shape and progress of the argument.

My advice to the reader is that you should use Miss Levett's Analysis to guide you through your first reading of the dialogue. The Introduction is for the slower reading and rereading that will follow.

In revising the translation and preparing the notes, I have inevitably made some controversial decisions. Any translation is also interpretation. In the case of a complex argumentative work like the

Theaetetus, a translator's view about the meaning of the text (even, at certain points, about what text to read) is closely intertwined with her or his sense of what the philosophical argument requires. This is not the place to debate technical issues of text and translation. The appropriate scholarly defence for my more controversial decisions, major or minor, will be provided elsewhere in an article called 'Notes on Plato's *Theaetetus*'.

The Introduction

It was Gilbert Ryle, a keen advocate of the Levett translation, who recommended that an introduction should be provided to bring out the continuing relevance of Plato's dialogue to present-day philosophical studies. This was when the 1977 reissue was in preparation at the University of Glasgow Press. It was hoped that Ryle would write the introduction himself. Platonic studies would have gained greatly had he done so. In the event the only additions in the 1977 reissue were Miss Levett's Analysis of the dialogue and a short Preface by D. R. Cousin. But when the late William Hackett invited me to write an introduction for a North American edition, the prescription he passed on was Ryle's: to bring out the continuing relevance of Plato's dialogue to present-day philosophical studies.

In attempting to meet this prescription I found that Part II of the dialogue required a longer and more demanding discussion than Part I, and Part III a longer and more demanding discussion than Part II. (As a first orientation, think of Part I of the Introduction as addressed to undergraduates, Part II to graduates, and Part III to colleagues in the Academy.) The reason for this is that Part II of the dialogue is shorter and more difficult than Part I, while Part III is shorter and more difficult than Part II. As the focus of discussion moves from perception in Part I to true judgement in Part II and on to accounts in Part III, the philosophical issues become more abstract, the writing less sensuous, and Plato leaves more and more of the thinking to his readers. Correspondingly, more help is needed from me and more demanding topics must be explored if the Introduction is to do justice to its dialogue.

The other side of this coin is that readers of the *Theaetetus* are required to contribute more and more as the dialogue proceeds. As I see it, your task in Part I is to *find* the meaning in the text and follow the argument to a satisfactory conclusion. In Part II you are challenged to *respond* to the meaning in the text by overcoming the problems and paradoxes that it leaves unresolved. In Part III the task is nothing less than to *create* from the text a meaning which will solve the problem of knowledge. What matters, then, is not how much experience you have of philosophy or of Plato, but your readiness to engage in philosophical reflection for yourself. It is for such readers, both younger and older, that the Introduction is written.

This is the place at which to thank the undergraduate class at UCLA and the very senior seminar in Tokyo who read an early version of the Introduction to Part I. Their lively and argumentative response encouraged me to think that the unorthodox approach I had adopted was achieving its aim.

I want also to thank the friends and colleagues without whose midwifery the project would never have been completed. The turning point came when Malcolm Schofield, besides offering valuable criticisms of what I had said about Part I, induced a total rewriting of the Introduction to Part II. The revised version, much clearer and kinder to its readers, was further improved by the keen eyes of David Sedley (who also helped with Part I) and Jonathan Barnes. Then, at a moment of despair about making sense of Part III, a conversation with Michael Frede helped me to see a way forward. The other decisive contribution to the approach I have adopted for Part III is a remark of John Cooper's, about deliberate ambiguity in the Dream, which has stayed with me since a memorable debate at Princeton in 1970. Finally, my understanding of the whole text, indeed of how to read and write about any Platonic text, owes much to Ruth Padel, on whose support and careful scrutiny of my sentences I have constantly relied.

Readers often expect from a preface some personal indication of how the author came to be interested in his subject. The answer in my case is a two-hour lecture on the *Theaetetus* that Bernard Williams gave at University College London in 1964. That was my first exposure to the interpretation of the argument of Part I which you will shortly meet as 'Reading B' and to other ideas of Williams's which have helped to shape the present Introduction. The lecture left me convinced that in the *Theaetetus* I had found a work of philosophy which would reward a lifetime's study. The conviction became knowledge during a joint seminar with him in 1968, and it was ultimately the undoing of a plan that we should collaborate in writing a philosophical commentary on the dialogue. The kind of definitive study we then intended is not to be written. The dialogue will always leave you with more questions than you have answered. In the Preface to the 1977 edition of the Levett translation D. R. Cousin spoke of 'the continuing search for understanding which the *Theaetetus* is so well adapted both to stimulate and to reward.' In that spirit I should like to thank Bernard Williams, not only for reading the whole Introduction in the final stages of its preparation and helping to clarify a number of important issues, but also for leaving me with one objection that I can only hope to be able to deal with in the future.

It remains to record my gratitude, first to William Hackett and then to Frances Hackett, for the trusting patience with which they awaited delivery of a project promised for October 1, 1979.

Robinson College, Cambridge   M.F.B.
March 31, 1989

INTRODUCTION

Plato's *Theaetetus* is a difficult but immensely rewarding dialogue. Because it is difficult, it has not been so widely read as dialogues like the *Phaedo, Symposium,* and *Republic,* nor so influential in the general current of ideas. But because it is so rewarding, it has long been valued within philosophy itself as being, of all Plato's works, the one with the most to say to a serious student of the subject.

Bishop Berkeley, for example, thought that in the *Theaetetus* Plato anticipated and approved the central tenets of his own theory of knowledge.[1] The eighteenth-century philosopher and moralist Richard Price recommended the dialogue for the opposite reason, for its *refutation* of the empiricist epistemologies made popular by Berkeley and Hume.[2]

That was a disagreement about the first part of the dialogue (151e–187a), which treats of the thesis that knowledge is perception. Plato's development and discussion of this thesis is one of the most elaborately sustained arguments in the whole history of philosophy, and while it bears (as Price and Berkeley recognized) on the assessment of empiricist theories of knowledge, it contains other riches as well: not least a section (166a ff.) in which the English pragmatist F.C.S. Schiller saw the pragmatist account of truth brilliantly expounded and then blunderingly condemned.[3] At the other end of the dialogue (201d–202b) Wittgenstein found an exemplary expression of the Logical Atomism which he and Bertrand Russell had once espoused.[4] The same passage prompted Leibniz, when he was writing an abridged translation of the *Theaetetus,* to comment: 'It is of great moment if rightly explicated.'[5] Moving on still further, the circularity which finally wrecks the dialogue's attempt

---

1. George Berkeley, *Siris: A Chain of Philosophical Reflexions and Inquiries Concerning the Virtues of Tar-Water* (1744), esp. §§ 311, 347–49.

2. Richard Price, *A Review of the Principal Questions in Morals* (1758), ed. D. D. Raphael (Oxford: 1974), 53–56.

3. F.C.S. Schiller, *Studies in Humanism* (London & New York: 1907), chap. 2; *Plato or Protagoras?* (Oxford & London: 1908).

4. Ludwig Wittgenstein, *Philosophical Investigations* (Oxford: 1953), § 46.

5. A. Foucher de Careil, *Nouvelles Lettres et Opuscules Inédits de Leibniz* (Paris: 1857), 138.

1

to define knowledge (209d–210a) has come to stand as an authoritative statement of a perennial difficulty for the project of analyzing knowledge in terms of true belief plus some appropriate sort of justification.[6]

The list could be enlarged. No other dialogue of Plato's speaks so directly to the concerns of the working philosopher in modern times. This is the case even when, or especially when, the line of thought is one that would not occur to a modern philosopher. The *Theaetetus* is not only the first major treatment of the problem of knowledge, a problem which has remained central to philosophy ever since; it is a classic treatment in the full sense of a work to which the philosopher can return time and again to find a challenge or stimulus to reflection. It is also a literary masterpiece, but with this difference from many Platonic dialogues, that in the *Theaetetus* Plato's artistic imagination is excited less by the interplay of the three characters who conduct the discussion than by the philosophical ideas themselves and the to-and-fro of dialectical argument.

What lies before us, then, is a drama of ideas and argument. It divides into three main parts, each a discussion precipitated by an answer to the question 'What is knowledge?'. Theaetetus' first answer is that knowledge is perception, his second that it is true judgement, and his third defines knowledge as true judgement with an account. Each proposal in turn is demolished by Socrates' relentless logic. We never learn what Plato thinks knowledge is. Nonetheless, we are clearly meant to see that the negative outcome of the inquiry is not defeat but progress.

At the end of the dialogue (210bc) we find Theaetetus both intellectually and morally improved. He has had more to say about knowledge than he could have without Socrates' help, and if he ever has any further ideas on the subject they will be the better for the testing he has undergone; meanwhile, he will be a gentler person through having come to appreciate what he does not know. What can this mean but that results, definite answers notched up as proven or learned, are not the sole criterion of progress either in education or in philosophy? There is as much or more to be learned from raising questions and then discovering *in detail* why a tempting but wrong answer is wrong.

This is a dialogue, not a treatise. As such it invites us not merely to witness but to participate ourselves in the philosophical activity

---

6. See e.g. Roderick M. Chisholm, *Theory of Knowledge* (Englewood Cliffs: 1966), 5–7, D. M. Armstrong, *Belief, Truth and Knowledge* (Cambridge: 1973), 153.

of the speakers. The most appropriate Introduction, therefore, is one that raises questions for readers to pursue in their own thinking. Not that I shall try to conceal my own views. That would be impossible, and besides, the invitation to participate is addressed to me as well as you. But my first concern will be to raise questions, to start lines of inquiry which will help you to see your way more clearly where things are difficult and to see that there are difficulties where things look clear. Some are questions of interpretation, some questions of philosophy. But anyone who really works on the dialogue will find that questions about Plato's meaning often turn into questions about philosophic truth, and vice versa. In the study of a great work of philosophy historical and philosophical understanding depend upon and reinforce each other.

Prologue and introductory conversation (142a–151d)

In the opening pages of the work the characters are introduced and the problem stated. Socrates meets Theodorus, an old and distinguished mathematician visiting Athens from Cyrene in 399 B.C.: the fateful year of Socrates' trial and death. They are joined by Theaetetus, a local lad of sixteen or even less and Theodorus' most brilliant pupil. Theaetetus will grow up to make original contributions to solid geometry and the theory of irrationals which rank him as one of the great mathematicians of antiquity. We will shortly hear of his first independent mathematical discovery (147d–148b), but already, in the little prologue which precedes the main dialogue, we have glimpsed him at the far end of his career, a famous man about to die after a battle in 369 B.C. It is scarcely surprising that this prologue has been read by many scholars as Plato's way of dedicating the dialogue to the memory of a recently departed friend and colleague. But we should not fail to think about the dramatic emphasis which Plato has contrived to place on the notion of *expertise*. In these early pages of the dialogue our attention is drawn both to an accomplished mastery in the person of Theodorus and to the process of acquiring it in the case of Theaetetus.

Expertise is specialized knowledge (knowledge which most people do not have), hence it is problematic if knowledge itself is problematic. It is in connection with expertise that Socrates first says he wants to ask what knowledge is (145ce with note ad loc.). And when Theaetetus gives his first answer to that question

(146cd), it is a list of branches of knowledge or areas of expertise, both theoretical (geometry and the mathematical sciences) and practical (cobbling and other crafts). Yet in reply Socrates insists (146d–147c) not only that a plurality of examples is something quite different from the unitary definition he requested, but also, more strongly, that they are in no position to know any examples of knowledge until they know what knowledge itself is.[7] The questions now begin.

(1) If we are debarred from saying we know that geometry is an example of knowledge, what does this imply for the dramatic role in which Plato has cast Theodorus and Theaetetus? Must we be uncertain about their expertise? Or should we, on the contrary, take their expertise as something which an adequate account of knowledge should cater for? That, however, might lead us to think of Theaetetus' first properly formulated definition, 'Knowledge is perception', as mistaken from the start. The discussion will later (161b ff.) dwell at length on the question whether the definition does or does not allow for the possibility of expertise, but at first glance to define knowledge as sense-perception hardly seems compatible with the existence of expertise in an abstract field like mathematics, or even in the more practical sphere of cobbling. Should we then say, with a distinguished modern philosopher, 'The definition "Knowledge is sense-perception" could have been dismissed at once by looking to Theaetetus' examples of knowledge'?[8]

(2) More generally, it is a problem to see how we can look for a definition, or discuss the merits of one that has been proposed, if we do not know any examples of the concept to be defined. Thus Wittgenstein complained, 'When Socrates asks the question "what is knowledge?" he does not even regard it as a *preliminary* answer to enumerate cases of knowledge'.[9] Wittgenstein's talk of a 'prelimi-

---

7. When Socrates asserts that a person who does not know what knowledge is does not understand names like 'geometry' and 'cobbling', he obviously does not mean that he and Theaetetus are in the same position as a foreigner who does not understand the language at all. They have the ordinary linguistic understanding which enables one to gloss 'cobbling' by 'knowledge of the making of shoes'. What they lack, through not knowing the definition of knowledge, is a clear philosophical understanding of what it is for cobbling to be knowledge of shoes and geometry knowledge of something else. So they cannot decide whether what ordinary language calls a branch of knowledge really is knowledge. For other examples of a philosophical nonunderstanding which presupposes ordinary linguistic understanding, see 184a, 196e, *Republic* 505bc, *Sophist* 243b.

8. P. T. Geach [10], 372. (Numbers in square brackets refer to works cited in the bibliography of further reading.)

9. Ludwig Wittgenstein, *The Blue and Brown Books* (Oxford: 1958), 20.

nary answer' suggests that it might help if we are allowed to have *beliefs* about examples, even if at this stage of the inquiry these beliefs cannot count as secure knowledge. We may believe that such and such or such and such are cases of knowledge, but we must hold ourselves ready to revise our beliefs in the light of the final decision on what knowledge actually is. Even this would meet with opposition in some quarters.

G. E. Moore has made famous a line of argument according to which there are many examples of knowledge which are *beyond question* examples of knowledge because they are much more certain than any philosophical principle used to impugn them could possibly be. No restrictive definition or tightened-up conditions of knowledge, implying that none of us knows, for example, that he has a pencil in his hand, could be anything like as certain as that we do have this knowledge.[10] Here is quite a challenge for Socrates. Admittedly, Moore's type of example, to do with pencils and hands, is very different from Theaetetus' citing of geometry and cobbling, but Socrates seems to exclude examples of any type. We may well wonder whether he will allow us to take anything at all for granted in advance of settling on the definition of knowledge. Have we any secure foothold to work out from? A full answer to these questions can only be obtained by carefully watching Socrates' procedure throughout the dialogue, but two passages are especially relevant: 146d–147c, where it is not easy to see what exactly Socrates is arguing for, and how; and the remarks at 196d–197a, where it is a question how much of what Socrates says is serious and how much ironical.

(3) Returning to expertise, we may further ask: What is the relation between individual items of knowledge (e.g. knowing that one has a pencil in hand or, to switch to the example with which Socrates starts us off at 152b, knowing that the wind is cold) and the mastery of a whole body of knowledge which is implied in the notion of expertise? Presumably expertise is not just knowing a vast number of items in a given domain: there must be some systematic grasp of relationships and dependencies between the items. But what exactly would that involve? This question will become important in Part III of the dialogue.

(4) Socrates' reply to Theaetetus' first suggestion implies that he thinks that the geometer's and the cobbler's knowledge (assuming they are knowledge) can and should both be brought under a single

10. G. E. Moore, *Some Main Problems of Philosophy* (London & New York: 1953), 119–26, and other references collected in Burnyeat [12].

account. He wants a single unitary definition to capture the essence common to both. But is this expectation realistic? Would Plato have done better to separate off practical from theoretical knowledge, perhaps along the lines of the distinction modern philosophers often make between knowing how to do something and knowing that something is the case?[11] Before jumping to a conclusion on these matters, one should look ahead to see how practical knowledge is actually treated in the discussion. Especially relevant is 177c–179b, where the doctor, the farmer, the cook, and other practical professions are cited for their ability to give expert judgements about the future. Specifically, they can say, in a given case, what will bring about health or an enjoyable dinner, and so on. The question to ask Plato now is this: Do judgements expressing knowledge of fact, e.g. knowledge of what will achieve a given end, exhaust the content of practical knowledge—in which case practical knowledge might well yield to the same analysis as theoretical knowledge—or are they merely the only aspect pertinent to the argument on hand?

*   *   *   *   *   *   *   *   *   *   *   *

After this bundle of questions we are ready to be introduced to the master of philosophical questioning, Socrates himself. His very first speech (143de) brings out his character as educator of the young, but he is no expert and what Theaetetus will get from him is something very different from the teaching of Theodorus. Socrates is like a midwife: his questions will direct a painful process of bringing to birth Theaetetus' own conceptions and then testing their soundness.

The passage (148e–151d) in which Socrates compares himself to a midwife is deservedly one of the most famous Plato ever wrote; it should be read with feeling as well as thought. It is an account of

---

11. The classic statement of the distinction is Gilbert Ryle, 'Knowing How and Knowing That', *Proceedings of the Aristotelian Society* N.S. 46 (1945/6), 1–16; also *The Concept of Mind* (London: 1949), chap. 2. The question how far Plato in the *Theaetetus* got clear about knowing how vs. knowing that is a main theme of Runciman [5]. But the clarity of the distinction itself has been challenged by Zeno Vendler, *Res Cogitans* (Ithaca & London: 1972), chap. 5, and by D. G. Brown, 'Knowing How and Knowing That, What', in O. P. Wood & G. Pitcher edd., *Ryle: A Collection of Critical Essays* (London & Basingstoke: 1971), 213–48. It is a further question how the modern distinction between knowing how to do something and knowing that something is the case lines up with the ancient distinction between practical and theoretical *branches* of knowledge.

a method of education which is at the same time a method of doing philosophy, and there are questions to ask about why it seems especially appropriate to *philosophy*, as opposed to geometry or cobbling, that its procedure should be a discussion in which Socratic questioning engages with one's own personal conception of things. But the passage is also an introduction to the discussion to come, especially its first part (the midwife figure is sustained all the way through Part I but then drops out of sight until the concluding remarks at 210bc). From 151d to 160e Theaetetus' conception of knowledge is being brought to birth; only when his child is fully born can the testing begin. This is an important piece of evidence for a major issue to which we must now turn, the interpretation of Plato's strategy in dealing with the definition of knowledge as perception.

PART I

'Knowledge is perception'

The overall strategy of 151d–184a

It is essential to try to get a sense of the whole discussion 151d–184a before getting stuck into its individual sections. How one reads the individual sections will depend a great deal on one's conception of the overall strategy into which they fit.

Three distinct theses are in play: Theaetetus' definition of knowledge as perception, Protagoras' doctrine that man is the measure of all things, Heraclitus' theory of flux. Protagoras' doctrine, as Plato interprets it,[12] maintains the relative truth of all appearances: however things appear to someone, things *are for this person* just the way they appear, and if they appear different to someone else,

12. The question how far Plato gives a faithful account of the teaching of the historical Protagoras need not concern us: see Kerferd [23], Vlastos [24], Jonathan Barnes, *The Presocratic Philosophers* (London, Henley & Boston: 1979), Vol. II, chap. 10. Protagoras was born early in the fifth century B.C. and had died some years before our discussion begins (cf. 164e, 168e).

then *for that person* they really and truly *are* different. Heraclitus' contribution is the thesis that everything is changing all the time, as summed up in the famous paradox 'You cannot step into the same river twice' (cf. 160d: 'all things flow like streams').[13] Two questions arise: How, in Plato's view, are the three theses related to one another in the discussion? What in fact are the underlying philosophical connections between them? It is on the answer to these questions that the disagreement between Price and Berkeley (p. 1) depends.

Here is one reading of Plato's strategy, which makes things come out in the manner Berkeley would wish.[14] Plato himself accepts the theories of Protagoras and Heraclitus, subject to certain qualifications: in particular the theories must be restricted (as their authors did not take care to restrict them) to perception and the world of sensible things. Sensible things are, Plato agrees, in a perpetual flux of becoming, and in perception each of us has a 'measure', i.e. an incorrigible awareness, of the sensible qualities whose coming and going constitute that flux. But Plato will then argue that this awareness, incorrigible though it be, is not *knowledge*, precisely because its objects belong to the realm of becoming, not being. It has been agreed from the start (152c) that any candidate for knowledge must pass two tests: it must be always of what is and it must be unerring. Thanks to Protagoras, perception passes the second test, but thanks to Heraclitus, in the end it fails the first. Thus the argument, taken as a whole, supports the view set forth at length in earlier dialogues like the *Phaedo* and *Republic*, the celebrated Platonic doctrine that true reality is a nonsensible realm of changeless being, the Forms, and it is in these alone that knowledge can find its objects.

To sum up this reading (call it Reading A): perception is something of which Protagoras and Heraclitus give a true account. But nothing of which these theories are true can yield knowledge. Therefore, knowledge is not perception.[15]

---

13. Again, there is controversy about Plato's historical understanding of Heraclitus: see W.K.C. Guthrie, *A History of Greek Philosophy* Vol. I (Cambridge: 1962), chap. VII, Charles H. Kahn, *The Art and Thought of Heraclitus* (Cambridge: 1979). The dates of Heraclitus' life are difficult to determine, but he was probably in middle age around 500 B.C.

14. See Cornford [2]. It would be fair to say that, in one version or another, this is the reading most commonly found in the scholarly literature on Plato.

15. Readers of Berkeley may wonder how he could endorse this conclusion, for did he not himself hold that perceiving is knowing (e.g. *Principles of Human Knowledge* [1710], §§ 1–6)? The answer is that in *Siris* Berkeley uses 'knowledge' to mean *science*, understanding the connections between the things we perceive and (in the *Principles*

Now for a rival reading (call it Reading B), more in harmony with the antiempiricist moral that Price wished to draw.[16] Plato does not accept the theories of Protagoras and Heraclitus. Theaetetus is made to accept them because, having defined knowledge as perception, he is faced with the question, What has to be true of perception and of the world for the definition to hold good? The answer suggested is that he will have to adopt a Protagorean epistemology, and that in turn will commit him to a Heraclitean account of the world. It takes Socrates until 160e to work out with Theaetetus these consequences of the definition of knowledge as perception, after which he shows that the three-in-one theory they have elaborated (Theaetetus' first-born child) leads to multiple absurdities, culminating in a proof (179c–183c) that if the theory were true it would make language impossible. Thus the structure of the argument is that of a *reductio ad absurdum*: Theaetetus → Protagoras → Heraclitus → the impossibility of language. Hence Theaetetus' definition is impossible.

This is only the barest outline of two ways of construing the elaborate argument of Part I. They are not the only possible interpretations, but they are sufficiently opposed to one another to focus the issue of strategy. You, the reader, must now watch for the stage-directions, as it were, which Plato scatters through the text to indicate how he views the three theses and their interrelations: e.g. at 151e–152c, 152e, 155de, 157cd, 158e, 160ce, 163a, 164d, 166ab, 168b, 177c, 179cd, 183ac. And you must consider for yourself which construal makes a better job of threading one section to the next to shape a philosophically coherent whole.

To illustrate: a key passage, on any reading, is 160de, centrally and emphatically placed at a turning point in the discussion. Socrates is summing up the whole process of bringing Theaetetus' conception of knowledge to birth before he turns to test it for soundness. He says that the three theses have been found to coincide: all three come to the same thing. In particular, he represents Theaetetus' view (160e) as the view that *since* all things change (Heraclitus) and man is the measure of all things (Protagoras), knowledge proves to be perception. In other words, he represents Theaetetus as relying on Protagoras and Heraclitus to support his definition. How are we to take this declaration?

---

sense) know. Cf. *Siris* §§ 253, 304–5. So what Berkeley thought the dialogue proves is that sense-perception is not science (expertise).

16. Sketched in Burnyeat [16] but originally formulated by Bernard Williams (cf. p. xiii).

On Reading A Socrates only says that all three theses come to the same thing because he has been making the best case he can for the definition of knowledge as perception. He will later refute 'Knowledge is perception' while retaining (some of) Protagoras and Heraclitus, so he cannot seriously think that all three stand or fall together. On Reading B this is just what he does think. Protagoras and Heraclitus provide sufficient conditions for Theaetetus' definition to come out correct (160e; cf. 183a). What Socrates has been arguing at length down to 160e is that they are the only sufficient conditions which could reasonably be devised. That means they are necessary conditions (Theaetetus → Protagoras → Heraclitus) as well as sufficient (Heraclitus → Protagoras → Theaetetus), and the three theses really do stand or, later, fall together.

That must suffice to set the question of strategy. It should whet the appetite for a closer examination of the part played by Protagoras and Heraclitus in the bringing to birth of Theaetetus' child.

Exposition of the three theses (151d–160e)

'Knowledge is perception' has a decidedly empiricist ring to it. In brief, empiricism is the doctrine that all knowledge has its source in sense-experience, although of course a bald statement like this admits of, and has been given, many different interpretations. If we may continue, nevertheless, to speak baldly and roughly, it can be said that, historically, there has been a tendency among empiricist philosophers to find the paradigm of knowledge and certainty in the immediate awareness of sensible qualities such as red or hot (Berkeleyan ideas, twentieth-century sense-data). We shall find something closely similar in the *Theaetetus*, and it was this, of course, that led Berkeley to identify the *Theaetetus* theory of perception with his own (p. 8). Once a view of that sort has been adopted, it is then one of the tasks of an empiricist epistemology to explain how on such foundations we can build the rest of knowledge, or at least, if that seems too ambitious, erect a structure of more or less reasonable belief.

Now the thesis that knowledge is perception breaks down into two propositions: (1) all perceiving is knowing, (2) all knowing is perceiving. The *Theaetetus* shows little recognition of the more generous empiricism that would result if the 'is' in (2) was changed to 'gets its content from' or, less stringently, 'is based on'. Nor is the dialogue interested in the (perhaps characteristically modern) idea that, where knowledge runs out, we may still seek reasonable belief. But the question whether the senses provide us with knowledge and certainty and, if they do, what kind of knowledge and certainty this is, goes to the heart of any empiricist programme. It is with this question that Part I of the dialogue is concerned.

However, propositions (1) and (2) are still vague. A precise meaning needs to be specified for them if philosophical progress is to be made. Socrates suggests (151e–152a) that the meaning is given, in different language, by Protagoras' doctrine that man is the measure of all things. This doctrine is expounded in terms of the example of the wind which feels cold to one person and not to another, and so according to Protagoras *is* cold for the one and not so for the other. And argument is given (152bc) to show that from Protagoras' Measure Doctrine we may derive proposition (1): all perceiving is knowing. (Question: what about proposition (2)? Could this also be derived from Protagoras? What role does (2) have in the sequel?) All perceiving is knowing because Protagoras' doctrine of the relative truth of all appearances enables perception to pass two tests which any candidate for knowledge must meet (p. 8). Every perceptual appearance is shown to be the *unerring* apprehension of *how things are* for the perceiver.

The logical analysis of the argument for this conclusion will provide a nice task for the reader's leisure. At present we should attend to the premise which is accepted by Theaetetus, without argument, at 152b: 'it appears' means 'he perceives it' or, rephrasing in the material mode, to perceive something is to have it appear to one.

From the example of the wind it is clear that the relevant kind of appearing is that which is expressed by such a sentence as 'The wind appears cold to me'. Recast in terms of the verb 'perceive', this will become: 'I perceive that the wind is cold'. So in its generalized form the premise may be stated thus: x appears F to a (where x is an object, F a sensible quality, and a a perceiving subject) if and only if a perceives that x is F. This means that the perceiving we will be concerned with is perceiving that such and such is the case, as contrasted with perceiving objects: 'a perceives that x is F' represents such constructions as 'He sees that the stone is white' (cf. 156e), 'He tastes the sweetness of wine' or 'He finds his food bitter' (cf. 159cd, 166e), 'He perceives the lyre to be out of tune' (cf. 178d), in contrast to: 'He sees the stone', 'He hears the lyre', and the like, which incorporate no reference to any sensible aspect the perceiver is aware of in the object perceived, and which do not say what he perceives it *as*.

This decision on how 'perceiving' is to be taken will prove critical
later (179c, 184b ff.), when questions are raised about the role of
judgement in perception. At this stage, however, we must ask
about the *status* of the identification of perceiving with appearing.
It seems to be supplementary to Protagoras' Measure Doctrine,
rather than part of it, for the Measure Doctrine, as stated, does not
mention perceiving. Hence to derive proposition (1) a supplementary premise is needed which does mention perceiving and identifies it with the key Protagorean notion of appearing. Is the extra
premise one that Plato inserts because he believes it to be true
(Reading A)? Or is the thought rather this, that Theaetetus will
need to take perception this way, to assume some element of judgement or conceptualization, or else he has no chance of making out
that perceiving is knowing (Reading B)? The text does not tell us.
We must decide as we go along which answer best illuminates the
whole discussion.

The next step (152ce) brings an analogous problem. The suggestion that perhaps Protagoras taught a secret Heraclitean doctrine is
not intended as a serious historical attribution—so much would
now be generally agreed—but it might nonetheless be serious as
philosophy. Reading A sees here nothing more than a humorous
device whereby Plato can introduce 'a fundamental principle of his
own philosophy',[17] that all sensible objects are perpetually changing
(p. 8). Others, however, are not so sure that so bald a principle
does accurately represent Plato's earlier views about the sensible
world,[18] or if it does, that we can assume that in the *Theaetetus* Plato
still adheres to it; maybe he wants to rethink his position.[19] It is
important, then, that Plato could quite seriously be maintaining
that all this Protagorean talk about things being what they are *for*
someone is something of a riddle (cf. 155de, 162a), which can be
clarified if it is translated into the Heraclitean idiom of becoming.
Thus '*x* is *F* for *a*' gives way to '*x* becomes *F* for *a*'. On Reading B
this would not be a commitment on Plato's part to a Heraclitean
theory of perception and the sensible world, but a commitment on
Theaetetus' part to clarify and develop the Protagorean epistemology he has just accepted.

17. Cornford [2], 36.

18. E.g. Alexander Nehamas, 'Plato on the Imperfection of the Sensible World',
American Philosophical Quarterly 12 (1975), 105–17; T. H. Irwin, 'Plato's Heracliteanism', *Philosophical Quarterly* 27 (1977), 1–13.

19. For a now famous scholarly controversy concerning the development of Plato's
views about flux in the sensible world, see Owen [18] *vs.* Cherniss [19].

What is gained by moving over to the idiom of becoming? Officially, it is to help with a certain problem about opposites. Opposite predicates like 'large' and 'small', 'heavy' and 'light', have the peculiar property that, when you find a thing to which one of the pair applies, it transpires that the opposite applies as well. (For the moment Plato leaves his readers to work out their own illustrative examples.) You cannot say 'x is F' and leave it at that (152d: 'there is nothing which in itself is just one thing'). You must add 'x is $*F$', where $*F$ is the opposite of F. But if F and $*F$ are opposites, in some sense they are incompatible with one another. The problem is to see how a thing can manage to be both F and $*F$.

There is no question but that this problem underlies many of Heraclitus' own paradoxical utterances,[20] but what is its relevance here? Does a Protagorean epistemology allow opposite predicates to be true of the same thing? If it does, how will the language of becoming help to make this intelligible? On any reading, the answer to these questions takes some while to emerge.

We are first (153ad) given some general considerations favouring a Heraclitean outlook on the world. (Do a count of the jokes in this bit. With a master dramatist like Plato, the tone of a passage can be an important guide to how we should respond.) Then come some rather more argumentative considerations (153d ff.) on behalf of Protagorean relativism, culminating in the statement and analysis (154c–155c) of a pair of puzzles about the opposites 'larger' and 'smaller', 'more' and 'less', puzzles which look to be structurally analogous to the original problem about 'large' and 'small', 'heavy' and 'light'. But the analogy is also an advance, inasmuch as the new puzzles are explicitly about relative predicates (e.g. the six dice are more *than four* and less *than twelve*). Their solution can thus serve as a perspicuous model for the thoroughgoing relativization which Protagoras recommends. When you add an explicit specification of the different relations in which opposite predicates hold of the same thing, the contradiction disappears. Finally, at 155d–156a the Heraclitean explanation of all this is at last announced. It becomes clear that relativization is not the complete answer to our problem, for Socrates proceeds to a complicated account (156a ff.) of perception, perceivers, and sensible things which spells out Protagorean relativity in the language of becoming.

---

20. E.g. 'Sea is the most pure and the most polluted water: drinkable and salutary for fishes, but undrinkable and destructive for men' (frag. 61); 'The path up and down is one and the same' (frag. 60); 'As the same thing there exists in us living

Let us look first at the Protagorean component of this account. It is recommended in the section 153d–154b by one of the most influential patterns of argument in the history of epistemology: the argument from conflicting appearances. It is a familiar fact of experience that the colour (taste, shape, temperature) of an object will appear different to different observers in the varying circumstances of observation. From this mundane starting-point it is inferred that the colour white, for example, is not inherent in the object, not a feature which characterizes the object in itself; white exists only in relation to a given observer, 'between' their eye and the object (154a), and it is therefore private to them (154a; cf. 161d, 166c), something of which only they can be aware.

That, in brief, is the argument from conflicting appearances as it is found in the *Theaetetus*, in the first of Berkeley's *Three Dialogues between Hylas and Philonous* (1713), in the first chapter of Russell's *The Problems of Philosophy* (1912), and in many other distinguished thinkers. The twentieth-century 'argument from illusion' for the thesis that what we perceive is sense-data (e.g. a private white), rather than whole physical objects, is a variant on the same theme, the main difference being that to call it the 'argument from illusion' presupposes we know which of the conflicting appearances is correct.[21]

It is worth pondering the argument both in the abstract and in the specific version presented here. What assumptions are required to validate the inference and how many of them does Plato make explicit? Does he need to have Socrates start from the extraordinarily strong claim (154a) that colour appearances are *never* the same between man and other animals, between one man and another, or even between one time and another within the experience of a single man? Why does Plato (unlike Berkeley and Russell, for example) couple the argument showing that white is not inherent in the object with another to show that neither is it inherent in the perceiving subject (154b)?[22] Most important of all, what (if anything)

---

and dead and the waking and the sleeping and young and old; for these having changed about are those and those having changed about are these' (frag. 88).

21. A well-known discussion of the argument from illusion is A. J. Ayer, *The Foundations of Empirical Knowledge* (London & New York: 1940), chap. 1.

22. There is one modern parallel for this second argument, in F. H. Bradley, *Appearance and Reality* 2nd edition (Oxford: 1897), 9–10, where it looks very likely that Bradley has our *Theaetetus* passage specifically in mind. However, on another interpretation (McDowell [3], 132) the second issue at 154b is not whether the perceiver's eye is white but whether he can be said, without qualification, to be seeing white.

does the conflict of appearances really tell us about the nature and objects of perception?

If these questions suggest lines of inquiry into resemblances and differences between modern empiricist theories of perception and the perceptual relativism which Plato develops out of Protagoras' Measure Doctrine, they may also prompt a further thought, which the history of epistemology amply confirms. It is that you cannot go far with this sort of theory without involving yourself, as both Berkeley and Russell did, with questions about the ordinary physical objects (sticks and stones, tables and chairs) which we ordinarily think, before we start to theorize, are the things we perceive. What implications does our theory bring for them? Notoriously, Berkeley held that a stone or a table can be nothing more than a 'collection of ideas': compare 157b. In *The Problems of Philosophy*, on the other hand, Russell thought that there was something more than appearances or sense-data, viz. the physical objects which cause us to have sense-data, but that what these physical objects are like in themselves could only be known with difficulty and by inference. If that idea seems alien to the approach followed in the *Theaetetus*, the contrast may itself serve to emphasize the extent to which the two propositions comprising Theaetetus' definition subordinate everything to the securing of certainty (pp. 10–11).

Thus, summing up the argument so far, from Theaetetus' definition we have the thesis (1) that perception, and (2) that perception alone, provides knowledge and certainty, and from Protagoras' Measure Doctrine we have a guarantee that every perceptual appearance will be the unerring apprehension of how things are for the perceiver; this secures for perception the certainty that Theaetetus requires. In addition, all through 153d–155c it has been brought home to us that what enables Protagoras to achieve this result is his strategy of relativization. And we can see why that should be so important. If there is no question of the wind being cold in itself, or not cold, but it is cold for one perceiver and not for another, then there is no question of one perceiver being right where the other is wrong about the temperature of the wind. There is no such thing as *the* temperature of the wind by which to correct, or confirm, someone who says that it is cold. There is no independent fact of the matter which they could be mistaken about. It seems reasonable to claim, therefore, that each perceiver is necessarily and incorrigibly right about all there is for them to be right about, namely, how it is *for them*. But what now becomes of the wind which we have described as cold for one perceiver and not for another, or the stone which is white for one person and a different colour for another? What about the perceivers themselves? And this coldness or whiteness existing privately for the one perceiver but not for the other? What sorts of item are these? The question is pressing, whether we take it as a question for Plato about the further development of his own theory (Reading A) or as a question for Theaetetus about the ontological basis for his Protagorean account of knowledge (Reading B). The strategy of a systematic relativization of sensory predicates makes problematic the whole nature of what we ordinarily think of as the physical world.

This brings us to the Heraclitean story set forth at 156a ff. The story teaches that there are no *things*, only processes—the world is a vast array of motions, some with active power and others passive. There are no *properties* of things either, but again only motions, produced in pairs by the pairing of an active and a passive member of the first group of motions, and distinguished from the latter inasmuch as the twin offspring are always swift motions while the parental pair are slow. As we ordinarily think of, e.g. visual perception, it is a relation between two things—say Socrates or, more narrowly, his eye, and a stone—one of which has the property of seeing and the other the property which is seen, e.g. whiteness. The Heraclitean story does away with things and properties, and would have us think instead in terms of four interacting motions:

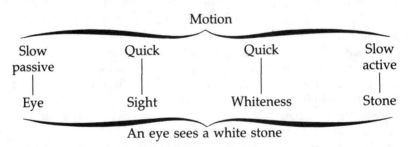

An eye sees a white stone

This is a remarkable theory. How exactly does it help the discussion forward?

One can interpret the theory in two very different ways, the first broadly speaking physical, the second metaphysical. To illustrate the difference, consider one detail, the description of whiteness and sight as moving through space between eye and object (156d). Is this literally meant as an account of what goes on in perception, so that we could think of colour and sight as rays of energy or streams of particles travelling from one place to another? The physical interpretation says: Yes, this is at least an outline framework for the sort of account Plato himself gives of colour vision in his cosmological work, the *Timaeus* (45b–46c, 67c–68d).[23] (The physical interpretation is thus a natural, though not perhaps an inevitable concomitant of Reading A.) The *Timaeus* account is all about particles of fire streaming out from the eye and coalescing with other fire particles emitted from physical objects, the varieties of the latter particles being coordinated with the varieties of colour seen. The *Theaetetus* story is less detailed, more of an outline than a completed theory, but it is making the same *sort* of claim and some of the same specific claims.

To this the metaphysical interpretation will reply that the *Timaeus* assumes stable objects to give off the particles and stable sense-organs to respond; the theory presupposes the notion of things having a continuing identity through time, which it is the very purpose of the *Theaetetus* story to deny.[24] Objects cannot have a continuing identity through time if every feature they manifest is relativized to a single perceiver and to the time of their perception, and every feature must be so relativized if perceptual awareness is to be incorrigible: stability through time, no less than objectivity between different observers, would constitute an independent fact of the matter by reference to which one perception could be counted right, another wrong. If that is the thought behind the theory, it goes well with Reading B: Theaetetus → Protagoras → Heraclitus. From this perspective it is not surprising that no mention is made of particles or stuff of a physical sort, or that no content is given to the contrast between swift and slow motions other than that the former involve two locations, the latter just one. If we stop expecting 'scientific' details of the type given in the *Timaeus*, we can take the talk of whiteness and sight moving through space between momentary eye and momentary stone as designed to bring out the point that seeing is seeing something *over there from here*, and whiteness is whiteness manifesting itself *there to me here*. Reference to two locations is intrinsic to the description of sight and colour in a way it is not intrinsic to the description of eye and stone, even though these also, on the theory, come into being, or occur, at their respective locations only as the stone acting and the eye responding

23. For elucidation of the *Timaeus* passages, see F. M. Cornford, *Plato's Cosmology* (London: 1937).

24. For other difficulties in the project of matching up the two dialogues, see McDowell [3], 139.

at the same moment of time. We can enjoy the picturesque detail without forcing it into a scientific mould. For the Heraclitean story which Plato recounts with imaginative delight is a metaphysical projection of a world in which the Protagorean epistemology holds good.

No doubt the physical interpretation can hit back by pointing out that at the metaphysical level the *Timaeus* would agree that ordinary objects are changing all the time (cf. *Tim.* 48e–52c); Plato need see no inconsistency in combining this, his usual metaphysical view (p. 8), with the sketch of a physical theory of perception. But the reader may now be left to follow the story to the triumphant climax of 160de, where the three theses come together to proclaim that no perceiver can fail to be a knower of that which they perceive. On the way you will recognize the first extant statement (157e–158e) of the now classic problems, whether it is possible to determine that one is sane and not mad, awake and not dreaming: problems which were to assume great importance in the first of Descartes's *Meditations* (1641). From the absence of any clear indication by which to tell which state one is in, Descartes is tempted to infer that, for all we know, any experience might be the illusion of a dream. The conclusion drawn in the *Theaetetus* is not this radical scepticism, but it is hardly less dramatic. It is not that any experience might be the illusion of a dream, hence false, but that any experience has as much right to be considered veridical as any other; all are on a par, all true for the individual subject who has them, no matter what the conditions (dreaming, madness, etc.) under which they occur. This disarms the objection of common sense that a dreamer perceives nothing real at all, while sickness makes one liable to misperceive.

To confirm the conclusion that there is no such thing as a false perception, the discussion then moves into a tricky argument (158e–160c) for a completely universal thesis of nonidentity over time. The healthy, sane, or waking Socrates who finds his wine sweet is totally distinct from the unhealthy, mad, or dreaming Socrates who finds his wine bitter, and there are two distinct wines as well. We end up conjoining, as it were, Berkeley's dissolution of physical objects into a series of ideas perceived with Hume's dissolution of the self into a series of perceptions.[25] Indeed, it is a question whether, at the end of the day, we are even allowed to construe the perceiving subject or perceived object as an aggregate of distinct

25. David Hume, *A Treatise of Human Nature* (1739), Bk. I, Pt. IV, Sect. VI.

perceptions/sensible qualities perceived. Compare 157b with 160b.
It is clear that 'people' employ names for such aggregates, not so
clear that this practice has the approval of the wise Heracliteans
whose story culminates in a decree of Necessity that ties each
momentary perceiver and its perceived partner to each other and
to nothing else.[26] Sorting all this out will challenge the reader to
reach at least an interim decision on the interpretative and philosophical issues we have been discussing.

On any account we have travelled a long way from Theaetetus'
first hesitant proposal of the definition of knowledge as perception
(151de). Thanks to Socrates' skill as a midwife of ideas, Theaetetus'
original conception has proved a larger thing than he foresaw.
It has grown into a whole theory of knowledge and the world,
astonishing not only for its anticipations of modern empiricist
themes, but even more for its own audacious combination of logical
rigour and philosophical imagination. It is time to see whether the
new-born child can survive in the cold light of Socrates' criticism.

Critique of the three theses (160e–184a)

When Theaetetus' travail is finally over and Socrates turns to examine the worth of his offspring, the first, and for much of the ensuing
discussion the dominant, issue is one the relevance of which is not
immediately obvious: whether the epistemology which Theaetetus
has borrowed from Protagoras allows for the possibility of wisdom.

The first point to make is that the Greek word translated 'wisdom'
has in this context the connotations of 'expertise'.[27] Remember also
that Socrates' question 'What is knowledge?' was originally
prompted by the idea that wisdom, that is, expertise, is (a matter of)
knowledge (145e, p. 3). The issue is not, of course, whether on the
account of knowledge we have elaborated with such care there can
be knowledge. The question whether there can be expertise is the
question whether there can be specialist knowledge (in geometry,
for example) such that one person is more knowledgeable than others, knows things that most people do not, has the truth where others are ignorant or wrong. That is how the discussion can treat the
following four propositions as equivalent: (i) each man is the mea-

---

26. The question of aggregates will come up again in Part III (p. 203). The difficulties
of deciding their status in Part I are discussed by McDowell [3], 143–45, Bostock [9],
66 ff., 153–54.

27. See note *ad* 145d.

sure of his own wisdom (161e, 169d), (ii) everyone is equally wise (162c), (iii) there is no such thing as wisdom/no-one is wise (166d), (iv) no-one is wiser than anyone else (161d). If no-one is wiser than anyone else, no-one is wise. If no-one is more expert than anyone else, no-one is an expert and expertise does not exist.

On the face of it, Protagoras' relativism is incompatible with expertise. As Plato argues elsewhere,

> If wisdom and folly exist [it has been agreed that they do], Protagoras' view cannot be the truth: for one person could not be truly wiser than another if whatever seems to each is to be true for him. (*Cratylus* 386c)

But in this dialogue a posthumous protest by Protagoras (162de) soon puts a stop to any such bare-faced appeal to common sense. You cannot just assert the existence of expertise against a philosophy which is designed precisely to eliminate the possibility of genuine disagreement between people.

Still, it is a legitimate question to ask, how far a Protagorean will have to go once he starts out on this line of thought. It is as a question that Socrates raises the point at 161c–162a. First, how, given his philosophy, can Protagoras set himself up to teach others? Then, more sharply, what, on Protagoras' account of truth, can be the point of philosophical discussion, including of course the present discussion of Protagoras' account of truth? We are also jokingly reminded (162c) that the young Theaetetus is supposed to be becoming more of an expert in the subjects he is learning from Theodorus, not to be already as good an expert as his teacher. There are phenomena here: teaching and learning, discussion and debate. Will a consistent Protagorean have to deny that they occur, which would seem frightfully implausible, or can he find some way of redescribing them to show that they are after all compatible with his philosophy?

Essentially, the question is a challenge. So far, the strategy of relativization has been applied only to the sensory predicates involved in perception (152c), although 'good' and 'bad' were slipped in at 157d, as was the typically empiricist idea that feelings like pleasure and pain, desire and fear, are species of perception (156b).[28] But we may wonder whether language comes in neat compartments such that relativization in one area will have no

---

28. Compare Hume, *Treatise*, Bk. I, Pt. II, Sect. VI: 'To hate, to love, to feel, to see; all this is nothing but to perceive'.

consequences elsewhere. The challenge is: How much further must a Protagorean go? Just as the strategy of relativization was seen to make problematic the whole nature of what we ordinarily think of as the physical world (p. 15), so also it makes problematic all those aspects of human life which involve communication. That is one possible answer to the question of relevance.

It is an answer that brings with it further questions. What right have we to discourse about human life in these terms after adopting the Heraclitean story (constant flux, universal nonidentity over time) about people and things? Does this question matter? How does it affect our two Readings A and B? Reading A has it that Plato is now embarking on argument to show that Protagoras' Measure Doctrine cannot hold beyond the field of sense-perception (p. 8). Reading B sees here the start of the process of bringing out the many absurdities to which Theaetetus' three-in-one theory will lead. Can either interpretation afford to ignore the questions just raised?

Whatever we decide about Plato's broadening the focus of discussion, it should come as no surprise to find that, in consequence, the application of the Protagorean formula 'x appears F to a' gets considerably extended. Instead of a sensible object appearing to a perceiver, in the following sections of the dialogue x may be, for example, a law or practice (167c) or someone's opinion (171a), a may be a whole city as well as any individual (167c, 172a), and the predicate term F may be 'just' (167c, 172a), 'false' (170d, 171a), 'persuasive' (178e). These are not sensory predicates. When we speak of a law appearing just, or an opinion false, to someone, in such cases 'it appears' means not 'he perceives it' but 'he believes it', 'it seems so to him.' If this raises in our minds questions about the relation of belief or judgement to perception, that is no doubt something Plato would wish to encourage (p. 12). It should also return our attention to the second half of Theaetetus' original definition, the thesis that all knowing is perceiving (p. 10, p. 15). If the Measure Doctrine says that however a thing appears to someone, so it is for them, and Theaetetus is brought to accept that this holds whether the appearing is to sense *or* to thought, how can he still maintain that all knowing is perceiving? Some of it must be simply believing or judging.

The stage is now set for a broad-ranging discussion of Protagorean relativism, taken in a more general form than was originally required for the elucidation of Theaetetus' definition. But first comes a section (163a–165e) which seems designed to emphasize the importance of opening up this broader perspective. It is a model demonstration of how *not* to go about criticizing the thesis that knowledge is perception, namely, by isolating the thesis from the epistemological and metaphysical concerns with which it has been connected hitherto and pointing to various sentential contexts in which 'knows' and 'perceives' are not interchangeable without loss of sense or truth. To an ear attuned to twentieth-century philosophy, one or two of the arguments are in fact quite impressive; notably some considerations after the manner of Gilbert Ryle to the effect that it is possible to see, but not to know, clearly or dimly, that it is absurd to say of knowing, what is true of seeing, that you can only do it from close by, and so on (165d).[29] But Plato makes it clear that in his view this sort of objection is no better than one which starts from the outrageous premise that a man with one eye covered both sees and does not see the cloak in front of him (165bc).

Readers can entertain themselves and exercise their logical wits deciding on the worth of the several objections. But you should also ask this question: Is it not a proper test of a proposed definition that it should supply a formula which is substitutable for the definiendum (in our case, the noun 'knowledge' or the verb 'to know') without loss of sense or truth? If not, why not? Is Plato really entitled to maintain that these substitution tests insist upon a too rigid and superficial verbal consistency instead of tackling the issues of substance (164c–165e, 166bc, 168bc)?

The issues of substance mentioned here are those that connect the definition with Protagorean relativism and Heraclitean flux (166bc). It is Protagoras himself who, in response to this parade of 'verbal' objections, brings the discussion back to the epistemological and metaphysical implications of the definition, and Protagoras who now widens our view of these implications still further. For at 166a we embark on an important section commonly known as 'The Defence of Protagoras' in which Socrates takes on the role of Protagoras replying to the challenge, What is he to say about expertise?[30] It is proclaimed that the challenge will be met head on.

29. McDowell [3], 163–64, feels constrained to offer a different reading just because otherwise the argument would indeed be a powerful one, which Plato should not so lightly brush aside!

30. It is generally agreed that Protagoras must have faced this challenge, at least in regard to his own profession as educator of the young. If he answered it in writing, Plato could be making use of genuinely Protagorean material in the central portion of the Defence (166d–167d). Many scholars think that he is; the talk of plants having perceptions, for example, has an archaic ring. Others think that 168c implies the opposite, that Socrates has had to construct the Defence from his own resources, without a written statement by Protagoras to guide him; that is why later on (169d–

Protagoras, in the mouth of Socrates, undertakes to show that expertise can exist, and the activities of experts can be described, compatibly with the relativism of the doctrine that man is the measure of all things (166d–167d). That done, he can restate relativism in the completely general form, 'For each person and each city, things are what they seem to them to be' (168b).[31]

This is the passage that F.C.S. Schiller seized upon for its persuasive recommendation of the pragmatist point of view (p. 1). Protagoras' central claim is that the expert (doctor, teacher, etc.) is one who effects an improvement in our perceptions, feelings, or thoughts. According to the Measure Doctrine, whatever we think or feel is true for each of us: so the state of mind which results from the expert's ministration is not *truer* than our previous state of mind. But it is *better* (167ab). Schiller supposed that by 'better' Protagoras meant that one is better adjusted to life and the world around (rather as when one's eyesight is improved); and he further maintained that this is only terminologically different from the full pragmatist thesis that the true or truer state of mind *is* the one which has the most satisfactory consequences, the one which selects itself as the most serviceable to live with.

Subtract this last claim, that Protagoras is virtually reshaping the notion of truth itself, not just appealing beyond it to considerations of what is better, and Schiller's interpretation is widely shared. The meaning of 'better' is disputed: Is it that which is most in accordance with the state of mind of a healthy subject, or that which most agrees with the perception and thought of one's fellows, or that which is most advantageous to the organism, or that which will seem better in the future? All of these have had their advocate.[32] Nonetheless, they have in common that they all provide a prag-

---

170a) he insists that the refutation must be based on statements made in Protagoras' book. It is not much use arguing that the Defence Socrates offers must be historically sound because there is no other way Protagoras could reconcile his philosophy with his profession (Cornford [2], 72, W.K.C. Guthrie, *The Sophists* (Cambridge: 1971), 172 n. 1). For, as we are about to see, the text leaves us guessing which of several different reconciliations Socrates-Protagoras might be offering.

31. Note the strict parallel between individual and city here. A modern philosopher would distinguish among relativisms between those that make truth relative to the judgement of an individual and those that make it relative to the standards prevailing in a group. The *Theaetetus* simply admits collective subjects on a par with individual ones, leaving aside questions about the relation between the judgement of the collective and the judgements of the individuals composing it.

32. Respectively, John Burnet, *Greek Philosophy, Thales to Plato* (London: 1914), 116; Taylor [4], 322–23; Kerferd [23]; Cornford [2], 73–74.

matic, if not strictly pragmatist, test for expertise. Results are the thing, on this interpretation, not truth. It is to results that Protagoras is looking to reconcile the Measure Doctrine with the existence of expertise.

Yet there are grounds for unease. If Protagoras takes this broadly pragmatic line of defence, but stops short of a Schiller-type redefinition of truth, he compromises his relativism in two places. First, whichever of the above-mentioned senses he gives to 'better', it becomes an objective matter that one of two states of mind is better than the other. The truth of the claim that one is better is not relative to how it appears either to the expert who effects the change or to the subject whose mind he changes. Second, and consequent upon this, it is an equally objective, nonrelative question whether experts exist. Schiller's suggestion that Protagoras was a full-blown pragmatist ahead of his time avoids the difficulty and secures consistency for the Defence, but unfortunately the text at 167ab insists strongly that, as regards truth, the better and the worse states of mind are on a par. It seems that we must abandon hopes of finding the pragmatist account of truth in the *Theaetetus*. In which case, all that remains for Protagoras, if he is not to compromise the Measure Doctrine, is the following:

> D1   State of mind S_1 is better *for a* than state of mind S_2 if and only if it seems to *a* that S_1 is better than S_2.

In other words, the test is whether *a* thinks or feels himself 'better off' for the change from S_2 to S_1. From which it is but a short step to

> D2   *x* is an expert *for a* if and only if it seems to *a* that he is better off thanks to *x*.

In other words, there are experts (doctors, statesmen, and the like) just insofar as, and *for* those people by whom, they are acknowledged as such.

On this basis Protagoras could argue that he resolves disputes over who is competent and who is merely a quack, be it in medicine or education, politics or agriculture, in exactly the same way as he had earlier dealt with disputes about whether the wind is cold or not cold. It is no objection that almost anyone might be found persuasive or improving by someone in some matter or other. For one thing, Protagoras is already on record, in Plato's dialogue *Protagoras*, as maintaining that virtue is taught by everyone to everyone.[33] For another, in strict logic nothing less radical than D1 and D2 will vindicate Protagoras' claim—a claim he does seem to make (167d, 168b)—that he can save his theory without compromising its generality.

It would be nice, and the history of philosophy would be an easier subject than it is, if philosophers never wavered from the requirements of strict logic. But of course they do. In advance of a close examination of the text we have no guarantee that the Defence does not compromise Protagoras' relativism and concede the objectivity of judgements of what is better. Let us focus on the formal definition of expertise from which the argumentative part of the Defence begins: 'I call wise . . . the man who in any case where bad things both appear and are for one of us, works a change and makes good things appear and be for him' (166d).

One thing this tells us is that the change to a better state of mind (described at 167ab) is a change to a state in which better things appear and are for one. That amounts to D1 if—but alas, only if— (i) 'Better things appear and are for someone' means the same as (ii) 'Things appear and are better for him'.

It is obvious enough why the uncompromising interpretation should offer (ii) as its elucidation of (i).[34] If things appear better than they were to someone, then on Protagorean principles they *are* better *for* the person who thinks them so. As we are forcefully reminded at 167a, and again at 167d, no-one can be wrong about anything, so no-one can be wrong if they feel themselves better off as a result of some putative expert's intervention.

The alternative, compromising view is that 'better' in (i) refers to things that are in fact better, regardless of whether they seem so to the person whose mind the expert changes. In more technical language, 'better' belongs to the subject rather than to the complement (predicate) of the verbs 'appear' and 'are'. The point is not that x appears better to a than it did before, with the result on Protagorean principles that it is better for a than it was. Rather, instead of x appearing F to a (for some as yet unspecified value of F), something better than x appears F to a, with the result on Protagorean principles that something better than x is F for a.

33. This is the theme of his Great Speech at *Protagoras* 320c–328d. So far as concerns his own teaching, Protagoras in that dialogue sometimes seems to promise objective benefits to his pupils (318a, 318d–319a), sometimes to accept that the test of his expertise as a teacher is whether his pupils *think* themselves better off for listening to him (316c, 328bc). Compare also *Republic* 488c.

34. So Vlastos [24], xxi–xxii with n. 47.

A nice choice. The wording of the definition of expertise quoted from 166d can be taken either way. So the next step is to consult the examples in the passage to see which construal they favour.

A doctor administers drugs which have the effect that your food tastes sweet instead of bitter (166e–167a). This fits (ii) quite well: tasting sweet instead of bitter is one way of tasting better, and on Protagorean principles a felt improvement is enough to make it true that for you the food is better. Or so the uncompromising interpretation can argue.

A politician makes wholesome things seem to a city to be just and admirable, and therefore to be just and admirable for that city, instead of the pernicious things which seemed (and therefore were for it) just and admirable before (167c). This does not fit (ii), because 'wholesome' is put on the subject side of 'seem'. The claim is not that the new conventions seem better but that better things seem just. The compromising interpretation infers, accordingly, that the improvement described here is objective: the new conventions are better whether or not they seem so. The uncompromising interpretation might think to reply that, if the new conventions are adopted because the politician has made them seem *more* just and admirable than the old, then 'wholesome' can be transferred to the predicate side of 'seem'; for seeming more just and admirable is one way of seeming better. But this looks like something the Defence ought to have said rather than what it does say. Yet another possibility would be a double application of the Measure Doctrine: things which seem and therefore are better (perhaps because they make the community's life more pleasant) come to seem just and therefore are just in that city for so long as the new convention holds.

The example of the sickly plants at 167bc is neutral. Given the archaic belief (shared by Plato, *Timaeus* 77b, and a few modern sentimentalists) that a plant can feel better off as well as be so, there is no telling whether the improvement effected by a gardener is dependent or not dependent on the patient's subjective responses.

Shall we then declare a draw? Of the three examples described in detail, one tells in favour of compromise, one against, and the plants help neither view. If this seems unsatisfactory, the explanation might be that the indeterminacy is deliberate: Protagoras has compromised, and later (171d ff.) Plato will hammer the point home, but it would be dramatically, and perhaps also historically, inappropriate to call attention to it now.[35] Unfortunately, when we get to the later passage, which does formulate the compromising interpretation in plain terms (cf. 171d–172b, 177cd), it turns out to be a question whether this is offered as a restatement of the Defence or as a modification of the Protagorean position (see below, p. 32).

What is at stake, philosophically, in the effort to find a satisfactory reading of this passage? Ultimately, it is nothing less than the place in human life of the notion of objective truth. Need it come in? Can a thorough-going relativist tell a *consistent* story about expertise, about teaching and learning, about discussion and debate, without conceding a role to objective truth? Should it come in? Can the relativist tell a reasonably *plausible* story without it? Or is Protagoras bound to compromise sooner or later, either to ensure consistency or as the price of plausibility? The Defence draws its examples from education and medicine, agriculture and politics, but are all the examples amenable to the same treatment (whatever treatment we decide is being offered)?

It could be said, for example, that D1 is a satisfactory enough principle for the medical case, since a doctor is supposed to make his patients feel better, but that the test of a politician is whether his proposals are objectively beneficial to the community. It could also be said, on the contrary, that a doctor's duty is to promote health, which is an objective benefit, whereas a good politician aims to give people a life that they themselves find satisfying. (Some years ago a British General Election was won on the slogan 'You've never had it so good'—would it be obligatory to construe this as an objective rather than a subjective appeal?) What, finally, of examples which Protagoras does not mention? The presence of Theodorus is a constant reminder of the problem of mathematical expertise (p. 4; cf. 169a, 170de). Do *any* of the interpretations canvassed above make decent sense of this? Since the question is particularly pressing for Theodorus himself, who was Protagoras' friend (161b,

---

35. Cf. McDowell [3], 167. I add 'perhaps also historically' because it might be that the best argument for the historicity of the Defence (cf. n. 30 above) was its very indeterminacy in the face of our puzzlement: maybe one cannot expect from fifth-century work precise and sophisticated answers to the questions that we, and Plato, want to press. Cole [25] prefers to think that Plato misinterpreted Protagoras and was unaware that the doctor example, which preserves Protagoras' original uncompromising view, is crucially different from the politician example, in which Plato tacitly incorporates the concession to objectivity that he is seeking to establish.

162a, et al.) and once his pupil (164e–165a, 179a), it is worth keeping an eye on his reactions now and in the sequel (168c, 171c, 179b).

We may hope for more help on these issues as we proceed. For whereas in the Defence Socrates makes the statement that some people are wiser or more expert than others on Protagoras' behalf, in the next section he sets himself to derive it directly from the Measure Doctrine as expounded in Protagoras' own book *Truth* (169d–170a, 171d). But this time the interpretation of the statement is quite unambiguous. Objectivity is admitted in both the places we were uneasy about earlier (p. 24): both what experts know and that they know it are equally matters of objective, nonrelative fact. We cannot, however, conclude straightaway that this is a retrospective clarification of what was intended in the Defence. For the tone of the discussion undergoes a dramatic change. Socrates is no longer the polite and helpful fellow defending Protagoras against some awkward questions. He makes Theodorus strip for action (169ac). The attack which follows leaves the old mathematician shocked and shaken (171cd). The proposition that some people are wiser or more expert than others is now (171d) not the centrepiece of a defence of Protagoras' relativism but the ignominious outcome of its self-refutation.

The argument by which Plato tries to show that a completely general relativism is self-refuting is of considerable philosophical interest in its own right, as well as an important step forward in the investigation of expertise. The essential trick is to move the discussion up a level. Instead of asking directly 'What is expertise? How can Protagoras describe it?', the question is raised, 'What do people in general *think* about expertise?' Answer: they think there are many areas of life in which some are knowledgeable and others ignorant, the difference being that the knowledgeable ones make true judgements and the ignorant false judgements on the matter in hand (170ab). But now, what people think and believe is the very thing the Measure Doctrine tells us about. It tells us that whatever people think and believe is true for them; no-one can be *wrong* about anything. So, by way of preparation for the self-refutation to come, let us consider the belief just mentioned, the widespread belief that people are sometimes ignorant and wrong, that false judgement does occur. If people are right to think that there is false judgement, there is. But equally, if they are wrong in this belief, there is false judgement (for here is an instance of it). But Protagoras must say—must he not?—either that they are right or that they are wrong: unless he is willing to go so far as to deny that people do hold this view about each other's ignorance and expertise. To deny that, Theodorus agrees, would be quite implausible (170c). So Protagoras is caught in a dilemma. Whichever answer he gives has the consequence that false judgement occurs, which the Measure Doctrine must deny.

Ingenious. But we must be careful, both in this dilemmatic passage and in the self-refutation argument to follow, about that little qualifying phrase 'for *a*' which distinguishes the Protagorean idiom from the language of ordinary people. It is acceptable to have the ordinary man express the view that some judgements are false, without qualification. That is exactly what the ordinary man wants to say. But is it acceptable to make Protagoras *comment on* this view with the statement that it is right (true) or that it is wrong (false), without qualification? Should he not rather express himself as follows? 'To be sure, people believe what some judgements are false. All I need say about their belief, however, is that it is true *for them*. It does not follow that it is true *for me*. So it does not follow that it is true *for me* that, contrary to my philosophy, some judgements are false (without qualification).'

The same question arises with the self-refutation argument beginning at 170e. At a critical moment (171ab) the relativizing qualifiers are dropped and Protagoras is made to speak of truth and falsity in absolute terms. What happens is this. We move from people's general belief that false judgement occurs to the specific belief that the Measure Doctrine in particular is false, and then on to the belief which Protagoras is committed to having *about* this belief if he believes his own theory. It is a self-refutation in that the Measure Doctrine, as a thesis about beliefs, is applied to beliefs about itself, to yield the conclusion that what it says about beliefs is not true for anybody. You need a clear head to follow the reasoning and to watch how Socrates handles the qualifiers:

Either (1) Protagoras himself did not believe the *Truth* he wrote, in which case, since no-one else does, it is not (sc. the truth) for anybody at all (170e). (No naughtiness with the qualifiers here.) Or (2) he did believe it, but the majority of people do not share his opinion, in which case two consequences follow. (a) The more the adherents of his *Truth* are outnumbered by people who do not believe it, the more it is not (sc. the truth) than it is (171a). (Does this mean it is more false than true, absolutely, or false for more people than it is true for?) (b) Protagoras himself must agree (171a) that his opponents' disbelief in his *Truth* is true (query: why omit 'for them' here?), and this leads eventually (query: how?) to the conclusion (171c) that Protagoras' doctrine is not true for anybody, not even for the Sophist himself. The final conclusion of (2) (b), like the conclusion of (1), is properly relativized. The question is whether that conclusion can be fairly derived without an illegitimate dropping of the qualifiers at the point queried above (171a). If it cannot—and this has been the common verdict—we have to decide whether the faulty step is a deliberate dishonesty on Plato's part or an inadvertent slip. If it can, we have to show how the reasoning remains sound when the qualifiers are restored in the appropriate places.[36]

The issue is too complex to enter fully into here. But it is very much worth wrestling with, and one substantive aspect should be mentioned. Isn't there something inherently paradoxical about someone asserting (or believing) that *all truth is relative?* That proposition sums up the message of a completely general relativism, but when asserted it is propounded as itself a truth. The reason for this is simple but fundamental: to assert anything is to assert it as a truth, as something which is the case. (Analogously, to believe something is to accept it as true.) The relativist may reply that 'All truth is relative' is not asserted as an absolute truth, which would indeed be self-refuting, but only as a relative one: *it is true for me that all truth is relative.* This is no help. This second proposition is less interesting (because it is no longer clear that the objectivity of *our* beliefs is jeopardized if relativism is true only for the relativist), but it is still an assertion. 'It is true for me that all truth is relative' is put forward as itself true without qualification. A commitment to truth absolute is bound up with the very act of assertion.

If this is correct, we may be able to salvage something from Plato's self-refutation argument even on the more pessimistic view that the omission of the qualifiers is a fatal flaw in the text as it stands. The omission, we may decide, was a fault in the execution of a well-aimed attack. Relativism is self-refuting, and for reasons that go deep into the nature of assertion and belief. One modern philosopher who contended that any formulation of Protagorean relativism must be self-refuting was the founder of phenomenology, Edmund Husserl, and he put it like this: 'The content of such assertions rejects what is part of the sense or content of every assertion and what accordingly cannot be significantly separated from any asser-

---

36. I have tried to do this in Burnyeat [28]; compare Waterlow [29]. For a logical defence of Protagoras, see Matthen [17].

tion'.[37] Other philosophical traditions express the point in quite similar terms.[38] There is impressive support for the idea that Plato in this passage was onto something of fundamental importance.

We can go further and propose a general perspective on Plato's critique of Protagoras as it has developed so far. Relativism is a philosophical tendency of perennial appeal. I have no doubt that many readers of this Introduction find themselves drawn to it. Recognizably Protagorean themes appear in important works of modern philosophy.[39] Of course, time and progress have brought an immense sophistication in the working out and advocacy of relativistic views. It would be foolish not to acknowledge this. But the questions we have seen Plato addressing to Protagoras are still worth asking in a contemporary context. It would be equally foolish to presume that the *Theaetetus* no longer has anything to contribute to the continuing debate.

The critique interrupted (171d–177c)

At this point we must break off to follow Plato into a digression of quite extraordinarily bitter eloquence. Digression is Plato's own word for it (177b), but the passage is bound to raise anew some of the questions involved in the decision between Reading A and Reading B. We should look first at the context which starts it off (171d–172c).

The self-refutation argument does not establish that there is *no* area of life in which what seems to each person or city is so for them, only that this is not the case in everything. If we are not to have that completely unrestricted relativism which has been shown to undermine itself, there must be some area or areas in which

37. Edmund Husserl, *Logical Investigations* 2nd edition (1913), trans. J. N. Findlay (London & New York: 1970), 139.

38. See Passmore [26], 67–68; J. L. Mackie, 'Self-Refutation—A Formal Analysis', *Philosophical Quarterly* 14 (1964), 193–203. Another version in McDowell [3], 171.

39. See, for example, in metaphysics and philosophy of language: W. V. Quine, 'Ontological Relativity', reprinted from *Journal of Philosophy* 65 (1968) in his *Ontological Relativity and Other Essays* (New York & London: 1969), 26–68. In philosophy of science: Thomas S. Kuhn, *The Structure of Scientific Revolutions* 2nd edition (Chicago: 1970). In moral philosophy: Gilbert Harman, 'Moral Relativism Defended', *Philosophical Review* 84 (1975), 3–22; B.A.O. Williams, 'The Truth in Relativism', reprinted from *Proceedings of the Aristotelian Society* N.S. 75 (1974/5) in his *Moral Luck: Philosophical Papers 1973–1980* (Cambridge: 1981), 132–43. In social philosophy: Martin Hollis & Steven Lukes edd., *Rationality and Relativism* (Oxford: 1982).

objectivity and expertise prevail. But the self-refutation argument alone does not determine in which area(s) the concession should be made.

Socrates reverts to the Defence of Protagoras to help him formulate an answer to this question (171d), but the reader has already been warned (p. 27) that it remains open to discussion whether the New Formulation, as I shall term it, should be understood as restating something already contained in the Defence or as reinterpreting its remarks about expertise along unambiguously objectivist lines. The back-reference on its own could be regarded either way. Two further clues may help decide the question, and should be taken into account by the reader who aims to reach a synoptic view of the whole issue. One clue is a statement at 172b, the purpose of which we will consider shortly, to the effect that the New Formulation, or at least one part of it, is endorsed by people who do not go so far as Protagoras. Another is Socrates complaining at 179b that the Defence forced him to be a measure even though he has no special knowledge.

Meanwhile, we proceed to the New Formulation and the digression arising out of it. The core of the New Formulation is a clear and unambiguous statement of the objectivity of judgements about what is to the advantage of or beneficial for an individual or a city.[40] The example given is judgements about what is good or bad for health. With these are contrasted judgements concerning (a) sensible qualities, (b) moral, political, and religious values. With regard to (a) what seems hot or sweet and the like, (b) what seems just or unjust, etc., the Measure Doctrine remains in force and is said (171d) to have a good chance of standing firm. From 171d to 172a this position is expounded by 'the theory', personified as a (somewhat chastened) spokesman for the Protagorean side of the debate. Then at 172b we hear, first, that 'men' are ready to deny the objectivity of values, and second, that 'even those who are not prepared to go all the way with Protagoras take some such view of wisdom'. We may take these additional items in order.

The first statement confirms the appropriateness of (one part of) Socrates' New Formulation of the Defence. The theory would not

---

40. For what it is worth, the New Formulation employs a somewhat different vocabulary from the Defence. The key word in the Defence was *chrēstos*, translated 'sound', 'wholesome'. This is now replaced by *sumpheron*, 'advantageous' or 'in one's interest' (172a), and *ōphelimos*, 'useful' (177d). Both passages employ the most general word of commendation, *agathos*, 'good'.

have a good chance of standing firm if it dared to deny the objectivity of advantage (172ab), but relativism with regard to (b) will get a sympathetic hearing from men in general. The second statement builds on the first: a lot of people are inclined to deny the objectivity of values, to incorporate that much Protagoras into their thinking, without going along with his parallel view of (a) and without, of course, doubting for a moment the objectivity of questions of advantage. Relativism about values is independently tempting; it need not be reached by way of a relativist epistemology. Indeed, it appeals to tough-minded characters (whether of the fourth century B.C. or the twentieth century A.D.) who have no time for the subtleties and the broad horizons of philosophical debate, to which the *Theaetetus* is devoted.[41] This is the cue for the Digression.

The central theme of the Digression is the relation of justice and prudence. If questions of advantage have objective answers but what is just or unjust depends upon and is relative to the fluctuating judgements of community or individual, then it becomes impossible to say that justice is in one's own best interests, that a prudent man who wants to lead a happy life will seek to acquire justice and moral virtue generally. There is no firm truth of the form 'Justice is necessary for happiness' if there is no definite and stable answer to the question 'What is justice?'. But now, exactly that question and that truth were the organizing principles of Plato's *Republic*. The *Republic* was designed to establish an objectively valid answer to the question 'What is justice?' from which it would emerge as an incontestable truth that justice is a requirement of prudence. The whole grand edifice would collapse if we were to accept the newly formulated separation, with regard to objectivity, between justice and prudence.

This is indeed, as Socrates describes it (172b), 'a greater discussion emerging from the lesser one'. The issues are both too large and

41. The reader should be warned that it is not easy to keep the translation of 172b neutral with respect to interpretation. Thus McDowell [3] has (i) 'they' in place of 'men' (the Greek is just a plural verb with no subject specified), 'they' being construed as the theorists of the theory which has been speaking so far; (ii) 'At any rate those who don't altogether assert Protagoras' theory carry on their philosophy on some such lines as these' where the present translation reads 'And even those who are not prepared to go all the way with Protagoras take some such view of wisdom'. My own view is that Miss Levett is correct on both counts: on (i) because 'they' makes 172b a mere repetition of 172a instead of support for it; on (ii) because, as urged by Cole [25], 113, the interpretation of wisdom is what the discussion is all about. These points of translation are inevitably to be connected with the question of the relation of the New Formulation to the original Defence.

too important to handle argumentatively within the framework of
Part I of the *Theaetetus*. They call for a work on the scale of the
Republic or the earlier *Gorgias*, and for specifically ethical and psychological explorations which would take us away from general
epistemology. On the other hand, Plato is deeply committed to the
view that the separation of justice and prudence is both false and
pernicious. So he interrupts the argument and launches into
rhetoric.[42]

We are invited to contemplate, not rival theories about the relation of justice and prudence, but the lives in which the rival theories
are put into practice. On the one hand, there is the life of the
philosopher, who knows that true happiness is to be found in
justice, because to be just is to model oneself on the pattern of
God's blessed perfection and thereby to take flight from the evils
of this world (176b).[43] Against this is set the life of the worldly man
of affairs who believes he is a tough guy, working the system to his
own best advantage, but who in reality is a slave of the system,
unaware that his unscrupulous conduct condemns his life to be its
own curse and punishment (176d–177a). The contrast is absolute
and unequivocal. There is no illusion about the cost, in worldly
terms, of the philosopher's devotion to justice. There is no hope of
a middle way which would allow a good man to be at ease with his
present surroundings. Even the talk of the philosopher having
abundant leisure for discussion (with which compare 154e, 187d)
is double-edged. In the actual world outside this philosophical
discussion Socrates has an appointment to meet—at a hearing of
the indictment which will lead to his trial and execution (210d).

After so much careful argumentation (soon to be resumed), all
this may seem a strange intrusion. One modern philosopher finds
it 'philosophically quite pointless', another assigns it the marginal

---

42. It is worth comparing *Protagoras* 333d ff. The question has arisen whether prudence and injustice are compatible; Socrates is shaping to argue that they are not, but
Plato allows Protagoras to interrupt with a rhetorical discourse about the relativity of
advantage. Another abortive discussion of the issue can be found at the end of
Republic Book I. In both these places and in the *Gorgias* one detects a strong sense
on Plato's part that short snappy abstract arguments are not going to carry conviction
with anyone who is genuinely concerned to know whether it is in their best interests
to be just.

43. The idea that to practise virtue is to become like God appears also at *Republic*
613ab, while at *Laws* 716cd it is associated with the dictum that God, not man, is
preeminently the measure of all things. Neither of these passages, however, makes
as much of the idea as the *Theaetetus*.

relevance of a present-day footnote or appendix.[44] But it had a tremendous impact. First, it stimulated a protracted debate, involving Aristotle and others, about the ideal form of life.[45] Then, in later antiquity (from around 100 b.c. onwards), the passage was endlessly excerpted and quoted from, both by pagan and in due course by Christian philosophers. The idea of virtue as becoming like God so far as one can (176b) was taken up as a common theme among philosophers of quite different persuasions.[46]

As the centuries passed, more and more readers responded sympathetically to the impassioned otherworldliness of the Digression,[47] which is stronger here than in any other dialogue except the *Phaedo*. Even today the Digression's disparagement of pride in one's ancestors and other social distinctions (174e–175b) can impress Plato's best-known philosopher-critic, Sir Karl Popper, as 'humanitarian'.[48] But this rejection of snobbery is embedded in a wholesale condemnation of ordinary human concerns which twentieth-century readers are more likely to find alien and repellent, even as we are gripped (despite ourselves) by the sweep and force of the rhetoric. The truth is, we here face an aspect of Plato which it is not easy for many of us to come to terms with. Nevertheless we must try. The Digression, being a digression, lies apart from the main line of the inquiry, but it is situated almost exactly at the midpoint of the dialogue. That suggests it is integral to the design of the whole. Another indication of design is the following.

When Socrates starts to characterize the philosopher, the very first thing he says about him—Socrates, of all people, whom every-

44. The verdicts of, respectively, Gilbert Ryle, *Plato's Progress* (Cambridge: 1966), 158, and McDowell [3], 174.

45. See Jaeger [31]; also note *ad* 174a.

46. Documentation of this claim may be found in Hubert Merki, *Homoiōsis Theōi: von der platonischen Angleichung an Gott zur Gottähnlichkeit bei Gregor von Nyssa*, Paradosis VII (Freiburg: 1952). For discussion, both learned and readable, which follows the theme from ancient into modern times, see Passmore [32].

47. For example, Plotinus, *Enneads* I 2 is an extended commentary on our text. But already Aristotle, *Nicomachean Ethics* X 7, has his own version of the theme, with the same emphasis on leisure.

48. K. R. Popper, *The Open Society and Its Enemies* 4th edition (London: 1962), Vol. I, 281. So impressed was Popper with this 'humanitarian' strain in the Digression that he postulated (*ib.* 320) an earlier edition of the *Theaetetus*, written long before the battle of 369 b.c. mentioned in the prologue at 142ab, indeed before the *Republic*. For Popper's book is an ardent denunciation of the 'antihumanitarian' ideals developed in the *Republic*, which he thought unreconcilable with the sentiments he admired in the *Theaetetus*.

body remembers as a habitué of the market-place—is that the philosopher does not know the way to the market-place, such is his
lack of interest in the world around him (173cd). We are surely
meant to be taken aback by this. And by the subsequent comment
(173e) that the philosopher does not even know that he does not
know these worldly matters (Socrates is famous above all for the
claim that his wisdom consists in his being acutely aware that he
does not have knowledge: cf. esp. *Apology* 20d ff., also *Theaet.*
150cd, 179b). Now, both cases are examples of the philosopher not
knowing something—not knowing them because to his way of
thinking they are not worth knowing. Perhaps this is the key to
Plato's intention. The discussion of what knowledge is is inter-
rupted so that we may be jolted into reflecting for a moment that
the question what knowledge is is important because there are
certain things it is important to know. The whole course of our life,
our happiness or lack of it, not to mention our fate after death (cf.
177a with note ad loc.), depends upon whether we know or we do
not know the right answer to the question about the relation of
justice to prudence.

Here, then, is one interpretation of the purpose of the Digression.
We are to be stirred to really serious reflection on what it is worth-
while and important to know. To make sure that we do not take
the issue lightly, Plato puts the full power of his rhetoric into an
extreme expression of his own vision of the human condition. The
moral aspect gets the chief emphasis, but, as in Book VII of the
Republic, the mathematical sciences—geometry and astronomy—
are important as well, since Platonic morality is not to be separated
from the quest for a total understanding of the nature of things
(173e–174a). No wonder old Theodorus finds the digression easier
and more pleasant than the rigours of dialectical argument (177c;
recall qu. (1), p. 4 above).

It is a feature of this interpretation that it gives the Digression the
weight which it is clearly meant to have, while leaving it a digression
which does not interfere with or contribute to the main inquiry. To
talk about what is worth knowing is not as such to say anything
about what knowing is. Formally speaking, it is far less restrictive
on possible answers to the latter question than the passage would
be if, instead of saying that worldly matters are not *worth* knowing,
Socrates had claimed that they are not the sort of thing that *can* be
known. Just this, however, is what Plato did claim in earlier dialogues like the *Phaedo* and *Republic*: in those dialogues the position
is that the sensible world is such that we can have no knowledge
of it, only opinion—knowledge is restricted to the unchanging

realm of the Forms (cf. esp. *Republic* V–VII; p. 8 above). Or so runs the general trend of interpretation.[49] And many scholars find it impossible not to see the *Theaetetus* digression as a reminder and reaffirmation of that earlier position.

Obviously, if the Digression does hark back to the *Republic*, this could be helpful to Reading A. A reaffirmation of the *Republic* would involve taking a stand on what can be known, which is anything but neutral as to what knowing is. Not that the text speaks explicitly to questions about what can and what cannot be the object of knowledge as opposed to opinion; and when geometry and astronomy are mentioned at 173e, Socrates does not commit himself to the *Republic* VII view that they are concerned with ideal nonsensible objects rather than with earthly surfaces and the visible stars. But there are echoes of the famous allegory of the Cave (*Rep.* VII, 514a–521b), as well as other parts of the *Republic*, and scholars who interpret these echoes as a reaffirmation of the *Republic* urge, first, that 174b does plainly refer to the Form Man, 175c to the moral Forms Justice and Injustice, and second, that whether or not 'the two patterns set up in the world' (176e) are themselves Forms, the phrase unmistakeably recalls the paradigmatic language in which Plato habitually spoke of his ideal Forms. In sum,

> The allusions to the allegory of the Cave, the passage about the true meaning of kingship, happiness, and justice, are intended to recall the whole argument of the *Republic*, with its doctrine of the divine, intelligible region of Forms, the true objects of knowledge. This is no mere digression; it indicates . . . the final cleavage between Platonism and the extreme consequences of the Protagorean thesis.[50]

You, the reader, now have before you two interpretations of the Digression. Your decision between them will go hand in hand with other decisions about Part I of the dialogue, and to some extent will depend on temperamental as well as intellectual factors. It is in part a matter of our own temperament whether we can imagine Plato's temperament being able to tolerate a separation of his moral vision from the restrictive epistemology and the Theory of Forms on which the *Republic* sought to ground it. But something had better be said

---

49. As always with Plato, to ascribe a position to him is to run into controversy. A respectable case can be made for the view that the above formulation is too strong: Crombie [6], 128 ff., Gail Fine, 'Knowledge and Belief in *Republic* V', *Archiv für Geschichte der Philosophie* 60 (1978), 121–39.

50. Cornford [2], 89.

about how one decides whether or not Forms are referred to at 174b and 175c.

The operative phrases are the interrogative 'What is Man?', asking for a definition of man in general (a philosophical account of human nature), and the title 'justice and injustice themselves', specifying that about which one asks 'What is justice? What is injustice? How do they differ from everything else and from each other?'. It is standard practice for Plato to use the locution 'X itself', where 'X' either is or is functioning as an abstract noun, to designate that which a definition defines; the terminology implies a contrast, which the *Theaetetus* contexts confirm, between the abstract or general thing to be defined and the various particular instances classified under it: the philosopher's next-door neighbour as opposed to man in general (174b), my injustice towards you or yours towards me as opposed to injustice itself (175c). If we now ask, 'What is Platonic Form?', the first thing to say is that the notion of a Form is the notion of that which a definition defines (cf. *Phaedo* 75cd). Hence 'X itself' does often import a reference to a Form. But the mere identification of something which a definition defines is not enough to constitute a *theory* of Forms. It is one thing to set out to define justice, quite another to say that justice as such exists on its own, separately from just men and just actions. We cannot properly speak of the Platonic Theory of Forms until this has been said. In dialogues like the *Phaedo* and *Republic*, which propound the Theory of Forms as a theory about the epistemological and ontological presuppositions of the Socratic method of definitional inquiry, the Forms are transcendent natures, existing independently of the empirical world, unchanging and divine, to be grasped only by reflective reasoning. In other dialogues, however, especially the early Socratic dialogues, 'X itself' is contrasted with its particular instances and definitions are sought, without any of this high-powered theoretical backing. (A good example is the use of 'knowledge itself' at *Theaet.* 146e.) So the question whether Forms are referred to at 174b and 175c is the question whether, *in those contexts*, the operative phrases are naturally taken to imply more metaphysics than is actually expressed. What is expressed is the idea that 'the philosopher is a theorist, a generalizer, and a spectator of the whole'.[51] We have to decide whether for Plato this immediately

51. Robinson [39], 9, who insists against Cornford that the description could perfectly well be applied to a nominalist and positivist philosopher. For an impassioned rebuttal of Robinson's critique of Cornford, see R. Hackforth, 'Platonic Forms in the *Theaetetus*', *Classical Quarterly* N.S. 7 (1957), 53–58.

implies believing in the Forms. And here again the temperamental factors mentioned earlier are likely to influence our answer—not improperly so, since a great work of philosophy demands a response which is more than merely intellectual.

One last question will bring us back to dialectic. On any interpretation the Digression emphasizes (esp. 175bc) that the philosopher does not concern himself with questions about examples of injustice or examples of happiness but proceeds from the general definitional questions 'What is injustice?', 'What is happiness in general?'. This has an obvious connection with a matter we discussed earlier (qu. (2), pp. 4–5 above). We must ask: Is it Plato's suggestion here that the philosopher would not be interested in considering examples *in the course of* the search for an adequate definition? The question is pressing because we are about to consider some examples of knowledge, or at least of competent judgement, licensed by the New Formulation of the Defence from which the Digression has been diverting us.

The critique resumed: (i) refutation of Protagoras (177c–179b)

The Digression over, the New Formulation is restated in summary form (177cd) and Socrates turns his attention to the one element of objectivity it allows, the objectivity of judgements about what is advantageous or beneficial. He points out that judgements about advantage are essentially forward-looking: they concern what *will* bring about some desirable state of affairs and so are one kind of judgement about the future (178a). (The reader might consider how this thesis can account for a past-tense judgement like 'Your assistance was most advantageous to us'.) It follows that any result proved for the whole class of judgements about the future will hold a fortiori for judgements about advantage. The result Socrates proceeds to argue for (178b–179b) is that judgements about the future cannot be admitted within the scope of the Measure Doctrine; their truth-conditions must be objective, not relative to the individual judgement-maker.

This confirms (cf. 178a), what has not previously been established (pp. 31–2), that Socrates was right to choose questions of advantage as the place to admit objectivity and the possibility of expertise in the wake of the self-refutation argument. But since the argument about the future is independent of the self-refutation, it is also an independent refutation of a completely general relativism, and is duly acknowledged as such by Theodorus at 179b. Our competing Readings A and B will draw different conclusions from this (p. 21), but the philosophical interest of the argument is by no means exhausted by that interpretative disagreement.

Consider

> (1) It seems to me on Monday that on Tuesday my temperature will be feverishly hot.

To hold that judgements about the future come within the scope of the Measure Doctrine is to hold that (in the striking phrase introduced at 178b) I have within myself the criterion of what will happen tomorrow, in this sense, that from (1) we may infer

> (2) It is true for me on Monday that on Tuesday my temperature will be feverishly hot.

But the Measure Doctrine also has something to say about Tuesday:

> (3) It is true for me on Tuesday that my temperature is feverishly hot if and only if on Tuesday I feel feverishly hot.

Now suppose that (as the doctor in 178b predicts) on Tuesday I do not feel in the least bit hot or feverish. Then (3) tells us that it is not true for me on Tuesday that I am hot—and doesn't this contradict the conclusion already drawn at (2)?

The best way to appreciate the force of this argument is to ask what resources a determined relativist could muster in reply. Evidently the contradiction, if it is one, is due to the supposition that the Measure Doctrine vests the authority to decide how things are for me on Tuesday both with my Monday's self and with my Tuesday's self, who may disagree.[52] But now, might our relativist challenge the assumption that the two selves can disagree in this way? There are occasions when my belief that I will enjoy a feast (an example from 178de) *brings it about that*, when the time comes, I do; and it is not difficult to imagine a similar story for Tuesday's temperature. Could this defence be extended to the other examples? What kind of a world would it be if *whatever* I predicted on Monday

---

52. Plato represents the disagreement as a disagreement on Monday between me and the doctor predicting, correctly, how it will be with me on Tuesday (178c), but for the present argument this comes to the same thing.

came to pass on Tuesday *because* I had predicted it? If that seems close to incoherent, we might imagine the relativist, on a different tack, exploiting the Heraclitean thought that Monday's and Tuesday's selves are two, not one and the same persisting person.

This would be analogous to a suggestion Protagoras has already made about the past. One of the 'verbal' objections to Theaetetus' definition of knowledge as perception had to do with memory: a man who remembers something he saw yesterday but does not still see now, allegedly both knows (because he remembers) and does not know (because he no longer sees) that thing (163d–164b). In his Defence Protagoras offers several alternative lines of reply, one of which is to deny that it is the same person who first sees the thing and then sees it no longer (166b, picking up the Heraclitean thesis of universal nonidentity over time from 158e–160c). The suggestion is not developed, but its effect is to break the objective connection we ordinarily assume to hold between memory and previous experience. And this could lead to a strongly verificationist reduction of the past to present memory experience: at any given time my past (what for me now was the case at earlier times) simply is whatever it now seems to me was the case earlier.[53] There would be no problem, on this view, if Monday's self and Tuesday's self have different impressions of what happened on Sunday (the two selves simply have different pasts), nor therefore if Monday's self and Tuesday's disagree about Monday: Monday's present does not become Tuesday's past. Now, could the relativist adopt an analogous strategy for the future? How would it work out? Are there asymmetries between past and future which would make it peculiarly difficult to transfer the strategy to the future?

If neither of these defences is satisfactory—neither collapsing the future into the present nor allowing future experience to be predetermined by present expectation—*and if* there is no other way out, the relativist is in real difficulty. There is more to it than the existence of one class of judgements for which relativism fails. In one way or another enormous numbers of present-tense judgements carry implications for the future; Plato's example was judgements about what is advantageous, but the reader will easily add more. Worse still, judgements about the near or distant future are

---

53. A verificationist account of the past with interesting affinities to the above was put forward by A. J. Ayer in 1936. See *Language, Truth and Logic* 2nd edition (London: 1946), 102: 'Propositions about the past are rules for the prediction of those "historical" experiences which are commonly said to verify them'.

intrinsic to action: an agent who does one thing for the sake of another typically chooses the first because it now seems to them that the second will result. But whether it *will* in fact result or not—that, on the present argument, is something the sense of which can only be given by saying, 'Wait and see.' The very notion of the future makes us submit to objectivity. So, then, does action. That is to say, life itself. Any readers of this Introduction who still incline to relativism had better look to their guns.

The critique resumed: (ii) refutation of Heraclitus (179c–183c)

Plato has now vindicated the objectivity of truth for a significant class of judgements, and thereby has secured a vitally important condition for expert knowledge. To be sure, he wants ultimately to establish not only that judgements about the future are objectively true or false, but also (178de) that experts are able to give better or more authoritative verdicts about the future than other people. But the question 'Is competence in judgement just a matter of getting it right, or is there more to it than that?' is held over to Part II of the dialogue, while the ensuing question 'What makes the expert's judgement better or more authoritative?' will concern us in Part III. Meanwhile, we return to perception.

So many present-tense statements carry implications for the future that we should by now be wondering where relativism can still stand firm. It could well be argued that the only present-tense statements which do not imply anything about the future are those that report the immediate perception of sensible qualities, e.g. 'I see (something) white'. Plato does not argue this, but in the light of the New Formulation (p. 32) it is no surprise to find that such perception is in fact his next target. We are to confront at last the question whether perception, as elucidated through the theories of Protagoras and Heraclitus, is knowledge.

The section opens at 179c with Socrates meditating on whether perceptions and perceptual judgements can ever be convicted of being untrue. Our first question must be, Why raise that issue now, so late in the proceedings? Have we not supposed all along (on Reading B for the sake of the *reductio ad absurdum* argument, on Reading A because we believe it ourselves) that every perceptual appearance is true for the person who has it? Part of the answer is that we have come back to perception after rescuing the objectivity of a very large range of judgements, and objectivity is closely connected with the possibility of getting things wrong (see 178a, 179a). Only where there is something to be wrong about is there a target for objective truth. Socrates is now wondering whether the critique of Protagorean relativism can be carried further, whether the Measure Doctrine can be dislodged from the ground where hitherto it has found its firmest footing, judgements concerning sensible qualities (cf. 178de for an earlier hint of this development). But perhaps the terms in which Socrates expresses his question are as important as the question itself.

For notice that perceptions and perceptual judgements are mentioned separately, side by side, as distinct things. At the beginning of Part I they were not clearly distinguished but amalgamated together by the equation of perception with appearing (152bc, p. 11). To mark off perception from perceptual judgement is to reveal that appearing is a complex notion, with these two things as its separate components.[54] Well then, if the notion of appearing is complex, the doctrine that every perceptual appearance is true for the person who has it is complex—and that complexity had better come into the open. For it will make a difference to the way perception itself is understood. And this in turn will have consequences for the relation of the Heraclitean theory of perception to the Protagorean theory of truth.

The Heraclitean theory of perception as expounded earlier certainly made provision for every sensible appearance to involve just that perceptual experience which is 'akin' (156c) or proper to the sensible quality displayed by the object perceived. The perception as such, the goings-on in eye or tongue, could hardly be convicted of being, in any sense, untrue or incorrect. But now that the other element in sensible appearances, the judgement identifying what is perceived as white, say, or sweet, has been marked off from the process of perceiving, we face a question that was not brought distinctly to our attention earlier: Does the Heraclitean theory guarantee that these judgements will always be true and correct?[55] Ac-

---

54. That Plato himself believed that appearing is a compound notion is made clear at *Sophist* 264b: 'What we mean by "it appears" is a blend of perception and judgement'. This would not of course apply to the extended use of 'appears' discussed p. 21 above.

55. Notice that Socrates in 179c speaks as if the predicates 'true' and 'untrue' apply both to perceptions as such and to the accompanying perceptual judgements, whereas at 186c we find him arguing that perception on its own cannot 'get at truth'. One of the tasks for a decision between Readings A and B is to explain this development.

cording to Reading B they must be correct if the Protagorean-cum-Theaetetan thesis is to hold good: that every sensible appearance is a case of the perceiver knowing, in virtue of their perception, how things are for them. The provision is no less important for Reading A, according to which we want to establish that every sensible appearance is, although not knowledge, nonetheless an incorrigible awareness of some quality in the flux of becoming (p. 8). Now that the element of judgement has been disentangled from perception, let us try to pinpoint exactly what the danger is that we still need to forestall.

The Heraclitean theory is a theory according to which, as we are shortly reminded (182ab), neither the object nor the subject of perception exists with any determinate properties of its own outside their mutual interaction. It is only within that interaction and for each other that the object can be said to be, or become, e.g. white, and the subject said to be, or to come to be, seeing (159e–160c). Thus a perceptual judgement like 'I see something white' identifies and records a momentary subject's momentary perception of a momentary object's momentarily occurring whiteness, a whiteness which exists privately for that perceiving subject alone. With judgements as exiguous in content as that, nothing that happens at any other time and nothing in the experience of any other person at the present time could be the basis for a charge of untruth. So much has already been secured (on behalf of Theaetetus' definition according to Reading B, on behalf of Plato's own philosophy according to Reading A) by the contributions of Heraclitus and Protagoras respectively (p. 17, p. 15). If there remains any basis at all for correcting a perceptual judgement, it must be found within the momentary perceptual encounter itself. This residual threat is what we still have to eliminate.

We are now in a position to appreciate that the issue at stake in the coming discussion is one that has been of the greatest importance for empiricist theories of knowledge. Socrates' question 'Can a perceptual judgement be convicted of being untrue?' is to be compared with the question often asked in modern epistemology 'Is it possible to be mistaken about one's own present sense-data?'. In the quest for certainty, both ancient and modern have to decide whether 'so long as we keep within the limits of immediate present experience' (179c) our judgements are completely and in every respect incorrigible. If they are not, there is no hope for the empiricist project of founding knowledge (or a structure of reasonable belief—pp. 10–11) on a base of experiential certainty.

There is an interesting difference, however, between the Platonic and modern approaches to this question. The traditional empiricist view, of Berkeley and others, is that in naming the colour one sees there is no room for genuinely factual error. If one says 'magenta' where 'crimson' is correct, it is either a deliberate lie (hence not a mistake in one's actual judgement) or a linguistic mistake about the meaning of 'magenta', e.g. the mistake of thinking it means the colour which is in fact called 'crimson'; in the latter case one is wrong about what the colour is called, not about what colour it is. A modern discussion will take up that view and argue for or against the proposition that judgements which keep within the limits of immediate present experience can be objectively incorrect.[56] By contrast, the conclusion Plato argues for is that in naming the colour one sees any and every answer is equally correct (182d–183a). It is not, or not in the first instance, that 'I see magenta' can be wrong, but that 'I see magenta' and 'I see blue' are both correct, and so is 'I'm not seeing but hearing' (182de). The conclusion is then generalized (183ab) in terms which imply that 'I see magenta' not only can be wrong but actually is wrong. Yet we are still not talking about the kind of error under discussion in the modern debate just mentioned. The point is that whatever I say is as wrong as it is right. Language is emptied of all positive meaning.[57]

This, then, is the final conclusion of the long discussion of the three theses which have been in play since the beginning of Part I. The problem for the reader is twofold: first, to see how the conclusion is arrived at, and assess the validity of the reasoning; second, to understand its significance for the three theses in general and more particularly for Socrates' question at 179c about the corrigibility of perceptual judgements. The two tasks are connected. For it will be remembered that on Reading A Plato himself accepts the theories of Protagoras and Heraclitus, so long as they are confined to perception and the world of sensible things (p. 8). He will hardly

---

56. For: A. J. Ayer, *The Problem of Knowledge* (London & New York: 1956), chap. 2; J. L. Austin, *Sense and Sensibilia* (Oxford: 1962), chap. 10. Against: A. J. Ayer, *The Foundations of Empirical Knowledge, op. cit.*, 78 ff.

57. All positive meaning because 183b seems—half-jokingly—to leave us with the option of a language of pure denial. See note *ad loc.*

want to accept an account of the sensible world from which the conclusion follows that it cannot be described in any positive terms at all. On the contrary, within their proper sphere, perceptual judgements ought to be infallible.[58] So the task for Reading A is to show that the damaging conclusion is not derived from the theory of perception adopted earlier but from a radical extension of it which Plato introduces quite deliberately, in order to draw attention to the absurd consequence it would involve. The absurdity will demonstrate where limits must be imposed on the Heraclitean flux of becoming; within these limits the earlier theory of perception can stand unimpaired, a firm Platonic basis for the proof that perception is not knowledge.[59]

For Reading B, however, denying as it does that Plato himself approves the theories of Protagoras and Heraclitus, the task is rather different: namely, to exhibit the section 179c–183c as the culmination of the long *reductio ad absurdum* which has been under way since Theaetetus' definition was first propounded (Theaetetus → Protagoras → Heraclitus → the impossibility of language). The extension of flux to the point where language is emptied of all positive meaning must be something to which Theaetetus is committed by the project of finding sufficient conditions for his definition to hold good (p. 10). In relation to Socrates' question at 179c, the price to be paid for making perceptual judgements totally incorrigible is that they then have nothing to say to us. If this is the moral of the argument, its interest is not confined to a convinced Platonist. It challenges anyone who appeals to immediate present experience

58. So Cornford [2], 92 with n. 1. Note that it would not be enough to leave the phenomenal world in radical flux and claim that the situation is saved by the postulation of unchanging Forms in addition to sensible things (so Cherniss [19]). The unpalatable consequence of flux cannot be avoided by flux plus Forms, for it is an elementary logical truth that, if a proposition entails an acknowledged absurdity, it continues to entail that absurdity no matter what further propositions you conjoin it with.

59. So Cornford [2], 92 ff., in large measure joined on this occasion by McDowell [3], 180–84, but with a disagreement as to the direction in which Heraclitean flux is extended and hence a disagreement on where limits must be drawn to save the theory of perception from the absurd consequence of extreme flux. For Cornford the extension that needs to be blocked is the extra claim that there is constant change even in the meanings of the words used to speak about perception: 'Plato's point is that, if "all things" without exception are always changing, language can have no fixed meaning' (p. 99). Similarly Ryle, *Plato's Progress*, *op. cit.*, 273. For McDowell it is the extension of change into the momentary perceptual encounter itself: 'if, as the [original theory of perception] implies, we can identify, e.g., whiteness and seeing, then it must be possible to say of each that it *is* just that' (p. 183–84).

for the kind of certainty which can serve as a base or foundation for the theory of knowledge. And readers of this Introduction who are attracted to the empiricist programme will note that, since the argument is a *reductio ad absurdum*, its starting point is not some alien Platonic premise they need not bother with, but a careful analysis and elaboration of their own initial conviction that the senses provide us with knowledge and certainty.[60]

What evidence does the passage offer to help us decide between these two interpretations? In favour of Reading A is that some time is spent on a portrait of contemporary Heracliteans in Ionia (179d–180d). These persons, who are as unstable as everything else in their philosophy, are often supposed to be wild extremists who would actually support the extended flux doctrine. In favour of Reading B is that the extended doctrine is reached by argument. Socrates offers a reason why a Heraclitean would be committed to accepting further elements of change into the theory of perception (181d–182a). One or other of these pieces of evidence must be discounted as not serious.

It would not be quite fair to recommend on this occasion (cf. p. 13) that the way to decide is to count the jokes. The Heraclitean portrait is indeed a witty matching of the men to their philosophy. So too the materialists at 155e–156a are tough, hard fellows like the bodies they believe in, and the 'One' who is Parmenides has the unruffled composure of his one unchanging reality (183e–184a with note ad loc.). But even a humorous sketch of invented characters[61]

60. On this understanding of Plato's argument (and subject to the qualification in n. 57 above about a language of pure denial), its closest modern analogue (noticed by K. W. Mills, 'Plato and the Instant', *Aristotelian Society Supplementary Volume* 48 [1974], 91) is Wittgenstein's celebrated argument for the impossibility of a private language: *Philosophical Investigations, op. cit.* §§ 243 ff. Wittgenstein sets out to show that on certain assumptions—assumptions which are often taken to be characteristic of empiricism—statements about immediate private experience, so far from being paradigms of certainty, say nothing even to the speaker himself. The argument proceeds, like Plato's, by taking the assumptions seriously and seeing where they lead. Two of the results to which (it is argued) they lead are worth highlighting here for comparison with Plato's conclusions. One is that, when I try to name my sensation, 'whatever is going to seem right to me is right. And that only means that here we can't talk about "right".' (§ 258). The other, connected point is that, for all the difference it makes, the private object could be constantly changing (§ 293).

61. Despite the apparent suggestion that the Heracliteans in Ionia are actual people whom Theodorus might have met (180b), we have no independent evidence of these goings-on at Ephesus, and it is not certain that it is not part of Plato's joke to represent the Heraclitean philosophy by a plurality of individuals springing up spontaneously on their own, each with their own claim to knowledge (180c). How

could be a device to signal that the extended flux doctrine is an inconsequential addition to what has gone before. So let us turn to the argument of 181d–182a.

A distinction has been introduced (181cd) between two kinds of motion or change: spatial movement and alteration (change of quality or character).[62] When the theory of perception was presented earlier, the dominant locutions were those of spatial movement, whether literally or metaphorically intended (pp. 16–18). Now the question is posed whether, when the Heracliteans say all things are in motion, they mean that everything is undergoing both spatial movement and alteration. Socrates has already expressed his opinion that they do mean this (181c). Theodorus agrees (181e), but with a hesitation which prompts Socrates to confirm the conclusion by the argument we are interested in. The argument is that if they left out one kind of motion, things would be at rest or not moving as well as moving, and it would be no more correct to say 'All things are in motion' than 'All things are at rest'; to eliminate all trace of stability, they must admit that everything is in every kind of motion at once.

With this conclusion we reach the extended flux doctrine. It is the addition of alteration which leads to the collapse of language. So it is vital to know how serious the argument is meant to be.

The ground for suspicion is that the argument turns on a contradiction which is 'obviously spurious'.[63] There is no inconsistency between 'All things are in motion' and 'All things are at rest' provided it is in different respects that they are in motion and at rest. Elsewhere Plato shows himself perfectly familiar with the point (e.g. *Republic* 436ce), which is too obvious for him or his reader to miss. Therefore, he cannot seriously mean to suggest that the extended flux doctrine is something to which a proponent of the theory of perception will be committed on pain of contradiction.

---

better to embody a philosophical thesis (universal nonidentity over time) which denies that one ever meets the same person twice? We do know of one extremist Heraclitean of the period, who 'finally did not think it right to say anything but only moved his finger, and criticised Heraclitus for saying that it is impossible to step twice into the same river; for *he* thought one could not do it even once' (Aristotle, *Metaphysics* IV 5, 1010a 12–15). This was Cratylus, whose view that sensible things are in flux and that there is no knowledge of them is also said by Aristotle (*Met.* I 6, 987a 32–b 1) to have been an early influence on the development of Plato's own thinking. If that sounds as though it could be helpful to Reading A (cf. Cornford [2], 99), a note of caution: Cratylus was an Athenian.

62. On the terminology here, see note *ad* 181d.

63. So McDowell [3], 180.

Abstractly considered, the objection appears sound enough. But Reading B will recall Socrates' question at 179c and the wider significance which the notion of stability has acquired in the course of the dialogue so far. If a thing is stable, or stable in some respect (the qualification makes no odds), that means there is an objective basis for correcting or confirming someone's judgement as to how it is, or how it is in that respect.[64] There is a fact of the matter, independent of the person's judgement. The whole point of eliminating first objectivity between persons and then identity through time was to ensure that there would be no basis in the experience of other times and other people for charging anyone with untruth. Accordingly, an element of stability within the perceptual encounter itself, although it would last for a moment only and would be inaccessible to anyone but the perceiver, would still mean that something has a determinate character independent of the perceiver's judgement about it. White is the colour I see, not pink; seeing is the perception it elicits in me, not hearing.[65] If I were to judge otherwise, I would be wrong. I would be wrong even if no other perceiver could ever be in a position to tell me so—incorrigibility by myself later and others now is not yet total incorrigibility or infallibility. Never mind what a bunch of wild Heracliteans in Ionia would say about that. The important thing is that Theaetetus cannot allow it. Stability, even for a moment, entails objectivity, even if only for that moment. This means that a perceptual judgement could, in principle, be wrong; hence we do not yet have it absolutely guaranteed that every sensible appearance is a case of the perceiver knowing, in virtue of their perception, how things are for them (p. 44). If Theaetetus is to maintain his position, every last remnant of stability must go.

Once this is understood, it becomes clear both that the argument of 181d–182a is serious and why it was an important move at 179c to replace the compound notion of appearing by its separate components, perception and perceptual judgement. The Measure Doctrine states that things are for each perceiver exactly as they appear to them to be at the moment of perceiving. Split the notion

---

64. Another place where the notion of stability is invoked to express the idea of objectivity is *Cratylus* 386de.

65. This is McDowell's understanding of the stability to be attacked (n. 59), with a different account of why it needs to be attacked: not to show the absurd consequences from which the Heraclitean theory of perception must be protected, but to show the absurd consequences to which Theaetetus' use of that theory will be committed.

Relativism

of appearing into two components, and the Measure Doctrine itself becomes two:

(i) Things are for each perceiver exactly as they experience them at the moment of perceiving,

and

(ii) Things are for each perceiver exactly as they judge them to be at the moment of perceiving.

For the Measure Doctrine to stand firm 'within the limits of immediate present experience', both (i) and (ii) must be secured. The Heraclitean theory of perception secures (i), but (ii) requires a guarantee that perceivers will not misinterpret their experience. How is this to be secured?

There is no mechanism in the theory of perception specifically designed to prevent perceivers misinterpreting their experience, and it would be an odd theory, to say the least, if it did in some way shackle a perceiver's judgement to match whatever perception occurred. Having one's judgement automatically determined by experience is no better than having one's future experience automatically determined to match whatever judgement of present expectation precedes (cf. pp. 40–1). Rather, the entire elaboration of the three-in-one theory takes it for granted, as do later empiricists like Berkeley, that perceivers will simply 'read off' the correct description of their perceptual experience from the experience itself. The weaknesses of that assumption will be further probed in the important concluding section of Part I (184a–186e). Meanwhile, the fact must be faced that so far there is nothing to prevent a mistaken judgement about what one's immediate present experience is. In more Protagorean idiom, 'x is/becomes F for a at time t' is itself an absolute form of statement: however momentary the state of affairs it claims to report, in principle it might fail to report correctly. To achieve total incorrigibility, therefore, we must make it impossible for a to be wrong if at time t they judge otherwise than that x is/becomes F for them.

At 182cd Theodorus, as spokesman for the compound theory, takes the only course open to it. He accepts Socrates' argument that there must not be even a momentary stability within the perceptual encounter, lest anything remain for perceptual judgement to be wrong about:

> There is a flux of this very thing also, the whiteness, and it
> is passing over into another colour, *lest it be convicted of
> standing still in this respect*. (182d)

Notice the verbal echo of Socrates' question at 179c. If the whiteness
could be convicted of standing still in respect of being/flowing
white, its stability would imply the possibility of convicting as
untrue the perceiver's judgement about which colour they see. This
is the reason for 'reimporting change into the atoms of change',[66]
or rather for introducing further change, viz. alteration, within the
momentary perceptual encounters which are all that remained of
ordinary subjects and objects of perception when the flux story
reached its climax at 160c. Without alteration the perceiver would
be wrong to judge that the colour they see is not white but (say)
yellow. The addition of alteration ensures that they would not be
wrong.

But now, of course, to complete the *reductio*, all Socrates has to
do is point out that nothing remains for judgement to be right about
either (182d). Any statement is as right, or as wrong, as any other
(183a).

Such is the devastating conclusion of the argument which spells
out the effect on the theory of perception of adding alteration to
spatial movement. There are plenty of questions to ask about the
passage. Should Theodorus have allowed Socrates to go through
with it? Would a Heraclitean be able to resist it? Are latter-day
empiricists better placed to defend the proposition that judgements
of immediate experience are incorrigible and yet meaningful? If you
pursue these questions seriously, you will find yourself led back
through all the philosophical and interpretative questions we have
had in view during this long discussion of Theaetetus' first definition. It is almost time to bring together the consideration of Plato's
stage-directions (cf. p. 9) and the assessment of his arguments to
reach a final decision on whether Reading A or Reading B, or some
third alternative, makes better and more coherent sense of Part I as
a whole.[67] But before leaving the three theses, Plato gives us one of

66. Owen [18], 86.

67. Let me repeat what I said at the beginning (p. 9), that Readings A and B are not
the only possible interpretations. I believe that they are the two most fruitful and
plausible interpretations if one is concerned to see the strategy of Part I as a whole.
They also have the expository advantage that the opposition between them enforces
a series of interpretative choices the effect of which has been to lay before the reader,
in sharp focus, the main problems which any alternative interpretation must address.
The reader who has been introduced to these problems in the terms proposed will

the most important of the stage-directions by which he guides our understanding of their role in the dialogue. And then, to conclude Part I, he takes up the definition of knowledge as perception once more, for a final discussion which is the most positive in the entire dialogue. To these matters we now turn.

Conclusion to Part I (184a–186e): perception and judgement

Nothing typifies the fascinating difficulties of a Platonic dialogue better than the question with which we approach the final section of Part I: Has the definition of knowledge as perception been refuted yet? That so basic an issue of interpretation should be in dispute is surprising, but true. The argument we have just been through concluded that the definition 'Knowledge is perception', being itself a statement in language, is no more true than false (182e). But according to Reading A, all that means is that the extended flux doctrine wreaks havoc with the definition as well as the theory of perception, so that a proponent of the definition must accept the restrained Heracliteanism of the earlier theory as the true account of perception (cf. p. 46). It still remains to show, on the basis of that account, that perception is not knowledge. On Reading A, this is the task which the final section undertakes.

Support for Reading A's account of the transition to 184a–186e is drawn from some remarks which follow the argument about the impossibility of language. When the argument is over, Socrates claims (183bc) that it completes the refutation not merely of some Heracliteans but of Protagoras and Theaetetus as well. Or rather, that is how it stands with Protagoras. About Theaetetus Socrates is more qualified: 'And we are not going to grant that knowledge is perception, not at any rate on the line of inquiry which supposes that all things are in motion; we are not going to grant it unless Theaetetus here has some other way of stating it'. This important stage-direction indicates a possibility left open which Theaetetus might take up. What is it?

According to Reading A it is the possibility of assessing the definition of knowledge as perception by the true Heraclitean the-

---

be well equipped to tackle alternative interpretations of Part I, in Sayre [7], for example, McDowell [3], or Bostock [9], or the various essays on particular passages mentioned in the bibliography.

ory of perception adopted earlier; for what has just been shown, and what the stage-direction points out, is that if the inquiry is pursued on the basis of the *extended* flux doctrine, the result is absurdity.

Reading B, however, takes a very different view. The conclusion that 'Knowledge is perception' is no more true than false is the final twist in the *reductio ad absurdum* of Theaetetus' definition (the collapse of language brings down not only the statements which come under the definition but also the definition itself). Recall that the *reductio* was set up by arguing that the theories of Protagoras and Heraclitus are the only sufficient conditions for Theaetetus' definition which can reasonably be devised; hence they are necessary conditions as well as sufficient (p. 10); hence when Protagoras and Heraclitus are refuted (the inclusion of Protagoras in the stage-direction is support for Reading B), the definition falls as well—unless Theaetetus can after all ground his definition on a different set of sufficient conditions, on an account of perception and the world which would avoid the disastrous consequences of the Heraclitean story. It remains in principle possible that he might do so.

The possibility is no sooner mentioned, however, than it is foreclosed. On Reading B, 184a–186e is a second refutation of 'Knowledge is perception', but this time it is a direct proof rather than an indirect proof or *reductio*. The difference between the two styles of proof is crucial. An indirect proof is one where the thesis under consideration supplies the materials for its own refutation; that is what has been happening so far. But in 184a–186e the argument proceeds, for the first time in the dialogue, from premises which Plato himself accepts as true (compare the stage-directions at 185e with those at 157cd). It follows that Reading B will not expect the account of perception given in this final section to be consistent with the Protagorean-Heraclitean account that has prevailed hitherto. Reading A will expect the contrary. Only now are we coming to the proof that perception is not knowledge, for which we have been preparing all along, so what is said about perception in 184a–186e should be consistent with what has gone before (subject, of course, to the limit which wards off the absurdity of extreme flux). These contrary expectations can be measured against the text to give us a final test of the two rival readings.

We begin with a grammatical contrast between two ways of expressing the role of the sense organs in perception. Is it more correct to say that we see *with* the eyes or *through* the eyes, that we hear *with* the ears or *through* them (184bc)? Socrates explains that he is not fussing about correct language for its own sake. He wants to use the grammatical contrast as the vehicle for an important philosophical contrast between two opposed views of the perceiving subject, as follows (184d).

To say that we see with the eyes, hear with the ears, etc., is to say that it is our eyes which do the seeing, our ears the hearing, and so on—the 'with'-idiom is intended to pick out that element in a person which is responsible for their perceiving. The difficulty then arises that this makes it sound as if there are a number of senses ensconced in us, like the warriors in the Wooden Horse at Troy, each doing its own perceiving with no coordination between them. To avoid such a strange suggestion we may prefer to say that what we perceive with, i.e. what does the perceiving, is a unitary centre to which the separate senses converge—the soul or mind. The 'through'-idiom can now be summoned to define the role of the senses: they are the instruments or equipment[68] through which we perceive with the soul, i.e. through which the soul perceives (cf. also 185c, 185d).

There is the contrast: on the one side, a plurality of perceivers; on the other, a single perceiving consciousness. It is not difficult to decide which to prefer. But the business of philosophy is argument, not preference. We shall need to see what argument Plato can muster for a single perceiving mind. First, however, we should dwell on the Wooden Horse model which Plato rejects. Does the rejection fit better with the expectations of Reading A or with those of Reading B?

At first glance the Wooden Horse model is strikingly reminiscent of the Heraclitean story elaborated from 156a to 160e. In that story not only is there no identity through time, since the perceiver we call Socrates at one moment is distinct from the perceiver we call Socrates at any other moment, but even of two perceptions occurring at the same time it cannot really be said that they belong to the same perceiver. If Socrates takes a drink of wine with his eye on the contents of his cup, the Heraclitean account of this will ascribe the seeing something white to an eye and the tasting something sweet to a tongue (156de, 159cd), where eye and tongue are distinct

---

68. The word is *organa*, which came to be, from Aristotle onwards, the general biological term for organs of the body, but it is here applied to the senses rather than the sense organs. Plato in this passage speaks indifferently of perceiving through a sense or perceptual capacity such as sight (184d, 184e–185a, 185b, 185e, 186b) and of perceiving through a sense organ, a proper part of the body (184c, 184de).

perceiving things and no less distinct are the white and the sweet things they respectively perceive. We may indeed speak of Socrates tasting sweet wine, but only on the understanding that this Socrates cannot be the subject, just as the wine cannot be the object, of any other perception (159e–160b). There is no more to this Socrates than his tasting tongue,[69] and no more to that than is given by the statement that it is tasting this sweet wine now; so if, similarly, Socrates is to be identified with his eye when he sees something white, it follows that the Socrates who tastes something sweet at a certain moment is distinct from the Socrates who sees something white at that moment.

A parenthesis may be of value here to those who find it hard to stomach the tasting tongues and seeing eyes in which the Heraclitean theory deals. In *The Problems of Philosophy* Russell argues,

> When I look at my table and see a certain brown colour, what is quite certain at once is not '*I* am seeing a brown colour', but rather 'a brown colour is being seen'. This of course involves something (or somebody) which (or who) sees the brown colour; but it does not of itself involve that more or less permanent person whom we call 'I'. So far as immediate certainty goes, it might be that the something which sees the brown colour is quite momentary, and not the same as the something which has some different experience the next moment.[70]

Russell's something or somebody, which does the seeing when I look at my table but is not necessarily me, is a twentieth-century relative of Plato's seeing eye, born of a similar quest for certainty, and when one thinks it through, hardly less puzzlingly problematic.

All this is fair game for Reading B. It is true that the Wooden Horse model is not Heraclitean. The hypothesis of constant change through time has been refuted, so the organs and objects dealt with in this section of the dialogue are the ordinary stable kind which continue in being from one moment to the next. But the Wooden Horse with its warrior-senses is a just representation of what remains of the earlier picture if flux through time is subtracted from

---

69. It is revealing, the way 159de switches indifferently from tongue to Socrates as the subject of perception.

70. Bertrand Russell, *The Problems of Philosophy* (Oxford: 1912), 19. For a helpful analysis and discussion of this type of theory, see Sydney Shoemaker, *Self-Knowledge and Self-Identity* (Ithaca: 1963), chap. 2.

it. Each organ or sense being an autonomous perceiving subject, the only role left to Socrates, if he is not to be identified with his eye when he is seeing and with his tongue when he is tasting, is that of a mere container, like the hollow horse, for the real subjects of these processes. No wonder Plato rejects the Wooden Horse model. His doing so is the natural corollary of rejecting Theaetetus' definition and everything that goes with it.

For Reading A, on the other hand, the Heraclitean story is still in force. Plato's present point is not that it gives the wrong picture, but that it cannot be the whole picture. Our sense organs are still to be regarded as mere motions or processes, as at 156a ff. But we must add[71] a central enduring mind to receive and coordinate the information they supply. The test question is: Can this be a mere addition, consistent with what has gone before and faithful to the letter and the spirit of the Heraclitean story? Berkeley would no doubt have it so. His approval of the *Theaetetus* theory of perception (p. 8) was certainly not meant to cast doubt on the substantial existence of an enduring mind, which was a mainstay of his own philosophy. Can he and his twentieth-century partisans sustain the interpretation all the way through the details of the theory of perception and its aftermath down to 160e?

Whichever explanation is preferred for Plato's rejection of the Wooden Horse model, reject it he does. He mounts a positive argument of considerable power for the thesis that we must recognize a central perceiving mind. We start (185a) from an occasion on which we both see a colour and hear a sound. There are a number of thoughts we can have about features common to this pair of sense-objects: that they both *are*, for example, and that they are *two*, that each of them is *one*, the *same* as itself and *different* from the other, and we can reflect on whether they are *like* or *unlike* each other (185ab). Such features as being and unity, sameness and similarity, and their opposites, are not, one would think, perceptible features of things. They are not properties we become aware of by the exercise of our senses. But can we prove this?

We can prove it if we accept either of the following principles:

P1 Nothing which is perceived through sight can also be perceived through hearing, and vice versa; similarly for the other senses.

P2 Colours and features of colours which are perceived

71. So Cornford [2], 105, McDowell [3], 143–44, 185.

through sight cannot also be perceived through hearing, sounds and features of sounds which are perceived through hearing cannot also be perceived through sight, and similarly for the other senses.

Both principles imply that each sense has its own proper objects—colours for sight, sounds for hearing, and we can add tastes, textures, temperatures, etc., for the other senses—but where P1 says that each sense is *confined* to its proper objects and can perceive nothing else, P2 leaves this open. P1 excludes, P2 allows room for, features like shape and size which are perceived through both sight and touch. Again, P2 but not P1 would allow Socrates to talk as he does later (192d) of seeing, touching, and hearing Theaetetus or Theodorus. It is natural to think that P1 is the principle stated in the text at 184e–185a, but P2 is all the argument will need. While P1 has the advantage of a generality lacking in P2, P2's advantage is that we are likely to think it true; from a commonsense point of view, P1 is soon seen to be false.

This is no objection, of course, if we adhere to Reading A, which looks upon commonsense falsehood as philosophical truth. P1 is precisely the principle we should expect to find at work in this section if the Heraclitean theory of perception is still in force.[72] Reading B can reply as follows. Certainly, the Heraclitean theory of perception is compatible with P1, but it is not compatible with the other premise of the argument, that a colour and a sound can share a common feature. For the Heraclitean theory expressly denies that two sense-objects can share a common feature (159a). We can regard the Heraclitean theory of perception as soundly refuted and still think there is a certain intuitive appeal to Socrates' statement at 185a that you cannot see what you hear. This is true of the examples cited in the immediately preceding context (184b, d). Let it be taken, therefore, as a way of focussing on that type of example and thereby *introducing* Theaetetus to the idea that each sense has its own proper objects which are inaccessible to the other senses. After all, why does Theaetetus give such ready assent? It is easier to imagine Plato sure that P2 or something similar is correct, though perhaps uncertain how to state it with persuasive generality,[73] than to think he means Theaetetus to find P1 an obvious

72. This is argued, independently of Reading A, by Modrak [38].

73. A correct principle for proper objects is in fact hard to formulate: see Holland [36] and Richard Sorabji, 'Aristotle on Demarcating the Five Senses', *Philosophical Review* 80 (1971), 55–79.

deduction from the original (restrained) Heraclitean theory of perception.

But this is just a preliminary skirmish. We must approach the main argument. It follows even from the weaker principle P2 that it cannot be through either sight or hearing that we are aware of the common features mentioned in our example. It cannot be through hearing if sameness and the rest are features of a colour, and it cannot be through sight if they are features of a sound. Some third mode of apprehension must be involved (185b).

The next step is to argue that the third mode of apprehension is itself perceptual only if we can find a sense or sense organ giving access to the feature in question; as, for example, it would be the sense of taste operating through the tongue that we would use if it were possible to investigate whether the colour and the sound were both *salty* (185bc). But no bodily organ or sense can be found to give access to the common features in our example. As a later philosopher might put it, there is no such thing as an impression of being or of sameness or of unity. Which proves that they are not perceptible features at all. They are not grasped through the senses but through the mind's own activity of thought (185ce).

This argument does a great deal more than prove a conclusion which was obvious all along. Certainly it establishes what Socrates wanted to establish (184d), that it is with one and the same part of ourselves that we do all our perceiving, contrary to the Wooden Horse model. But it proves this by showing that there is something in us, the soul or mind, which can think and reason about whatever we perceive. The unity of the perceiving subject is demonstrated from the unity of the thinker who surveys and judges the proper objects of different senses, for which purpose the thinker must also be a perceiver capable of exercising and coordinating a plurality of senses. Plato's achievement in this passage is nothing less than the first unambiguous statement in the history of philosophy of the difficult but undoubtedly important idea of the unity of consciousness.

Question: Does the emergence of this idea fit better the expectations of Reading A or those of Reading B? A correlative question is which reading best accounts for the status of the sensible qualities in the present argument. This 'being' that is shared by a colour and a sound, indeed by everything whatsoever (185c): is it the relative 'being' that was earlier run in tandem with the Heraclitean idiom of becoming (160b, p. 12, p. 50) or the absolute 'being' which a Heraclitean would excise from the language (157ab)? If it is the latter, the argument implies that, just as the perceiving mind has its own nature and identity apart from particular perceptions, so too do the sensible qualities perceived. The total picture as seen by Reading B is in thoroughly commonsensical counterpoint to the Heraclitean theory of the earlier discussion and its commitment to doing away with personal identity on the one hand and an objective world on the other.

We are now ready to demolish (for the second time, according to Reading B) the thesis that perception is knowledge. The essential premise has been established: being is not grasped through the senses but through the mind's own activity of thought (185ce). But if perception on its own cannot grasp being, neither can it get at the truth about anything, and getting at truth is very evidently a necessary condition of knowledge (cf. 152c, 160cd). Therefore, perception never amounts to knowledge (186ce).

The argument is brief. It has an air of confident finality. The conclusion refutes both halves of Theaetetus' original definition, both (1) 'All perceiving is knowing' and (2) 'All knowing is perceiving' (p. 10; cf. p. 21).[74] With such momentous consequences in the offing, it is obviously important to take a closer look at the concept of being, on which everything now depends.

The principal guide to understanding here is the link which the argument appeals to between being and truth. For reasons to be made clear later, I shall sketch three, instead of the usual two, competing lines of interpretation. The first is that of Reading B.

(1) A true judgement states what is the case. If 'The wind is cold' is true, the wind is cold. The term 'being', then, is no high-flown abstraction: it is simply the general notion corresponding to the ordinary everyday use of 'is'.[75] Any judgement, even the most minimal, is a judgement as to what is the case, making explicit or implicit use of the verb 'to be'. Any judgement, in other words, calls upon the capacity to think that something is thus or (185c) that it is not thus (compare 183ab). It requires the mind's own activity of thought and cannot be accounted for as an exercise of the powers of our senses. Thus the inability of perception to get at being is its

---

74. Cornford [2], 102, finds an argument against (2) in the section up to 185e. No such argument is announced and none is needed, since the final conclusion 'No perceiving is knowing' is simply convertible. The task of 184a–85e is to secure the premise for this conclusion.

75. Readers who know some Greek can be referred on this point to the admirable discussion in Charles H. Kahn, 'Some Philosophical Uses of "to be" in Plato', *Phronesis* 26 (1981), 105–34.

inability to frame any proposition at all. Socrates could hardly have found a more conclusive reason for denying that perception ever amounts to knowledge.

(2) Reading A, it will be recalled, was designed to reinforce the epistemological theories of dialogues like the *Phaedo* and *Republic*, which declare that, because the sensible world is the realm of becoming, not being, it is the province of opinion, not knowledge. From this perspective what perception cannot do, given that the Protagorean and Heraclitean theories are true of it, is grasp the changeless being of the Forms. It is incapable of establishing the truth of definitions (cf. p. 38). Therefore, perception is not knowledge.

Readings A and B are now very far apart. To sustain Interpretation (2) Reading A requires us to take 'being' and 'truth' at 186c in a restrictive and specialized sense, laden with Platonic metaphysics from earlier dialogues or at least ready to be filled with metaphysical content in due course. Interpretation (2) also requires us to view the argument as resting on the assumption that a definition is a necessary condition of knowledge. This idea is the pivot of the epistemology of the *Phaedo* and *Republic* and will become the object of critical attention in Part III of the *Theaetetus*. But it has already been invoked, without metaphysical implications, in the *Theaetetus*; for it is the guiding principle of Socrates' argument at 146c ff. that one is in no position to know what is an example of knowledge until one knows what knowledge itself is (p. 4). Reading A can therefore plead that there is no difficulty about supplying it as an unexpressed assumption of the final proof that perception cannot be knowledge. It is an idea that Plato can expect to be vividly present to every reader of his works.

In the end, therefore, the opposition between our two Readings A and B comes down to a choice between two global approaches to Plato. Shall we read Part I of the *Theaetetus* in its own terms, as a self-sufficient critique of empiricism (Reading B)? Or shall we determine its meaning from the horizons of expectation established in earlier works of the same author (Reading A)? Finally, if Reading B is preferred, there is the further question how the critique of empiricism relates to those earlier expectations.

If one turns back to the *Phaedo* and *Republic* after studying the *Theaetetus*, one soon notices that, while they are full of hostility towards perception and everything it represents, this hostility depends upon, and is motivated by, the idea that perception is intrinsically judgemental. The charge against perception is that it offers itself as a dangerously seductive rival judgement-maker to reason (*Phaedo* 65a–67b, 79cd, 81b, 82e–83e, *Republic* 523a–525a, 602c–603a). The *Theaetetus* began from a similarly judgemental notion of perceiving that such and such is the case (p. 11), but the final outcome of Part I is that this analyzes out into two distinct components: perceiving something (e.g. hardness) and judging that it is such and such. The moral is that even in the sensible world it takes the abstract judgemental capacities of a thinking soul, not merely to have knowledge, but to be aware of anything *as* anything at all. And the question is: Was this the teaching of the earlier works, or does Reading B force us to acknowledge a change of course, or at least a striking new emphasis, in Plato's epistemology?

Afterthought

That virtually completes my account of the two readings. It is, of course, *my* account of the two readings: less coercive than if I had presented a single line of interpretation in the assertive mode, but coercive nonetheless insofar as I have asked you, the reader, to consider these questions rather than others. You should also be aware that I as author am able to write more sympathetically and compellingly for Reading B, which I have helped to work out and believe in myself, than for Reading A.[76] But my chief act of coerciveness was to insist at the outset (p. 7) that we look for an overall strategy behind the long discussion of the definition of knowledge as perception. I made it a constraint on the interpretation of individual passages that they fit into a coherent architectonic. And the reader is entitled to wonder how we would have fared if we had been less mindful of that constraint.

Let us, therefore, to complete our examination of Part I, suspend questions of overall strategy and consider on its own independent merits a third interpretation of this final section, an interpretation which challenges the results both of Reading A and of Reading B. It is best motivated by confronting a certain grave difficulty which

---

76. As stated earlier (notes 14, 16), Reading B is primarily the work of Bernard Williams, Reading A the account most commonly found in the scholarly literature. I have contributed some of the detailed elaboration of Reading B, particularly in connection with the collapse of language argument at 179c–183c, and I would claim to have done better at certain points for Reading A than its adherents have usually done; e.g. according to Cornford [2], 108–9, Plato wants us to extract from the text of 186cd *both* Interpretations (1) and (2) and accept them both.

is concomitant to Interpretation (1). Interpretation (1) acknowledges the difficulty and says 'Such is the price you pay to be a Platonist'. This new Interpretation (3) aims to eliminate the difficulty without going over to the highly restrictive understanding of 'being' and 'truth' advocated by Interpretation (2). Interpretation (3) thus seeks a middle path between Interpretations (1) and (2).

We left Interpretation (1) at a point (pp. 59–60) where it would not have been inappropriate to invoke Immanuel Kant's famous dictum 'Intuitions without concepts are blind'.[77] Plato's critique, like Kant's, is directed against the empiricist assumption that at least some of the things we perceive—even if it is only the colours, sounds, etc., which are the proper objects of the several senses— are peculiarly self-intimating, in that we have only to sense them to know them immediately for what they are, with a certainty that establishes a secure foundation for the interpretations and inferences which constitute the rest of knowledge. Against this view Socrates insists at 186b that it is one thing to feel the hardness of something hard or the softness of something soft, quite another to reach the thought that it *is* hardness. One is not aware of hardness as being hardness except in contrast and opposition to softness. Only a mind that can step back, as it were, from a particular occasion of perception and make contrasts and comparisons with other per- ceptions can tell that what it is perceiving is hardness—the percep- tion by itself is blind and can tell us nothing, even in a simple case like this. In more complex cases (186ab) judgement will need to bring to bear upon the perception the resources of memory and past learning which Plato goes on to study in Part II of the dialogue. All this does indeed presuppose a central enduring mind with a unified consciousness capable of far more than the mere reception of isolated data.

But impressive as that sounds as the note to conclude on, how is Interpretation (1) to respond to the following question: Once the contrast is set up between perception on the one hand and all thought on the other, what becomes, for example, of the difference between someone feeling warmth and warmth affecting him in ways which do not amount to his perceiving it? Socrates' talk at 186c of 'experiences which reach the soul through the body' may imply that some of the things that happen to the body do not reach the soul, but can he explain the difference without bringing in some

---

77. Immanuel Kant, *Critique of Pure Reason* (1781), A 51. Cf. A294: 'In the senses there is no judgement whatsoever, neither a true nor a false judgement'.

trace of awareness, consciousness or judgement—the very things he wants to contrast with perception?

A more deeply probing version of the same difficulty is this: with perception so barely characterized, what sense can be made of the purposive behaviour of nonhuman animals who have perception only, without the coordinating capacity of interpretative judgement (186bc)? If Protagoras appeared to obliterate the difference in cognitive powers between man and beast (161c, 171e with 154a, 162e, 167b), Plato has gone to the opposite extreme and made it impossible to speak of animals using their senses to get information about the environment. Descartes was to uphold a similar view, with the claim that animals are just mechanical systems. Aristotle, on the other hand, who took biology seriously, found it necessary to promote a rich concept of perception such that the faculty of perception, which all animals share, brings with it both a considerable degree of judgemental capacity and the unity of consciousness. The debate is still with us today. It is one of the most difficult and pressing problems in philosophy to decide which concepts we may properly use in explaining the abilities of animals other than ourselves.[78] Let this be the cue for Interpretation (3).

(3) It is obvious that the above difficulty, which confronts Plato's position as seen by Interpretation (1), would be mitigated if we could ascribe to Plato a less impoverished idea of what perception on its own can achieve. The snag is that the more capacity one builds back into perception, the larger the assumption that has to be supplied for the final proof that perception cannot be knowledge because it does not get at being and truth; this was illustrated in our discussion of Interpretation (2) (p. 60). The aim of Interpretation (3) is to find a reasonably mundane, nonmetaphysical sense of 'being' and 'truth' such that (a) attaining to being and truth in this sense is uncontroversially a necessary condition of knowledge, (b) perception cannot achieve this, (c) perception is not thereby deprived of all cognitive content.

Accordingly, we allow that perception on its own is capable of identifying its own proper objects (this being the least step we can

---

78. Aristotle, *De Anima*, esp. II 6 and III 1–2; Descartes, *The Philosophical Works of Descartes*, edd. and trans. E. S. Haldane & G.R.T. Ross (Cambridge: 1931), Vol. I, 116–17, Vol. II, 103–4; Jonathan Bennett, *Linguistic Behaviour* (Cambridge: 1976); Norman Malcolm, 'Thoughtless Brutes', reprinted from *Proceedings of the American Philosophical Association* 46 (1972–73) in his *Thought and Knowledge* (Ithaca & London: 1977), 40–57; Stephen P. Stich, 'Do Animals Have Beliefs?', *Australasian Journal of Philosophy* 57 (1979), 15–28.

take to realize condition (c) and therefore the least likely to violate conditions (a) and (b)). Perception is aware of red as red, of hardness as hardness. What it cannot do is go beyond this awareness to determine what is objectively the case in an interpersonal world. It is not, for example, just by using my eyes that I decide that red *really is* the colour of something before me, nor just by the sense of touch that I conclude that what I am sitting on is *genuinely and truly* hard. For that involves, among other things, considering whether current conditions of perception are normal and can be relied upon to continue. It involves, that is, reflection and prediction, which means a level of thought that cannot be ascribed to perception as such.

This line of objection to the thesis that perception yields knowledge should strike a chord in the reader's memory. Considerations about prediction and the future refuted Protagoras earlier (177c–179b, pp. 39–42). Interpretation (3) brings them back for the final refutation of Theaetetus. The essential thought is that any claim to truth and objectivity goes beyond what is given within the confines of present perception, so perception on its own cannot get at being and truth.

That must suffice to sketch Interpretation (3).[79] The best way to get a fuller picture is to undertake the exercise of fitting this interpretation to the text. See for yourself what further details emerge and whether the groundplan just given requires modification. Does Interpretation (3) attribute to Plato a credible view of the nature and powers of perception? Does it accord with the recent emphasis on the unity of the perceiving consciousness and the claim that the senses are just instruments for the mind to work through (184de, p. 54)? How well does it cope with the grave difficulty we started from just now (pp. 61–2)? Is there any better way of satisfying conditions (a)–(c)? Take, in particular, the statement at 186c that calculations about being and advantageousness come, when they do, only as a result of trouble and education. The 'education' adverted to and contrasted with the power of perception—the former being something acquired, the latter inborn throughout the animal kingdom—will be very different kinds of

---

79. It was originally proposed by Cooper [35] as marginally preferable to Interpretation (1). An alternative version in Modrak [38] suggests a richer sense for 'being' and 'truth' and consequently does less well by conditions (a)–(c). A very detailed survey of the territory (presupposing some knowledge of Greek) is undertaken by Yahei Kanayama, 'Perceiving, Considering, and Attaining Being (*Theaetetus* 184–186)', *Oxford Studies in Ancient Philosophy* 5 (1987), 29–81.

learning for each of our three interpretations. Does Interpretation (3) give Plato a more reasonable contrast than Interpretations (1) and (2)? What, finally, of the questions of overall strategy we suspended a while ago (p. 61)? Is Interpretation (3) powerful enough to force us right back to the beginning of Part I to think again about the quest for a unitary design?

The last question amounts to a renewal of all previous questions. But that is as it should be for an Introduction which began by emphasizing the value of raising questions and then discovering in detail why a tempting but wrong answer is wrong (p. 2). The point is emphasized in the dialogue itself (151cd, 160e–161a, 187a, 187c, 210bc). Any reader of this Introduction who sets out to show that both Reading A and Reading B are misconceived will learn an enormous amount about Plato, about the *Theaetetus* and about the philosophical problems we have been discussing.

PART II

'Knowledge is true judgement'

Structural preliminaries

The first thing to note about Theaetetus' second definition of knowledge, 'Knowledge is true judgement', is that it is an example of false judgement.[1] To demonstrate its falsehood, Socrates says, only a brief argument is required—but he does not say this, nor produce the brief argument, until right at the end of Part II (201a). The bulk of Part II (187d–200c) is devoted to a discussion of the question whether false judgement is possible. A series of attempts to explain how false judgement can come about ends in confessed failure (200cd). Only then does Socrates proceed to prove that Theaetetus' second definition is an example of the very phenomenon they have been struggling, in vain, to account for.

1. Theaetetus' reasoned decision in its favour at 187b is reaffirmed with less hesitancy at 187c.

A dramatic artist like Plato is unlikely to be unaware of this relationship between the false definition and the long discussion it precipitates about whether false judgement can occur. The question is, What does he intend by it? We could take the point to be simply a down-to-earth reminder. Of course false judgement occurs, as we ordinarily believe it does (187e; cf. 190e); for here, in the definition with which Part II begins, is an example of it. If we keep firmly in mind the fact that false judgement does occur, we will appreciate that the failure of repeated attempts to explain how it can occur reveals that there is an error somewhere in the assumptions guiding the inquiry. Part II of the *Theaetetus* is to be a challenge: Spot the false judgement which makes it appear that false judgement is impossible.

A stronger and more intriguing suggestion about the role of the false definition would be the following. The false judgement which makes it appear that false judgement is not possible is none other than the false judgement which reminds us that false judgement is possible, namely, Theaetetus' definition of knowledge as true judgement. If that were so, the failure of repeated attempts to explain the undoubted fact of false judgement would constitute a sort of *reductio ad absurdum* of Theaetetus' second definition, to be followed by the direct refutation, from premises which Plato himself accepts as true, in the brief argument that begins at 201a.[2] We had better be cautious about this suggestion, for Plato has left it to us to spot the erroneous assumption. But this much at least he makes clear, both at the end and at the beginning of the discussion of false judgement, that in his view the perplexity about the possibility of false judgement stems from some assumption about knowledge.

First, the conclusion of the discussion of false judgement is that it was a mistake for Socrates and Theaetetus to embark on that inquiry before they had an adequate grasp of what knowledge is; a better understanding of knowledge is the precondition for solving the problem of false judgement (200cd). Second, the problem of false judgement is initially posed when Socrates states a puzzle based on considerations about knowledge (188ac), considerations which appear to leave no room for false judgement to occur, and this puzzle continues to be felt as a constraining influence on subse-

2. This suggestion was made long ago by the great historian of ancient philosophy Eduard Zeller: see his *Plato and the Older Academy*, trans. Sarah Frances Alleyne & Alfred Goodwin (London: 1876), 171–73. It makes a striking parallel with Reading B's map of the structure of Part I: p. 53.

quent attempts to show how false judgement is possible (cf. 191ab, 196bc, 199ac, 200b). Clearly, it will be important to see whether we can diagnose the assumptions about knowledge which give rise to Socrates' puzzle.

These are not the only signs that Part II is written as a challenge. Socrates does not say that he believes the conclusion to which his puzzle leads, namely, that false judgement is impossible. Rather, he indicates that he is deeply perplexed: false judgement is a problem we should investigate (187d, 188c). But instead of reexamining the puzzle, he leads off on a different approach (188d–189b), and then another (189b–190e), both times hoping to explain how false judgement is possible but reaching the result that false judgement is impossible. Instead of a solution to the original puzzle, we end up with three independent arguments which show, apparently, that false judgement is impossible. And that, Socrates says firmly (190e), is an absurd and shameful position to be in.

At this point Plato gives us one of the most memorable images of the entire dialogue. If we do not make strenuous efforts to think our way out of confusion and puzzlement, we shall be laid low, like seasick passengers who allow themselves to be trampled over by the sailors (190e–191a). It is as if Plato is saying to each of his readers: Are you going to let these arguments trample all over you or will you stand up and fend for yourself?

The attentive reader will appreciate the image. The three arguments against the possibility of false judgement have been knotty and abstract. Examples have been few and scantily developed. We have been left to ourselves to formulate the distinctions which would give us some insight into what is going on. The image of ourselves as seasick passengers implies that all this has been deliberate policy on Plato's part. But the image is also the cue for the discussion to take a more constructive turn. Socrates shows the way to respond to the challenge to stand up and fend for ourselves by developing two thoroughly positive models for explaining how false judgement can occur. One is the famous model of memory as a block of wax (191c ff.), the other the model of understanding as an aviary (197d ff.). Significantly, both models attempt to extricate our thought from the constraints of the considerations about knowledge which in Socrates' initial puzzle appear to leave no room for false judgement to occur. We cannot complain that Plato leaves us with no resources to cope with the difficult questions he wants us to think about.

Yet both models fail—or so Socrates will argue. The challenge continues. Is the help offered by the two models really no help at all? Why is it that even these splendidly imaginative constructions do not get to the heart of the problem? Plato is prepared to be helpful to his readers, but not so helpful that nothing remains for us to do on our own. Throughout the discussion, from Socrates' initial puzzle to the final collapse of the Aviary model, he will be challenging us to think, to formulate distinctions, and above all to diagnose the false judgement which makes it appear that false judgement is impossible.

Accordingly, my account of the arguments will have a double design. First, I shall try to help the reader keep enough control of the complexities of the issues we shall be discussing not to become more than momentarily seasick. But second, I hope that you will feel able and willing to pursue in your own way the various questions and lines of inquiry on which this effort of control will concentrate. For Plato is not playing games with his readers. He is drawing you into some of the most difficult and fundamental questions of philosophy. What is at stake in the discussion of false judgement is nothing less than the mind's relation to its objects.

* * * * * * * * * * * *

So now to work. I have offered a preliminary overview of the course and character of Part II. We should prepare to face the initial puzzle, which purports to show that false judgement is impossible, by looking more closely at the one example of false judgement that has been put before us so far.

'Knowledge is true judgement' has the form of an identity statement: according to Socrates at 201c, the definition claims that knowledge and true judgement are the same; the refutation shows that they are different things and not the same. This is an identity statement (a false one) the terms of which are abstract things. We shall meet other examples of identity statements, both true and false, which deal with abstract things (universals, as in this case, or numbers), but we shall also be discussing true and false identity statements about concrete particular things such as persons. I shall speak of the former as abstract identifications or misidentifications, of the latter as concrete identifications or misidentifications.

Now it is a feature of abstract misidentifications that they can lead to false judgements of a different logical form: false descriptions as contrasted with false identifications. If Theaetetus believes the false identity claim that knowledge is true judgement, he will treat a person's having true judgement about something as sufficient grounds for describing them as knowing it. And if knowledge and true judgement are in fact different things, there will be cases, like that of the jurymen in the brief argument of 201ac, where this is a mistake, a misdescription. The jurymen judge truly and reach the correct verdict, but it is wrong to describe them as *knowing* who committed the crime. Plato often stresses the danger for politics and for life in general arising from abstract misidentifications; the misdescriptions they lead to in particular cases can have serious practical consequences (cf. 176cd). But in the present discussion the issues he is concerned with are more logical than ethical, and for this purpose the important thing is to bear in mind the difference in logical form between the misidentification 'Knowledge is true judgement' and the misdescription 'The jurymen know who committed the crime'. It is not that Plato himself draws our attention to the distinction. But there will be moments in the sequel when we have to bring it into our interrogation of his text.

Another thing to bear in mind is that the Greek noun *doxa* and its cognate verb *doxazein*, which are here translated 'judgement' and 'to judge', can also be rendered by 'belief', 'believe', or 'opinion', 'opine'. 'Belief' makes the connection with modern epistemology: what awaits us in the brief argument of 201ac is Plato's version of the familiar thesis that knowledge cannot be equated with true belief (below, p. 125). 'Opinion' usefully evokes the two-world theory of the *Republic*: one important question about the brief argument of 201ac is whether it retracts Plato's previous view that the sensible world is the province of opinion (*doxa*), not of knowledge (below, p. 127). These alternative translations should, however, be held in the reader's mind rather than put down on the page, for the following reasons.

First, *doxa* is initially described as an experience (187d) or episode (187e) occurring at a particular time and place. In due course it will be defined as a statement made silently to oneself (190a). All this is better suited to 'judgement' than to 'belief', which stands for a continuing state of mind or, on some philosophical views, a disposition. Second, although 'opining' can, unlike 'believing', refer to an act or episode, 'opinion' imports a *contrast* with 'knowledge' and would make Theaetetus' second definition seem absurd rather than merely false. The solution is to prefer 'judgement' in the translation[3]

3. McDowell [3], 193, sides with Miss Levett and translates 'judgement' throughout. Cornford [2] starts off with 'judgement' but switches to 'belief' or 'notion' from 200d. Further reason to prefer 'judgement' will emerge in Part III, p. 179 with n. 62.

but to remember that judging can be thought of as coming to believe something or forming an opinion.

The puzzle (188ac)

Can you judge (1) that something you know is something else you know? Or (2) that something you don't know is something else you don't know? Can you judge (3) that something you know is something you don't know? Or, conversely, (4) that something you don't know is something you know?

Put like that, without context, examples, or explanation of what is to count as knowing something, these are mind-darkening questions. But Theaetetus does not hesitate, does not press for further information before replying. He answers 'That would be impossible' to question (1) even before Socrates illustrates question (2) with the only example in the entire passage: 'Is it possible that a man who knows neither Theaetetus nor Socrates should take it into his head that Socrates is Theaetetus or Theaetetus Socrates?' (188b). It is true that Socrates offered an argument for the impossibility of case (1): anyone who made such a judgement would be ignorant of, i.e. would not know, the very items he knows, which is a contradiction. But Theaetetus does not pause to wonder whether the contradictory consequence really follows. To all four questions he gives the same firmly negative answer (but cf. 191b). We must ask: In which cases, if any, is he right to do so? And again: In which cases, if any, would Plato think him right to do so? Thirdly: What should we conclude if the answers to the two previous questions are not identical?

But the puzzle is not yet complete. Socrates claims that cases (1)–(4) are all the forms that false judgement could take (188c). He claims this on the strength of a proposition that has the ineluctable appearance (but is it only an appearance?) of a logical law: with everything whatsoever, and therefore with every object of one's judgement,[4] one either knows it or one does not (188a). The puzzle

4. The phrase 'object of judgement' represents Plato's use of the verb 'to judge' with a direct accusative. Thus if someone judges that X is Y, Plato's Greek describes him as judging X and judging Y (188a, 189c, 190d), and X or Y as judged by him (cf. 209ac). 189e, 195de, and 209ab impress a similar direct accusative construction on the verb 'to think' (Miss Levett translates 'think of'). 190c does the same with the verb 'to state' (she translates 'makes a statement about'). The accusatives specify the object or objects (concrete or abstract) with which the judgement, statement, or thought is concerned.

now has us trapped. If, as Theaetetus accepts, cases (1)–(4) are all impossible, and if, as Socrates has argued, they are all the forms that false judgement could take, no false judgement can occur (188c).

We have already raised questions about Theaetetus' replies. What of Socrates' part in the proceedings? In particular, how do we assess his argument that cases (1)–(4) are all the forms that false judgement could take? It is natural to read (1)–(4) as attempting to list the possible varieties of false *identity* statement; the example 'Socrates is Theaetetus', a concrete misidentification, pushes us in the same direction. But then it is equally natural to object that these are by no means all the forms that false judgement could take. For example, we have no grounds yet for denying the possibility of misdescriptions like 'Theaetetus is stupid'.[5] Let us call this the Objection.

Can we read (1)–(4) differently, so that misdescriptions are included? Try it on questions (1) and (3), so as to make them ask: Can you judge that something you know, e.g. Theaetetus, is something else you know, e.g. stupid, or that he is something which you don't know, e.g. stupid? It may seem hard to make sense of *stupid* as something one knows or does not know (for we are not of course considering the judgement 'Theaetetus is stupidity'). But the main difficulty is that the revised questions (supposing that they are intelligible) would lure no-one into the trap that Socrates is setting. They no longer tempt one to reply immediately 'No, that would be impossible'. For the revised question (1) could equally well have been 'Can you judge that something you know, e.g. Theaetetus, is something else you know, e.g. intelligent?', to which the natural answer is an unhesitating 'Yes'.

The point can be put more formally as follows. The original questions speak of two distinct items and of judging that one is the other. With a judgement of identity such as 'Socrates is Theaetetus', this specification guarantees that the judgement is false; it is false precisely because the items are two, not one and the same. But the falsehood of 'Theaetetus is stupid' is not a consequence of Theaetetus and *stupid* being distinct items. For Theaetetus and *intelligent* are equally and in the same way distinct, yet 'Theaetetus is

---

5. Since the forms of false statement are as many as the forms of statement, the list of omissions can be extended by as many additional forms of statement as we, or Plato, wish to recognize. One notable absence is negative falsehoods of any form: 'Theaetetus is not the son of Euphronius of Sunium', 'Theaetetus is not intelligent', etc.

intelligent' is true. Once descriptive judgements are included, the specification 'judging that one thing is another' no longer picks out false judgements to the exclusion of true ones and no longer makes manifest that and why they are false. Hence it is no longer tempting to think that, if you know the two items, you could never judge that one is the other.

This line of argument suggests that the Objection is not to be evaded by saying that the puzzle does cater for misdescriptions and shows them to be impossible as well as misidentifications.[6] In which case our response to the Objection must acknowledge and offer some explanation of the fact that Socrates has not listed all the forms that false judgement can take.

(a) We might suppose that Plato's real concern is just with false judgements of identity. It is these that he is puzzling over, both here and in the most substantial of the later sections, where he invokes the model of memory as a block of wax to vindicate the possibility of concrete misidentifications (191c ff.) and the model of understanding as an aviary to account for abstract misidentifications (197d ff.). The initial gesture at a completely general problem applying to all forms of false judgement is not sustained. In retrospect, it is best regarded as part of the dialectical puzzle-making which prepares us to welcome the models and follow through the lines of solution they suggest.

(b) Another answer to the Objection would be to question its assumption that the difference in logical form between misidentifications and misdescriptions was clear for all to see at the time the *Theaetetus* was written. There is evidence that it was a struggle for Plato himself to reach an adequate understanding of the logical issues involved in the distinction.[7] He can be found hard at work on them in the *Sophist*, a dialogue which presents itself as a sequel to the *Theaetetus* (*Soph.* 216a, *Theaet.* 210d) and continues its concern with falsehood. Maybe, then, the puzzle is designed to elicit the very objection we are considering. Try stating the Objection without the kind of terminology I used when I spoke of 'the difference in logical form between misidentifications and misdescriptions'. Such language is available to us now because Plato began the practice of logical analysis. He began it by presenting puzzles such as this one,

6. For contrary views, see Williams [43], Fine [45], who read back into the initial puzzle the concern with misdescription which is evident in the third approach to false judgement (189b–190e).

7. See Owen [46].

where it is easy to sense that something has gone wrong but you need to formulate subtle distinctions to say what it is. Anyone who raises the Objection will be joining Plato on an intellectual journey that will carry them forward into the complexities of the *Sophist*.

(c) A third approach would be to suggest that for Plato, in this dialogue at least, misidentifications are somehow fundamental. We have noted already that a misdescription may derive from a prior abstract misidentification (pp. 68–9). We will shortly reach a section (189b–190e) which suggests the view that misdescription always involves misidentification. To judge that Theaetetus is stupid, for example, is to mistake the fact of the matter, Theaetetus' intelligence, for its opposite, stupidity. The conclusion is that if this sort of misidentification is impossible, so is misdescription—the Objection is overcome. (You may want to question Plato's way of representing what it is to misdescribe something, but that is a different objection, which we can think about later.)

Meanwhile, the several solutions just sketched to the problem of the scope of the puzzle (and a fourth consideration to be added below—p. 80) are an invitation to the reader to ask not only 'Which gives the best account of the ensuing inquiry?', but also 'Can a still better account be put together by combining elements of each?' The puzzle remains puzzling, however, even if it is confined to the sphere of identity statements. It is surely not to be believed that no-one ever gets these wrong. Our chief problem is with the claim that misidentification is impossible.

Alternative diagnoses

One thing should be clear. Plato's intention is to provoke us into looking for a faulty assumption that makes Theaetetus accept so unacceptable a conclusion. The faulty assumption that generates the puzzle may or may not be identical with the false assumption about knowledge which prevents Part II from solving the problem of false judgement (p. 66). But if there are two distinct errors to spot, not just one, they are likely to be closely related, such is the influence of the puzzle on the whole subsequent discussion.

Little else is clear, owing to the abstract bareness with which the puzzle is presented. Plato leaves it to us to discover how to proceed with the search. Since, however, the puzzle is based on the dichotomy between knowing and not knowing, there should in principle be two avenues of approach. Either it is wrong to think that *knowing* something is incompatible with misidentifying it, or it is wrong to think that *not knowing* something is incompatible with misidentifying it. It could also be that both are wrong, but on the whole the modern response (as I shall call it) emphasizes the first error, while an alternative response gives more weight to the second.

The modern response will come naturally to many readers, as follows. It is with case (1) that the bad mistake is made.[8] Consider a detective whose investigations of a kidnapping cause him to meet Castor in one context and Pollux in another. Let his dealings with Castor and with Pollux be such that any of us would describe him as knowing both of them. He can still judge, and be mistaken in judging, that Pollux is Castor in disguise. Or, to vary the example, if Pollux explains that they are twin brothers, the detective may nonetheless disbelieve him and judge that they are one and the same person. So the question becomes: What is the false assumption which blinds Theaetetus to the fact that case (1) misidentifications can and do occur?

That being the question, it is natural to look for clues to the answer in cases (2)–(4), where at least one of the terms is an unknown. For it is reasonably clear what guides Theaetetus to say that *these* are all impossible (188bc). It is the principle

J1 If something is to be an object of one's judgement, one must know it.

The idea is that one cannot so much as take it into one's head to think about Castor unless one knows Castor; hence there can be no judgement, false or true, about something or someone one does not know. To which the modern response is, typically, a qualified nod of approval: given the right understanding of what it is to know something, principle J1 is correct and important—but given that understanding, it does not exclude case (1) misidentifications.

The right understanding of J1 is this. If the detective is to make a judgement about Castor, he must know who it is that he is referring to.[9] Our example shows him in possession of such knowledge about Castor, and independently about Pollux, and thus able to judge, mistakenly, that one person he knows is another person

---

8. This is the emphasis in Ackrill [40], 385–87, McDowell [42], 182–83, McDowell [3], 196–97, 219. Although Fine [45] reads (1)–(4) broadly, to include misdescriptions, she too focusses her attack on (1). Williams [43], 293 roundly states that (1) is the only case where Theaetetus is wrong to think that a false judgement of identity is impossible. Cornford [2], 113, by contrast, is equally confident of the opposite view: 'It is true that when two known objects are clearly before the mind we do not judge that one is the other'.

9. Ackrill [40], 387, McDowell [42], 188 and [3], 196; cf. Fine [45], 71.

he knows. If Theaetetus thinks otherwise, insisting that the detective cannot judge that Castor is Pollux, this must be because he has made a mistake about the kind or extent of knowledge required by J1. He must suppose that it entails knowing that Castor is a different person from Pollux. This mistake about the kind or extent of knowledge required by J1 is the faulty assumption we are looking for, which blinds Theaetetus to the fact that case (1) misidentifications can and do occur.

Accordingly, the modern response, as I am calling it, suggests that the way to clear up the puzzle is to correct the wrong understanding of J1 which guides Theaetetus to say that case (1) misidentifications are impossible. This is actually a harder and more challenging task than it may appear. It calls for a charting of the connections and divergences among a group of subtly distinct notions: knowing that it is Castor one is referring to, knowing what the name 'Castor' refers to, knowing who Castor is, knowing Castor, knowing Castor from Pollux, knowing Castor from everyone (everything) else one knows, knowing Castor from everything else, knowing that Castor is a different person from Pollux. The reader who tries to make an analytic chart of all these different notions will soon begin to sympathize with Theaetetus for having gone astray. And perhaps you will come to suspect, as not a few scholars have done, that it is not just Theaetetus, but Plato himself, through his spokesman Socrates, who is in the grip of a mistaken conception of knowledge.[10]

The interest of this exercise in conceptual clarification is increased by a close resemblance, both in content and in resulting difficulties over identity statements, between J1 and a principle maintained in this century by Bertrand Russell:

> Whenever a relation of judging or supposing occurs, the terms to which the supposing or judging mind is related by the relation of supposing or judging must be terms with which the mind in question is acquainted. This is merely to say that we cannot make a judgement or supposition without knowing what it is that we are making our judgement or supposition about.[11]

10. McDowell [3], 196–97, White [8], 169–70, Robinson [39], 25 ff.

11. Bertrand Russell, 'Knowledge by Acquaintance and Knowledge by Description', *Proceedings of the Aristotelian Society* 11 (1910/11), 118; repr. in his *Mysticism and Logic* (Harmondsworth: 1953), 207. McDowell [42] is an exemplary exploration of this common ground between Plato and Russell. The most penetrating defence of 'Russell's Principle' on the contemporary scene is Gareth Evans, *The Varieties of Reference*, edited by John McDowell (Oxford & New York: 1982); not a book for beginners.

This statement of Russell's may even be the origin of the modern response, the influence which has made J1 so appealing to a present-day reader. What is certain is that through Russell the inquiry will lead on to numerous current debates. What is it for a judgement or statement to be *about* something? What is it to know what one is thinking or speaking of? What is the analysis of 'knowing Castor'? What is the correct account of identity statements? In short, to make the modern response to the puzzle is to welcome Plato into the centre of current philosophical discussion.

But there is an alternative to consider. At 191ab Socrates declares that they were wrong to deny the possibility of misidentification *in case (3)*. Contrary to his and Theaetetus' earlier agreement, it is in fact possible to judge that something one knows is something one does not know. This dramatic reversal brings with it a rejection of principle J1. For Socrates and Theaetetus are now envisaging that one can make a judgement about a person whom one does not know. Shortly afterwards (191d) Socrates introduces the Wax Block model, which amounts (as we shall see in due course) to replacing J1 by the more generous principle

> J2 If something is to be an object of one's judgement, one must *either* know it *or* perceive it.

The admission of case (3) misidentifications is an alternative to the modern response previously sketched because it does not claim that knowing something is compatible with misidentifying it, but rather that not knowing something is compatible with misidentifying it. Instead of distinguishing between a right and a wrong understanding of J1 (and perhaps reconstructing a confusion which could move Theaetetus from the one to the other),[12] the alternative response invites us to reject J1 altogether. J1, on this alternative diagnosis of the puzzle, *is* the faulty assumption we are meant to catch. (Whether J2 is adequate to be accepted in its stead is a further question, to be decided when we come to assess the merits and shortcomings of the Wax Block model.)

Here, then, are two ways of responding to the initial puzzle, the one leading straight into contemporary philosophical discussion, the alternative suggesting that the Wax Block will provide the help

---

12. Two very different attempts at such a reconstruction are McDowell [42], who locates the confusion in Plato himself, and Fine [45], who argues that it is not Plato's but Theaetetus' confusion and that it is what lends plausibility to his definition of knowledge as true judgement.

we are looking for. At this early stage readers need not feel bound to decide that one response is wholly right, the other wholly wrong. Each may enable you to see interesting and important points in the discussion which grows out of the puzzle; each will obscure features that the other brings into sharp focus. Our job, the job Plato has laid upon his readers, is to discover how to see the whole clearly and steadily. It may be helpful, therefore, before proceeding to the next section, to attempt a brisk summary, in fresh terminology, of the difference between the two responses.

The puzzle makes out that a necessary condition for mistaking X for Y is also a sufficient condition for not mistaking X for Y. The necessary condition is that one know X and know Y. But this, it is claimed, is a sufficient condition for knowing that X is not Y. The modern response, roughly and summarily, is to deny that the condition is sufficient for knowing that X is not Y. The alternative response is to deny that the condition is necessary for mistakenly judging that X is Y. The alternative response may come less easily to us, because when we reflect on the question we are so sure that it is possible to judge that something one knows is something else one knows. But in reading the text we should keep our minds open to the possibility that Plato's vision is different from ours.

Different approaches (188c–190e)

At 188cd Socrates wonders whether they have not been going about the question of false judgement in the wrong way. Perhaps it would be better to approach it by way of the idea that false judgement occurs when someone thinking about something judges about it *things which are not*. We naturally read this as: judging about something things which are not the case, i.e. ascribing to it features which it does not in fact possess. We seem to be all set for an analysis of misdescription.

But an imaginary questioner inserts a distinction (188d) between (i) judging what is not about one of the things which are, and (ii) judging what is not 'just by itself'. (i) is a restatement of the account of false judgement that Socrates is now proposing; (ii) represents the idea, common in paradox-mongering of the period,[13] that the object of a false judgement is—nothing at all. (ii) leaves out, while (i) takes care to mention, that the false judgement judges what

13. See, for example, *Euthydemus* 283e ff., *Cratylus* 429d ff., *Sophist* 236e ff.

is not *about something* (something that is)—therein lies the crucial difference between them.

Socrates then does something he has just proved to be impossible. Mistaking (i) for (ii), he develops a scandalous analogy between judging what is not and seeing or touching what is not there to be seen or touched. Touching/judging what is not → touching/judging nothing → not touching/judging at all. The conclusion, that there is no judging what is not, is a *reductio ad absurdum* of (ii) presented as a refutation of (i) as well. (Notice the hesitant tone of Theaetetus' responses as the argument nears its conclusion.)

This is grand fun. A model on which judgements relate to the world in the same sort of unstructured way as perceiving or (we may add) naming, will tie anyone in knots when it comes to the question 'What is a false judgement the judgement/name of?'.[14] The only available answer, when the judgement is taken as an unstructured whole, appears to be: Nothing. And finding oneself in knots is the best way to appreciate the importance of the qualification 'about something' which (i) includes and (ii) leaves out. The qualification points to a structural complexity within the false judgement which the scandalous *reductio* ignores. It is true of perceiving, as of naming or mentioning, that without something to perceive/name/mention the act does not come off at all. But once you have succeeded in perceiving or mentioning Theaetetus, who is something that is, you can go on to misdescribe him as old or aquiline. This is what it means to judge things that are not about something that is. Precisely because there is a distinction between what a judgement is about and what is judged about it—a distinction with no parallel in perceiving or naming—there is a difference between judging what is not about something and judging without anything to judge.

However, it is one thing to take note of this difference, another to articulate a theory which explains it. The precise analysis of what is wrong with the unstructured model of judgement, and with the abstract misidentification that Socrates perpetrated when he mistook (i) for (ii), is a serious and difficult business: the main business,

14. Witness G. E. Moore, *Some Main Problems of Philosophy, op. cit.*, chap. 14, who finally concludes, in all seriousness, that 'to say of a belief that it is true is merely to say that *the* fact to which it refers *is;* while to say of it that it is false is merely to say that the fact to which it refers, *is not*—that there is no such fact' (p. 269). 'How', an imaginary questioner could ask, 'can you refer to a fact which is not there to be referred to?'

in fact, of Plato's *Sophist*. It is also in the *Sophist* that Plato undertakes the examination of Eleatic monism (the thesis that the only reality is one single, completely changeless thing) which was promised at *Theaetetus* 180d–181b but put off at 184a. The two tasks are intimately connected, since Parmenides argued against change and plurality from the principle that 'you cannot speak or think of what is not'.[15] An ancient reader would know at once that it is Parmenides' principle that Socrates has been exploiting, and that it is chief among the 'unmanageably vast issues' which at 184a Socrates said must not be allowed to sidetrack them from the investigation of knowledge. We had better heed this warning ourselves.[16]

Moreover, beyond the *Sophist*, and presupposing its appreciation of the distinction between what a judgement is about and what is judged about it, lie further puzzles of not-being. Consider the case of a hallucinating drunk who imagines that he sees pink rats and judges that they are coming closer. No rats for him to see, so none for him to make a judgement about—though he, poor fellow, thinks otherwise. Does he really make a judgement (a judgement about nothing) or should we say that, just as he fails to see anything, so he fails to make a judgement—he only thinks he does?[17] The *Sophist* offers no help towards an answer. It is content to vindicate the possibility of falsehoods like 'Theaetetus is aquiline'. Correspondingly, my readers must be content with the promise that that vindication will be forthcoming if you go on to the sequel-dialogue.

Even so, one problem remains. What is the significance, for the *Theaetetus* investigation of whether false judgement is possible, of Socrates' backing away from what at the time was the most notorious argument for thinking it is not? Must we regard any positive result achieved as conditional on our being able to answer the questioner who persists in saying 'But false judgement *is* judging what is not, so how can it be possible?'? Or is this the explanation of the confessed failure of the *Theaetetus* inquiry, that the problem

15. The argument may be studied in Parmenides, Fragment 8 (see G. S. Kirk, J. E. Raven, & M. Schofield, *The Presocratic Philosophers*, 2nd edition [Cambridge: 1983], 248–52)—the longest piece of pre-Socratic philosophy to have survived intact. Its influence on subsequent Greek philosophy, down to Plato's *Sophist* and beyond, was enormous.

16. If the *Theaetetus* conveys an invitation to the *Sophist* (cf. 210d), that need not imply that while writing the *Theaetetus* Plato already knew everything he was going to say in the sequel dialogue, only that he knew what problems he had to tackle.

17. The deep issues raised by this question are a main theme of Evans, *op. cit.*

of false judgement can only be solved by the more sophisticated analytical tools made available in the *Sophist?*[18] A third option would be to go back to our earlier discussion (pp. 72–3) of misidentification vs. misdescription. Could we say, keeping (i) properly distinct from (ii), that misdescription involves judging about something things which are not, but in a misidentification both terms are things which are? Our dialogue's concentration on false identity statements would then be altogether responsible. Misdescriptions must wait for the *Sophist's* analysis of not-being; misidentifications need not.

Whichever answer be preferred, the discussion from this point on accepts the constraint that the terms of a false judgement must be things which are. At 189bc Socrates turns to a new approach, a new definition of false judgement as 'other-judging', and he emphasizes that it conforms to this constraint. We are given to understand that 'other-judging' (the name is newly coined by Plato, as if to signal the novelty of the conception) is judging, i.e. asserting to be the case, one of the things which are in place of another of the things which are. That this is the meaning of 'other-judging' is confirmed—apparently—when a show of initiative by Theaetetus provides us with an example (189c): someone judges 'ugly' instead of 'beautiful' or vice versa. We recall Theodorus' judgement about Theaetetus (143e) and Socrates' recent correction of it (185e).[19] And here it cannot be that both terms are things which are in the sense appropriate to (i), viz. both are the case (p. 77). It is precisely not the case that Theaetetus is ugly. The effective meaning must be: both beauty and ugliness exist,[20] neither is a thing which is not in the sense appropriate to (ii), viz. nothing at all. Of two real things, Theodorus picked the wrong one to ascribe to his pupil.

If that sounds to the reader quite a reasonable account of what false judgement is, or at least of what misdescription is, remember

18. So Cornford [2], 110–11, 115, 140, whose view is that both the problem of knowledge and the problem of error are solved in the *Sophist* by the Theory of Forms; for a vigorous criticism, including doubts about whether the Theory of Forms is to be found in the *Sophist*, see Robinson [39]. A very different view of the whole passage, and consequently of its relation to the *Sophist's* analysis of not-being, can be found in McDowell [3], 201–2: Plato believed in the scandalous *reductio* when he wrote the *Theaetetus*, so that in the *Sophist* he is criticising his own earlier self.

19. It is the same Greek word, *kalos*, which is translated 'beautiful' at 143e and 'handsome' at 185e.

20. Plato would normally express this by saying that each of them *is* something: e.g. *Phaedo* 64c, *Republic* 477b, 583c, 584d, *Hippias Major* 287cd, *Sophist* 246e–247b.

that the same is true of the previous definition, (i). The *Sophist* will
in fact defend (i) as a reasonable account of misdescription by
analyzing 'saying about something things which are not' as 'saying
about something things *other* than the things which are about it'.
Does Plato realize that Socrates is mistaken in the *Theaetetus* when
he introduces 'other-judging' as something wholly different from
(i) (189b)? Or are the puzzles in Part II of the *Theaetetus* part of
Plato's education as well as his readers'?

But in fact 'other-judging' in the *Theaetetus* is more—apparently—
than the bare notion of saying one thing (the wrong thing) in place
of another (the right) thing. It is doing this as a result of *substituting
the one for the other in one's thought*. Behind the misdescription lies
a misidentification. In some way or other Theodorus must have
mistaken beauty (the feature Theaetetus does possess) for ugliness,
or else he would not have judged that Theaetetus is ugly instead
of beautiful. But in what way? Since Socrates will argue (189d–190d)
that misidentification in thought is impossible, the first question
for us should be: Is misidentification in thought necessary for misdescription? Unless

(i) Theodorus judged Theaetetus ugly when the fact is that
   Theaetetus is beautiful implies
(ii) In his thought about Theaetetus, Theodorus substituted
   ugliness for beauty,

there will be no need to despair about the possibility of misdescription when it turns out that the abstract misidentification (ii) is
impossible.

The question presupposes that (i) and (ii) are distinct elements in
the account of 'other-judging', (ii) being intended as the explanation
required by (i). So understood, this third approach to the problem of
false judgement is the first to include an explanation—an important
step forward, even if to claim that (i) *implies* (ii) is to claim that the
only possible explanation of misdescription is an impossible misidentification. But some readers may wonder whether (i) and (ii) are
really different. 'Substituting ugliness for beauty' *can* be construed
as just another way of expressing the point that ugliness is the wrong
feature to ascribe to Theaetetus, beauty the right one, in which case
it is trivially true that (i) implies (ii), because (ii), instead of explaining
(i), is merely an alternative description of the same event.

Other readers may feel that Socrates does have two distinct elements in mind when he speaks of 'other-judging', but that he
presents them as one. His account of 'other-judging' commits the

very fault he is describing. (ii) is indeed impossible, but, as in the previous section (p. 78), it is only by mis-taking (i) for (ii) that he makes it appear that (i) is refuted as well. Alternatively, he mistakes one construal of (ii) for the other: to launch the account of 'other-judging' he construes (ii) as equivalent to (i), but for the refutation he reconstrues it as the impossible misidentification.

Yet other readers may find themselves (as I have done) vacillating between these various interpretations, repeatedly substituting one for another in their thought as they read and reread the account of 'other-judging' at 189bc in the light of the argument which follows.[21] The section we are now embarking on is arguably the trickiest in the entire dialogue. It is no accident that it is the section immediately preceding the seasickness image (p. 67). Here more than anywhere else we are likely to wonder whether the seasickness is ours alone. Is Plato fully in control of the confusions he is challenging us to sort out, or is the captain laid low with the passengers?

To complete this review of the difficulties before us, let us plunge into the argument (189d–190d) which purports to show that misidentification in thought is impossible. It is structurally analogous to the initial puzzle about knowing, but this time the connection between the mind and its objects is expressed in terms of thinking and judging.

How can anyone mistake X for Y in their thought? A necessary condition for doing so is that one's thought set both X and Y before one's mind to be objects of one's judgement, in a single moment of attention. But if both are before someone's mind in this way, they cannot possibly judge that one is the other. No-one, even in sleep, would say to themselves that X is another thing, Y. In sum, a necessary condition for one's thought to judge that X is Y is a sufficient condition for it not to do so. Hence the misidentification is impossible.

The context, and the examples mentioned at 190bc, show that Socrates is gunning for the kind of abstract misidentification which (he claims) is involved in 'other-judging.' But the argument itself is expressed in completely general terms (that is why I used 'X' and 'Y', corresponding to 'one thing' and 'another' in the original text). If valid, it is valid against all misidentification in thought, abstract or concrete. Imagine, for example, our detective sitting at home by himself, not perceiving either of the two suspects but simply pondering the case in his mind. He cannot, according to the present argument, judge that Castor is Pollux. The consequences for ab-

---

21. The key sentence at 189bc is itself unclear in several ways: see note *ad loc.*

stract misidentification are no less surprising: 'Knowledge is perception' and 'Knowledge is true judgement' are strictly *unbelievable*, so there was no need for Plato to write a dialogue showing that they ought not to be believed.

As before, it is obvious that something has gone wrong. But it is a good deal more of a challenge than in the previous sections to say exactly what it is. One complication to be wary of is the type of example Socrates cites to instantiate the schema 'judging that one thing is another'. 'Beauty is ugliness', 'A cow is a horse', and the like (190bc),[22] are indeed judgements that no-one is likely to make (though how about 'A sloop is a schooner'?), but is this because they involve judging that one thing is another or for other reasons? If misidentification is impossible, a fortiori abstract misidentification is impossible; if abstract misidentification is impossible, a fortiori it is impossible to judge that beauty is its opposite, ugliness. But the converse inferences do not hold.

This complication means that readers who are stirred to defend 'other-judging' against Socrates' critique cannot confine themselves to finding fault with the general argument that no-one can judge that one thing is another. It is specifically the mistaking something for its opposite that Socrates connects with 'other-judging'. If, for example, the possibility of judging 'ugly' in place of 'beautiful' stands or falls with the possibility of judging that beauty is ugliness, and this latter judgement is impossible for reasons other than those given by the general argument, then 'other-judging' falls. Thus even when we have sorted out the puzzle about judging that one thing is another, there will still be work to do. We will need to go back to the account of 'other-judging' to reconsider the first question we raised about it (p. 81): Is misidentification in thought necessary for misdescription?

Only when both tasks have been satisfactorily completed will we have a clear understanding of how a discussion which starts from the innocuous-seeming idea of a man who judges 'ugly' in place of 'beautiful' ends up contemplating a man who judges, absurdly, that beauty is ugliness.

Alternative diagnoses

The general argument against judging that one thing is another, as sketched above, turns on two contentions. The first lays down a

22. On the construal of these examples, see note *ad loc.*; a contrary view in Williams [43], Fine [45].

necessary condition for mistaking X for Y in thought, namely, that one should be thinking of X and thinking of Y, in a single moment of attention (190d with 189e). The second contention is that having both X and Y before one's mind in this way is a sufficient condition for realizing they are different and not judging that X is Y (190cd). The second contention is more prominent, however, since it is preceded and explained (so Socrates claims at 190c) by a lively account of what thought and judgement are.

Thinking, says Socrates, is the soul's discussion with itself. While the soul asks itself questions and is divided between answering 'Yes' and answering 'No', it is thinking. When one answer prevails, this is its judgement on the issue in question—judgement is a statement made silently to oneself (189e–190a).

A preliminary comment might be that this is very much an intellectual's picture of thinking. That is to say, it is a picture of intellectual thinking rather than, for example, of the thought and concentration with which an athlete runs, an artist paints, or a child reads a story.[23] Even as a description of the philosophical thinking which has been going on in this dialogue, it omits much that is important. Most conspicuously, it omits all mention of reasoning.

A more challenging topic to pursue is the analogy between external and internal speech. In talking to someone else I can surprise or amuse them, teach them something or deceive them. I can say something without meaning what I say, or fail to express adequately what I want to say. How many of these things can I do to myself? I suggest that the more features of external speech you find it plausible to transfer to internal speech, the less plausible you will find it to *identify* a person's internal speech with their thought.

These comments are critical—unduly so, you may feel. For the present account of thought and judgement (which is reaffirmed in the *Sophist*, 263e–264a; cf. *Timaeus* 37b) has one undeniable virtue. It forces us to attend to the point that thought and judgement have the logical characteristics (propositional structure, etc.) of speech and assertion. And this is in fact the one point used for the argument. The definition of judgement as a statement made internally to oneself allows Socrates to formulate the premise that someone who judges one thing to be another is actually *saying* (to themselves)

---

23. For a modern philosophical attempt to rectify the one-sided intellectualism of Plato's account of thinking, see Gilbert Ryle, *On Thinking*, ed. K. Kolenda (Oxford: 1979), esp. chap. 2. Interestingly, however, Ryle's approach runs into difficulty when he tackles intellectual thought.

that the one is the other (190a). It is this premise which is supposed to make it clear that no-one would or could judge one thing to be another. When we look at the verbal form of the judgement, 'X is Y', we see that in order to have two things distinctly in mind (the agreed necessary condition for misidentification), the judgement-maker must speak of two distinct things, X and Y, even while saying they are one.

So what? Speaking of two distinct things is not necessarily speaking of them as two or as distinct. Saying 'X is Y' is not the same as saying 'X is another thing, Y'. The falsity of the latter judgement is manifest in the very meaning of the sentence; the falsity of the former is not. Likewise, the falsity of 'Beauty is ugliness' is manifest in the very meaning of the sentence; not so the falsity of 'Knowledge is true judgement'. Understanding the meaning of 'X is another thing, Y' or 'Beauty is ugliness' is indeed a sufficient condition for not judging them true.[24] But understanding the meaning of 'X is Y' or 'Knowledge is true judgement' is not.

However, it is one thing to register this difference, another to articulate a theory to explain it. Such a theory entered modern philosophy with Gottlöb Frege's celebrated paper 'On Sense and Reference' (1892).[25] By distinguishing between the sense and the reference of the referring expressions which flank the 'is' of identity, Frege showed how an identity statement—his example was 'The morning star is the evening star'—can have a content which is true but informative, i.e. not manifestly and trivially true like 'The morning star is the morning star'. The statement 'The morning star is the evening star' is true because the expressions 'the morning star' and 'the evening star' refer to the same thing, the planet Venus. But its truth is not manifest in the very meaning of the sentence because 'the morning star' and 'the evening star' have different senses (different meanings, in one sense of 'meaning').

Admittedly, Plato's problem is not how, if an identity claim is

---

24. This is not to deny that such sentences can on occasion be seriously and sincerely used, e.g. for deliberate paradox. At a moving moment in Sophocles' play *Ajax* (394–97), Ajax expresses his wish to die with the words 'O Darkness, my light, take me to dwell with you'. A dogma of early modern ethics collapsed under the impact of the remark 'Everything is what it is and not another thing, unless it is another thing, and even then it is what it is' (W. K. Frankena, 'The Naturalistic Fallacy', *Mind* 48 [1939], 472; repr. in Philippa Foot ed., *Theories of Ethics*, Oxford Readings in Philosophy (Oxford: 1967), 58).

25. Now to be found most conveniently in Peter Geach & Max Black edd., *Translations from the Philosophical Writings of Gottlöb Frege* (Oxford: 1960), 56–78.

true, it can fail to be manifestly true, but how, if it is false, it can fail to be manifestly false. But are these two distinct problems or one? Is not the solution to the puzzle about misidentification simply this, that an identity claim 'X is Y' can be false without being manifestly false, just so long as 'X' and 'Y' refer to what are in fact different things by way of different but logically compatible senses?

More than one famous philosopher has been trapped in paradox and difficulty by the notion of identity,[26] and modern philosophy has grown used to the idea that Frege's distinction between sense and reference, or some variant of it, is the great solvent for clearing away the mess. We cannot unthink our inheritance, and it would be foolish not to take advantage of the Fregean perspective on the *Theaetetus* discussion of identity judgements. But we will be better placed to appreciate its value if we also make the imaginative effort of asking ourselves: What was it like to confront the puzzle of identity at the time when Plato wrote the *Theaetetus*? Reading Plato as fully as we can involves both the use of the best modern resources and the ability to distance ourselves from them, so that we stay alert to the possibility that Plato has resources of his own which are different from ours.

Recall the contrast between the modern and the alternative response to the initial puzzle about knowing (pp. 76–7). Frege's theory offers a semantic basis for distinguishing *what* you think of from what you think of it *as*. But if the same distinction could be made on a different basis, that would be an equally effective way to undermine the contention that having both X and Y before the mind in thought is a sufficient condition for not judging X to be Y. In due course the Aviary discussion will suggest an alternative account, expressed in epistemic rather than semantic terms, of how it is possible to think of X without thinking of it as X. After the Wax Block has provided resources to help with the initial puzzle about knowing, the Aviary does the same for our present problem about misidentification in thought. But in fact the Wax Block has a bearing on both puzzles. One can perceive X without thinking of it as X, indeed without thinking of it as any determinate kind of thing at all. This suggests a different alternative response which fastens on the contention that having both X and Y before the mind *in thought* is a necessary condition for mistakenly judging that one is the other.

26. Most famously, Hume in *A Treatise of Human Nature*, Bk. I, Pt. IV, Sect. II. A comparison between Hume and Plato's treatment of 'other-judging' is developed by Williams [40], 292.

We have already anticipated the point that the Wax Block model allows, in contrast to the initial puzzle of 188ac, that an item (one of the things which are) may come before the mind to be an object of judgement otherwise than by being known. But it also allows, in contrast to the puzzle here at 189d–190d, that an item may come before the mind to be an object of judgement otherwise than by being thought of. It is enough that the item be something perceived, where perception is distinguished not only from knowledge, but also from thought; for in the Wax Block section (look ahead to 195cd) the contrast between perception and thought is as sharp as it was in the closing pages of Part I (184a–186e).

The relation between knowledge and thought will be of the first importance to us later. For the moment we need only notice one consequence of the Wax Block's distinguishing perception not only from knowledge but also from thought, namely, that besides and parallel to the move from J1 to J2 (p. 76) there appears to be a move from

> J1a If X is to be an object of one's judgement, one must be thinking of it (as X)

to

> J2a If X is to be an object of one's judgement, one must *either* be thinking of it (as X) *or* perceiving it.

A clarification of this move will be offered later (p. 94). For the moment it is enough to say that the parenthetical 'as X' is needed because the only means envisaged so far for having an abstract term like beauty before the mind in thought is that the person uses a phrase like 'the beautiful' in internal speech: to think of beauty one speaks of beauty as such. Thus understood, J1a is what guides Theaetetus to agree that, if one's thought is to mistake beauty for ugliness, it must affirm 'Beauty is ugliness'. From J2a it follows directly that the alleged necessary condition is not in fact necessary. Someone can mistakenly judge that beauty is ugliness without thinking of beauty as beauty—provided they can perceive it instead. The Wax Block thus offers an alternative to the modern response inspired by Frege. We can appeal to perception to explain how it is after all possible in certain cases 'to set down a thing in one's thought as another thing and not itself' (189d).

Objection: The examples in the Wax Block section are perceived persons. We are shown how someone who perceives Theaetetus can judge him to be Theodorus instead of Theaetetus, and can

judge this without thinking of Theaetetus (as Theaetetus), but that
is a concrete misidentification. Where abstract misidentifications
are concerned, we are no better off than before. Answer: Sensible
qualities are not concrete particulars, and Plato treats them as items
that can be perceived, e.g. hardness and softness at 186b. The Wax
Block model can at least accommodate a case like the misidentification of hardness as softness.[27]

Second objection: Beauty and ugliness are not sensible qualities,
according to Plato in this dialogue, not features we can perceive
(186a).[28] So we are no further forward with the abstract misidentification behind Theodorus' judgement that Theaetetus is ugly. True,
but we can make progress on the question whether Theodorus'
misdescription implies that in his thought about Theaetetus he
mistook beauty for ugliness. For we know quite a lot about how
this particular judgement came to be made. It was Theaetetus' *visual
appearance* (snub nose, bulging eyes—143e, 144de) that the old man
was going by. He perceived it accurately enough, but his thought
mistook what he saw for ugliness. He had not yet learned the lesson
of 186a, let alone Socrates' preliminary point at 185e that in judging
of beauty one should go by the quality of a boy's mind, not his
body. In fact, we need not suppose that Theodorus *thought of* beauty
at all. Hence, whatever the reason why it is impossible to judge
that beauty is ugliness, fortunately he did not have to.

These two answers are, of course, highly speculative. The very
idea that the main example in the passage alludes to Theodorus'
mistake about Theaetetus is a connection I have made with earlier
parts of the dialogue, not something explicit in the text. Philosophically, the move from J1a to J2a involves the grave difficulty we
discussed at the end of Part I (pp. 61–3): how can something come
before the mind through perception without any assistance from
thought? More on perception and thought below. The one thing I
am confident of is that Plato has designed this whole stretch of text
as an invitation to his readers to engage in the *kind* of thinking or
internal dialogue which I have been sharing with the readers of
this Introduction. The seasickness image will challenge us to do
whatever we can to stop the argument trampling all over us (cf.

---

27. I trust that readers will not be disturbed by the implication that an abstract
universal can be perceived. All it means is that I can be said to see *the same thing*,
the colour red, when I look first at a red flag and then at a red ball. The distinction
between universal and particular is a different distinction from Plato's distinction
between nonperceivable and perceivable.

28. Contrast *Phaedrus* 250de.

also 191c). The least we can do, given the resources provided by the Wax Block model, is show that, thanks to perception, some abstract misidentifications are possible and that misidentification in thought is not in every case necessary to explain misdescription (cf. the two tasks distinguished on p. 83).

This is also the second time that I have contrasted two ways of looking at and responding to Plato's puzzle-making, one of them characteristically 'modern', the 'alternative' having some *prima facie* support in later portions of the text; the one linking Plato with our own philosophical concerns, the other offering to show us a different and unfamiliar vision. Perhaps the alternative response seems less promising on this occasion than on the last. If so, that is a philosophical judgement on our own part which it should be instructive to elucidate and defend. If, on the other hand, readers are inclined to pursue the alternative response in a positive spirit, they will find that it leads to further questions which relate closely to the concerns of the *Sophist*.

To account for certain mistaken judgements in terms of thought misidentifying a perceived property is to isolate the predicate part of the erroneous judgement from its subject and to treat misdescription as simply a matter of the predicate missing its perceived target (cf. 189c). But is this good enough? Does misidentifying hardness as softness while feeling a hard object amount to making a mistake *about* the hard object? Did Theodorus, on the suggested account, make a mistake *about* Theaetetus, or did he merely err in his vicinity?

These questions bring back the issue of structure which was raised, only to be set aside for the *Sophist*, in the section on judging what is not (pp. 78–9). So far as misdescription is concerned, the discussion in the *Theaetetus* remains abortive. Both judging what is not and 'other-judging' come to grief. But they both come to grief, it is now beginning to appear, for reasons which advertise the importance of looking into the subject-predicate structure of descriptive statements in which something is said *about* something. What the *Sophist* will show is that, to understand misdescription, one must recognize that description itself has a logical complexity of a different order from the complexity of identity claims. A false judgement of identity may be characterized as a joining of two terms, each of which is something that is (cf. p. 80), but to understand how a descriptive judgement can be false, one must start from the fact that description involves a fitting together of two terms, a subject and a predicate, which are essentially unlike.

An Introduction to the *Theaetetus* can do no more than point out the places, and the issues, which tie this dialogue to the *Sophist* (pp. 72–3, pp. 78–80). Of the three approaches to false judgement which precede and lead up to the seasickness image, I took the first to be concerned with misidentification, the second with misdescription, and the third with both. And I have tended to suggest a division of labour between the *Theaetetus* and the *Sophist*: the *Theaetetus* sets puzzles both about misidentification and about misdescription, but for positive progress with misdescription we must go on to the *Sophist*. I very much hope that readers will go on to the *Sophist*, both for its own sake and in order to consider whether it confirms this suggestion about how the problem of false judgement is shared between the two dialogues. For remember that the distinction between misidentification and misdescription is itself a distinction I drew at the beginning (pp. 68–9) and imported into our subsequent interrogation of the text. While I believe that the text is written in such a way as to challenge us to formulate the distinction for ourselves, you may feel, on the contrary, that the chief act of coerciveness in this part of my Introduction is the way the whole discussion has been organized around a distinction—between the structure of identity statements and the subject-predicate structure of descriptive statements—which is not explicit in the text and which Plato does not analyze until the *Sophist*.

The Wax Block (191a–195b)

Suddenly and decisively Socrates declares that he and Theaetetus were wrong when they agreed (188c—case (3)) that it is impossible to judge that something you know is something you don't know.[29] Theaetetus immediately comes up with an example. Sometimes Theaetetus, who knows Socrates, has seen someone else in the distance, someone whom in fact he does not know, and thought that he was Socrates (191b).[30] This example is the simplest of several we shall be working with, so it will be as well to pause and take some bearings.

---

29. On the face of it, a mistake about something being impossible is a mistake of a type which none of the approaches that have been or will be tried out in the *Theaetetus*, or subsequently in the *Sophist*, comes near to explaining.

30. Note the past tense of the example, suggesting perhaps that the boy has long been eager for a meeting with Socrates (cf. 148e). Note also that Theaetetus is using his memory—the very faculty which is now going to help us make some progress with the problem of false judgement.

The essential novelty which the Wax Block model contributes to the understanding of misidentification lies in its vivid depiction of perceiving and memory-knowledge as two independent ways an item can come before the mind to be an object of judgement.[31] It will be argued that I can mistake X for Y provided I perceive X and know Y. I may, in addition, know X and/or perceive Y, but these extras, while they complicate the examples, seem to add little or nothing to their explanation. The replacement of J1 by J2 is sufficient to break the prohibition on case (3) misidentifications (cf. p. 76). And here of course it is vital that Part I has established that to perceive something is not, as such, to know it; otherwise J2 would collapse back into J1. We may add, with an eye to our discussion of 'other-judging' (pp. 86–7), that Part I secured this result by proving that to perceive something is not, as such, to think of it as or judge it to be anything in particular; otherwise J2a would collapse back into J1a.

The model envisages two operations. One operation is learning or memorizing something perceived, by getting its 'signature' stamped on the block (191ce). The other operation is that of fitting an imprint to a new perception in the attempt to identify its object (192b, 193cd, et passim).[32] Theaetetus' knowing or remembering Socrates is then very simply represented as his having the imprint of Socrates on his block ready for use when needed (191de).

We are not told, however, what this identifying knowledge consists in (cf. p. 75). Nothing is said to distinguish between knowing (remembering) what Socrates looked like yesterday, knowing (remembering) what Socrates looks like, knowing (remembering) who Socrates is, knowing (remembering) Socrates—to mention just a few of the notions which an analytical treatment would wish to scrutinize (cf. the recognition scene at the beginning of the dialogue, 144bd). We are told, in luxuriant detail, how the capacity for learn-

---

31. The relation of perceiving and memory-knowledge was, of course, unsatisfactorily discussed in Part I, 163d–164b, 166b. How many principles of Protagoras' philosophy are denied by the Wax Block model?

32. Socrates also says that we can use the block to memorize things we think of or conceive ourselves (191d); these imprints are applied to identify, successfully or unsuccessfully, what we are thinking of on a later occasion (195a). He gives no example to illustrate what he intends by this additional facility, but it could easily be applied to imaginative constructs like the Wax Block model itself. As we go through Parts II and III we shall repeatedly have occasion to ask: Is this the same conception as before? For another, quite different account of thought-imprints, see n. 40 below.

ing and retention varies from one person to another according to
the qualities of their wax (191cd, 194c–195a). But the description
leaves it quite unclear how, or even whether, Plato intends us to
translate into nonpictorial language the difference between, for
example, a distinct and an indistinct imprint of Socrates.[33]

Thus readers may properly wonder what happened the first time
Theaetetus perceived Socrates. How did he recognize Socrates as *a
man*? How did he distinguish him as *this particular* man? It would
seem that both these cognitive achievements are presupposed by
the operation of getting the 'signature' of Socrates stamped on
Theaetetus' wax block. Yet both require a cooperation between
perception and thought or judgement more complex than the simple identification of perceived properties, one by one, on which the
dialogue has largely concentrated hitherto.

There is material that bears on this topic in Part III of the dialogue
(cf. esp. 209bc). But so far as Part II is concerned, the initial stamping
operation (learning, *coming* to know) remains shrouded in brilliant
metaphor. Socrates remarked earlier (188a) that learning and forgetting, which are 'intermediate' between knowing and not knowing,
are irrelevant to the argument, and in fact it is only the second
operation envisaged by the Wax Block model, the fitting of a pre-
existing imprint to a new perception, which he puts to use in the
argument. In more logical terms, the argument is about judgements
which attempt, successfully or unsuccessfully, to reidentify something previously perceived. And for this purpose the Wax Block
model is a highly effective means to make us separate, in imagination, the new perception from the 'signature' applied to it. In accepting the model 'for the sake of the argument' (191c), we accept the
thesis that perceiving and knowing are distinct and independent
ways to 'get hold of something with the soul' (cf. 190cd)—the very
thing needed to break out of the absurd predicament in which the
discussion of false judgement has stuck (190e–191a).

For a twentieth-century reader this is one of the most fascinating
moments in the dialogue. Given the question 'How can a judgement
of identity, "*X* is *Y*", be true/false without its truth/falsity being
manifest in the very meaning of the sentence?', both the modern
and the alternative response suggest that this is possible if, and
only if, the route by which *X* is brought before the mind to be an
object of the judgement and the route by which *Y* is brought before

33. Notice the distancing effect of 'they say' at 194c, where 'they' remain unidentified.

the mind to be an object of the judgement are distinct and independent ways to 'get hold of something with the soul'. Then, and only
then, is it possible for someone (speaker, hearer, or solitary thinker)
to understand the sentence and still be left with a genuine question,
to which a mistaken answer can without absurdity be given, as to
whether X is Y. Thus far the modern and the alternative response
agree. But where Frege proceeds to speak of the different senses
of 'X' and 'Y', distinguishing two *semantic* routes from linguistic
expression to thing, Plato speaks of perceiving X and knowing Y,
distinguishing two *epistemic* routes from mind to thing. The truly
fascinating question is: How much difference does this difference
make to the understanding of misidentification?

Theaetetus' misidentification of the stranger certainly invites
treatment in Fregean style. Just put his mistake into words such as
'The man I see in the distance is Socrates' and point to the difference
of sense between the name 'Socrates' and the definite description
'the man I see in the distance'. The trouble is that, once the solution
is cast in semantic terms, the special role which the Wax Block
model assigns to perception would appear to lose its rationale. The
Fregean treatment is equally available for mistakes where perception is not involved, yet for these Plato later feels the need to
introduce new apparatus, the Aviary. How so, if perception in the
Wax Block was no more than the source or ground of descriptions
like 'the man I see in the distance?'[34]

A more special difficulty arises from this dialogue's bleak view
of the powers of perception. The use of a definite description like
'the man I see in the distance' involves thought and a preliminary
classificatory judgement as well as perception. But the Wax Block
model assures us only that perception by itself is an independent
way to 'get hold of something with the soul'; it offers no such
guarantee for perception aided by thought. Strictly speaking, any
verbal expression for the perceived term in Theaetetus' misidentification will involve thought, but the minimal sentence 'That is Socrates', where the demonstrative 'that' does not describe the perceived

34. For this line of reasoning, see Ackrill [40], 391–92. White [8], 167–68, prefers to
say that the Wax Block does apply the treatment and Plato wrongly supposed that
perception is crucial to it. McDowell [3], 216–17, is more charitable: if Plato thinks
perception is crucial, he 'has come quite close to a satisfactory way of dealing
with the difficulty raised by the argument of 187e–188c, without, apparently, quite
grasping the essential point.' Rudebusch [41] argues that in the *Theaetetus* Plato not
only understood the general form of Frege's solution but gave good reasons for
rejecting it.

item as anything in particular, would be more faithful to the Wax Block analysis than 'The man I see in the distance is Socrates'.[35] A bare 'that' (as opposed to 'that man') could never serve on its own to pick out an object of judgement; at most it registers (and tells one's audience) that some object is independently accessible through perception.

A modern philosopher might argue that this is a semantic solution after all. Certainly, perception is crucial when Theaetetus says, to himself or another, 'That is Socrates'. But what it is crucial for is securing the reference of the demonstrative 'that'. The sense of an expression is the way in which its reference is secured. So to say that the reference of 'that' is secured through perception (plus other contextual factors) is to start explaining the sense of the demonstrative in Theaetetus' judgement. We are still in the sphere of semantics.

It is important, however, that Plato does not say that the reference of 'that' is secured through perception. He does not speak of reference or of demonstratives and does not call attention to the words Theaetetus used for his judgement. What he emphasizes is the contrast between perception on the one hand and knowledge or thought on the other. The question (to repeat) is: How much difference does this difference make to the understanding of misidentification?

This is the point at which to offer the clarification promised earlier (p. 87) of the move from J1a to J2a implied at 195cd. We should distinguish the question whether the perceived term in Theaetetus' misidentification is thought of from the question whether thought is the route by which it comes before the mind to be an object of his judgement. To concede that it is thought of, because judgement is verbal and must include some designation of the stranger in the distance, is not yet to concede that thought does the work of connecting the mind to its object. On the picture put before us at 195cd it is only the known term which thought brings before the mind to be the object of a mistaken judgement of identity; this term must indeed be thought of as that which one knows it to be. The other term

---

35. At 202a 'that' and 'this' appear in a list of terms which can be applied to anything whatsoever. At 209b, in a context which returns to the Wax Block model, the example is 'This is Theaetetus'. As for the 'Socrates' part of the sentence 'That is Socrates', notice that Theaetetus uses 'Socrates', not 'you', in reporting his mistaken judgement *to Socrates* at 191b; this implies that he is reporting the expression he used to himself at the time, not just its reference. He might have used 'the son of Phaenarete' instead (cf. 144c, 149a): the essential thing for the illustration is not the use of a proper name like 'Socrates' or 'Theaetetus' but the identifying knowledge it represents.

comes before the mind through perception. Hence it need not be thought of as anything in particular, and thought responds by trying to decide what it is; this is the attempt to fit an imprint to the perception (cf. 194a). The sequence is: you perceive something, you think (ask yourself) 'What is that?', you think of Socrates, whom you know already, and you think (judge, assert to yourself) 'That is Socrates' or words to similar effect. If Plato leaves it to his readers' imagination to supply a suitable sentence for Theaetetus' judgement, we can be confident that, in his view of the Wax Block solution, the sentence and the semantics of its constituent expressions are secondary to the contrast between epistemic routes.

No doubt, if Plato were to go beyond the gross contrast between perceiving and knowing to discriminate more finely among modes of 'getting hold of something with the soul', he might in the process come closer to modern ways of treating judgements of identity. For it is not the case that Frege solved the whole problem once and for all. His theory of sense and reference has been a formative influence on the modern debate, but the debate goes on, and at the heart of it is the question how the semantic aspects of reference are related to the epistemic aspects.[36] But this must be left as a suggestion for the interested reader to pursue, since the gross contrast is all that the Wax Block allows. A more refined set of distinctions will become available when we reach Part III.

Meanwhile, there is a rival interpretation to note. The point of distinguishing two routes, epistemic or semantic, is to provide an enabling condition for an identity statement 'X is Y' to express genuine information if it is true and genuine misinformation if it is false. But, as so often in philosophy, the solution to one problem leads on to another. When we ask what this information or misinformation is that 'X is Y' conveys, it is exceedingly difficult to answer without moving up a level and describing it as information or misinformation about the two routes themselves, to the effect that they lead to one and the same thing. This is the motive for an alternative interpretation of the whole section, as follows.

The purpose of the Wax Block model is to explain, or explain away, Theaetetus' judgement 'That is Socrates' as, in reality, a judgement of the form 'This perception matches my memory-im-

---

36. See esp. Saul Kripke's influential essay *Naming and Necessity* (Oxford: 1980) and Evans, *op.cit.* For a profound discussion of the bearing of these issues on the relation of language and thought, see Michael Dummett, 'The Philosophy of Thought and Philosophy of Language', in J. Vuillemin ed., *Mérites et limites des méthodes logiques en philosophie* (Paris: 1986), 141–55.

print of Socrates'. The replacement of J1 (J1a) by J2 (J2a) is still the crucial novelty on this interpretation, but it plays a different role. The importance of the independence of perceiving from knowing is no longer that they are distinct routes for items to come before the mind to be the objects of a mistaken judgement of identity, but that perceptions and imprints are themselves distinct items for the mistaken judgement, which asserts, not of course that they are identical, but that they match or that they converge on a single person, Socrates.[37]

Such a manoeuvre avoids the puzzle of identity statements because it *replaces* the notion of identity by a different relation, the relation of matching, which holds or fails to hold between psychological entities (perceptions and imprints), not between the human entities one meets about town. Philosophically, it is an interesting question whether this style of analysis should be regarded as an evasion of the original problem or as a solution to it. Textually, the interpretation requires us to look closely, as Socrates discourses at length about fitting imprints to perceptions, for signs that he intends this to analyze what Theaetetus asserts by his statement 'That is Socrates', rather than what an onlooker asserts by the statement 'Theaetetus judges that the person he sees is Socrates'. In other words, does the fitting of an imprint to a perception represent the content of Theaetetus' judgement, or does it represent what goes on in his mind when he makes the judgement? Or does Plato simply fail to be clear about the difference between these two things?

Having canvassed several strategies for interpreting the philosophical achievement of the Wax Block, we may now return to the example with which Theaetetus starts us off at 191b. We should notice that, as he states the example, the order of the terms is the reverse of the order in the general formula it is designed to illustrate. Socrates had said that it is possible to judge that something you know is something you don't know (191ab). Theaetetus presents his own personal concrete misidentification as a case of judging that someone he does not know is someone he knows (191b). The known item shifts from first to second place, in disregard of the distinction at 188c between cases (3) and (4). Now, from a logical point of view, the distinction between cases (3) and (4) is empty.

37. So Ackrill [40], 392–93, followed by Williams [43], 301–2. This alternative interpretation has its own counterpart in Frege, whose earlier work *Begriffschrift* (1879) took the view that an identity statement 'X is Y' is a statement about the actual expressions 'X' and 'Y', to the effect that they stand for the same thing. See *Translations, op. cit.*, 10–12, and Frege's later rebuttal of the idea in 'On Sense and Reference', *ibid.* 56–57.

The order in which an identity claim arrays its terms makes no difference to its content and is likely to be determined pragmatically, by the presuppositions of the context. (Thus 'That is Socrates', with the known item in second place, would be appropriate in answer to the question 'Who is that?', while 'Socrates is that one', with the known item in first place, would be appropriate in answer to the question 'Which is Socrates?') The same principles apply when an identity claim is reported and discussed by someone else. There should be no objection, therefore, if Plato sticks to the logical content of the identity claim and treats his formula 'judging that X is Y' as reversible, i.e. as equivalent to 'judging that Y is X'. This practice does, however, create unclarity when Socrates enumerates a series of combinations in which each of X and Y is either known or perceived or neither or both, and if both, either with or without the knowledge being correctly lined up with the perception (192a ff.). (Readers with combinatorial skills will enjoy deciding how many cases he overlooks and whether or not he is trying to enumerate all possible combinations.) So I shall use the nonreversible English formula 'mistaking X for Y', where X is the item which has to be perceived for misidentification to occur and Y the item known. In Theaetetus' example, X is the stranger seen at a distance, Y is Socrates. And to make the next stage easier for my own readers than Theaetetus found it (192cd), I shall present in tabular form the outcome of Socrates' search for the combinations where false judgement is conceivable:

$Y\rightarrow$	KP	K$-$P	$-$KP	$-$K$-$P
X $\downarrow$ KP	(i) 192cd 193bd 193e—194a	(ii) 192c 193d 194a		
K$-$P				
$-$KP	(iv)	(iii) 191b 192c		
$-$K$-$P				

(K = known, P = perceived, $-$K = not known, $-$P = not perceived)

The task is to discover under what conditions it is possible to mistake X for Y. All but four squares are eliminated as soon as we see that the Wax Block model requires P in the X-line, K in the Y-line. Of the remaining combinations, (iii) is that of Theaetetus' first simple example: stranger seen, mistaken for Socrates. Combinations (i) and (ii) are described (twice) at 193b–194a: (i) Theaetetus and Theodorus seen (both of them known to Socrates), Theaetetus mistaken for Theodorus and vice versa, (ii) Theaetetus alone perceived, and mistaken for Theodorus. What of combination (iv): a stranger and Theaetetus perceived, the stranger mistakenly identified as Theaetetus? Readers may speculate on the reasons why it is not mentioned, but it is certainly possible. The omission underlines the unimportance, in the present context, of the fact that the Y-item may be perceived as well as known (p. 91).

But now comes the big question. Is it equally unimportant that the X-item may be known as well as perceived? Having said at 191ab that they were wrong about the impossibility of false judgement in case (3) of the initial puzzle, Socrates takes a second look back at 191e and says they were wrong *in case (1) also.* He thereby presents combinations (i) and (ii) as counterexamples to his earlier thesis

> K It is impossible to judge that something one knows is something else one knows.

It is thanks to the provision that at least one term, the X-item, is perceived that (i) and (ii) can appear in this light (cf. 192cd), but appear in it they do. Is the appearance deceptive?

I would like to suggest, though readers should think twice before agreeing with me, that the answer is 'Yes and No'. Take combination (ii). In the story which the Wax Block has to tell of this misidentification, the imprint holding Socrates' knowledge of Theaetetus plays no part. It remains inert in the block while Socrates tries to fit his knowledge of Theodorus to the perception of Theaetetus. Combination (i) is a slightly different story. Socrates' knowledge of Theaetetus does play a part—but not in the misidentification of Theaetetus. (i) is simply twice (ii): two separate misidentifications, each of which the model explains in the same way as (ii). In neither (ii) nor (i) is the knowledge of X active in the misidentification of X.

Thus Socrates' retraction at 191e is a lesser thing than it looks. He does not endorse the modern response to the initial puzzle, since he remains adamantly opposed to the combination (K–P, K–P) which we illustrated by the detective judging 'Castor is the same person as Pollux' when not perceiving either suspect (192a, 192e–193a; cf. p. 74, p. 82). He does not suggest that a correct understanding of what is involved in knowing X will show it to be compatible with misidentifying X (cf. pp. 73–4), but rather that knowing X (whatever that involves) is compatible with misidentifying X in circumstances such that the knowledge plays no part in bringing X before the mind to be an object of the judgement.

These observations continue to apply, *mutatis mutandis*, when Socrates at 193d quietly describes combination (i) as an admissible case of 'heterodoxy' or 'other-judging'.[38] The implication of this surprising comeback is that both terms are *thought of* as well as perceived; they may even be thought of *as* Theaetetus and Theodorus respectively. Yet although the mistaken judgement involves thinking of Theodorus (as Theodorus) and thinking of Theaetetus (as Theaetetus), the thought of Theodorus plays no part in the misidentification of Theodorus, nor the thought of Theaetetus in the misidentification of Theaetetus. It is perception, not thought, that makes Theaetetus available for the misidentification; it is knowing him, not the perception, which makes one think of him as the person he is, and likewise with Theodorus. The mistaken judgement is 'This is Theodorus and that is Theaetetus', not 'Theaetetus is Theodorus' or 'Theodorus is Theaetetus'. Thus if the Wax Block's treatment of combination (i) is meant to be a counterexample to Socrates' earlier thesis

> T It is impossible to judge that something one is thinking of is something else one is thinking of,

it appears no less halfhearted than it does when viewed as a counterexample to thesis K. For it does not suggest that a correct understanding of what is involved in thinking of X will show it to be compatible with misidentifying X, but rather that thinking of X (as X) is compatible with misidentifying X in circumstances such that the thought of X (as X) plays no part in bringing X before the mind to be mistaken for Y.

The reader is entitled to find all this somewhat puzzling. Why in combination (ii) does Socrates' knowledge of Theaetetus remain inert in the block? Why in combination (i), where Socrates' thought is actively using his knowledge of Theaetetus, does this knowledge or thought not connect up with the perception of Theaetetus? Help-

---

38. 'Heterodoxy' was introduced at 190e as a variant for 'other-judging': see note *ad loc.*

ful as it is to have perceiving brought into the discussion as an independent way of getting hold of something with the soul, the Wax Block model raises more questions than it answers about the mental activity of the soul which owns and uses the block. It presupposes a distinction (as our questions bring out) between merely having some knowledge (an imprint stamped on the block) and actively using it in one's thought, but it is singularly inactive about bringing the distinction to the forefront of our attention.

The Aviary model, by contrast, is all about the difference between having knowledge and using it. Moreover, the Aviary is expressly designed to circumvent thesis K. It is to the Aviary, then, that we must turn if we want to understand why that thesis has so far received only circumspect and halfhearted criticism.

*   *   *   *   *   *   *   *   *   *   *   *

Before moving on, however, there is an opportunity not to be missed of gaining a historical perspective on our own philosophical vocabulary. Consider this passage from Locke's *Essay concerning Human Understanding* (II 29.3):

> The *cause of Obscurity* in simple *Ideas*, seems to be either dull Organs; or very slight and transient Impressions made by the Objects; or else a weakness in the Memory, not able to retain them as received. For to return again to visible Objects, to help us apprehend this matter. If the Organs, or Faculties of Perception, like Wax over-hardned with Cold, will not receive the Impression of the Seal, from the usual impulse wont to imprint it; or, like Wax of a temper too soft, will not hold it well, when well imprinted; or else supposing the Wax of a temper fit, but the Seal not applied with a sufficient force, to make a clear Impression: In any of these cases, the print left by the Seal, will be *obscure*. This, I suppose, needs no application to make it plainer.

Here is the Wax Block model still thriving in the seventeeth century. Locke appears to reinvent *Theaetetus* 194c–195a. Yet there is a critical difference. Plato keeps memory quite separate from perception. The first impressions on the wax are memory-knowledge, derived from perception by a deliberate act of memorization (191d). In Locke a perception is already the receiving of an impression, which memory can then retain. What Locke has and Plato lacks is the notion, so important in the modern philosophical tradition, of a *sense-impression*.

It was Aristotle who first applied Plato's Wax Block metaphor directly to perception: 'We must take it that sense is that which can receive the perceptible forms without their matter, as wax receives the imprint of the ring without the iron or gold' (*De Anima* II 12, 424a 17–20). After Aristotle, the Hellenistic philosophers, especially the Stoics, made it standard philosophical practice to discuss sense-perception in terms of impressions.[39] Aristotle's move was sharply polemical, part of the rich concept of perception he advocated in opposition to *Theaetetus* 184a–186e (p. 63). Aristotle and Locke, for all their differences, are both defending an empiricist theory of knowledge against contemporary Platonism. Both maintain that, at least at the level of simple sensible qualities, the senses can identify what is presented to them. That is the philosophical issue behind this history. We naturally think of an impression as carrying information about its cause (the 'signature' is a record of the seal). So the notion of a sense-impression is an apt metaphor for the empiricist claim that sense-perception is a form of awareness in its own right. Plato, by contrast, who gave philosophy its first and most compelling description of the Wax Block model of which empiricists, ancient and modern, have been so fond, reserves the identifying capacity it represents for the higher level of thought and judgement.

Criticism of the Wax Block (195b–196d)

After this brief historical excursus, a surprise. The Wax Block model, on which so much time and care has been spent, is curtly dismissed on the grounds that it fails to explain mistakes where perception is not involved—for example, the mistake of thinking that five and seven are eleven. Why, the reader may wonder, is this a criticism *of the Wax Block?* Surely it was not the aim of the Wax Block model to deal with arithmetical mistakes. The result with which Theaetetus professes himself well satisfied at 195b, and again at 195d, is the proof that false judgement is possible because *some* misidentifications are coherently conceivable. Other mistakes may need other

---

39. For the Stoics, see Sextus Empiricus, *Adversus Mathematicos* VII 228–41, 248–52. Aristotle uses the Wax Block model for memory also (*De Memoria* 450a 29–32), because, like Locke, he thinks of remembering as retaining an impression got originally in perception. Conversely, a later Platonist like Plotinus argues (*Enneads* IV 6) against the thesis that memory is the retention of sense-impressions on the grounds that perception does not involve the receiving of impressions.

models, but that is no reason for Socrates to deprecate the achievement of the Wax Block in the way he seems to do at 195bd.

A closer examination of the text discloses, however, that Socrates'
objection is not so much to the use that has been made of the Wax
Block to answer the question 'How is false judgement possible?' as
to the answer which it implies—more precisely, which an imaginary
questioner construes it to imply—to the definitional question 'What
is false judgement?', namely, that false judgement is the misfitting
of perception and thought (195cd; cf. 196c). At the start of the
inquiry into false judgement (187d), Socrates raised both questions
together, as if they were interdependent, and while the question
'How is false judgement possible?' has been at the forefront of the
discussion, the definitional question has put in several appearances
(189b, 190e, 194b). We may feel that Socrates could have relaxed
his ruling that perception is a necessary condition for mistaken
identifications without jeopardizing the achievement of the Wax
Block within the narrower sphere where perception can contribute.
But once the imaginary questioner has formally construed the misfitting of perception and thought as a *definition* of false judgement,
any such adjustment will take on a more drastic appearance and
seem to be a discarding of the whole preceding discussion (196c).

Pause for a glimpse into the future: the relation of definitional to
other questions is the subject of an uneasy interlude a little way
ahead at 196d–197a, and the imagery of the Wax Block recurs near
the end of the dialogue at 209c, as if to tell us that our reading of
the *Theaetetus* will not be complete until we have worked out how
much can be salvaged from the Wax Block section.

Meanwhile, if the mistake of thinking that five and seven are
eleven is possible, as Theaetetus agrees (196b), how are we to
explain it? At 196ab Socrates invites Theaetetus to accept the inference 'If a man judges that five and seven are eleven, he judges that
twelve is eleven'. Theaetetus accepts, with reluctance, and Socrates
concludes that their only choice, if they are to vindicate the possibility of arithmetical mistakes, is to reexamine thesis K; for the man
under discussion is someone who, if he does judge that twelve is
eleven, thereby judges that one thing he knows is another thing he
knows (196bc).

Does this mean that Socrates will undertake to show that it is
indeed possible to judge that twelve is eleven? Theaetetus has just
agreed with the imaginary questioner that, on Wax Block principles,
this is impossible (195e)—as impossible as the imaginary questioner's other example of the combination $K-P$, $K-P$, judging that a

certain man, whom one is not observing, is a certain horse, which also one is not observing (195d). And perhaps the imaginary questioner is right about these examples. Even a critic who disputes the Wax Block principles which rule out 'Theaetetus is Theodorus' (193a) or our own 'Castor is Pollux' could agree that 'Twelve is eleven' and 'Socrates is Black Beauty' are manifestly absurd. On the other hand, if Theaetetus is unwilling to accept that it is possible to judge that twelve is eleven, what is he to say about Socrates' inference at 196ab, 'If a man judges that five and seven are eleven, he judges that twelve is eleven'?

Socrates at this point has taken over the role of that tricky customer, the imaginary questioner (195e), which suggests that Plato intends to catch his readers in the same dilemma as Theaetetus. Are we meant to agree with the imaginary questioner that it is not possible to judge that twelve is eleven? We should have learned by now that imaginary questioners are not to be trusted (cf. 188d, 163d, 165be). Or are we meant to agree with Socrates that if a man judges that five and seven are eleven, he judges that twelve is eleven? We should have learned by now that Socrates too can be a tease, not least when an imaginary questioner gets him going (cf. 188e).

Let us look back over the passage which leads up to Socrates' inference. Theaetetus, defensively holding on to the Wax Block model, has said that someone seeing or touching eleven things could take them for twelve, but he could not judge that the eleven he has in his thought is the twelve he has in his thought (195e). We need not be surprised at the claim that someone who is thinking of eleven and thinking of twelve cannot judge that the one is the other. That sounds all too like the example 'Two must be one' which helped to refute 'other-judging' at 190c; the Wax Block has certainly offered no means of challenging it. But what of the claim that one can perceive eleven things and think they are twelve? To bring this under the two epistemic routes of the Wax Block model is to imply, what Socrates will shortly confirm (196ab), that an imprint holding the knowledge of twelve can be added to the imprints of our friends and acquaintances. And this in turn puts 'Those are twelve', said of a perceived group of eleven men, parallel to earlier examples like 'That is Theodorus' said of Theaetetus seen at a distance. Yet if 'Those are twelve' and 'That is Theodorus' are of the same form, both are identity statements, and it would appear that Theaetetus treats the number of the men perceived as nothing different from the men themselves. Has he forgotten that in Part I we learned

(Theaetetus volunteered the point himself—185cd) that numbers are not perceptible features of things and a fortiori not perceptible things themselves?

Pause for a second glimpse into the future: in Part III of the dialogue Socrates subjects Theaetetus to a lengthy 'proof' of such propositions as these, that the number of an army is the same as the army (204d), that six is nothing different from four and two (204c), and quite generally that a whole is identical with the parts which make it up (205a). Theaetetus puts in a valiant resistance to this 'proof', but he does not command the analytical resources to say what is wrong with it. But if something is wrong with it, as we are clearly meant to see, we must be prepared to distinguish, not only the number of men perceived from the men themselves, but also, more surprisingly, the number of five and seven from five and seven themselves.

A modern reader is likely to feel that Socrates behaves no better here at 196ab when he takes over from the imaginary questioner and describes a mistake of pure thought, where perception is not involved. He alleges that in asking the question 'How many are five and seven?' a man considers the five he has imprinted on his block and the seven he has imprinted on his block. Not only does this account make it appear that the man is using his knowledge of five and seven in the very act of inquiring how many they are, but Socrates then achieves the inference 'If the man judges that the answer is eleven, he judges that twelve is eleven' by simply referring to the two items under consideration as 'the twelve on the block'. He treats knowing five and knowing seven as no different from knowing twelve, considering five and seven as no different from considering twelve. That is how he makes it appear that someone who considers five and seven and judges that they are eleven is someone who considers twelve and judges it to be eleven. Well may we share Theaetetus' reluctance to admit that this is what happens in a mundane miscalculation like 'Five and seven are eleven'.

Evidently we are back in choppy water.[40] The smoother sailing

40. This is the place at which to confess that a less provocative interpretation of the whole section 195b–196d can be obtained from McDowell [3].

(1) At 195d he translates

'And you say', he'll go on, 'we couldn't ever think that man—something we only have in our thoughts, but don't see—is horse, which, again, we don't see or touch, but only have in our thoughts, and don't have any other perception relating to it.'

Where Miss Levett (like Cornford) has the imaginary questioner start with two sensible objects which are currently unobserved, moving on at 195e to numbers, we enjoyed when the Wax Block model was introduced is to be no excuse for relaxing the effort to think for ourselves. A modern reader may side initially with Theaetetus against Socrates. But it is Socrates who will be steering us through the second constructive section of the discussion of false judgement, and it is Socrates' inference which motivates its central task, the reexamination of thesis K.

The Aviary (196d–199c)

The Aviary is introduced as a daring, even shocking breach of philosophical principle. In earlier dialogues Plato makes Socrates insist that definitional questions have priority over certain other questions. Sometimes the claim is that in order to know examples of a concept you must first settle its definition (*Republic* 505a–506a, 520c, 534bc, *Hippias Major* 304de; perhaps also, by implication, *Lysis* 223b). We met a version of this principle at the beginning of the *Theaetetus* (146c–147c; cf. pp. 4–5, p. 39, p. 60), and it returns here when Socrates expresses dismay at the lax manner in which they have allowed themselves, while still seeking the definition of knowledge, to use verbs of knowing to instance things they know and do not know. At other times the claim is that until you have defined a concept, you cannot give knowledgeable answers to ques-

---

which ought to be classified as unobserv*able,* McDowell's alternative translation starts from the concepts or kinds *man* and *horse,* in a manner reminiscent of the example 'A cow must be a horse' at 190c.

(2) Connected with this is the suggestion (McDowell [3], 214–16, 218–19, following Ackrill [40], 394–95; cf. Bostock [9], 177–78, 181–82, 264) that 'Those are twelve' should be seen, not as an inapposite use of the Wax Block's analysis of mistaken judgements of identity, but as an extension of the model to cover descriptive judgements in which a predicate is applied to the item perceived. Already at 191d Socrates announced that the block can be used to record things we think of or conceive as well as things we perceive; McDowell and others suggest that this allows for imprints representing the grasp of a predicative concept.

My objection to (2) is that at 195a the application envisaged for thought-imprints is precisely not to (describe or classify) objects perceived but to (identify) objects of thought; cf. n. 32 above. My objection to (1) is partly that I find it a less natural rendering of the Greek, partly that the context suggests that the imaginary questioner should start by resuming (so as to build his challenge on) a case ruled out in the preceding exposition of the Wax Block. Now the example used earlier to rule out the combination K–P, K–P, was 'Theaetetus is Theodorus' (193a; cf. 192a), a concrete misidentification where the two items are unobservable but not unobservable. 'Socrates is Black Beauty' is a quite manifestly absurd example of the same type from which the imaginary questioner can then *argue* ('Doesn't it follow from this theory . . . ?') that the abstract misidentification 'Eleven is twelve' should fall under the same ban.

tions about it. Just as, until you know who Meno is, you cannot know whether he is beautiful or the opposite, so too until you know what virtue is, you cannot say *what it is like*, e.g. whether it is teachable (*Meno* 71ab, 86c–87b; cf. *Republic* 354bc). Be the subject concrete or abstract, descriptive knowledge waits upon knowledge of identity. All of that is mulled over from 196d to 197a as Socrates prepares himself to describe, with the aid of the Aviary model, what he does not yet know: knowing itself.

Readers will find it difficult to decide what, in the final outcome, his attitude is to his own methodology, or how to assign different levels of irony as between Socrates and the 'expert in contradiction' who upbraids him at 197a. Plato leaves us wondering whether he shares Socrates' unease over certain principles he had previously taken for granted. Perhaps he intends an ironic jolt to the expectations which his own earlier works have formed in his readers. Perhaps the methodological principles, since they speak of a priority *in knowledge*, rule themselves out of court in the context of an inquiry into that very concept.

Be that as it may, the description of knowing contributed by the Aviary model is in fact based on a prior identification of knowing as 'the possession of knowledge' (197ab). The point of this statement, which has the form but hardly the content of a definition, is to contrast possession and use. It is one thing to know something, i.e. possess some knowledge, quite another to have the knowledge actively in use, e.g. to answer a question. The Aviary model likens the first to having a bird in one's cage, the second to having a bird in hand. In more logical terms, the first is a power or capacity (197c), the second the exercise of a power or capacity.

One could think of this contrast as a distinction between two senses of 'knowing' or between two ways of knowing.[41] Thus Aristotle, who was a keen student of the *Theaetetus*, frequently alludes to the distinction between knowing in the sense in which a person who has learned grammar may be said to know it even when they are asleep or thinking of other matters, and knowing in the active sense which English would describe as exercising knowledge, as when a scholar uses their knowledge of Greek grammar to read the

---

41. So Cornford [2], 130, Ackrill [40], 397, Lewis [48], 262. The text does distinguish two senses for the verb 'to have' (197c; cf. 198b), but not for the verb 'to know'. Both senses of the Greek verb 'to have' were in fact used in expounding the Wax Block: e.g. 'holding' and 'keeping' at 192b, 193d, render the exercise sense, 'possess' and 'have' at 192a, 193bc, the capacity sense.

Theaetetus.[42] But in fact Socrates reserves the verb 'to know' for the capacity (possession of knowledge), and he affects some puzzlement about finding appropriate terms to describe the exercise of knowledge (198a, 198e–199a). Aristotle also tends to take it that what one knows, in one or the other of his senses, is a whole field or branch of learning, such as grammar. Socrates makes use of the idea that a well-stocked aviary will contain the art of arithmetic (198ab) or the knowledge of the alphabet which is exercised in reading (198e–199a). But his distinction between possessing knowledge and having it in hand is introduced and explained for the individual birds which represent the knowledge of eleven, the knowledge of twelve, and so on for each separate number. Is the art of arithmetic just the sum total of these separate pieces of knowledge? Are we to imagine that a man who has completely mastered arithmetic has an infinity of birds in his soul (cf. 198b)? If not, what is the relation between, on the one hand, the mastery of a whole branch of learning and, on the other, the individual pieces of knowledge falling under it (recall qu. (3), p. 5)?

Analogous questions arise already at the level of these 'pieces of knowledge'. It is easy enough to grasp the distinction between having a bird in one's aviary (knowledge as capacity) and having a bird in hand (knowledge actively in use): same bird, two ways it can be present in the mind. But what exactly is a bird? What scope of knowledge does it comprise? What assures us that it is a genuine 'element' in our understanding of arithmetic and not itself a multiplicity of pieces of knowledge?

Some of these questions must wait for Part III. Others are best

42. *The distinction in Aristotle*. Whereas in Plato the distinction needs a model to explain it and make it vivid in our minds, Aristotle is able to use his version of Plato's distinction as the model for a metaphysical distinction which is central to his whole anti-Platonic philosophy of mind: the distinction between first and second actuality. Briefly, as knowledge in the capacity sense is to active knowledge, so is the soul to the various activities making up the life of a plant, animal, or human being; hence to speak of the soul is to speak of nothing more mysterious than the capacity for living a certain kind of life (*De Anima* II 1). Again, as knowledge in the capacity sense is to active knowledge, so too is a sense like sight to the actual seeing of colours; hence to speak of our awareness of colour is to speak of nothing more mysterious than the exercise of a capacity which we and other animals are born with (*De Anima* II 5). Other important Aristotelian uses of the distinction between two senses of 'knowing' may be observed at *Nicomachean Ethics* VII 3, *Metaphysics* XII 7, *De Anima* III 4. Aristotle uses the verb 'to have' to mark the capacity rather than the active sense, thereby reversing the change Socrates makes when he borrows the formula 'having knowledge' from unidentified contemporaries (197ab).

studied in the context of the Aviary's solution to the problem of arithmetical mistakes. Our first task is to understand how the distinction between a capacity and its exercise breaks the impasse over mistakes of pure thought. The Aviary proposes to vindicate the possibility of abstract misidentification where perception is not involved, by making it conceivable that one should judge that something one knows is something else one knows (196bc). How does this work?

The argument against case (1) misidentifications has all along been that, if you were to judge that something you know is something else you know, it would follow that you both know (*ex hypothesi*) and do not know (because you misidentify) the same things, which is a contradiction (188b, 191b, 196bc). But if 'knowing something' signifies the possession rather than the use of knowledge, the contradictory conclusion does not follow. Misidentification does not entail that you do not know the thing. What follows is that *either* you do not know it *or* you are not using the knowledge you possess. There is no contradiction in the idea of someone possessing knowledge but failing to make active use of it (199ac).

This is very far from a conversion to the 'modern' view (cf. pp. 74–5) that knowledge is a condition of mistake, as J1 maintains, because to make a judgement about something (be it true or false) one must know what one is referring to. That view implies not merely that knowing something is compatible with misidentifying it, but that some knowledge must be actively in use for the misidentification to occur. By contrast, it is because the knowledge need not be actively in use that Socrates is prepared to agree that knowing something is compatible with misidentifying it. He does not reject outright the inference from misidentification to ignorance which served to rule out case (1) misidentifications. He qualifies it, saying, in effect, 'We must allow for people's failure to use their knowledge as well as for ignorance. Knowing something is a capacity, and a capacity is to be distinguished from its exercise. Hence, just as your failure to recognise Theaetetus when you see him does not necessarily show that you did not memorize his features when you met him before, so likewise, if you meet a number in the realm of thought and fail to identify it correctly, this does not necessarily show that you did not learn your arithmetic properly at school'.

But how close is this analogy with the Wax Block, and how, if you please, does one 'meet a number in the realm of thought'? The metaphor is mine, not Plato's, but it points up a genuine parallel between the two models. Just as the imprints on the block are used to identify objects perceived, so the birds in the aviary are used to identify numbers. There is a bird for each number you know (198ab). Numbers themselves are not perceived, though some of the things which have number are perceived. What corresponds in the Aviary to the Wax Block's fitting of an imprint to a perception is *counting*. Counting is the attempt to identify, not the items themselves, abstract or concrete, which have number, but their number.

The chief evidence for these assertions of mine is Socrates' description of the arithmetician at 198c. We hear that the man who has birds for all the numbers in his aviary may proceed to do some counting, either counting to himself the numbers themselves or counting some external thing which has number. We also hear that counting is considering how large a number actually is. Now, to ask how large a number is is the same as to ask which number it is: 'How large is five and seven?' is the same question as 'What is five and seven?' And we are bound to ask, What number is this that he is considering and trying to ascertain how large it is/which number it is? The answer can only be the number of, for example, seven men and five men or the number of five and seven themselves (196a). It is to identify this number that the arithmetician activates his knowledge of twelve, the mistake-maker his knowledge of eleven.

There is a certain foreignness, for the modern reader, in this manner of speaking about numbers and counting. Some more explanation is in order. We need to see that the Aviary is not just an addition to the Wax Block. The new features transform the whole picture of arithmetical mistake.

Already in our discussion of the Wax Block we found it necessary to bring out the distinction between active and inert knowledge (p. 100). The Aviary allows us to recognize that an imprint, like a bird, is essentially a capacity. To put wings on such capacities is then simply to make vivid the point that Socrates may have the capacity to identify Theaetetus and yet not exercise it when he meets him. Where before we said that Socrates' knowledge of Theaetetus remains inert on the block while he tries to fit his knowledge of Theodorus to the perception of Theaetetus, now we can say that the knowledge of Theaetetus eluded his grasp, and he got hold of the knowledge of Theodorus instead.

Well and good. The distinction between knowledge as capacity and knowledge actively in use is a perfectly general one which holds for any kind of knowledge. It is therefore available, if we take the initiative, for a retrospective clarification of the Wax Block. But we had better not mix the imagery of the two models. For when it comes to the knowledge of numbers, the twelve-bird is not simply our old friend, the imprint of twelve, with wings on.

The imprints on the block are memorized from perception. The birds in our aviary are gained by education (198b) or independent inquiry (197e). The aviary is empty in childhood (197e). It is not the place where you put your knowledge of Mummy and Daddy, but where you house later learning of a more intellectual and more systematic kind: the capacities involved in counting and reading. So while a bird is like an imprint in being a capacity to identify something, it is a capacity of the understanding, not just of memory.

This goes with an improved conception of number. The phrase 'external things which *have number*' in Socrates' description of the arithmetician at 198c is important. The Aviary model enables us to progress beyond Theaetetus' treatment of the number of the men perceived as nothing different from the men themselves (195e, p. 103). The imagery reflects this progress: imprints presumably resemble the objects they are used to identify, the birds do not. Birds fit better than imprints with Part I's insight that numbers are not perceptible features of things (185cd).

The Aviary also corrects Socrates' earlier account of arithmetical reflection. Whereas the man at 196a considers the five and the seven imprinted on his block, with the result that he seems to be using his knowledge of these numbers in the very process of inquiring how many they are (p. 104), the arithmetician at 198c is simply said to count either the numbers themselves or some external thing (collection) which has number. The five-bird and the seven-bird are not in the picture, only five and seven.

But how, you may ask, can he speak or judge of five and seven without using the knowledge of five and the knowledge of seven? And what about a bird for the operation of adding one number to the other? The questions derive from the modern presumption that knowledge is a condition of mistake (pp. 74–5). We may think that knowledge must be exercised in judgements or questions about anything whatsoever, but Plato's imagery would translate that into the idea that the arithmetician must get into his aviary and grab two birds in order to go looking for a third. Nothing so bizarre is put before us here. To repeat: the five-bird and the seven-bird are not in the picture, only five and seven; still less is there any hint of a piece of knowledge concerning five-and-seven being represented within the aviary, either by the twelve-bird itself or by some more advanced ornithological crossbreed.[43] So far as the text is concerned, the only bird a mathematical thinker works with is the bird he takes up for his answer: the capacity to identify twelve, if he gets it right, the capacity to identify eleven, if he makes the mistake we are interested in (199b).

But what, you may ask, is this capacity to identify twelve if it is not, precisely, the capacity to identify twelve as the number of, e.g., five and seven? Socrates makes it sound as if the knowledge of numbers involved in arithmetic was like the knowledge of letters involved in reading, a bundle of separate capacities, one for each item to be identified, and no questions asked about how the knowledge of twelve can exist independently of and prior to the knowledge that twelve is five and seven. Quite so. Part III will make it difficult for us to be that simplistic even about the knowledge of letters.[44]

Thus the success of the Aviary model depends upon the twelve-bird remaining caged up while the mistake is made of thinking that five and seven is eleven. The mistake-maker does not recognize twelve for what it is when he meets it in the realm of thought, even though he has the capacity to recognize it. Asking oneself 'What is five and seven?' is like wondering what it is that one sees in the distance. Answering 'Eleven' when the right answer is 'Twelve' is like misidentifying Theaetetus as Theodorus. So you can judge that twelve is eleven, just as you can judge that Theaetetus is Theodorus—in cases where this does not involve the illicit thought 'Twelve is eleven' or 'Theaetetus is Theodorus'. If you know twelve/Theaetetus as well as eleven/Theodorus, you will then be judging that something you know is something else you know—this is possible, but only because in the cases described your knowledge of twelve/Theaetetus is not active in linking the mind to twelve/Theaetetus (cf. p. 99).

43. Cornford [2], 137–38, argues that Plato ought to have recognized a five-and-seven bird; Ackrill [40], 398–99, disagrees. The question is reopened by Lewis [48], who argues that birds ought to represent numbers *under certain designations*, with one bird for knowing twelve under the designation 'twelve' and a distinct bird for knowing it under the complex designation 'the sum of five and seven'. The 'ought' in these views represents an attempt to solve a problem (we will come to it shortly) the importance of which is precisely that it is not to be solved by invoking more birds than are mentioned in the text; i.e. it is not to be solved in terms of *knowledge*.

44. The reading example which is worked into the Aviary at 198e–199a is an important link to Part III, suggesting that Part II expects help from any lessons we can learn about letters and syllables in Part III.

All in all, the analogy with the Wax Block is closer than one might have expected. But an important question remains: What in the Aviary model corresponds to the role of perception in the Wax Block? What connects the mind to twelve as, in the analogous Wax Block example (combination (ii)), the route to Theaetetus is through perception? In the case of twelve it cannot be perception, and it cannot be knowledge. For perception can at most put us in touch with 'one of the external things which have number', and the only knowledge actively in use is the knowledge of eleven. We are forced to recognize that principle J2 is not generous enough. There must be a third way, besides perception and knowledge, to 'get hold of something with the soul'.[45]

Let us return to the arithmetician at 198c 'considering how large a number actually is'. The next sentence is revealing: 'Then it looks as if this man were considering something which he knows as if he did not know it'. The implication is that asking oneself, 'How large a number is five and seven?' or 'What is five and seven?' is indeed a way of considering twelve. If so, it is a way of encountering twelve without recognizing it for what it is, without activating one's knowledge of twelve—exactly what is needed to complete the analogy between the Wax Block's explanation of concrete misidentifications and the Aviary's explanation of abstract misidentifications.

This interpretation is interesting because it shows Plato opting once again for an epistemic solution to a problem that Frege solves in semantic terms. Finding himself in a world full of dunces who judge that five and seven is eleven and make other mistakes of pure thought which the Wax Block model cannot explain, Plato invokes a third epistemic route from mind to thing. He does not suggest that the reason why the dunce can judge that five and seven is eleven, and thereby mistake twelve for eleven without entertaining the illicit thought 'Twelve is eleven', is that the expressions '5 + 7' and '12' have the same reference but different senses. The moral of the Aviary is rather this, that because the dunce does not use his knowledge of twelve when his thought misidentifies twelve as eleven, there must be such a thing as *unknowingly thinking of* twelve, i.e. thinking of twelve without recognizing it *as* twelve. The reason why the dunce can judge that five and seven are eleven, and thereby mistake twelve for eleven without entertaining the illicit thought 'Twelve is eleven', is that there are two different and independent

45. This is the important conclusion missed by scholars (n. 43 above) who invoke more birds than are mentioned in the text.

ways for a number to come before the mind in thought to be an object of judgement: it can be actively known and recognized, or it can be thought of without being actively known and recognized. J2 and J2a were separate and therefore partial glimpses of this truth. They can now be seen, in retrospect, as fragments of a larger principle:

> J3 If something is to be an object of one's judgement, one must *either* know it and be actively using one's knowledge *or* perceive it *or* be thinking of it unknowingly.

But of course an interpretation should not be accepted just because it is interesting. I have placed more emphasis than other scholars do on the fact that the arithmetician at 198c is said to consider a number he knows as if he did not know it. This is the textual basis for my talk of a third epistemic route which completes the parallel with the Wax Block. But is it enough to build an interpretation on? Even if the interpretation is found persuasive, readers will want some explanation of this third epistemic route, 'thinking of something unknowingly'. For it is one thing to include questioning as a part of *thinking*, as Plato did earlier (189e–190a), quite another to develop this into the suggestion that the question 'How large a number is five and seven?' can be a way of considering or *thinking of* the number twelve without realizing that you are doing so.[46]

Socrates accepts that 'considering something he knows as if he did not know it' is a way of speaking that people can all too easily make a puzzle of (198c). This arouses an expectation that in due course he will show the puzzle to be merely superficial. A deeper issue is the following. Suppose it granted that, where Frege distinguishes between thinking (speaking) of X as X and thinking (speaking) of X as Y, Plato distinguishes between thinking (speaking) of X knowingly and thinking (speaking) of X unknowingly. How great is the difference between the two distinctions? A modern philosopher might argue that the Platonic distinction is after all a semantic solution dressed up in epistemic terms (cf. p. 94). To assess this judgement we must watch to see how the contrast

---

46. Nonetheless, it was the need to get clear about *thinking of* which prompted Socrates' account of thought and judgement at 189e–190a. Perhaps the restricted scope of that account, which I criticised on p. 84, was designed to match the uses to which the account is put: first, in the discussion of 'other-judging', the thinking of involved in judgement, and now the thinking of involved in questioning.

between knowledgeable and unknowledgeable thinking develops in the sequel.

Fortunately, Socrates expands his account of arithmetical self-questioning from 198d to 199b. He distinguishes two phases of the hunt for knowledge. There is the hunt you were engaged in when you wanted to learn the numbers for the first time; this phase, if successful, effects the passage from ignorance to knowledge. Afterwards there is the hunt we are interested in, when, having learned your lesson, you want to use it to answer a question; this phase, if successful, effects the passage from capacity-knowledge to active recognition. Socrates makes the second phase sound even more puzzling than before when he describes it as setting out to learn again from yourself something you have already learned (198de). But that paradox is easily dissolved in the light of the distinction between a capacity and its exercise (198e–199b). The real surprise comes at 199b, where the self-questioner is described as hunting for one piece of knowledge but getting hold of another by mistake.

This is a surprise because it seems to imply that he is hunting for the knowledge of twelve. He is not simply looking to lay hands on *whichever* bird will answer the question; there is a particular bird he is hunting for. This cannot be the eleven-bird, which he gets hold of by mistake, so it must be the twelve-bird. Yet he cannot be aware that it is the twelve-bird he is seeking, or else he would already have the answer to his question. He hunts the twelve-bird and no other, without being aware of the fact, and does so *in virtue of* asking himself 'What is five and seven?'. I suggest that this confirms that in asking the question he is unknowingly thinking of the number twelve. For hunting the twelve-bird means attempting to (activate his capacity to) recognize the number twelve. It is twelve he is trying to recognize and that is why, when he seizes the eleven-bird, he can be said to think that eleven is twelve (199b). He does not have the illicit thought 'Eleven is twelve'. What he says to himself is 'Eleven is (the number of) five and seven'. But in so saying he thinks of eleven (knowingly) and thinks of twelve (unknowingly) and judges that one is the other.

By now the reader may (should) be getting impatient with me. I have been pressing my own interpretation more strongly than usual, just where an interpreter has less than usual to go by in judging Plato's intentions.[47] I cannot claim that the text contrasts

47. E.g. Bostock [9], 186–89 accepts that the dunce is hunting for the twelve-bird, asserts that he cannot fail to be aware of the fact, and concludes that Plato is in a hopeless muddle.

actively recognizing and unknowingly thinking of something as explicitly as it contrasts the former with the capacity-knowledge it exercises, or as emphatically as the Wax Block section contrasted knowing and perceiving. So how can it be justified for me to suggest that the moral of the Aviary is that we should accept J3 and the idea of a third epistemic route?

I have been treating the discussion of false judgement as a double dialogue. There is the written dialogue between Socrates and Theaetetus, and through it arises the unwritten dialogue between Plato and his readers. I have been making up my own part as I go along, and encouraging you to do the same. But to do this we have to assume that our interlocutor, the controlling author, is indeed in control. He knows what he is saying, and has reasons for it. Maybe, however, Plato has himself been floundering in all the puzzlement and confusion we have struggled through. It was not purposively structured, to goad our thought into responding to his. The captain is the person who is seasick, and the best we can do as readers is offer sympathy and the appropriate twentieth-century remedies.

Or maybe he has been seasick some of the time, some of the time on his feet and in control, and the best verdict to pass on the Aviary is that it is a partial success: Plato needs a third epistemic route to complete the analogy with the Wax Block, but, if he is thinking of it, he does not recognize it clearly and distinctly *as* a further way, besides knowledge and perception, to get hold of something with the soul.

Maybe. You must decide. Let me simply remind you that when we were thinking about the Wax Block, we found that it presupposed a distinction between merely having some knowledge (an imprint stamped on the block) and actively using it in one's thought, but was singularly inactive about bringing the distinction to the forefront of our attention (p. 100); the Wax Block made us feel in need of the Aviary before we came to it. The relevance of this reminder to the question whether the Aviary presupposes J3 and the idea of a third epistemic route is that a third epistemic route is what Theaetetus will propose in the next section, when Socrates unleashes a devastating objection to the Aviary's account of false judgement.

Criticism of the Aviary (199c–200c)

Attentive readers may have noticed that, whereas Socrates began the Aviary resolved to show how it is possible to judge that twelve is eleven (196bc), he ends by showing how it is possible to judge that eleven is twelve (199b). The known item shifts from second place to first. We remarked earlier (pp. 96–7) that reversing the order of terms is logically legitimate. There should be no objection, therefore, if, having concentrated throughout the Aviary section on the item which is not actively known, Socrates demands that the actively known item take first place in our attention for a change.

The trouble, as he points out (199d), is precisely that this item is *actively known*. How, then, can it be mistaken for something else?

Socrates' objection is that we have explained one mistake by another. According to the Aviary model, the dunce makes his mistake about twelve by activating his knowledge of eleven. The result is that he makes a mistake *about eleven:* the mistake of thinking that eleven is five and seven. This time we cannot save the situation by invoking the distinction between knowledge and its exercise. For here he is actively exercising his knowledge of eleven. Worse, his actively exercising the knowledge of eleven is what produces the mistake about eleven. The Aviary account has it that knowledge makes you go wrong—an absurdity on a par with the idea that ignorance could make you know something or blindness make you see (199d).

Question: If this objection is sound, does it not wreck the Wax Block as well? If the mistake of judging that twelve is eleven can be viewed not only as a mistake about twelve, but also as a mistake about eleven, then presumably the mistake of judging that Theaetetus is Theodorus can be viewed not only as a mistake about Theaetetus seen at a distance, but also as a mistake about Theodorus recalled in memory. If it is absurd to suggest that activating one's knowledge of eleven could lead to a mistake about eleven, why is it not equally absurd to suggest that applying one's imprint of Theodorus could lead to a mistake about Theodorus?

It is at this juncture, when the entire constructive effort of Part II hangs on the balance, that Theaetetus introduces the idea of a third epistemic route. In a longer speech than usual, which earns a compliment from Socrates (199e), he suggests that there are *pieces of ignorance* flying about in the soul as well as pieces of knowledge. He has taken Socrates' point (199d) that it is unreasonable to say that when actively exercising his knowledge of eleven the man goes wrong about eleven. He reasons that what the man is exercising (holding in his hand) is something other than the knowledge of eleven. It is a capacity (birds stand for acquired capacities of the soul), but a capacity for misapprehension rather than for recognition. False judgement is to be explained by a flock of capacities for going wrong.

That sounds mysterious. We would normally expect a mistake to be explained by the *absence* of a capacity for getting it right, not the presence of a capacity for getting it wrong. The 'want of knowledge' of which Socrates speaks at 199d sounds like the mere absence of a capacity for recognition, but a 'piece of ignorance' such as Theaetetus describes is clearly meant to be a positive presence in the soul. It is not ignorance in the ordinary sense of the absence or want of knowledge, but some positive capacity different from knowledge which allows, and perhaps even encourages, the committing of mistakes.[48]

But even if we fail to recognize this capacity under the name that Theaetetus gives it, we should be able to see that from Theaetetus' new suggestion it follows immediately that something can come before the mind to be an object of judgement even if it is neither actively known nor perceived. There must be such a thing as thinking of something ignorantly, when one's thought exercises a capacity which is not knowledge.

We have now found thinking which is not the exercise of knowledge at both ends of the judgement that five and seven are eleven. According to Socrates in the Aviary section, the dunce is unknowingly thinking of twelve, and, according to Theaetetus' latest move, he is also exercising his 'ignorance' of eleven. Are these two examples of unknowledgeably thinking of something the same sort of thing? Have we added one epistemic route to active knowledge and perception, or two?

Let us put this question aside for the moment and take a third glimpse into the future. The discussion in Part III sets out from the position that the number of epistemic routes from mind to thing is three: knowledge, perception, *and true judgement* (202b). A person may be in a state of truth concerning something and yet at the same time be in a state of *ignorance* about it (202c), namely, when they have true judgement without knowledge.

Should we then conclude, with foresight, that Theaetetus' pieces of ignorance are in fact true judgements about individual numbers?

---

48. Suggestions about what a 'piece of ignorance' is include: a false belief one has been taught, e.g. that five and seven are eleven (Cornford [2], 138, Bostock [9], 192); a misconception of twelve in the form of a twelve-bird labelled 'eleven' (so, in effect, Ackrill [40], 399–401); an erroneous eleven-bird masquerading as the twelve-bird (Lewis [48], 282–83).

The idea would be that to have learned part of the truth concerning something is the precondition for going wrong about it; it *enables* you to go on to other judgements which are false. Our dunce has a hold on eleven and can make it an object of the judgement that eleven is five and seven because, and only because, he has already learned some truth or truths about eleven, e.g. that it is nine and two.

The idea sounds promising. But if we take it up, we should be clear with ourselves that we are responding to the written dialogue, not deciphering it. The statement 'Pieces of ignorance are in fact true judgements which fall short of knowledge' does not give the hidden meaning of the text, but our own contribution to the dialogue with Plato. What happens in the text is that Socrates tells Theaetetus to think again about pieces of ignorance (199e). The two of them agree that having an ignorance-bird in hand is just like having a knowledge-bird in hand. Your attitude is that of one who is exercising knowledge; you think you are exercising knowledge, though you are not. But this means that we have again explained one mistake by another. The mistaking of eleven for twelve only happens because the dunce mistakes an ignorance-bird for a knowledge-bird: he thinks he is exercising his capacity to recognize eleven when in fact he is activating a capacity of an altogether different sort. Socrates now (200ac) brings back the expert controversialist of 197a, who gleefully announces that we are stuck again in the initial puzzle of 188ac and will need a whole new set of blocks or aviaries to extricate ourselves from the difficulty of understanding how the mistake-maker mistakes a piece of ignorance for a piece of knowledge.

The next move is up to us. Do we let the expert's challenge stand? Or do we think again ourselves about pieces of ignorance? Perhaps it is we who have been mistaking pieces of ignorance for pieces of knowledge, in which case we shall indeed have to go back to the initial puzzle and rework the entire discussion. For to suggest that true judgement is a third way for the soul to have hold of something is to abandon Theaetetus' second definition, which holds that there is no difference between true judgement and knowledge. If true judgement and knowledge are different, an account of that difference will be the account the expert demands of the difference between knowledge and ignorance—if by 'ignorance' is meant what 202c describes as the soul being in a state of truth and ignorance about something. In other words, the best reply to the expert is to rework Part II in the light of Part III.

If, on the other hand, Theaetetus maintains his definition, it would then appear that the expert is right to object that we will be unable to tell the difference between a piece of ignorance and what we have been calling, up to now, a piece of knowledge. Both are capacities which consist in the soul's having learned part of the truth about something. If Theaetetus persists in calling this 'knowledge' and agrees that mistakes cannot be due to the exercise of knowledge, he must admit that they cannot be the product of ignorance either—a paradox indeed.

The reader is now invited to recall the suggestion mooted long ago (p. 66) that the false judgement which makes it appear that false judgement is impossible might turn out to be none other than Theaetetus' definition of knowledge as true judgement.

True and false judgement in retrospect

We are now at the end of the discussion of false judgement. Theaetetus cannot answer the expert's refutation (200c). Socrates comments, and Theaetetus accepts, that the refutation is reproving them for trying to understand false judgement without first getting an adequate grasp of what knowledge is (200cd). This is not only an invitation for us to think again about the entire discussion. It is a strong hint that the way to do this is indeed to consider the possibility that, in the final analysis, it is Theaetetus' equation of knowledge and true judgement which makes it appear that false judgement is impossible.[49]

Suppose that, on reflection, the suggestion meets with our approval, so that the lesson we prepare to carry forward to Part III from the puzzles of Part II is that knowledge is not simply true judgement. Isn't that rather a mouse of an idea for our mountainous labours to have brought forth? No modern philosopher would take such a long and tortuous path to the conclusion that knowledge is not the same thing as true judgement or belief. All that Theaetetus' second definition would merit in a modern book on the theory of knowledge is an intuitively persuasive counterexample (such as the gambler who judges correctly, by lucky guesswork, which horse

---

49. Cf. Fine [45], 77–78, who, however, differs from Zeller (n. 2 above) in holding that the source of the trouble is not the equation as such but an assumption needed to make it plausible, viz. that any grasp of a thing confers total knowledge of it, that there is no middle state between total knowledge and total ignorance. It was this assumption, according to Fine, which gave rise to the initial puzzle of 188ac.

will win), plus a quick argument to clinch the point that correct judgement is not yet knowledge.[50] A quick argument and a persuasive counterexample is exactly what Plato provides in the next and final section of Part II (200d–201c). Why should he have felt the need to do more? Why make us work so hard to see a distinction that is so easy to see?

But surprise is relative to expectations. If we are surprised at Plato's using the long discussion of false judgement to bring us to reject Theaetetus' second definition, that may be because twentieth-century philosophy does not expect to *do* very much with the distinction between knowledge and true judgement or belief. The distinction has to be noted. It is a fact about our notion of knowledge that there is more to knowing than being right about something. But for us the interesting questions in epistemology only begin when we go on to the question 'What does that "more" consist in?'—when we turn to a study of the justification or explanation of true belief.

Our expectations should be quite different if, as readers of the *Theaetetus*, we decide that Theaetetus' second definition is not merely wrong but is itself the main obstacle to understanding what goes wrong when our minds mistake one thing for another. We will learn a great deal from seeing, *in detail*, why this wrong answer is wrong (cf. p. 2). The whole discussion—both the puzzlement and the limited progress that Socrates and Theaetetus were able to make with it—should be transformed if we think it over again from the beginning in the light of our realization that it ignored (was conducted in ignorance of) the need to distinguish knowledge from true judgement. The distinction itself may be an obvious truth, but it is not obvious what difference it would have made, at each stage, if we had had at our disposal the idea of true judgement as a third epistemic route from mind to thing.

Consider, to begin with, the effect on our two models of the suggestion just made (pp. 117–9) that not only 'pieces of ignorance', but also the imprints and birds which have hitherto been called knowledge, might be regarded as examples of true judgement falling short of knowledge. The Wax Block remains adequate for mistaken identifications where perception is involved; the only failing charged against it was that it does not explain mistaken identifications where perception is not involved. It works by contrasting

50. E.g. A. J. Ayer, *The Problem of Knowledge, op. cit.*, 29, D. M. Armstrong, *Belief, Truth and Knowledge, op. cit.*, 150.

perception with another epistemic route, and its success is unaffected if we reclassify the imprint route as true judgement instead of knowledge. Likewise, the Aviary can account for mistaken identifications of thought, where perception is not involved—*provided* the birds are refused the title of knowledge. For the failing charged against the Aviary was that it is absurd to explain error as the exercise of knowledge, and this difficulty was removed by Theaetetus' postulation of 'pieces of ignorance'. The difficulty would never have arisen if the birds had been called true judgement, for it is not absurd to explain error as the product of true judgement which falls short of knowledge.

The exercise of reading through again to consolidate this unobvious lesson of Part II (supposing it is what Plato intends) will be particularly valuable for twentieth-century readers like ourselves if we remember that a number of the problems we encountered on our first reading were problems which Frege has taught us to deal with through the philosophy of language (p. 85, p. 93, p. 112). We will understand our own philosophical heritage better if we can enter imaginatively into an alternative approach which deals with the problems epistemologically, by distinguishing different capacities of the mind and the different kinds of hold it may have on something in asking questions and making judgements about it. We may in the end decide that the two approaches are closer in certain respects and more comparable than they look (cf. p. 94, p. 113). If so, we will be better placed to appreciate the maxim that in philosophy it is often small differences that matter most.

There are several issues which a retrospective reading should consider. The first is the fate of thesis K. Refuted though it is by combinations (i) and (ii) in the Wax Block (p. 98) and by the Aviary's proof that you can judge that something you know is something else you know (p. 111), it returns in a modified or clearer form when Socrates concludes the Aviary discussion by insisting that *active* knowledge is incompatible with mistakes (199d). In other words, if you do judge that something you know is something else you know, you are not using your knowledge; conversely, if you use your knowledge, you cannot go wrong. In yet other terms,

> K′ It is impossible to judge *either* that something one actively knows is something else one knows *or* that something one actively knows is something one does not know.

If this is Plato's final verdict on the initial puzzle of 188ac, it confirms a deep divergence between the modern response we started from (p. 74) and the alternatives developed in the constructive sections of Part II. Correspondingly, a modern philosopher's response to K' is likely to be that it is simply and straightforwardly *wrong* about knowledge. But readers of the *Theaetetus* should ask: How do we decide when a philosopher is wrong about a concept and when they are working with (or advocating) a different concept from the one we are used to? Is Plato's apparent approval of K' the false judgement which vitiates his stance in the unwritten dialogue, or is it a true judgement about *his* notion of knowledge?

A second issue for retrospective consideration is the fate of thesis T. A number of ways have emerged in which you can be thinking of X and thinking of Y and still judge that X is Y. First came the halfhearted counterexample to thesis T where you are thinking of Theaetetus when you judge that Theaetetus is Theodorus and are able to do so because the thought of Theaetetus plays no part in bringing him before the mind to be mistaken for Theodorus (193d, p. 99). The vital point here was that perceiving Theaetetus does not entail thinking of him as Theaetetus. Then the Aviary prompted the suggestion that you can be thinking of X unawares, i.e. thinking of X without recognizing it as X (198c, p. 112). The vital point here was that to be wondering what some number is is precisely not yet to have determined the answer. This disposes of the contention that thinking of two distinct things, X and Y, is a sufficient condition for realizing they are different and so not judging that X is Y (p. 84); but one could wish for more explanation than we are given of how it is that asking 'What is five and seven?' is a way of considering the number twelve. Thirdly, Theaetetus' postulation of 'pieces of ignorance' implies that you can be thinking of X, even thinking of it as X, and still judge that it is some other thing, Y, which you are thinking of; you can do this, I have conjectured, if you have true judgement about X which falls short of knowledge.

Thus it seems clear that by the end of Part II thesis T is fairly and squarely refuted. It is also clear that damaging implications for Theaetetus' second definition of knowledge ensue once we recognize that much thought is not knowledgeable, not the exercise of capacity-knowledge. What is not clear is how, more positively, we should characterize the unknowledgeable thinking on which our attention has increasingly come to focus. In particular, we have not yet faced the question raised earlier (p. 117) whether unknowingly thinking of twelve is the same sort of thing as ignorantly thinking of eleven.

Here is a suggestion. Recall that in Part III Plato will want us to think of 'five and seven' as a simple enumeration of the constituent parts making up a whole number, and that he will be challenging us to say whether twelve *is* (identical with) five and seven or whether it is rather the number they have or make (p. 104). The *truth* of 'Five and seven are twelve' is an elementary fact of arithmetic. But if it cannot be taken for granted that it is an *identity*, we must tune into the language of parts and whole. Very well. The dunce who judges that five and seven is eleven makes a mistake both about twelve and about eleven (p. 116). He makes a mistake about twelve because the whole of which five and seven are the constituent parts is twelve, not eleven. He makes a mistake about eleven because the constituent parts of which eleven is the whole are not five and seven but, say, five and six. Thus at one end of the judgement he considers the constituent parts of twelve without recognizing the whole they make up; at the other end he considers a whole number, eleven, without recognizing its constituent parts.

This is the merest sketch of a suggestion, but it should be enough to show that our two examples of unknowledgeable thinking may not be so disparate as they seem at first sight to be. They are connected through the topic of parts and wholes, which will be the subject of a lengthy discussion in Part III. It is also in Part III that the dialogue takes explicit cognizance of true judgement as a third epistemic route. The moral would seem to be that for a full understanding of Part II we must negotiate the dialectic of parts and wholes in Part III.

Last but not least, we should apply the lessons we have learned to the false judgement which reminds us that false judgement is possible, namely, Theaetetus' misidentification of knowledge as true judgement. The mistake shows that Theaetetus was not using, and may well not have, knowledge of knowledge itself. But K' also implies that he was not using, and may well not have, knowledge of true judgement either. If he was thinking of knowledge and thinking of true judgement, in both cases this was unknowledgeable thinking. He set down knowledge as true judgement in his thought and on that basis proceeded to misdescribe the owners of blocks and aviaries as having knowledge when all they have is true judgement.

So we end, as we began (pp. 68–9), with the idea that abstract misidentification leads to misdescription. But we have not made much progress with the question whether misdescription is always the result of a misidentification (p. 73, p. 89). That question awaits the detailed analysis of misdescription in the *Sophist*.

The Jury (200d–201c)

We come at last to the brief argument and persuasive counterexample which is all it takes to prove the nonidentity of knowledge and true judgement. No tricks or complications here to threaten seasickness. We can relax and allow Socrates to persuade us of what we will all agree is the correct conclusion.

Question: If that is all we do, will our grasp of this correct conclusion be any better than that of the jurymen in the counterexample, who are persuaded of the correct verdict but do not know it is correct? Theaetetus, we have come to see, does not have an adequate grasp of what knowledge is (200d). Does he even now *know* (grasp) what it is not, or is his acceptance of the conclusion that knowledge is not the same as true judgement itself only an example of true judgement, not yet of knowledge?

There is in fact matter for more leisurely philosophical reflection in the details of Socrates' case for the nonidentity of knowledge and true judgement, not least the emphasis he puts on the fact that Athenian court proceedings are governed by the clock (compare 201ab with 172de). The trouble with the art of rhetoric, he suggests, the reason it cannot teach adequately the truth about something and must resort to persuasion, is that the advocate has only a limited time to present his case. The implication is that, if the time-limit was removed, so that advocate and jury had the leisure for a detailed consideration of all the relevant issues, the advocate could teach the jury adequately. He could bring them to *know*, not merely persuade them, that the accused is the guilty party or that he is not.

But this implication is contradicted by something else that Socrates says, with equal emphasis, at 201bc: what happened at the scene of the crime can only be known by an eyewitness. Obviously, no amount of teaching could put the members of the jury in the same position as an eyewitness who saw what happened with his own eyes. In this case, and in any other where seeing is a necessary condition for knowing, teaching can do no better than persuasion. The jury can never know.

A resolution of this conflict is not necessary for the success of Socrates' proof that knowledge is not the same as true judgement. For this, we need only to accept *that* the jury's verdict is a counterexample, a case of true judgement without knowledge. We do not have to understand *why* it is not knowledge. Hence we do not have to choose between the two conflicting explanations Socrates dangles before us: (a) the constraints of the clock and the methods of persuasion it imposes, (b) the fact that the jury did not see for themselves what happened and so must judge 'upon hearsay', on the basis of testimony. But if we want to conclude Part II with understanding, not mere true judgement, we had better take the time to do some thinking for ourselves about the conflict between (a) and (b).

The first inclination of a reader versed in twentieth-century epistemology is likely to be towards Explanation (a). It is not just that Explanation (b) has the immediate and paradoxical effect of making historical knowledge impossible (none of us witnessed Socrates' death in 399 B.C. or Theaetetus' in 369). Explanation (a) is attractive in its own right because it leads easily and naturally to the conclusion that what the jury lacks, due to the circumstances in which they make their judgement, is adequate grounds. They have the right answer, but because the advocate has not had the time and has not used the methods that would be needed to teach adequately the truth about what happened, their grasp of this truth is not adequately grounded. And it is predominantly in the adequacy of the grounds for a true belief that twentieth-century philosophy has sought the differentia between knowledge and true judgement or belief.

There are of course objections to the analysis of knowledge as well-grounded true belief; it needs elucidation and qualifications, sometimes of labyrinthine complexity, before being accepted as our credo. But it remains, by and large, the key idea from which we expect discussion and debate about knowledge to begin. What more natural, then, than for Plato to point our thoughts in that direction as we prepare to embark on Part III?

On the other hand, a reader versed in earlier works by Plato will hear a familiar theme in Explanation (b). A famous passage in the *Republic* (518bc) proclaims that education is not what it is ordinarily thought to be, a matter of putting knowledge into a soul where there was none before. That would be like trying to put sight into blind eyes. We already have the power of intellectual vision; if we turn it in the right direction, we will see the truth for ourselves. This is said with special reference to mathematical knowledge and knowledge of the Good, but another well-known passage in the *Meno* (97ab) has it that the difference between someone who knows the road to Larissa and someone who merely has correct opinion about it is due to the former having travelled the road and seen it with their own eyes. So although Explanation (b) subverts the commonsense idea that teaching and testimony can convey knowledge from one person to another, Plato has controverted common sense before, both about mathematical and about empirical knowledge.

Our own philosophical tradition too bears witness to the idea that knowledge must be firsthand or it does not deserve the name. Thus Locke (*Essay* I 4.23):

> For, I think, we may as rationally hope to see with other Mens Eyes, as to know by other Mens Understandings. So much as we our selves consider and comprehend of Truth and Reason, so much we possess of real and true Knowledge. The floating of other Mens Opinions in our brains makes us not one jot the more knowing, though they happen to be true. What in them was Science, is in us but Opiniatrety, whilst we give up our Assent only to reverend Names, and do not, as they did, employ our own Reason to *understand* those *Truths*, which gave them reputation.

What more natural, then, than for Plato to close Part II by insisting on the gulf between secondhand opinion and firsthand knowledge? Socrates was much too glib when he described mathematical teaching—to Theaetetus, of all people—as handing over birds of knowledge (198b). Mere true judgement can be acquired that way, but knowledge is something we must achieve for ourselves.

Thus both Explanation (a) and Explanation (b) have their attractions. Yet if we accept everything that Socrates says, we accept a contradiction: that the jury could in principle come to know and that they could not, that teaching is possible and that it is not, that knowledge is well-grounded true judgement and that it is not. So we conclude Part II, as Socrates began it (187d), in a state of quandary. What should our attitude be?

First, a question of interpretation. Does Plato make Socrates behave like this because he is determined that we should think for ourselves even where Theaetetus does not? Even if we accept the idea of an unwritten dialogue between Plato and his readers, we cannot infer that he has calculated every move; authorial control is not divine omniscience. On the contrary, a real philosophical dialogue would be one in which Plato shared with us both his insights and his problems, in which he set out to educate himself as well as his readers (cf. pp. 72–3, p. 115). Plato might be quite confident that the distinction between knowledge and true judgement is of crucial importance for understanding both the potential achievements and the failings of the human mind, and yet remain torn himself between Explanation (a) and Explanation (b). Or he might simply be unaware of the conflict. Second, a question about Plato's epistemology. The claim that *only* an eyewitness can know what happened at the scene of a crime is doubly challenging. It rules out historical knowledge and debars most of our everyday empirical beliefs from counting as knowledge. (Ask yourself how much knowledge you would have left if you had to establish every truth entirely by your own resources, or for that matter if you accepted information only from authorities whose reliability you had conscientiously verified for yourself.) But the claim also rules out the metaphysical thesis that the sensible world is the province of opinion, not of knowledge. For it implies that the eyewitness *can* know mundane empirical facts. Is Plato retracting the epistemology he propounded in the *Phaedo* and *Republic*, or is the contrast between eyewitness and jury only an analogy to get us to appreciate that knowledge must be firsthand?[51]

Third, a question of pure philosophy. Why is the jury example so compelling? Do juries *never* know? What is it about the concept of knowledge which makes it so easy for philosophers to arouse sceptical suspicions about testimony and information derived from someone else?[52] On the other hand, is it any easier to believe philosophical theses of the form 'Facts of kind K can *only* be known by someone who has come to believe them by method M'?

Lastly, it is worth noticing that the entire dialogue was presented to us in the Prologue (142a–143c) in such a way as to raise the question, Is it testimony or not? Is Eucleides telling us what Socrates and Theaetetus said to each other, or are we listening to them directly? Perhaps Plato's meaning is that we can read the dialogue either way. We can be passive recipients of testimony, or we can be actively present with the discussion. The choice is ours. But only active participation, which means doing philosophy for ourselves and getting into interesting quandaries of our own, will bring us to know—really know—what a discussion with Socrates was like.

51. This question, which is obviously important for proponents of Reading A's account of Part I, has aroused fierce controversy. Scholars who deny that Plato is retracting include Cornford [2], 141–42, and Jaako Hintikka, *Knowledge and the Known* (Dordrecht & Boston: 1974), 27, 63–64. In the opposite camp may be found Runciman [5], 37–38, McDowell [3], 227–28.

52. Classic texts on this question include Augustine, *De Magistro* (*On the Teacher*), who argues that no man can teach another anything, and Hume's discussion of the testimony for miracles in *An Enquiry Concerning Human Understanding* (1748), Sect. X. See also Manley Thompson, 'Who Knows?', *Journal of Philosophy* 67 (1970), 856–69, C.A.J. Coady, 'Testimony and Observation', *American Philosophical Quarterly* 10 (1973), 149–55.

PART III

'Knowledge is true judgement with an account'

Part III of the *Theaetetus* opens with an air of solemn indeterminacy. A theory is stated which will shortly be described (203e) as 'a great and imposing theory'. Leibniz said much the same: 'It is of great moment if rightly explicated'.[1] Wittgenstein found it fascinatingly reminiscent of certain theses of his own *Tractatus Logico-Philosophicus*. Many scholars (not all) have agreed that it is an impressive theory, even while disagreeing with each other over what it says. But Socrates and Theaetetus are not only impressed. They also make it clear that they have difficulty knowing what exactly the theory maintains. Much of the discussion in Part III is in fact a search for an answer to the question: What is the theory we are discussing?

There is good reason for this perplexity. The more you think about the theory, the more questions you discover that it leaves unanswered, the more explanations you feel the want of. It is a thoroughly indeterminate theory, and a reader's first task must be to register its indeterminacies.

The theory comes into view in three stages. First, Theaetetus reports a theory he has heard, but which he is unable to elaborate or explain (201cd). Second, Socrates offers what he calls a dream in return for Theaetetus' dream. This is the explanatory elaboration that Theaetetus could not give, but it is done at such an abstract, formal level that it raises many more questions than it answers (201d–202c). Only at Stage Three (202c–203c), when the theory is filled out in terms of the model of letters and syllables, does it acquire enough content for critical assessment to begin. Even then, the main strategy followed in the critical section (203c ff.) is to

---

1. Reference at Part I, n. 5 above. For clues to what Leibniz might have had in mind, see his *Monadology* (1714).

suggest ways of making previous indeterminacies determinate and show that none of them will do.

From this preview of the discussion to come, it should be clear that the question 'What is the theory we are discussing?' has no complete and final answer. To read Part III effectively we must be prepared to tolerate ambiguity. We shall also find that some of Part III's most important ideas are merely suggested, not developed. They signpost alternative paths that the inquiry might have followed. They can be read as directions for us to travel on our own, for in the dialogue itself the ways actually chosen to make the various indeterminacies determinate are only a selection from a range of possibilities. In the same spirit, I shall deal with the problem of ambiguity by trying to open up, at each stage, as many different lines of interpretation as the text allows.

All this will mean more exposition and fewer questions than before. The patient exposition of alternatives is less dramatic than a question mark, but I hope that by now you will find it an equally good stimulus to philosophical reflection. Just 13 sparely written pages of the dialogue remain. They are as intricate and philosophically as ambitious as the entire preceding 79.

The theory at Stage One: Theaetetus' report (201cd)

Socrates having completed Part II by arguing that knowledge and true judgement are not the same thing, Theaetetus suddenly remembers that this is exactly what he once heard a man say (201c). The reader can hardly fail to remember that the argument with which Socrates established that knowledge and true judgement are not the same was an argument which contrasted firsthand appreciation, necessary for knowledge, with judgements made upon hearsay, which cannot count as knowledge even when they are correct. The least we can conclude is that the theory Theaetetus is about to propound, on the strength of this other man's say-so, is not something he knows to be true—even if it is true.

The theory is a conjunction of two distinct theses. One is a definition of knowledge:

Def. K Knowledge is true judgement with an account (*logos*).

The other, logically independent of the first (see below), asserts a surprising asymmetry between two classes of thing:

The things of which there is no account (*logos*) are unknowable; those which have an account are knowable.

This much Theaetetus can report, because he heard it. But when he is asked how the author of the theory established the distinction between knowable and unknowable things—in effect, when he is asked for an account of accountability—he is unable to discover it for himself. He can only say that he could follow someone else's explanation (201d).

Thus Theaetetus' relation to the theory is the partial grasp we earlier associated with true judgement that falls short of knowledge (pp. 117–8). Not only does he not know whether the theory is true, he is unable to tell us in detail what the theory is. When Socrates elaborates an explanation of the distinction between knowable and unknowable, Theaetetus follows well enough, and he says that it is precisely what he heard (202c). But this only reinforces the impression that he is like a juryman who has to judge on the basis of what he is told by other people; when supplementary questions arise, he has nothing of his own to answer with. You may ask: Where does that leave us, the readers who will be following the discussion of the theory he has introduced? How are we to judge the theory if, like jurymen, we have to rely on Theaetetus and Socrates to tell us what it is?

Important as this question is, it is too soon to attempt an answer. We have two theses to examine, both of them pregnant with alternative possibilities.

Throughout the discussion of false judgement in Part II knowledge was treated as the capacity to identify something, whether the something was a concrete object like Theaetetus and Theodorus or an abstract object like twelve. Led by this, we might read Theaetetus' third definition as an account of what it is to know an object:

Def. K_o Knowing o is having true judgement concerning o with an account of o,

where o is any object, concrete or abstract. Def. K_o stands in obvious contrast to any reading of the third definition which construes it as a thesis about knowing propositions. Let p be any proposition. Then the contrast is between Def. K_o and

Def. K_p Knowing that p is having true judgement that p with an account of the proposition p.

Def. K_p would follow appropriately on the final Jury section of Part II, where what the jurymen can judge but do not know is *the truth of what happened* (201b). Def. K_p also brings to mind important theories of knowledge in ancient and modern philosophy.

Aristotle, for example, held that knowing a proposition is being able to provide a proof of it which is both demonstrative and explanatory. Roughly and summarily, knowledge for Aristotle is the ability to explain scientifically why something is so. Now one meaning of 'account' is explanation, and it may well be with the *Theaetetus* in mind that Aristotle declares that knowledge is always 'with an account'.[2] So we could take Def. K_p more specifically as

Def. $K_{p(e)}$ Knowing that p is having true judgement that p with an explanation of why it is the case that p.

We would then expect Part III to turn our thoughts towards structures of explanation, so as to illuminate the difference between true judgements which are informed by an expert understanding of their subject matter and true judgements which merely 'get it right' (cf. p. 42).[3]

On the other hand, Def. K_p readily suggests to a modern reader the familiar idea that knowledge is true judgement or belief with adequate grounds to justify it:

Def. $K_{p(j)}$ Knowing that p is having true judgement that p with adequate justification for the judgement that p.

'An account' can very well refer to a justification or statement of grounds. Inadequate grounds was one diagnosis we considered earlier for the jury's failure to achieve knowledge (p. 125). So a discussion inspired by Def. $K_{p(j)}$ would be relevant to (the last section of) Part II as well as to modern debates about the analysis of knowledge.[4]

Nonetheless, I propose that, to begin with, we stick to Def. K_o.[5] I do not mean that Def. $K_{p(e)}$ and Def. $K_{p(j)}$, or the philosophical concerns they bring with them, can be set aside as irrelevant. Theaetetus' statement of Def. K, taken by itself, is indeterminate

2. *Posterior Analytics* II 19, 100b 10, *Nicomachean Ethics* VI 6, 1140b 33.

3. Such an approach to reading Part III is recommended by Burnyeat [54], Annas [53], Nehamas [62].

4. Such an approach to reading Part III is taken for granted by the modern philosophers cited in Part I, n. 6. A more comprehensive approach is pursued by Fine [52], who regards Def. K_o as no more than a special case of Def. K_p and Def. $K_{p(e)}$ as no more than a special case of Def. $K_{p(j)}$ (pp. 366–67). Her reading of Part III aims to pick out the common pattern in the options I have distinguished.

5. With White [8], 176–77, and others.

enough to allow all three readings, and not only these, as we will see. But as the theory develops, it becomes increasingly clear that it is couched in terms of knowing objects. Both Socrates' elaboration of the theory in his dream at Stage Two and all the subsequent criticisms of the theory treat it as a theory about knowing objects. So it is from knowing objects that we must start. This will help us draw connections with the main body of Part II, where knowledge was of objects like Theaetetus and twelve. We may still hope to find a place in the discussion for explanation, justification, and the knowledge of propositions. We may want to say, for example, that knowing an object involves knowing propositions about it or having a certain kind of explanation of it. But any such conclusion will have to be reached by way of elucidating Def. K_o, not by going back to Def. K_p. The question will be: Which types of proposition are involved in knowing an object, and how are they involved?

This decision about Def. K dictates that the asymmetry thesis be read, correspondingly, as dividing knowable from unknowable objects. It is an obvious consequence of Def. K_o that, for any object o, o is knowable only if an account can be given of o. But Theaetetus speaks of 'the things of which there is no account' and Socrates of 'these knowables and unknowables' (201d), implying an existential claim,

AL$_o$ There actually are some objects of which there is no account, and others that have an account,

which is not entailed by Def. K_o. Def. K_o could be true even if everything was accountable, or nothing was.

Another consequence of Def. K_o is of course that, for any object o, o is knowable only if there can be true judgement concerning o. Socrates' reference to 'these knowables and unknowables' presupposes that for some objects at least, viz. the knowable ones, true judgement is possible also. Call this the true judgement presupposition. We can defer until later (p. 174 ff.) the question whether there can be true judgement concerning the unknowables of the theory. For the argument Socrates is interested in (cf. 203ac) takes the true judgement presupposition for granted and proceeds from the conjunction of Def. K_o and AL$_o$ to the conclusion

AK$_o$ Some objects are unknowable, others knowable.

('AL' stands for 'asymmetry as to *logos* or account', 'AK' for 'asymmetry as to knowability'; the true judgement presupposition is required for that part of the conclusion which asserts that some objects are knowable.)

It is worth mentioning, however, that Theaetetus' statement of the asymmetry thesis, taken by itself, is like his statement of Def. K in being indeterminate enough to allow propositional as well as object-oriented readings. The deduction would then come out differently:

Def. K_p Knowing that p is having true judgement that p with an account of the proposition p.

AL$_p$ There actually are some propositions of which there is no account, and others that have an account.

AK$_p$ Some propositions are unknowable, others knowable.

The object-oriented version, Def. K_o, AL$_o$, AK$_o$, is only forced upon us by Socrates at Stage Two. The interest of the propositional version is that, if it was the preferred reading, many philosophers would know at once how they wanted to respond.

AK$_p$, they would say, is intolerable and must be rejected. Since the deduction is valid (granted as uncontroversial a propositional rendering of the true judgement presupposition), one of the premises is at fault. But not AL$_p$, for whether 'account' means explanation or justification the process of explaining/justifying one thing in terms of another must come to a stop somewhere; there must be some propositions for which no account (explanation/justification) can be given. So it is Def. K_p that should be rejected or modified.

This line of argument is not watertight (I leave it to readers to locate the weak point), but it has had a powerful influence in philosophy. There is a strong tradition in favour of modifying Def. K_p by allowing that *some* propositions are known without an account. Thus Aristotle held that the propositions which are most fundamental to a scientist's knowledge of his field are *self*-explanatory,[6] while empiricist theories of knowledge have often maintained that propositions about immediate experience can serve as the foundation for the rest of our knowledge because they do not *need* justifying. The moral is that Def. K_p holds for all knowledge except the most basic, whether this is the most basic in the order of explanation (Aristotle) or the most basic in the order of justification (traditional empiricism).

6. Aristotle, *Posterior Analytics* I 4, 73b 16–18, I 24, 85b 24–25; II 19, the very last chapter of the treatise, discusses the undemonstrated knowledge of first principles.

Would a parallel response be appropriate to the object-oriented version we are to be faced with at Stage Two? AK_o is no less of a surprise than AK_p. At Stage Three Socrates will make clear that he does not like it (202de), and he sets it up for a lengthy refutation (202d–206c). But AL_o does not have the same immediate plausibility as AL_p. Hence it is not so clear that Def. K_o, like Def. K_p, should be rejected or modified. Maybe we should hold on to Def. K_o and find fault with AL_o.

This, we shall discover, is the central conundrum of Part III. Plato does not tell us the answer, and it is hard even to begin thinking about it until we have a more determinate idea what an 'account' (*logos*) of an object *o* might be.

The Greek word *logos* has a wide spread of meanings. It is 'speech' or 'discourse' in general, and also particular kinds of speech such as 'argument'; it is 'statement' in general, and also particular kinds of statement such as 'theory', 'explanation', 'definition';[7] it may even mean a 'tally' or 'list'. We have already begun to explore the possibilities allowed by this indeterminacy. Clearly, it would be much more of a surprise to learn that some objects cannot be expressed in a statement than to be told that some objects cannot be defined or explained. The latter seems just what one would expect, given that the process of defining the terms used to define other terms, like the process of explaining one thing in terms of another, must come to a stop somewhere.

But we have seen that Theaetetus does not know enough about the theory to tell us how the division between knowable and unknowable was made. He cannot give an account of accountability. Can Socrates?

The theory at Stage Two: Socrates' dream (201d–202c)

Socrates explains AK_o by correlating AL_o with a metaphysical distinction between elements and complexes. Elements are the things

---

7. Thus within Part III not only do all the numerous occurrences of 'account' translate *logos*, but so also does 'theory' at 202e, 203d, 203e, and 'argument' at 204b, 205c, 205e. Elsewhere *logos* is, for example, the entire 'conversation' that Eucleides wrote out (143b), the third new 'discussion' broached at 172d, or the 'account' demanded of the worldly man of affairs at 175c. Again, it is both the 'talk' which the soul has with itself when thinking (189e) and the silent 'statement' with which that talk concludes (190a).

which have no account and are therefore unknowable. An account is always of a complex, so complexes alone are knowable.

Socrates also explains why an account is always of a complex. The reason is that an account is essentially a complex of names woven together and presupposes a matching complexity in what it is an account of (202b). An element, therefore, since it is noncomplex, i.e. simple and incomposite,[8] cannot be what an account is of. It can only be part of what an account is of, just as its name cannot be an account but only part of one.

All this is extremely abstract, and somewhat mysterious. But the most mysterious feature is the claim with which Socrates opens, that 'the primary elements, as it were, of which we and everything else are composed, . . . can only be named' (201e).

As regards complexes, this is helpful, for it tells us that 'we and everything else' are complexes. 'We and everything else' ought to be objects rather than propositions, so it is complex objects which have accounts and are knowable. Socrates' opening claim determines (subject to one challenge we can ward off later—p. 157 ff.) that the theory is to consist of Def. K_o, AL_o, AK_o, rather than the propositional versions we compared them with at Stage One.

But as regards elements, the claim is a mystery as dark as anything in the dialogue. It is one thing to say that an element corresponds to a name in an account, quite another to say that it can *only* be named or that 'a name is all that it has' (202b). How could there be anything as impoverished as that?

No examples of elements are given, and it is not easy to see how any could be given. It would seem absurd for Socrates to list a number of items and ask us to agree that they all have the peculiarity that they can only be named. (How would we decide what to answer?) On the other hand, if he were to introduce us to some elements by giving an account of an object *o* and saying that the elements of *o* are what correspond to the names in this account, he would be claiming knowledge of *o*, and that is something he does not like to do (cf. 150cd, 179b, 207a, 210c).

In the absence of examples, we can only get at elements by thinking in the abstract about the idea that they correspond to the names in an account which expresses knowledge of *o*. Any convincing interpretation of the thesis that elements can only be named must be linked to an equally convincing interpretation of

8. This is implied by the very terms of the contrast between element and complex and is confirmed in retrospect at 205c.

the suggestion that, where complexes are concerned, having an account of one is the differentiating condition of knowledge.

But we have seen that 'account' (*logos*) has a wide spread of meanings. Later in Part III (206c ff.) Socrates will acknowledge three meanings in particular as meanings which the theory might intend by the word. The account added to true judgement concerning *o* to yield knowledge of *o* might be (a) a *statement* putting into words one's judgement concerning *o*, or (b) an enumeration of all the elements of *o*, i.e. a completed *analysis* of *o*, or (c) a *differentiation* of *o* from other things. The implication is that the theory as stated was indeterminate between the three meanings, to which we may add that a text which is indeterminate between three such disparate meanings is likely to allow other meanings of 'account' (*logos*) as well, each linked to a different understanding of the thesis that elements have no account but only a name.

Now Plato could easily have contrived to tell us right at the start of Part III which meaning of 'account' is appropriate to the theory. Not only does he not do this, but he later calls attention to the fact that he did not do it by having Socrates go through (a), (b), and (c) only to find that none of them is philosophically satisfactory. This may suggest that he wants us to think for ourselves about the question which meaning of 'account' is appropriate to the theory. We are to think about it in the way Socrates thinks about (a), (b), and (c), by considering which meaning would produce a philosophically satisfactory theory of knowledge. In other words, the answer to the question 'What is the theory we are discussing?' is 'Make it and see.' We will then be able to judge it for ourselves, without relying on hearsay (p. 130; cf. 203a).

The strongest interpretation of the thesis that elements can only be named would doubtless be that there is nothing whatsoever you can do to or with an element except name it. This, however, runs into conflict with Socrates' statement that, although elements are unaccountable and unknowable, they are nonetheless perceivable (202b). In due course we shall have to consider what Socrates might mean by saying that elements are perceivable. (One thing it establishes is that he is not referring to microscopic entities like atoms.) But if you can perceive an element, it is not the case that you can do nothing with it at all except name it. We can set this interpretation aside as unconvincing.

[a] The next strongest interpretation would appeal to the first of the three meanings of 'account' that Socrates will examine later. You cannot make any *statement* about an element; there is no *linguis-*

tic action you can perform on or with an element except name it. This interpretation too runs into conflict with Socrates' statement that, although elements are unaccountable and unknowable, they are nonetheless perceivable. First, Socrates' statement is itself a statement about elements; so too, of course, is the self-refuting statement that no statement can be made about an element. Second, if it is true that elements are perceivable, a host of other things must be true as well, about what elements are perceived by whom, and when and where; it is hard to see how these detailed truths could one and all be unstateable.

Yet *logos* does often mean 'speech' or 'statement' and some readers may feel that the objections just made are not overwhelming. Even though Socrates makes statements about elements, an incoherence in his exposition of the theory does not necessarily prove incoherence in the theory. Even if it does, an incoherence in the theory (which Socrates himself, after all, is going to refute) is not necessarily an objection to the interpretation's attempt to say what the theory is. The most convincing evidence for the interpretation is the way Socrates expands the claim that elements can only be named:

Q1 Each of them, in itself, can only be named; it is not possible to say anything else of it, either that it is . . . or that it is not . . . .[9] That would mean that we were adding being or not-being to it; whereas we must not attach anything, if we are to speak of that thing itself alone.

This certainly can be read, and often has been read, as denying that you can make any statement about an element. Alternatively, Q1 rules out descriptive statements such as '*e* is yellow' while Socrates' next remark rules out statements of identification like 'That is *e*':

Q2 Indeed we ought not to apply to it even such words as 'itself' or 'that,' 'each,' 'alone,' or 'this,' or any other of the many words of this kind . . .

And if there is nothing to say about elements, that seems as good a reason as one could have for calling them unknowable. Conversely, it sounds good that complexes are knowable because they can be described and statements can be made about them.

But look at the argument again:

---

9. Dots added for the reason given in the note *ad loc.*

Def. K₀ Knowing o is having true judgement concerning o with an
account of o.

AL₀ There actually are some objects of which there is no account, and others that have an account.

AK₀ Some objects are unknowable, others knowable.

Even though the inference to AK₀ goes smoothly if we understand
'account of' in AL₀ as 'statement about', with this understanding
of 'account of' Def. K₀ becomes utterly feeble. It says that you know
a (complex) object o if you have true judgement and a statement
about o. Later in Part III (206ce) Socrates will allow the possibility
of so understanding Def. K₀. (This confirms that Def. K₀ is genuinely
indeterminate.) But he says that it would make the theory nonsense. Anyone who can speak can put their judgement into words
and produce an account in sense (a): statement. There must be
more to the difference between knowledge and true judgement
than the ability to put the true judgement into the words of a
statement.

It is hard to disagree with this verdict. Take the very simple
recognition scene at the beginning of the dialogue (144bd). A lot
more is involved in Socrates' knowledge of Theaetetus than his
ability to judge and state that Theaetetus is the son of Euphronius
of Sunium. Interpretation [a] leaves knowledge much too simple
and easy an achievement.

The point can be strengthened. In the later passage just referred
to, Socrates describes the process of putting one's judgement into
the words of a statement as a mirroring in sound of the thought
within (206d). The description should recall the account of judgement he gave in Part II (190a). Judgement as silent statement and
statement as audible judgement are but two sides of the same coin.[10]
Interpretation [a] has the consequence that there is no difference of
substance between Theaetetus' third definition of knowledge and
his second. Socrates is hardly exaggerating, therefore, when he
objects that, if 'account' means 'statement', no-one will have correct
judgement without knowledge (206de; cf. 201c). The third definition will keep us stuck in the problems of Part II unless we pass on,
as Socrates does, to other meanings of 'account'.

---

10. Likewise, the problems encountered by a view of judgement as silent statement
(p. 84 above) are related to the problem posed for a view of statement as audible
judgement by the existence of lies and insincerity.

Interpretation [a] also needs to provide some philosophical motivation for postulating elements about which nothing can be said.
On what grounds would anyone become convinced that

AL(st. about)$_0$ There actually are some objects about which no
statements can be made, and others about which
statements are possible?

Can you imagine coming across some objects which you found it
was impossible to say anything about? That seems too grotesque
for words. The grounds for AL(st. about)$_0$ must lie in some more
abstract reflection on statements and their relation to the things
they are about.

The best place to look for such reflection would seem to be
Socrates' remark at 202b that an account is essentially a complex of
names. One way to read this is the following: an account is essentially one name after another. Socrates has just said that when the
names of elements are woven together they become an account of
something. Now he supports this by a general rule, which we may
take as his definition of account: any account is a complex, i.e. (on
the present reading) a sequence, of names. *Logos*, we remember,
can mean a tally or list (p. 134).

Does Socrates mean that any account is a sequence of names of
elements? If so, and if 'account of' means 'statement about', we get
the niggardly result that the only way you can make a statement
about a complex object is by listing (some or all of) its perceivable
elements. So far from helping to explain why anyone would think
there is nothing to say about elements, this immediately prompts
the question why anyone would think there is so little to say about
complexes. Consider Theodorus' description of Theaetetus at 143e–
144b: how much of it could be represented as a listing of the perceivable elements of Theaetetus? It is true that the Heraclitean theory
in Part I included the suggestion (157bc) that what people call a
man or a stone is really just an aggregate of (transitory) perceived
qualities. If Theaetetus is conceived as an aggregate of perceived
qualities, these could be his elements.[11] But the Heraclitean theory
was refuted. To go back to it now would seem to be a drastic
regression to earlier themes. You may prefer to struggle with the
difficulties—we shall find that they are considerable—of a more
charitable version of Interpretation [a] whereby Socrates means that

11. Cf. Sayre [7], 121–30.

to make a statement about something is to issue a sequence of names, each of which designates an elementary *or a nonelementary* constituent of the thing.

Caution: there is no need to take either 'element' or 'constituent' in a crudely physical sense. Quite apart from the perceived qualities of the Heraclitean suggestion just recalled from Part I, within Part III itself at 209bc Theaetetus' peculiar snubnosedness will be listed along with eyes and mouth as things he 'has' or 'is made up of'. Without examples of elements we are in no position to decide whether elements are simple parts or ingredients of some sort, or simple qualities. Parallel considerations apply to nonelementary constituents: they could be parts, ingredients, qualities, or any other aspect of a thing that might be mentioned in statements about it.

Another point for caution is the status of words like 'is' and 'that', as discussed in Q1 and Q2. Are they names too? Are they just connecting devices (joining name to name or name to thing) which do not contribute *essentially* to what a statement conveys? Or does Socrates' definition of account simply ignore them?

A related problem is the status of names like 'Theaetetus' and noun phrases like 'a boy', which specify the complex a statement is about. Are these counted in the list or not? Is it e.g. 'Theaetetus— ABC' that we should be thinking of when Socrates says that a statement is a complex of names, or just 'ABC'? All we can be confident about is that, on the present reading of the definition, a list of names gives you, so to speak, the substance of a statement, its whole informative content. Subtract the comparisons from what Theodorus told Socrates about Theaetetus at 143e–144b and you are left with a plain list of his features: 'ugly, snubnosed, eyes that stick out, etc.'.

Now consider any statement (the informative content of which is given by) listing the constituents of something, in the generous sense of 'constituent' just adopted: eyes, mouth, snubnosed, white, or whatever. Do those constituents themselves have nameable constituents? In other words, is there any further description to give of eyes, mouth, snubnosed, white, or whatever constituents were mentioned in the first statement? The question will work out differently for different sorts of constituent (the description of a quality like white, for example, could surely not involve parts in the way that the description of a part such as mouth could involve qualities), but that might seem no barrier to the a priori deduction that talk cannot go on forever. You cannot have an endless series of descriptions of descriptions of descriptions. . . . Maybe no-one has got to a stopping point yet, but there has to be one. There must be perceivable constituents for which no list of nameable constituents can be assembled. Which means, given a model of statements as lists, that they admit of no statements being made about them. They can only be named.

The deduction is shaky in the extreme—just try to work it out in detail. For a start, some strong empiricist assumptions will be needed to guarantee a *perceivable* terminus to every tracing of the constituents of constituents of constituents. . . . But the main problem is with the very first premise: the model of statements as lists. The problem is the same for the niggardly version, which lists only the names of elements, and for the more charitable version. What, we may ask, does a *false* statement list? A model on which statements relate to the world in the same sort of unstructured way as a list of names threatens to make falsehood impossible in a manner reminiscent of the second puzzle of Part II (188d–189b, p. 78), where judging what is not was put on a par with perceiving (or, we added, naming) what is not there to be perceived (named). If you cannot perceive, name, or mention one thing without something to perceive/name, you cannot perceive, name, or list several things without a corresponding multiplicity of things to perceive/name.

Worse follows. If Interpretation [a] requires the list model to motivate AL(st. about)$_o$, and the list model makes false statements impossible, but any true statement about something counts on Interpretation [a] as an expression of knowledge, then we are back with (a generalized version of) the initial puzzle of Part II: knowing a thing is both a necessary condition for speaking or judging of it and a sufficient condition for not going wrong about it. The opening page of Part III would mark no progress whatever.

All in all, Interpretation [a] is liable to many objections. Notice, however, that none of the objections I have been through finds fault with Interpretation [a] for not fitting the text of the Dream. They are objections to the theory which emerges when Interpretation [a] is fitted to the text. The charge against Interpretation [a] is one of philosophical and literary incompetence. It yields a feeble theory of knowledge and sends Part III circling back to the puzzles of Part II (not to mention the Heracliteanism of Part I) instead of advancing the progress of the dialogue.

[b] Let us return to the passage quoted as Q1. It can also be read

with the emphasis on 'in itself' and 'if we are to speak of that thing itself alone'. This suggests a weaker interpretation: there is no linguistic action you can perform on or with an element *by itself* except name it. Interpretation [b] is weaker than Interpretation [a] because linguistic actions which import other terms besides the element—in particular, those which import the being and not-being involved in predication—are not excluded. The point is not that you cannot describe an element but that, if you do, you are adding to it, not speaking of the element itself alone. For the element is not identical with being (cf. 185c, 186a) or with the feature you ascribe to it when you say it is such and such. No doubt the same holds for describing complexes: description is precisely 'saying one thing of another' (cf. pp. 71–2). But the elements of a complex are internal to it. So you are not adding to the complex if you speak of it by an account which weaves together the names of its elements. Therein lies the difference between element and complex. Both can be described, but when considered in itself a complex can be analyzed as well as named, whereas an element considered in itself cannot be analyzed but only named.

An element can of course be *referred to* otherwise than by its name. Socrates refers to one when he uses the words 'if we are to speak of that thing itself alone'. In a sense, therefore, Socrates speaks of that thing itself alone, otherwise than by naming it, in the very act of denying that one can speak of that thing itself alone otherwise than by naming it. In a sense his thesis is self-refuting. (Compare, on Interpretation [a], the statement that no statement can be made about an element.) Q2 is his acknowledgement of the point. He ought not to use the words he used in Q1, on pain of inconsistency.[12]

But again readers may feel that the inconsistency is a pardonable flaw in Socrates' exposition of the theory, not a defect in the theory itself. No-one would call the phrase 'that thing itself alone' an account of that thing itself alone. For terms which apply to everything (all elements, all complexes) can be definitive of none. Socrates explains:

---

12. All the words listed in Q2 were used in Q1, except 'this'. Campbell [1], 213–14 notes that in the Greek of Q2 all the words except 'this' are introduced by the definite article, the backward-glancing force of which might be rendered by translating thus: 'Indeed we ought not to apply to it even that word [*sc.* the word we have just used] 'itself,' or those words 'that,' 'each,' 'alone'—or 'this' or any other of the many words of this kind'.

Q3 for these go the round and are applied to all things alike, being other than the things to which they are added, whereas if it was possible to express the element itself and it had its own proprietary account, it would have to be expressed without any other thing.[13]

It is obvious that I have moved on to the second of the three meanings of 'account' that Socrates will examine later: (b) a completed analysis or enumeration of all the elements of o. The advantage of Interpretation [b] is that it yields a more significant reading of Def. K_o than Interpretation [a]: namely, you know a (complex) object o when you have true judgement concerning o and you can analyze o into its ultimate perceivable constituents. This is very abstract still, but at least we can see that knowledge of an object would be a difficult and rare achievement. (Who would venture to enumerate the ultimate perceivable constituents of a human being like ourselves?) Later in Part III (206e), when he gives 'the enumeration of elements' as a second relevant meaning of 'account', Socrates not only allows that Interpretation [b], like Interpretation [a], gives a possible way of understanding Def. K_o. He evidently finds it superior and worthy of a careful, quite lengthy refutation.

Another advantage of Interpretation [b] is that it is easy to comprehend why anyone would become convinced that

AL(anz.)$_o$ There actually are some objects which cannot be analyzed, and others which can.

The reason is simply that no analysis, of whatever type, could go on and on forever. *Elementary* constituents are precisely those that can be analyzed no further.

Consequently, Interpretation [b] has no need to read Socrates' remark at 202b that an account is a complex of names as endorsing a list model of statements. A list model of analysis or definition will do instead. An unstructured list of names is exactly what Socrates envisages when he makes the shift to Interpretation [b] and the second meaning of 'account' (206e–207c). Indeed, he implies that any answer to a question of the form 'What is o considered in itself?'

---

13. The explanation is not pellucid, because in the most obvious sense of 'being other' *all* words, including the element's own name, are other than the things to which they are added or applied. But the recapitulation at 205c makes it clear that 'other than' is to be glossed 'alien to', i.e. 'not proprietary to', and this does distinguish the words listed in Q2 from the element's own name. McDowell [3], 238–39 offers a different but avowedly bizarre solution to the difficulty.

will come out as a list of elementary or nonelementary constituents. An account, which expresses knowledge, has to be a list of *elementary* constituents (207c). (Notice that Interpretation [b], unlike Interpretation [a] (pp. 139–40), has no problem over the range of names included in 202b's definition of account. The names of nonelementary constituents never combine to form accounts in sense (b), as they might combine to form accounts in sense (a).) But the unknowledgeable answer which is all that Socrates can manage in reply to the specimen question 'What is a wagon?' is still a list: 'Wheels, axle, body, rails, yoke' (207a). It is a list of names of nonelementary constituents.

In this particular example the constituents are physical parts. But they are also functional parts and the wagon is in any case only an example. My previous caution (p. 140) can stand: we are in no position to rule out constituents which are not physical parts. What Interpretation [b] does require is that 'constituent' be restricted to items that can be cited in answering a question of the form 'What is *o* considered in itself?'. Both elementary and nonelementary constituents must be parts, ingredients, or qualities which help to make *o* what it is. I shall therefore call them essential constituents. As such they are to be contrasted with any other parts, ingredients, or qualities that might be mentioned in statements about *o*.

This in turn means that Interpretation [b] carries no general threat to the possibility of falsehood. The question 'What does a false statement list?' does not arise, only the question 'What does a false analysis list?'. Interpretation [b] is thus compatible with a decent appreciation of the structure of ordinary misidentification and misdescription. I do not mean of course that Interpretation [b] solves all the problems of *Theaetetus* Part II (but see below, p. 177 ff.) and the *Sophist*. Rather, it directs our attention to a narrower topic of its own, which we will discuss in due course: the question whether the structure of analysis is adequately represented by accounts in sense (b). For the moment I shall continue to speak as if an enumeration of elements was exactly the same thing as a completed analysis (or definition). Doubts about that identification can wait.

So far, then, we have two interpretations of the thesis that elements can only be named. On Interpretation [a], elements can only be named because they are literally indescribable, whereas complexes have accounts in the sense of statements about them. On Interpretation [b], elements can only be named because considered in themselves they are unanalyzable, whereas complexes have accounts in the sense that you can enumerate their elements. Both interpretations have found adherents,[14] and readers may like to join in the battle for themselves, marshalling further grounds for the interpretation they favour and rebutting the objections. But we have also seen that Socrates will later admit that the text is open to both interpretations, at least so far as concerns the meaning of 'account' (*logos*). (And how can the ambiguity of 'account' fail to spread ambiguity throughout the passage?) It is a dream, after all, and dreams are inherently open to (multiple) interpretation—in the Greek tradition as in ours. 'Dreams are baffling, their meaning impossible to judge, and they are not in all ways fulfilled for men.'[15] Perhaps, therefore, the proper response is to tolerate the ambiguity, while trying to be clear ourselves about the alternatives between which the theory at Stage Two is unclear.

I have already declared my preference for tolerating ambiguity and for making the choice between Interpretation [a] and Interpretation [b] on philosophical, not on textual grounds (p. 129, p. 141). I would like to think, though I surely cannot prove, that Plato designed this whole stretch of text to be readable *either* with 'account' as 'statement' *or* with 'account' as 'completed analysis'. You choose one meaning or the other and all the pieces move together to form, in their totality, the two theories we have been comparing. It is true, and important, that on every point of comparison Interpretation [b] makes a better theory and a better development for the dialogue. But it remains equally true that Interpretation [a] fits the text as well. The ambiguity is systematic and deliberate, and Socrates' subsequent examination of the philosophical consequences of taking his dream one way or the other—as a theory of statements or as a theory of analysis—is a model set within the dialogue of the kind of response that Plato would like from his readers.

My readers, however, may want to hear about the alternative approaches available to those who are less enthusiastic than myself

---

14. In favour of [a], including the list model of statements: Cornford [2], 143–45 (cf. 253), McDowell [3], 231 ff. Unlike Sayre (cited n. 11 above), neither makes a clean decision between the niggardly and the charitable version. They work with the former but hope to allow for the latter, not by essaying the shaky deduction sketched above (pp. 140–1), but by borrowing Interpretation [b]'s notion of analysis (Cornford [2], 144–45, McDowell [3], 231). Is this consistent with the rest of Interpretation [a]? Can it explain why elements are indescribable?

In favour of [b], Burnyeat [54], 117–22, Fine [52], 370–78, Bostock [9], 202–09.

15. Homer, *Odyssey* XIX 560–61.

about ambiguity and indeterminacy.[16] From the very beginning of this part of the Introduction ambiguity and indeterminacy have been its controlling themes. It would have been no less coercive had I pressed you to go for a single determinate interpretation, as I did in Part I (p. 61). But still, it is a fair question to ask: Why not plump for one interpretation or the other? What is the price of univocity?

Suppose, first, that you are engaged in single-minded advocacy of Interpretation [a]. Interpretation [a], as we have seen, is open to serious objections, some philosophical, others pertaining to the literary organization of the dialogue. I think you will find it difficult to acquit Plato of them all.

The traditional answer[17] is to shift the charge of philosophical incompetence onto other shoulders. The theory which Theaetetus reports and Socrates expounds appears to derive from another thinker. For convenience we can use the name of the most likely candidate, Antisthenes, whom we will be meeting later, but it makes no difference if another candidate is preferred or he remains an anonymous unknown. The argument depends solely on the claim that the whole theory is the invention of someone other than Plato. Just as in Part I (on Reading B) the detailed elaboration of the theories of Protagoras and Heraclitus tells us nothing about Plato's own beliefs, so too with the details of the Dream. The list model of statements, indescribable elements, a feeble theory of knowledge— these reveal the quality of Antisthenes' thinking, not Plato's.

Very well. But now you must explain why Plato should devote Part III of this dialogue to the views of so incompetent a thinker. The theories of Protagoras and Heraclitus did not come into Part I because Protagoras and Heraclitus happened to hold them. They were elaborated at length (on Reading A as well as Reading B) because relativism and flux were found relevant to the discussion of the definition of knowledge as perception. Either they are required for the definition to work (Reading B) or they represent Plato's own belief (Reading A). The suggestion we are considering is that the details of the Dream are not Plato's own belief. What,

16. For alternative ways of working out the idea that the Dream is deliberately designed for multiple interpretation, see Morrow [51]; Amélie Oksenberg Rorty, 'A Speculative Note on Some Dramatic Elements in the *Theaetetus*', *Phronesis* 17 (1972), 227–38.

17. Exemplified by Cornford [2], 143–45 (cf. 111).

then, is the relevance of, for example, the list model of statements? Is it a necessary presupposition of the definition

Def. K$_{o(st.)}$ Knowing o is having true judgement concerning o with a statement about o

—a definition, remember, which has in substance already been refuted (p. 138)? It would be interesting to try to discover whether this can be shown. If it can, you may also be able to show that the niggardly version of the list model is a necessary presupposition of the definition of knowledge as perception (cf. p. 139). The only thing I would insist on now is that, if you want Antisthenes to carry the can for the philosophical defects of Interpretation [a], some relevance must be found for his alien ideas. Otherwise Plato's literary competence is impugned.

An alternative move for a single-minded advocate of Interpretation [a][18] is to vindicate Plato's literary competence by saying that he was himself gripped, or at least tempted, by the list model of statements. It is only in the *Sophist* that he wins through to an adequate appreciation of the structural complexity of various kinds of statement and a satisfactory analysis of falsehood (cf. pp. 72–3). Earlier he found falsehood a problem. Not that he ever seriously doubted its existence. Rather, certain assumptions and lines of thought which he found plausible—the list model of statements being one of them—appeared to make false statement and false judgement impossible.

This view is widely held among students of Plato who have been educated (as I have been) in the tradition of analytic philosophy. Some of the influences which have helped to give it currency will be considered when we turn, in the next section, to Wittgenstein's *Tractatus*. But it should be obvious at once that it implies a more grudging assessment than I gave earlier of the progress made in Part II. Once the list model of statements is housed in Plato's own thinking, the puzzles of Part II are bound to be regarded as puzzles by which Plato himself is enmeshed, not puzzles which Plato is challenging and encouraging his readers to overcome. Part II as a whole, instead of being the dialectic of challenge and response which I tried to share with you, becomes (at best) a record of honest perplexities which Plato is not yet (fully) competent to resolve.

Many scholars do read Part II that way. It is an approach that

---

18. Exemplified by McDowell [3], 231 ff.

consorts naturally with the conviction, which analytic philosophy has inherited from Frege, that such puzzles require a semantic not an epistemological solution and are therefore likely to be caused by primitive semantic views, of which the list model of statements would be a prime example. This is not the place for me to reopen discussion of Part II. It is you who must do that, if you want the list model to be Plato's own. The only thing I would insist on now is that the issue is global, not local to the Dream.

Single-minded proponents of Interpretation [b] have an easier ride. Interpretation [b] yields a better theory and carries the discussion forward in a manner that does not call into question either Plato's literary or his philosophical competence. Other things being equal, it is a sound maxim for historians of philosophy to prefer the best theory your text will bear. But other things are not quite equal now.

For why, if Interpretation [b] is unambiguously correct, does Plato turn the discussion later to the ambiguity of 'account'? At 206c it may seem that Socrates simply wants to consider the abstract impersonal question: What could be meant by 'account' in the definition 'Knowledge is true judgement with an account'? But by 206e it has become clear that his question is rather this: What might the theorist whom Theaetetus heard have meant by 'account' when he defined knowledge as true judgement with an account? It is speaker's meaning he is after, not lexical variety, and the speaker in question is the person he has previously spoken of, in the singular, as the author of the whole Dream theory (compare 206e with 202e and 208c). It does not matter whether this person is an actual historical thinker or a dramatic fiction. Why even raise the suspicion that he might have meant 'account' in sense (a): statement?

True, all Socrates acknowledges at 206ce is that the person Theaetetus heard might have meant 'account' in sense (a) when he defined knowledge as true judgement with an account. Nothing is said about the rest of the theory. By this stage in the discussion AK_0 has been refuted and set aside (205e, 206bc), and it is not at all clear how much of the original theory is to be thought of as still in play. So it is only one part of Interpretation [a], its reading of the third definition of knowledge, that Socrates explicitly invites us to consider. But he does, explicitly, invite us to consider it. And if, in considering it, we are moved to look back to the Dream to check whether the whole thing can be read with 'account' in sense (a), we find that, lo and behold, it can.

I do not wish to suggest that Interpretation [b] is not correct, only that at Stage Two it is not unambiguously correct. It *becomes* unambiguously correct at Stage Three, when Socrates fills out the theory with the model of letters and syllables; a back-reference at 207b implies that both Socrates and Theaetetus now take it to *have been* correct. But the suspicion raised at 206ce that Interpretation [a] *might* have been correct, coupled with the fact that at Stage Two it *could* have been correct, is an invitation—I need put it no more strongly—to keep Interpretation [a] in mind, if only for purposes of comparison, as the discussion proceeds. The potency of this enigmatic text should be savoured to the full. We should be alert to what it might have said about statements as well as to what it turns out to have said about analysis. That is my proposal.

All I have done so far is state the alternatives as clearly as I can, pointing out the advantages and disadvantages of each. But clarity, while desirable, is not enough. What are the philosophical aspirations of a theory of complexes and elements? Without some idea of what such a theory is *for*, it is difficult to be greatly concerned whether elements are indescribable or merely unanalyzable. It is not surprising that single-minded advocates of one interpretation or the other have looked outside the dialogue for help in understanding what, at a deeper level, the Dream is about.

Wittgenstein and the Dream

One philosopher to whom scholars have gone for guidance—both those who think of accounts as statements and those who prefer the notion of analysis—is Ludwig Wittgenstein. Wittgenstein's *Tractatus Logico-Philosophicus* is a modern classic called in to assist with the old. This, therefore, is the moment for an excursion into modern philosophy. I call it an excursion, not a digression, because the Dream has itself played a small but significant part in the course of modern philosophy. What is more, the reception of the Dream into modern philosophy has fed back into Platonic scholarship in ways that it is important to become aware of, particularly when discussing this very text, the Dream.

The reception of the Dream into modern philosophy took the form of a comparison between the Dream and the *Tractatus*. One version of the comparison was advanced by Wittgenstein himself, another and *prima facie* quite different version, with a different moral, by Gilbert Ryle. The effect was to create a powerful presumption that Plato's concerns in Part III of the *Theaetetus* have much in common with the *Tractatus,* and hence that the *Tractatus* can be used to illuminate the Dream.

Now readers will recall that, whereas in introducing Part I my practice was to draw parallels with later philosophy, in dealing with Part II I emphasized a contrast between Plato's epistemological approach to the problems we were discussing and Frege's explicitly semantic approach. In this section I shall renew that contrast (much of the *Tractatus* is a meditation upon Frege's philosophy), but with an extra purpose. Previously I hoped that, by keeping ancient and modern perspectives apart, we could appreciate and learn from both. The extra point now is that, where the Dream is concerned, one factor which makes it hard to hold the two perspectives apart is the spellbinding effect of the *Tractatus.*

It was in fact an interpretation more like Interpretation [b] which led Wittgenstein to compare the elements in Socrates' dream with the 'objects' of his own *Tractatus.* In the following passage Wittgenstein purports to be explaining the indescribability of his objects and Socrates' elements, but the sense in which they are indescribable turns out to be precisely that they admit of no internal analysis:

> 'In a certain sense, an object cannot be described.' (So too Plato: 'You can't give an account of one but only name it.') Here 'object' means 'reference of a not further definable word', and 'description' or 'explanation' really means: 'definition'. For of course it isn't denied that the object can be 'described from outside', that properties can be ascribed to it and so on.[19]

Like Socrates' dream, the *Tractatus* gives no examples of simple objects but is totally confident that we would reach them at the end of a completed analysis. As in the Dream, so in the *Tractatus:* 'Objects can only be *named'* (*Tr.* 3.221). But to offer examples, by actually naming some, would be to claim to have completed an analysis. For the same reason, if we ask 'Are objects simple parts or ingredients of some sort, or simple qualities, or what?', the *Tractatus* does not volunteer an answer (cf. p. 140).[20] As Witt-

19. Ludwig Wittgenstein, *Philosophical Grammar* (Oxford: 1974), 208. The *Tractatus* was first published in 1921. The material in *Philosophical Grammar* is from manuscripts of the early 1930s.

20. Wittgenstein's discussion of simple objects in *Philosophical Investigations, op. cit.,* §§ 47–48, is illustrated with examples of all these kinds: bits of wood, molecules, atoms, coloured squares, segments of curves, colours, types of letter. But this is by way of repudiating, not elucidating, what he meant in the *Tractatus.*

genstein once wrote (and Socrates would surely agree—p. 135), 'we do not infer the existence of simple objects from the existence of particular simple objects, but rather know them—by description, as it were—as the end product of analysis, by means of a process that leads to them'.[21]

Much better known than the passage quoted above is that Wittgenstein chose to make the comparison between the Dream and the *Tractatus* one of the means through which he would present his later philosophy. In the *Philosophical Investigations* he quotes a portion of 201d–202b and comments: 'Both Russell's "individuals" and my "objects" . . . were such primary elements'.[22] There follows an extended (and very interesting) critique of the errors which he now diagnoses as common to the Dream and the *Tractatus*—the idea that names really signify simples, that reality is composed of simple constituent parts, that a sentence or proposition is a complex of names, and so on. It is this critique which has made Socrates' dream part of the philosophical consciousness of our time, helping thereby to form the expectations which a present-day reader brings to the text before us. If these expectations are never wholly fulfilled, and the relation between the two works remains elusive, it is because the simple objects of the *Tractatus* are notoriously as obscure as the elements of the Dream.[23]

One thing, however, is entirely clear in the *Tractatus*, and predictable from its background in Frege's philosophy of language. The process which leads to simple objects has a *semantic* bias. The techniques involved are logical analysis and definition. Their purpose is to display the exact meaning of propositions and thereby to determine what is the case when the propositions are true:

> It is obvious that the analysis of propositions must bring us to elementary propositions which consist of names in immediate combination. (*Tr.* 4.221)[24]

21. Ludwig Wittgenstein, *Notebooks 1914–1916* (Oxford: 1961), 50.

22. *Phil. Inv.*, § 46. That Wittgenstein quotes only the portion he does is not without its significance, as will be seen below, n. 45.

23. In fact, while commentators on the *Theaetetus* have looked to the *Tractatus* for inspiration, students of Wittgenstein are as likely to turn to the *Theaetetus* for guidance in understanding the *Tractatus*. See, for example, Irving M. Copi, 'Objects, Properties, and Relations in the "Tractatus"', reprinted from *Mind* N.S. 67 (1958) in Irving M. Copi & Robert W. Beard edd., *Essays on Wittgenstein's Tractatus* (London: 1966), 184–85, or Norman Malcolm, *Nothing Is Hidden: Wittgenstein's Criticism of His Early Thought* (Oxford: 1986), 34, 44. (Beginners will find both these books a helpful introduction to the problems and pleasures of reading the *Tractatus*.)

24. Cf. *Phil. Gram.*, 211.

These names 'cannot be dissected any further by means of definition' (*Tr.* 3.26). They are simple signs for simple objects (*Tr.* 2.02,
3.201 ff.). The doctrine of the *Tractatus* is that at the end of the
process of analysis we would see that the reality described by our
propositions consists entirely of simple objects in various combinations or arrangements. The objects themselves are permanent and
unalterable; it is their changing configurations which produce this
state of affairs or that (*Tr.* 2.027–2.0272).

Such is the abstract cosmology that Wittgenstein found prefig-
ured in the *Theaetetus*. Plato did not have available to him the
techniques of logical analysis on which Wittgenstein was relying
(especially Russell's Theory of Descriptions), but he did know about
definition; indeed, the great emphasis placed on definition in subsequent philosophy owes much to his writings. Accordingly, since
one common meaning of *logos* is 'definition' (p. 134), it is possible to
think—we have seen that Wittgenstein did think—that in Socrates'
dream, as in the *Tractatus*, the process which leads to simple elements has a semantic bias. You analyze (not in Plato's case whole
propositions but) terms for complex objects, until all definable
words have been defined and you are left with an account consisting
of indefinable names in immediate combination. These are the
names for simple elements.[25]

Socrates does not say that his elements are permanent and
unalterable, combining and recombining to produce this complex
object or that. But contemporary readers may well have inferred
it, for a number of pre-Socratic theorists had held such views and
the word 'element' was coming to be the vogue term for reporting
them.[26] It could easily suggest permanence and unalterability. If
elements are perceivable (202b), that rules out microscopic entities
like the atoms of Democritus—and the elements of Plato's own
physical theory in the *Timaeus* (56bc). But it would not rule out
other theorists' elements, such as earth, air, fire, and water, or
fundamental qualities like 'the hot' and 'the cold'. In any case we
should not imagine that Socrates has some particular theory of
elements in mind. It would take knowledge to *name* the primary
elements of which we and everything else are composed.[27]

So much for Wittgenstein's own reading of the Dream as aspiring

25. Some such process is assumed by Cornford [2], 144–45, Burnyeat [54], 117 ff.
26. Cf. *Sophist* 252b, *Timaeus* 48bc.
27. Cf. Wittgenstein, *Notebooks 1914–1916, op. cit.,* 68: 'Our difficulty was that we
kept on speaking of simple objects and were unable to mention a single one'.

to discover the unalterable substance of the world (cf. *Tr*. 2.021 ff.) through semantic analysis. 'The requirement that simple signs be possible is the requirement that sense be determinate' (*Tr*. 3.23). Since sense is determinate—this is the large assumption which the later Wittgenstein will challenge—reality must ultimately be composed of the simple objects which our language presupposes. I turn now to another and *prima facie* quite different version of the comparison between the *Theaetetus* and the *Tractatus*, to be found in an influential paper of great brilliance on 'Plato's *Parmenides*' which Gilbert Ryle published in 1939.

Note the date. Ryle promoted the idea of comparing the Dream with the *Tractatus* long before the publication of the *Philosophical Investigations* in 1953 revealed that Wittgenstein had made the comparison himself, and Ryle had the greater impact on Platonic scholarship. His paper exercised a formative influence on the study of late Plato within the tradition of analytic philosophy, for it established, on a much wider basis than Wittgenstein's critique of the Dream in the *Philosophical Investigations*, a sense of kinship between Plato's philosophical concerns and ours, and opened up a whole new range of questions for scholars to debate: especially questions about Plato's progress and achievements in the philosophy of language. Besides, Ryle came to praise Plato for anticipating the best insights of the *Tractatus*, not, like Wittgenstein, to bury him along with the errors of the *Tractatus*.

Ryle's suggestion was that the way to understand the Dream is to think of the *Theaetetus*, with the *Parmenides* and *Sophist*, as concerned with issues of 'logical syntax' of the kind that preoccupied Wittgenstein in his *Tractatus*.[28] Already we detect a change of emphasis, by comparison with Wittgenstein's own remarks on the Dream; syntax has to do with the joining of one word to another rather than with the analysis or definition of a given word. Next, Ryle read Plato differently, taking 'account' in the *Theaetetus* to mean

---

28. Ryle [55], 316, 325, also cites Russell, Carnap, and some older philosophers, but he wishes to emphasize 'more than any other, nearly the whole of Wittgenstein's *Tractatus Logico-Philosophicus*'. Ryle's main interest in this paper is of course the *Parmenides*. The *Theaetetus* is discussed rather briefly at pp. 317–21, but readers can now consult, not only Ryle [57], published some 20 years later, which is more explicit in its references to the Dream, but also Ryle [56], a famous, long unpublished paper on the *Theaetetus* read to the Oxford Philological Society in 1952—a paper which, through the circulation of its ideas among Oxford-based scholars, undoubtedly added to the influence described above.

'sentence' or 'statement' rather than 'definition'. This put him initially on the side of Interpretation [a], but what followed was an
entirely novel development of Interpretation [a]'s understanding
of 'account'. According to Ryle, the Dream is more interested in
statements and complexes than in the names and elements of which
they are composed. The great lesson to be learned, in fact, is the
special logical complexity of what a sentence states. An immediate
corollary (since both knowledge and belief or judgement are expressed in statements) is an identical complexity in what we know,
believe, or judge.

The complexity at issue, which we have touched on before (p.
89), is not a matter of being complicated, as an arrangement of wires
or a pattern of coloured dots might be complicated. Take the least
complicated of statements—one of Plato's examples in the *Sophist*
(263a) is 'Theaetetus sits'. Already this is logically or semantically
complex in that it involves a fitting together of two terms, a subject
and a predicate, which are essentially unlike. It is not just two
names in a row (as 'Theaetetus, Theodorus' or 'Theaetetus, sitting'
would be), nor is it a composite name (like 'The Mona Lisa' or 'Part
III of Plato's *Theaetetus*'). What it states, viz. *that Theaetetus sits*, is
not the sort of thing you *can* name. Conversely, things you can
name, like Theaetetus and the Mona Lisa, are not the sort of thing
you can state. What there can be statements of and what there can
be names of are as different from each other as statements are from
names.

This lesson was important to Russell and Wittgenstein early in
the twentieth century.[29] It was still important to Ryle in 1939, when
he proposed it as a worthy lesson for Plato to have been teaching
in the fourth century B.C.[30] For on Ryle's reading, the Dream's
contrast between elements and complexes is precisely the contrast
between nameable and stateable, between things there can be
names of and things there can be statements of. The thesis that
elements can only be named does not deny the possibility of any
statement *about* a nameable element. It denies the possibility of any

29. See the first section of 'The Philosophy of Logical Atomism' (1918), in Bertrand
Russell, *Logic and Knowledge: Essays 1901–1950*, ed. Robert Charles Marsh (London:
1956), 178–88; Wittgenstein, *Tractatus* 3.142, 3.144, 3.3, 4.032.

30. Ten years later Ryle can be found rebuking Carnap for having learned the lesson
rather less well than Plato: Gilbert Ryle, *Collected Papers* (London: 1971), Vol. I, 234
(a discussion, reprinted from *Philosophy* 24 [1949], of Rudolf Carnap, *Meaning and
Necessity*).

statement *of* an element. This requires a word of explanation and some grounding in the text.[31]

We must first reread Socrates' remark at 202b that an account is essentially a complex of names. Instead of saying that a statement or, on Interpretation [b], an analysis is a sequence of names (p. 139, p. 143), it now says the opposite, that the complexity of statements is not to be parsed as a mere sequence of names. The names are arranged or 'woven together' in a definite way to form a unified whole which, like 'Theaetetus sits', has structure as well as components. The same structure unifies the nonlinguistic correlates of 'Theaetetus' and 'sits' to form the complex truth (or falsehood) *that Theaetetus sits.*

Some of you may find it difficult to make the Gestalt switch to a Rylean reading of 202b because you would not normally call 'sits' (in contrast, perhaps, to 'sitting') a name. If you feel more comfortable calling it a term instead, that will still be in keeping with Ryle's intentions and Plato's Greek. Plato's terminology in the *Sophist* (261d–262a) distinguishes *onoma* (name or noun) from *rhēma* (predicate or verb) as two types of *onoma* in the generic sense of name, term, or word. The definition of account at *Theaetetus* 202b uses *onoma*, but Ryle is entitled to take the word in its generic sense, which covers any kind of term. The definition will then be compatible with the *Sophist*'s doctrine that a string of nouns like 'lion stag horse' or a string of verbs like 'walks runs sleeps' can never make a statement; the simplest statement is a complex formed by the fitting together of a noun (*onoma* in the specific sense) and a verb, as in 'Theaetetus sits'. The important point for Ryle is this: from the fact that the Dream does not distinguish different types of name or term, you cannot argue that only one type is intended. You might even commend Socrates' definition of account for being properly neutral as to the specific structures a statement might display.[32]

31. The next five paragraphs are my own attempt to show Plato cooperating with Ryle's expectations. For Ryle left it to his readers to relate his suggestive, but all too briefly sketched interpretation to the details of the text. As a result, he is often misread and criticised for holding views he did not hold, e.g. that there are no statements about elements (Fine [52], 371 ff.).

32. A technical complication here (on which McDowell [3], 233–34, is excellent) is that, even if the component names of a statement were all of the same type, structure could still be expressed by their order or arrangement. Plato's much-admired claim in the *Sophist* that the simplest statement requires two unlike components, a noun and a verb, is false in principle even if it is true of Greek, English, and related natural languages. See Wittgenstein, *Tr.* 3.14–3.1432, *Phil. Inv.* §§ 48–49. Conversely, it is most unfair of the later Wittgenstein (*Phil. Gram.*, 56) to see in the *Sophist* no more

We may now proceed to the thesis that elements can only be named. According to Interpretation [a] this meant: no statement *about* an element. According to Ryle it means: no statement *of* an element. The difference is all-important. 'Theaetetus sits', for example, is a statement about Theaetetus, but what it is a statement *of* is the truth or the falsehood (whichever it be) *that Theaetetus sits*. Let us work this out for elements.

A statement about an element would be, for example, '*e* is yellow' (a description) or 'That is *e*' (an identification). According to Interpretation [a], both kinds of statement are ruled out by Q1, or alternatively Q1 excludes the former and Q2 the latter (p. 137). But let us take a second look at Q3, where Socrates gives a reason for the prohibition on 'that' and 'this' in Q2. This time we are to understand 'account' as 'statement' rather than 'definition' or 'analysis', with a matching sense for the verb 'to express':

> Q3 for these go the round and are applied to all things alike, being other than the things to which they are added, whereas if it were possible to express (state, say)[33] the element itself and it had its own proprietary account, it would have to be expressed (stated, said) without any other thing.

Socrates' point here is that identification, like description, uses words which do not belong uniquely and exclusively to the element in question. The extraordinary implication, if 'account' means 'statement', is that the kind of statement he is looking for, and failing to find, is one that would use words belonging exclusively to the element; no other words would be used. If such a statement were possible, it would express *e* itself without saying anything *about* it, without even identifying it *as e*. It would be a statement *of*

---

than another version of his *bête noire*, the idea that all words are names. Plato should be admired for insisting that statements have structure, regardless of whether the simplest structure he could discern is truly the simplest there can be.

33. The parenthetical gloss is mine. 'Express' is appropriate for a translation designed to keep the options for interpretation open; e.g. in the context where Q3 was quoted before (pp. 142–3), 'express' can be understood as 'express in an account, define'. But the verb so translated is the ordinary Greek verb for 'say, state' (*legein*, cognate with *logos*). It is, of course, strained to talk of 'stating an element'. When *legein* occurred with a comparable direct object construction at 190c, it was translated 'makes a statement *about*' (cf. Part II, n. 4). But on Ryle's interpretation a linguistically strained and logically improper form of thought is exactly what the text should display. The same gloss would then be appropriate for the verb 'speak of' at the end of Q1.

e in the sense that the answer to the question 'What does the statement express, say or state?' would be just: *e*.

No such statement is possible. The only word that belongs uniquely and exclusively to an element is its name. Hence the only linguistic role which is unique and exclusive to an element is that of being named. This is Ryle's interpretation. You can say as much as you like *about* elements. What Q1 maintains you cannot do is say or state *them*. Conversely, although this is not explicit in the text, the things you can state, you cannot name.

The corollary may now be drawn:

> There must be a complex of distinguishable elements as well in what I know as in what I mistakenly or correctly believe. What I know are facts, and facts always have some complexity. So 'simples' could not be facts, though they would be elements in facts. Only a proper name could directly stand for a simple, and only a sentence could state a fact.[34]

The complexity of what knowers know is the logical or semantic complexity of what is said by a sentence or statement. It is not the complexity of a complicated object.

The obvious objection[35] is that in the text it is 'we and everything else' that accounts and knowledge are of. The complexity of what knowers know, according to the Dream, is precisely the complexity of those very complicated objects, ourselves. That, of course, was my reason for preferring Def. K_o to Def. K_p at the start (p. 135). If Ryle's interpretation was correct, we would have to go back to Stage One and begin again with Def. K_p.

I am not going to suggest that Ryle's interpretation can be sustained. But it is not to be so quickly defeated as the obvious objection makes out, and much can be learned from exploring further to see how far, and at what price, the objection can be stalled. Another reason for exploring further is that many who find the objection conclusive have nonetheless been gripped by Ryle's *Tractatus*-inspired vision of what, ideally, the Dream should be about. Let me explain.

Ryle's interpretation has one advantage over Interpretation [a]: it does not postulate, and so does not have to concoct reasons for believing in, elements about which nothing can be said. It shares

34. Ryle [55], 318.
35. McDowell [3], 232, 240, White [8], 194 n. 48, Annas [53], 99, Bostock [9], 206.

one major disadvantage of Interpretation [a]: if we understand 'account of' as 'statement of' in

Def. K$_p$ Knowing that p is having true judgement that p with an account of the proposition p,

the result is as feeble as Def. K$_o$ with 'account of' understood as 'statement about', and for the same reasons (p. 138). But plusses and minuses of this sort look trivial, or at least uninteresting, when compared, on the one hand, with the exciting prospect that was opened up by Ryle's attribution to Plato of so enlightened a view of statements, and, on the other, with the damaging and very obvious textual objection which Ryle's interpretation, unlike Interpretation [a], has to confront. Few scholars have accepted Ryle's interpretation as it stands,[36] just because of the obvious objection. But few wish to deny Plato the enlightenment so manifestly achieved in the *Sophist*. One common compromise is to infer that Plato in the *Theaetetus* is *on his way to* the insights of the *Sophist*.

The compromising inference can be put like this. Plato is not, in the Dream, proceeding from the enlightened view of statements that Ryle ascribed to him; this much the objection makes clear. Therefore he is proceeding from an unenlightened view of statements, the candidate nearest to hand being our old friend the list model, which Plato will overcome and reject in the *Sophist*.[37] In short, if you accept from Ryle that Plato's starting-point in the Dream, like Wittgenstein's in the *Tractatus*, is a concern with the nature of propositions or statements, but the obvious textual objection dissuades you from accepting Ryle's account of Plato's conclusions, you will be driven back to Interpretation [a] and to the reevaluation of Plato's progress in Part II which is called for once the list model of statements is housed in Plato's own thinking (p. 147).

This should be enough to explain why I think it is worth taking the trouble to describe two ways one might try to meet the objection that in the text it is 'we and everything else' that accounts and knowledge are of. Neither reply is finally convincing, but the second, when pursued far enough, will bring us to the limits of the

36. An important, if partial, exception is G.E.L. Owen, 'Notes on Ryle's Plato', in Wood & Pitcher edd., *Ryle: A Collection of Critical Essays, op. cit.*, 356, 364–65; also in G.E.L. Owen, *Logic, Science and Dialectic: Collected Papers in Greek Philosophy*, ed. Martha Nussbaum (London: 1986), 94, 99–100.

37. A lucid formulation of this response to Ryle may be found in McDowell [3], 231–39 (cf. 248–50). Many other writers on Plato wittingly or unwittingly take it for granted.

likeness between the *Tractatus* and the Dream. Once these limits are fixed, the spell of the *Tractatus* should be broken. It should become easier to see that the semantic bias of the *Tractatus* illustrates just one way—a characteristically twentieth-century way—of filling in the indeterminacies of the Dream.

For a start, we could disarm the objection by supposing that the Dream was deliberately designed to draw the distinction between nameable and stateable in the wrong way.[38] Here is how the story might go. Socrates casts 'we and everything else' as the complexes that accounts are of, and declares that an account is 'essentially a complex of names'. The result, assuming that 'account of' means 'statement of', is a twofold disaster: the complexity of the stateable is equated with the complexity of a complicated nameable object, and the complexity of a statement is reduced to that of a composite name. AL_0 becomes

AL(st. of)$_0$ There actually are some objects of which there is no statement, and others which there are statements of.

But Socrates will impale the Dream theory on a dilemma. As it turns out, either elements are as knowable as complexes or complex objects are as unaccountable and unknowable as elements (205de). Now, if this is the inevitable result of treating the distinction between nameable and stateable as a distinction between simple and complicated objects, then the distinction between nameable and stateable had better be drawn differently. Contrary to the second conjunct of AL(st. of)$_0$, no object, however complicated, is such that there is a statement *of* it. Contrary to the first conjunct of AL(st. about)$_0$, no object, however simple, is such that there is no statement *about* it. That is why we should go back to Stage One and start again with Def. K_p. What we should be discussing is propositional knowledge *about* objects.

This reply extracts the great lesson from the demolition of the Dream instead of the Dream itself. It has the merit of audacity. It founders on the fact that the dilemma, when we reach it, will have a much broader target than the distinction between nameable and stateable. It attacks a certain misconception of complexity as such. The lesson is not that we should not be thinking about complicated objects, but that we should be thinking about all complex things differently.

There is, however, another way to draw the sting of the objection.

---

38. Cf. Gerold Prauss, *Platon und der logische Eleatismus* (Berlin: 1966), 161 ff.

The Dream would be even more reminiscent of Russell and the early Wittgenstein if analysis showed that the complexity of 'we and everything else' was after all an example of, or at least unexpectedly similar to, the logical complexity of statements.

Take Theaetetus. As Ryle presents his interpretation, Theaetetus could perfectly well be an element. For on Ryle's reading of the Dream, 'element' is to be understood in a purely logical sense. An element is a logical or semantic atom—an elementary component in the constitution of truths and falsehoods. It is a nameable but not stateable component in something said or stated (a component because nameable, an elementary component because not itself stateable). Just so, Theaetetus is a nameable (indeed a named) component in what is said by the statement 'Theaetetus sits', and Theaetetus cannot himself be stated. However many physical atoms he is composed of, he is one logical atom in the truth *that Theaetetus sits*. It is only in relation to the complexity of what is said or stated that an element has to be incomposite or 'simple'. Theaetetus can perfectly well be simple in this logical sense without being, in any ordinary sense, simple. His simplicity, in the logical sense, just is the fact that he can be named but not stated, and this fact about him derives entirely from the fact that 'Theaetetus' is only a name, not yet a statement.

The obvious objection to Ryle's interpretation can now be put as follows. The interpretation, as so far presented, allows Theaetetus to be an element, but the rubric 'we and everything else' counts him a complex. To be consistent with the text, Ryle ought therefore to say that 'Theaetetus' is not a name but already a statement, or at least more like a statement than a name. Which is absurd.

The reply is that, according to the most distinguished philosophers of our time, the supposed absurdity is no absurdity at all, but a plain truth of logic.[39] One of the main tenets of what is loosely called 'Logical Atomism', in the form or forms expounded by Russell and Wittgenstein early in this century, is that ordinary proper names like 'Theaetetus' are not *logically* proper names. Several lines of thought led to this view, of which the most relevant for our purposes is the argument from mortality.

Theaetetus is mortal, in fact dead. When he died, he ceased to exist, but his name lived on. Histories of mathematics can still speak about him and his achievements because the name 'Theaetetus' did not lose its meaning in the battle of 369 B.C. where Theaetetus lost

---

39. That this is the reply Ryle himself would favour is indicated in Ryle [56].

his life and ceased to exist. It follows that Theaetetus is not the
meaning of the name 'Theaetetus'. And from this it follows that
Theaetetus is not after all a component in what is said by 'Theaetetus
sits'. A fortiori it is wrong to count him a nameable (indeed a
named) but not stateable component in what that statement says.
Logically speaking, therefore, it is wrong to count 'Theaetetus' a
proper name. Ordinary language calls it a proper name, but it turns
out not to be functioning as one when the statement 'Theaetetus
sits' is subjected to logical analysis. Thus 'Theaetetus' is not, logically, a proper name, and Theaetetus is not an element.

So much for what Theaetetus and 'Theaetetus' are not.[40] What
are they? We need not go into the modern techniques of analysis
(Russell's Theory of Descriptions and Wittgenstein's adaptations of
it) which can be called upon to elucidate the statement 'Theaetetus
sits' in such a way that what looks like a reference to or naming of
the man Theaetetus is shown to be really an *assertion* of the unique
instantiation of certain properties or a *statement* about the constituents of the man and the relations obtaining between them.[41] Close
to hand in Part III of the dialogue itself is the idea that Theaetetus
might be regarded as made up of a nose plus eyes plus mouth, etc.,
the nose snub, the eyes bulging, and so on, each in a unique way
(209bc). Recall also, once again, the suggestion in Part I that what
people call a man or a stone is really an aggregate of perceived
qualities (157bc). All we need now, to rebut the obvious objection
to Ryle's interpretation of the Dream, is Platonic licence for regarding the name 'Theaetetus' as a kind of shorthand for the statement
that those constituents (or enough of them, or the essential ones) are
or (when the name is used today) were appropriately combined.[42]

40. For an elegant presentation of the reasoning, see Wittgenstein, *Phil. Inv.* §§ 39–
40, and compare Russell, 'Knowledge by Acquaintance and Knowledge by Description', *op. cit.*, 118 ff. (*Mysticism and Logic, op. cit.*, 208 ff.). If at first it sounds too
anachronistic to be useful for the interpretation of Plato, try comparing the argument
in Plato's *Timaeus* (49a ff.) for the conclusion that no quenchable fire can properly
be named 'fire' or 'this fire'. 'Fire' is also one of Russell's examples ('The Philosophy
of Logical Atomism', *op. cit.*, 183) of a single word expressing a fact, the full expression of which requires a sentence.

41. Russell, 'On Denoting' (1905), in *Logic and Knowledge, op. cit.*, 39–56. Cf. *Tractatus*
2.0201: 'Every statement about complexes can be resolved into a statement about
their constituents and into the propositions that describe the complexes completely'.
The interested reader may consult Anthony Kenny, *Wittgenstein* (Harmondsworth:
1973), 35–39, 77 ff.

42. The idea that an ordinary proper name might be an abbreviated statement is not
so anachronistic as it may seem: witness *Cratylus* 396a ff.

It is true (and damaging to Ryle's interpretation) that there is not the slightest hint of any such view of 'Theaetetus' in the Dream. The Dream offers no view of 'Theaetetus' at all. But suppose it did. Suppose that the text, besides implying (as it does) that Theaetetus is not an element, also gave some indication (as it does not) that 'Theaetetus' is more like a statement than a name. This would be enough to rebut the obvious objection, but it would not be enough to establish Ryle's interpretation and make the Dream an early contribution to the philosophy of Logical Atomism. The crucial item still missing is the argument: Theaetetus is not an element *because* 'Theaetetus' is not in the requisite sense a name.

The aspiration of Logical Atomism, as its own name implies, was to derive metaphysical insights from the logical analysis of language. Twentieth-century metaphysics has shared that aspiration ever since. One might call it the modern dream. Consequently, the parallels between the *Tractatus* and the Dream make it enormously tempting for a twentieth-century reader to find the same semantic bias in the *Theaetetus*. But it is not there. The reason it is not there is simple. Just as it would take knowledge on Socrates' part to name some primary elements, so also it would take knowledge to say which methods of analysis can disclose them.

This point works against Wittgenstein's version of the comparison with the *Tractatus* as well as Ryle's. The divergence between them is ultimately just a difference in the ways they supplement the text so as to find in it the semantic bias of twentieth-century philosophy. They ask: When Socrates propounds the thesis that elements have only a name, not an account, does he imply, by contrast, that complexes have a (definable) name as well as an account, or is the contrast that complexes have no name at all, they can only be stated (and anything that looks like the name of a complex must really be a statement in disguise)? Wittgenstein proposes the first answer, Ryle the second, but neither answer has any basis in the text.[43]

Socrates does not say that the account of a complex is an account of the name of the complex, or that it is reached by defining the meaning of the name, or that it has any connection with the name

---

43. The difference between the two answers will be further lessened to the extent that, when Wittgenstein looks back to the role of definition in the *Tractatus*, Russell's Theory of Descriptions is often the paradigm he has in mind. Compare *Phil. Gram.*, 211, on Russell and definition with 199–201 on the mistake of assimilating the complexity of complex objects and the complexity of states of affairs.

at all. Unlike Wittgenstein, he does not so much as offer a view of 'Theaetetus', or 'man', or any other word for complex things. Consequently, if we do understand 'account' in the Dream as definition, we should not assume that a definition has to be a semantic definition which analyzes the meaning of a word. It may be a real definition which gives the essence of some thing in itself, without regard to its linguistic expression. Here it is perhaps worth glancing back to 147ac: Socrates does speak of understanding the name 'clay', but the understanding he aims for—knowing that clay is earth mixed with liquid—sounds more like a scientist's than an ordinary speaker's understanding of the term.[44]

Equally, if 'account' in the Dream is understood in Ryle's way as statement or proposition, there is nothing in the text to show that it is through the analysis of what statements say that we are to reach the primary elements. Hence there is nothing to vindicate Ryle's assumption that the elements Socrates is speaking of are logical or semantic elements in the constitution of truths and falsehoods.

Yet neither does Socrates mention physically dissecting a complex object—with a knife, for example. If we ask, 'How does one discover that clay is earth mixed with liquid? From a dictionary? With a knife? By some other means?', no answer is forthcoming. As regards methods for reaching the primary elements, the Dream is completely indeterminate.

This indeterminacy goes along with another. Socrates does not say what makes a complex complex, nor which of many different modes of complexity he has in view. Wittgenstein and Ryle assume that what makes a complex complex is something to do with the complexity of its linguistic expression; otherwise the question to which they give divergent answers would not arise. It is only natural they should assume this, given their assumption that it is by logical or semantic analysis that one unravels the complexity to get at the primary elements. In effect, both are assuming that the main direction of discovery is from language to the world. But when Socrates propounds the thesis that elements have no account, only a name, while complexes have an account, which is a complex of names, it is no less compatible with the text to assume that what makes a complex complex is something other than the complexity of its linguistic expression, so that the complexity of accounts ('an account being essentially a complex of names') is a response to, not the cause of, the complexity of the things that accounts are of.

44. Cf. Part I, n. 7.

Not only is it no less compatible with the text to assume this, but it is more natural to do so, given that Socrates' reason for citing the linguistic complexity of accounts is not to explain the complexity of complex things but to explain why an account is always of something complex (p. 135). Whether 'account' is 'statement' or 'definition', this strongly suggests that the complexity of a complex thing is independent of, not derivative from, the linguistic complexity of its account. The complexity of the things is mirrored in and recorded by the linguistic complexity of their accounts, not explained by it.

The upshot of this examination of the comparison between the Dream and the *Tractatus* is that the Dream is significantly more indeterminate than the *Tractatus*. Like the *Tractatus*, the Dream gives no examples of elements, and in addition, unlike the *Tractatus*, it offers no hint as to how they are to be reached. It is indeterminate about methods of analysis, and correspondingly indeterminate about how the elements are 'woven together' to form the complexes that analysis would unravel. Reflection on meaning is not excluded, but it is not at the forefront of attention as Wittgenstein and Ryle assume.[45] Theirs is one way—a characteristically twentieth-century way—to *make* a theory out of the indeterminate schema that Plato provided. Other ways of filling in the indeterminacies will make other theories, as we will see. This is not to say that the comparison with the *Tractatus* has proved unilluminating. Far from it. Only that it tells us as much about ourselves as about the Dream.

Antisthenes and the Dream

But students of the Dream have looked for ancient as well as modern sources of inspiration. Admittedly, Socrates is rather elusive about

45. Plato devoted a separate dialogue, the *Cratylus*, to the question whether reflection on meaning could yield insight into reality. His answer is negative, but it takes a long and complicated discussion to reach it. On the relationship between the Dream and the *Cratylus*, see Annas [53].

It is worth noting that Wittgenstein's quotation from the Dream in *Phil. Inv.* § 46 stops at the words which Miss Levett renders 'an account being essentially a complex of names' (202b). In the English version of *Phil. Inv.* these words appear as 'For the essence of speech is the composition of names', which, though questionable as a translation of the German translation of Plato that Wittgenstein is quoting, is exactly how the Dream theory is understood and criticized in *Phil. Inv.* §§ 48 and 49, viz. as a theory of speech in general. On looking back to the original dialogue, you see that Wittgenstein has lopped off the connection with AK_o to which Socrates proceeds in the very next sentence: 'Thus the elements are unaccountable and unknowable . . .' One effect of this is to cover up a significant divergence between the Dream and the *Tractatus*: *Tractatus* simples are not unknowable (2.0123, 2.01231). The more whether his dream comes from anywhere but his own head. It is something he *thought* he heard from some 'people' (201d). Yet Theaetetus speaks robustly enough of what 'a man' said and how he put it (201cd). And if, as Theaetetus at least implies, the theory does derive—in whole or in part—from an actual historical thinker, the most likely candidate is Antisthenes, a follower of Socrates about whom a certain amount is known from Aristotle and other sources.[46]

Antisthenes' writings included a four-book work on opinion (*doxa*) and knowledge, now lost, and some imaginary speeches by heroic characters, in one of which (entitled *Ajax*) much ado is made about jurors judging without knowledge of an affair at which they were not present. Would this have put contemporary readers on the alert to recognize Antisthenes as the author of the theory which Theaetetus is reminded of by the conclusion to the Jury section of Part II?

Much has been conjectured about Antisthenes on the assumption that he is indeed the author of the Dream theory, and a target of allusion elsewhere in Plato.[47] The idea is that the indeterminacies of our text would be eliminated if only we had access to Antisthenes' own statement of the theory which Plato is putting up for criticism. On the other side, much has been written to prove that he is not the author of the theory. The argument is that, although one obscure report in Aristotle (*Metaphysics* VIII 3, 1043b 23–32) can be read as ascribing to Antisthenes a theory of unanalyzable/indescribable elements, the passage does not match up with the details of the Dream.[48] I shall spare you the complexities of controversy about

---

important effect is to narrow the discussion to the domain of language; epistemology is excluded.

46. It was common practice when writing about contemporary theories (as opposed to the theories of long-dead philosophers like Heraclitus and Protagoras) not to identify their authors by name. Antisthenes, though older than Plato, was probably still alive when the *Theaetetus* was being written.

47. Esp. *Sophist* 251ac, where the 'late-learners' are frequently identified with Antisthenes. Add this identification to the assumption that Antisthenes wrote the Dream and you can paint quite a detailed portrait of the man. See, e.g., C. M. Gillespie, 'The Logic of Antisthenes', *Archiv für Geschichte der Philosophie* 26 (1912–13), 479–500, and 27 (1913–14), 17–38, who finds resemblances with Hobbes; a more sober sketch in G. C. Field, *Plato and His Contemporaries* 3rd edition (London: 1967), 164–69, 192–96.

48. Winifred Hicken, 'The character and provenance of Socrates' "dream" in the *Theaetetus*', *Phronesis* 3 (1958), 126–45; Burnyeat [54], 108–17. A brief synopsis of Aristotle's report appears in n. 54 below.

this passage, partly because it is too obscure for the issue to be decidable, but also because neither side allows for the more lively possibility that Socrates in the *Theaetetus* is not restating Antisthenes but making creative use of some Antisthenean materials. This would give a nice point to the change from the external voice reported by Theaetetus to the inner voices of Socrates' dream. Instead of pursuing the scholar's question 'Who is the author of this theory, and what exactly does he maintain?', Socrates appropriates other people's ideas for his own thinking and formulates the theory for himself.

What is certain is that Antisthenes had a theory of accounts. This could be relevant to the Dream even if it was not accompanied, as in the Dream, by a distinction between elements and complexes.

The best clue to follow up is the striking phrase 'its own proprietary account' (*oikeios logos*) in Q3, which recurs in Aristotle's clearest and most important reference to Antisthenes (*Metaphysics* V 29, 1024b 32–4). According to Aristotle in this passage, Antisthenes maintained that nothing can be spoken of except by its own proprietary account (*oikeios logos*), which implies, Aristotle continues, that contradiction is impossible and virtually abolishes falsehood.[49]

Here we must pause. If Socrates' use of the phrase 'proprietary account' owes anything to Antisthenes, it becomes an urgent question whether, despite the efforts of Part II, he means to embrace in his dream the paradoxical consequences of Antisthenes' theory: no contradiction, no falsehood. Two people contradict one another if they say conflicting things about the same subject, while a falsehood states about a subject something different from all the things that are true of it (cf. p. 81). If a subject can only be spoken of by its own proprietary account, any statement different from the proprietary account, and a fortiori any statement both different from and conflicting with the proprietary account, will fail to be a statement about that subject; at best it will be a statement about something else. Thus a necessary condition for speaking of a thing is simultaneously a sufficient condition for describing it correctly.[50]

This formulation of the paradox should sound familiar. Socrates' dream is that an account of a complex should distinguish knowledge from mere true judgement. If the account which accompanies true judgement to constitute knowledge of *o* was the only statement

49. Antisthenes' denial of contradiction is confirmed by Aristotle, *Topics* I 11, 104b 20–21, Diogenes Laertius III 35, IX 53.

50. For an amusing version of this argument, see *Euthydemus* 285e ff.

to be made about o, we would be back with (a generalized version of) the initial puzzle of Part II: knowing a thing is both a necessary condition for speaking or judging of it and a sufficient condition for not going wrong about it. The opening page of Part III would mark no progress whatever.

We have been here before. Last time it was the list model of statements which threatened to make falsehood impossible and drive us back to Part II (p. 141). It is not surprising, therefore, that the list model of statements has often been attributed to Antisthenes and Interpretation [a] combined with the historical hypothesis that Antisthenes is the author of the Dream in the straightforward sense that he composed it and Plato copied it out for criticism. This, as we saw (p. 146), is a convenient way to shift the philosophical defects of Interpretation [a] onto other shoulders than Plato's.

By itself, however, a model of statements as lists would be insufficient to explain the point which Aristotle emphasizes, that according to Antisthenes only *one* statement can be made about each thing, this one statement being the proprietary account. Why should there not be a number of statements about a given thing, each listing a different selection of its parts or qualities? This is not excluded by Interpretation [a] as developed so far. Nor by Interpretation [b], which holds that for each complex there is indeed only one account (sense (b): definition or analysis into elements) but numerous other statements. On neither interpretation is it the case both that 'account' means 'statement' and that each complex has only one account.[51] Antisthenes' theory of accounts is stronger and stranger than anything we have met before.

But that does not make it incompatible with the text of the Dream. True, Socrates' one mention of proprietary accounts is negative: a proprietary account of its own is what an element does not have (202a). He does not expressly claim that the accounts which complexes have are proprietary to them in some Antisthenean sense. But if we wish to infer that he means this, there is nothing to stop us doing so. The language Socrates uses to recount his dream is so abstract and indeterminate that it is perfectly possible to read him as saying that each complex has just one statement to be made about it. A moment's thought will confirm this. If the text is genuinely ambiguous between Interpretation [a], which takes 'account' as

---

51. This does happen on Ryle's interpretation, but only because for Ryle a complex is the truth or falsehood which an account is the statement *of*, not a complex object which an account is a statement *about*.

'statement', and Interpretation [b], which includes only one account per complex, it is bound to permit a third interpretation—by conflation of the previous two—according to which there is only one statement per complex.

But why would anyone entertain so strange a view? And why would Plato wish to put us in mind of it? Aristotle's report suggests an answer to the first question which may also help with the second. For he implies that it was precisely by ignoring the distinction between account in sense (a) and account in sense (b) that Antisthenes arrived at the conclusion that nothing can be spoken of or stated except by a unique account of its own. If Antisthenes could serve Aristotle as an awful warning of where you end up if you do not separate definition or analysis from statement in general, he might do the same for Plato.

Here is Aristotle's report, with the word *logos* translated 'account' to facilitate comparison with the *Theaetetus* and italics marking the place where I find his diagnosis of Antisthenes' mistake:

> An account is false when it is of things that are not, insofar as it is false. That is why every account is false of anything other than what it is true of, as the account of circle is false of triangle. *Of each thing in a sense there is one account, that of its essence, but in another sense there are many, since the thing itself is identical in a sense with itself qualified, as Socrates with musical Socrates* (a false account is not an account in the strict sense of anything). *That is why* Antisthenes was thinking simplemindedly when he maintained that nothing can be spoken of except by its proprietary account, one account for one thing, from which it followed that contradiction is impossible and falsehood virtually impossible too.[52] (*Metaphysics* V 29, 1024b 26–34)

Not only does Aristotle insist that *logos* as definition (the account of a thing's essence) must be distinguished from *logos* as descriptive

---

52. Aristotle's qualification 'virtually' is perhaps meant to concede that, while a statement which fails to be about *o* could not be said to *contradict* the proprietary account of *o*, it could at a pinch be called *false* on the grounds of its missing *o* altogether. Alternatively, or in addition, the qualification marks the impossibility of falsehood as Aristotle's inference, not the point Antisthenes was expressly arguing for (the references in n. 49 above establish that the denial of contradiction was the thesis for which Antisthenes was celebrated). But since Aristotle's inference, if such it be, is obviously correct, and must have been as obvious to Antisthenes as it was to Plato (*Euthydemus* 286c), it would be idle not to treat the two paradoxes as a pair.

statement (e.g. 'Socrates is musical'); otherwise put, that the essential constituents of a complex must be marked off from nonessential ones (cf. p. 144). He goes so far as to call Antisthenes simpleminded for not restricting his theory to accounts in sense (b), with regard to which it is true that each thing has only one.

Not that Aristotle would expect Antisthenes to agree to the narrowing, or even to the distinction between *logos* as definition and *logos* as statement. In his other substantial reference to Antisthenes, the obscure passage of *Metaphysics* VIII 3 which I set aside earlier, he counts Antisthenes as someone who disputes (or at least raises a difficulty about) the very possibility of definition. In Aristotle's book such an attack on definition shows a deplorable 'want of education'.

Now Aristotle was a contemporary reader of the *Theaetetus*—the only one about whom we in the twentieth century have enough information to say both that he studied Part III of the *Theaetetus* carefully and that he knew about Antisthenes. We can imagine him reading the Dream. He notes that Socrates is in danger of repeating the views of that simpleminded fellow Antisthenes unless sense (a) of 'account' is distinguished from sense (b) and the question posed: Which meaning of the word is appropriate to the theory Socrates is expounding? It is also clear to him that only in sense (b) could it be reasonable to suppose that each thing has a unique account of its own. He is already doing what Socrates will do later in the dialogue (206c–207a). Spurred by his recollection of Antisthenes, he is making the shift from Interpretation [a] to Interpretation [b] as he reads and reflects on what the Dream theory might reasonably intend us to understand by 'an account of *o*'.

I make no apology for invoking imagination here. It is a real possibility—not of course a certainty—that Socrates is alluding to Antisthenes when he uses the phrase 'proprietary account'. We can neither avoid asking what the sense of the allusion might have been nor answer the question with confidence. What we can do, with Aristotle's help, is try to imagine, as rigorously and clearly as we can, how a contemporary reader's knowledge of what Antisthenes said about accounts would affect his response to the Dream.

Back, then, to Aristotle. Besides emphasizing that for each thing there is only one statement, its proprietary account, Aristotle's report on Antisthenes gives equal weight to the converse point that each account is of or about no more than one thing. This suggests that Antisthenes' concern was not only with the nature of statements, but as much or more with the question what it is for a statement to be *about* an object *o*. Later in Part III, when Socrates examines the third meaning of 'account': (c) a differentiation of *o* from other things, he will be considerably exercised by the parallel question what it is for a certain kind of *judgement* to be about Theaetetus rather than anyone else. More precisely, and anticipating some details of the interpretation to be defended later, his question is this: Could knowledge of Theaetetus consist in being able to add an account of Theaetetus in sense (c) to a true judgement of identification concerning Theaetetus? No, he argues, because you will not produce a judgement identifying someone as Theaetetus rather than Theodorus or Socrates unless you are already thinking of everything that (would be mentioned in an account which) differentiates Theaetetus from others and makes him the particular person he is (209ac).

Suppose, then, that Antisthenes maintained that an account of *o* must differentiate *o* in the sense that it must identify *o* and distinguish it from other things. The account must include the constituents that make *o* what it is, if it is to be a statement about *o* rather than about something else similar to it in the respects listed. (To maintain this is to require that what or whom a statement is about be specified unambiguously within the statement itself; reference is to be secured without help from any action of the speaker's or contextual clues.) Paradox would ensue when the demand for differentiation joined up with Antisthenes' unwillingness to countenance a distinction between account as statement and account as definition or analysis. For without that distinction there would be no circumscribing the tally of things that make *o* what it is. There would be no saying 'These parts and those qualities make *o* what it is and are essential to its identity; the rest just happen to belong to *o*.' A truly differentiating list would swell to include every part and quality of *o*. There could be no more than one such list, which would be the one and only statement that was genuinely about *o* and nothing else. It would be a statement that was simultaneously the simplest adequate identification of *o* and an exhaustive description of *o*.[53]

---

53. This would not be the rejection of predication associated with the 'late-learners' of the *Sophist*, nor quite the view often ascribed to Antisthenes that every (legitimate) statement is a statement of identity, but rather a *merging* of description, analysis, and identification in one paradoxical notion of account.

Of course all this is speculation. No interpretative story about Antisthenes can be verified.[54] Let us, nonetheless, take stock.

Antisthenes has led us on an advance tour of the three meanings of 'account' that Socrates will later acknowledge as meanings which the theory might intend by the phrase 'an account of o'. We have imagined how, by rejecting or ignoring precisely the distinctions that Socrates will later draw for us, Antisthenes could arrive at the strange conclusion that nothing can be spoken of except by its own proprietary account. There is no denying the relevance of this imagined Antisthenes to our understanding of the Dream. But equally he cannot be, in any straightforward sense, its author. The Dream neither affirms nor denies that there is only one statement you can make about a complex. Rather, the voices which Socrates seemed to hear (a noteworthy plural: every other reference to the Dream theorist is singular) are hospitable to either broader or narrower meanings of 'account' without obliterating the distinction between them. The indeterminacy of the Dream leaves the reader free to fall into the Antisthenean paradoxes and free to avoid them by making the necessary distinctions.

It would be rash to conclude that the imagined Antisthenes is identical with the real Antisthenes of history. But even as an imagined possibility he can be a useful way to think about the Dream. His is the worst theory you can make from the text before us, combining the defects of Interpretation [a] with others peculiar to

54. Certainly not by the obscure passage of Aristotle (*Metaphysics* VIII 3, 1043b 23–32) which I set aside at the beginning (pp. 165–6). What Aristotle reports here is a puzzle propounded by 'the Antistheneans and similarly uneducated persons' to the effect that you cannot define/delimit what a thing is ('for a definition is a long *logos*'), though you can teach what it is like. The illustration given is: you cannot say what silver is, though you can say that silver is like tin. Is the point about definition being a long *logos* an echo of the reasoning we have just been through? Is it significant that 'Silver is like tin' is a relational statement which does not purport to be about silver *and nothing else*? Unfortunately, Aristotle does not elucidate. Unfortunately also, when he goes on to a contrast between definable (because composite) substances and their indefinable primary constituents (1043b 28–32), it is impossible to tell whether this is continuing the Antisthenean train of thought or resuming his own. No doubt it is significant that his reference to Antisthenes' puzzle is sandwiched between some objections to the idea of definition as an unstructured list (1043b 4–14) and a discussion of the sense in which a definition must be finite and complete (1043b 32 ff.). But it remains very unclear how his report of the puzzle fits into this wider context. In the end, with so many question marks over the passage, the only information it is safe to take from it, and the only information I have relied on (p. 169), is that Antisthenes cast doubt on the possibility of definition.

himself. Yet Antisthenes' theory of proprietary accounts bears a striking family resemblance to the best theory presently in sight. For consider Interpretation [b] with a list model of analysis (p. 144). This is a theory of accounts whereby contradiction and falsehood are impossible *when* an object is spoken of or expressed by a special account (analysis) of its own. No implication that this is the one statement you can make about the object, only that it is the one analysis you can give of it. Any list of elements differing from the special account will fail to be an analysis *of* that object; at best it will list the elements of something else. And this may be thought not a paradox but a rather good argument for viewing the special account as the differentiating condition of knowledge.[55]

Such a theory, moreover, would be an appropriate response to Socrates' response to the puzzles of Part II, where we saw him rejecting the idea that knowing a thing is a necessary condition for speaking or judging of it, but sympathetic to the idea that knowledge (at least when active) is a sufficient condition for not going wrong about a thing (at least in questions of identity). How better to realize this condition than by a complete account of what a thing is?

Another feature shared with Part II is the assumption that knowledge is a one-to-one relation between the mind and an individual knowable object (concrete or abstract) considered in and by itself. In Part II the imprints on the wax block were described as 'proper' (*oikeios*) to that which they are the imprints of, and vice versa (193c, 194b); likewise the birds in the aviary were each concerned with a single number. Then the imprints and birds were knowledge; now perhaps they are some kind of true judgement and something more is required for knowledge. But the something more—the analysis of *o* into its elements—is still, like the imprints and birds, concerned with *o* and nothing else. Each knowable object is to be grasped in and by a condition of the soul which Antisthenes would have every reason to describe as proprietary to *o*. His simpleminded, paradox-

---

55. Aristotle, for example, while rejecting the idea that a definition is an unstructured list (see previous note), was prepared to argue—at least on occasion, with qualifications and for certain types of example—that there is really no such thing as a false definition. When asked a question of the form 'What is *o*?', you either get the answer right or you miss *o* altogether. See *Metaphysics* IX 10, 1051b 27–1052a 4, *De Anima* III 6, 430b 26–31; Richard Sorabji, 'Myths about nonpropositional thought', in Malcolm Schofield & Martha Nussbaum edd., *Language and Logos: Studies in Ancient Greek Philosophy Presented to G.E.L. Owen* (Cambridge: 1982), 295–314; and the unitalicized parenthesis in the quotation on p. 168 above.

producing essay in semantics has been transformed into a challenging thesis in epistemology.

No imagination is needed to see that this epistemological challenge is one that Plato takes seriously. The assumption that knowledge is a one-to-one relation between mind and object is a major concern of the dialogue. In retrospect it can be seen to have ruled the discussion, save in one or two places,[56] ever since Theaetetus' tentative suggestion that knowing something is perceiving it (151e). But it will come under severe strain when the critical section of Part III gets going. So much so that, when Part III is finished and all its interpretations of Theaetetus' third definition have been thoroughly refuted, one moral we might wish to draw from the negative outcome of the whole dialogue is that knowledge is *not* the one-to-one (proprietary) relation it has by and large been assumed to be.

True judgement in the Dream

Closer to hand than any external source of inspiration is the context established for the Dream by its position in the dialogue. I hope that readers enjoyed the discussion of Wittgenstein and Antisthenes and found it instructive. But in each case it became clear that their semantic concerns, though not irrelevant, are marginal to the Dream. Let us therefore turn back to the central epistemological themes of the dialogue. Can these illuminate the aims of a theory of complexes and elements and tell us what the Dream is about?

The chief novelty of Part III, by comparison with what has gone before, is the separation of true judgement from knowledge. There are now three epistemic routes—perception, true judgement, and knowledge are all mentioned in the Dream—instead of the two explicitly acknowledged in Part II. Looking further back, we can see that the dialogue is at last separating out the three elements which the definition of knowledge as perception fused together to make the single epistemic route acknowledged in Part I.

The process has been gradual. In fact it is continuing still. In Part I true judgement was a necessary component of (Protagorean) perceptual awareness. In Part II it was separate from perception but not from knowledge. In Part III we have a choice. Interpretation [a] achieves no more than a nominal separation of true judgement

---

56. Most notably, in the final section of Part I (184a–186e) and the final section of Part II (200d–201c), the two places where we can be most confident that Socrates speaks for Plato himself.

from knowledge; two of its three epistemic routes are in substance one and the same (p. 138). But Interpretation [b] does bring out true judgement as a distinct presence on the stage. It is still a part of knowledge. But it is an independent part, which can and does occur separately in its own right. Neither Wittgenstein nor the imagined Antisthenes had anything helpful to say about true judgement. We must go back to the text and manage for ourselves.

At first reading the theory makes it one of the distinguishing features of complexes that they can be the objects of true judgement (202b). Elements, that is to say, cannot be the objects of true judgement.

If this is correct, the knowable is not just that of which there can be accounts but also that of which there can be true judgement. The two constituents of knowledge, accounts and true judgement, range over the same territory. Both demand a complex object. Of elements, by contrast, there are no accounts and no true judgements either.

This first reading poses no problem for Interpretation [a]. Elements which admit of no statement (= audible judgement) necessarily admit of no judgement (= silent statement) about them. But it does set a problem for Interpretation [b], which maintains that elements are unanalyzable, not that they are indescribable and cannot have statements made about them. If a statement such as '*e* is yellow' or 'That is *e*' could be true of an element, surely the corresponding judgement that *e* is yellow, or that that is *e*, must be possible as well?

One expedient for Interpretation [b] is to argue that Socrates does not in fact commit the theory to the view that true judgement concerning elements is impossible. Look more carefully. When Socrates says that elements are perceivable and does not say that complexes are, no-one infers that complexes ('we and everything else') are not perceivable. So, likewise, he says that complexes can be the objects of true judgement and does not say that elements can be too, but we should not from this silence infer that they cannot be the objects of true judgement.[57]

Alas, the two cases are different. The remark about elements being perceivable is a pause or reassurance inserted into the middle of a summing up of the difference between elements and complexes. We might fear that if elements are unknowable, we have no epistemic access to them at all. Socrates pauses to reassure us

57. So Fine [52], 373.

that we can get at elements through perception, and then resumes his summing up of the difference between elements and complexes. For the two cases to be alike he ought to have concluded his characterization of complexes with 'but they can be the objects of true judgement', in parallel to 'but they are perceivable' at the end of his characterization of elements. As it is, he says 'and they can be the objects of true judgement'. The whole balance of the sentence is against the suggestion that elements can be the objects of true judgement. That first reading was correct.

If one expedient fails, try another. A change in the meaning of 'account' may imply a corresponding change in the treatment of true judgement. When talking about 'account' in the first and widest of his three meanings, Socrates allows equally wide scope to the notion of true judgement. The content of a true judgement can be anything that anyone thinks about something, so long as the thought is correct (206de). But when he moves on to 'account' in sense (b), an enumeration of elements, he illustrates correct judgement by the list of nonelementary constituents, 'Wheels, axle, body, rails, yoke', which is all that he can manage in answer to the question 'What is a wagon?' (207ac). This correct judgement is an intermediate-level analysis. Is Socrates pretending that an intermediate analysis of the kind illustrated is the only type of correct judgement there can be? That would be very hard to believe. But he may be thinking that it is the only type of correct judgement relevant to the definition of knowledge. For when he develops the poet Hesiod's suggestion that expert knowledge of the being of a wagon requires adding to true judgement a complete enumeration of the 'one hundred timbers' of a wagon, the true judgement he is referring to is plainly his own 'Wheels, axle, body, rails, yoke' (207bc).

Interpretation [b] has much to gain and nothing to lose from following the example set by Socrates within the dialogue and narrowing the scope of true judgement to match its narrower sense of 'account'. First, the problem about how it can deny true judgement of elements is solved without doing violence to the sentence at 202b. If true judgement concerning *o* responds at the intermediate level to the same question, 'What is *o* considered in itself?', that the added account answers at the level of elements, then the denial of true judgement concerning elements follows at once. Unanalyzable elements have neither elementary *nor* nonelementary constituents.

Second, the narrowing has philosophical advantages. The definition 'Knowledge is true judgement with an account' is importantly vague and indeterminate about the relationship between the two constituents of knowledge. In fact, 'True judgement with an account' is essentially a list, like 'Wheels, axle, body, rails, yoke'; hence Socrates' willingness, on occasion,[58] to reverse the order and say 'An account with true judgement' (e.g. at 208b). Accordingly, one task for an interpretation is to *specify* a relationship as part of the theory. It is not enough for Interpretation [a] to say that true judgement concerning o is any true judgement you like and the added account simply a statement about o. The statement added to true judgement to constitute knowledge must be the verbalization *of* the true judgement (as it is at 206de), or else a true judgement that o is red plus a true statement that o is round would constitute knowledge of o. Comparable hotchpotch cases will arise for Interpretation [b] unless it too specifies a suitable relationship between true judgement and account.

Consider someone who can already provide a list of wagon elements '$e_1 \ldots e_{100}$' on demand. He then makes the judgement (as true now as it was in Hesiod's day) that every farmer needs a wagon. Does this improve his claim to have expert knowledge of the being of a wagon (207c)? What if he announces, correctly, that that thing rumbling down the hill towards us is a wagon? Such judgements, about wagons in general or some particular wagon, are ordinarily within the capacity of anyone. Readers may be able to imagine unusual circumstances in which judgements like these would be evidence that someone possessed and was using expert knowledge of what a wagon is. But they do not seem at all plausible as a *part* of that expertise itself. The correct judgement 'Wheels, axle, body, rails, yoke', on the other hand, fits into place immediately. Especially if Socrates is thinking, as Hesiod was, of the knowledge needed to *build* a wagon.[59]

Both the intermediate analysis (the true judgement) and the elementary analysis (the account) are concerned with the essential constituents of a wagon: constituents that help to make a wagon what it is (p. 144). Both analyses, moreover, are arguably necessary constituents in an expert's knowledge of what a wagon is. Socrates' correct judgement 'Wheels, axle, body, rails, yoke' is not enough

---

58. More occasions than Miss Levett's translation reveals.

59. The objection to hotchpotch cases under Interpretation [b] is well made by Nehamas [62], esp. 22–23, arguing against Fine [52] and Burnyeat [54], 188. But it is premature to reject, as Nehamas does, the whole idea of adding an account to true judgement to make knowledge. The narrower kind of true judgement which Socrates illustrates deserves a hearing.

by itself, because it invites further questions, 'What is a wheel?' or 'How is a wheel made?'[60] Equally it would be a poor sort of expertise that could list $e_1 \ldots e_{100}$ but had nothing to say about wheels, axle, and other nonelementary parts. Would you accept as a mechanic someone who could catalogue all the least components of a modern car—each nut and bolt, knob and wire—but had nothing to say about the engine or the lighting system? Would you be any happier with someone who had no idea of the internal mechanisms of these larger functional parts? It does seem that both levels of analysis are essential; they complement each other. True judgements that give an intermediate analysis of something are relevant to the kind of expert knowledge Socrates is now discussing, in a way that other true judgements are not.

Let us then allow Interpretation [b] to restrict the scope of true judgement to intermediate analysis. A remarkable consequence follows. We can rectify a number of the faults and obscurities in the Aviary's account of intellectual mistakes.

I have just mentioned the fact that Socrates is now analyzing expertise. This should remind us of earlier occasions, both in Part I (161c) and early in the Aviary section of Part II (198ab), when the focus of discussion changed from a conception of knowledge so mundane that any man (even, in Part I, any pig) can have it, to types of expertise which are transmitted by specialist teaching and learning. The dialogue has oscillated between these two poles ever since the opening scene (compare 144bd with 143d–144b and 145ce). The shift from Interpretation [a] to Interpretation [b] at 206e is the latest in a series of returns to the topic of expertise. But if you compare this occasion with the earlier ones, especially the Aviary, you will see that Socrates is now formulating important new points about the complexity of expertise.

He is still assuming, as in the Aviary, that knowledge is a one-to-one (proprietary) relation between the mind and its object (the being of a wagon). But now the object itself is complex, because analyzable, and the knowledge of it is complex, comprising both true judgement and an account, i.e. both intermediate level analysis and an enumeration of elements. It is the recognition of these matching complexities which permits a less simplistic account than

---

60. We may assume that his judgement is indeed correct. 'Axle' (in the singular) implies a vehicle with two wheels, not four. Further technical details, with pictures, in H. L. Lorimer, 'The Country Cart of Ancient Greece', *Journal of Hellenic Studies* 23 (1903), 132–51.

Socrates gave earlier of the dunce who judges that five and seven are eleven.

But first another preliminary point about the transition from Interpretation [a] to Interpretation [b] at 206e. Socrates starts to make more of a distinction than he has done before between true judgements and accounts, on the one hand, and the ability or capacity to produce them when asked, on the other. Strictly speaking, the constituents of knowledge are the capacities, not the performances in which they are expressed.

There was never any doubt that in the third definition of knowledge the phrase 'with an account' is shorthand for 'having an account' or 'being able to give an account'. The Dream soon expands 'without an account' into 'cannot give and take an account' (202c) and the remainder of Part III follows the same pattern. What knowledge requires is that you have and can give an account (206de, 207bc, 208b, 208c).[61] But with true judgement the distinction between act and ability is less clear—for reasons which take us back to the gradualness with which perception, true judgement, and knowledge have been separated from one another in the course of the dialogue.

Readers may have noticed an inconcinnity in Part II's treatment of the notion of judgement. Judgement is defined as a statement made to oneself (190a) and discussed throughout as an experience (187d) or episode (187e) occurring at a particular time and place. False judgements *happen*, as when Theaetetus, seeing a stranger in the distance, thinks that he is Socrates (191b). For true judgements the story is the same (e.g. 199b). Yet Theaetetus' second definition equates true judgement with knowledge, which is categorized, implicitly in the Wax Block (p. 100) and explicitly in the Aviary (p. 106), as a capacity. How can an episode be one and the same with a capacity?

Exactly this question could have been asked about Theaetetus' suggestion 'It seems to me that a man who knows something perceives what he knows' (151e). In effect, it was asked. Look back to the superficial linguistic arguments of 163a–165e and you will see that the more telling blows reflect the fact that, while perceiving is an episode, knowing is not. Plato makes it very clear, however, that in his view this sort of objection is not the right way to prove that knowledge is not perception. And by the end of Part I we find him introducing a distinction between the activities of seeing,

61. Recall that 197c distinguished two senses for the verb 'to have'.

hearing, etc., and the capacities or powers (185a, 185c, 185e) through which they are effected.

Similarly, Plato never objects that true judgement cannot be knowledge because it is not a capacity. He simply writes into Part III a distinction between the capacity for a certain kind of true judgement and the episodes of judging in which it is expressed. The distinction is not evident in the Dream, where the description of true judgement as the soul being in a state of truth about something (202bc) would fit either capacity or performance. Nor is it evident when Socrates considers Interpretation [a] at 206de. It *becomes* evident as he passes to Interpretation [b], saying that 'Wheels, axle, body, rails, yoke' is the best answer he would be *able* to give to the question 'What is a wagon?' (207a) and continuing thereafter to treat the capacity, not the act of truly judging something, as what knowledge conjoins with the ability to give an account.[62]

We are now ready to resume the double dialogue of Part II.

Recall that the failing charged against the Aviary was that it is absurd to explain error as the exercise of knowledge (199d). The dunce who judges that five and seven are eleven cannot be exercising *knowledge* of eleven. I had already urged the need for a third epistemic route which, unlike perception, would involve thinking and judging but which, unlike knowledge, would be compatible with mistakes (p. 112 ff.). Theaetetus promptly suggested that the dunce is exercising a 'piece of ignorance' concerning eleven (199e). I responded by proposing that we might identify a 'piece of ignorance' with what the Dream calls ignorant true judgement (p. 117). And I obscurely conjectured that it would have something to do with the mind grasping an object in part but not whole or whole but not in part (pp. 122–3).

Interpretation [b] can now offer a more precise specification. The dunce is exercising a capacity for intermediate analysis of eleven. He has learned, perhaps, that eleven is nine and two, and this partial grasp of eleven enables him to think of eleven and judge that it is five and seven. No breach of K' occurs, because what he is using is a capacity for true judgement concerning eleven, not knowledge.

Suppose he has also learned that twelve is ten and two. He has a capacity for intermediate analysis of twelve. It would be difficult

---

62. This confirms that Miss Levett was right to translate *doxa* as 'judgement' throughout Parts II and III; cf. p. 69 above. Belief is neither an episode nor a capacity, though it is often the result of an episode of judging.

to imagine him wondering 'What is ten and two?' and answering 'Eleven' by mistake.[63] That would indicate that he had not yet learned his lesson properly. But twelve units differently arranged, as in the question 'What is five and seven?', would not necessarily activate the lesson. In asking the question he can be thinking of twelve without recognizing it as twelve, even though twelve is a number concerning which he has true judgement.

The key innovation here is that one partial lesson can be independent of another. To have learned that twelve is ten and two and that eleven is nine and two is not necessarily to have learned that twelve is five and seven or that eleven is five and six. A fortiori someone who can divide eleven into nine and two does not thereby have full knowledge of eleven. Nor yet does someone who can enumerate or count all the elementary units of which eleven is composed. Both capacities must be acquired, not to mention further intermediate divisions (cf. 204bc), before we can say, 'Here is a person who really knows eleven—knows it through and through. You won't catch them judging that five and seven is eleven.'

Readers are now invited to go back over pp. 115–19, pp. 122–3, to form their own assessment of how far matters have improved. What are the prospects for an account of unknowledgeable thinking which appeals, not to a semantic distinction between the different descriptions under which a number can be thought of,[64] but to an epistemological distinction between the different partial lessons that the thinker can activate? As before, it is a delicate matter to calibrate Platonic devices with the modern techniques we are familiar with. For that very reason it is philosophically rewarding to try.

I trust that no-one will object that, even if Interpretation [b] has the resources to do better than the Aviary with the dunce who judges that five and seven are eleven, Part III does not resume the discussion of false judgement. We can resume it, if we care about the problem. Even without Antisthenes, Interpretation [a] is a constant reminder of the puzzles of Part II. It would be a slow mind that refused to see that if, on Interpretation [b], the *addition* of a capacity for elementary analysis to a capacity for intermediate analysis gives a person knowledge and excludes mistakes, then, with the *subtraction* of the former capacity from the latter, it ought to

63. He might do it because he was not concentrating or in his cups, but that is not the sort of case we were discussing. The Aviary was designed to explain real, not accidental, mistakes of calculation (196b).

64. As proposed by Lewis [48]—Part II, n. 43.

become intelligible how mistakes occur. In short, if the idea of a double dialogue is valid, Plato has every right to expect us to use the resources he has provided.

In any case, the Aviary was designed to do more than explain false judgements of pure thought, where perception is not involved. It was also a positive picture of true judgements and knowledgeable thinking, in cases where perception is not involved. The positive picture is undoubtedly improved by Interpretation [b]'s emphasis on the complexity of expertise and a corresponding complexity in the object known. Gone is the simplistic assumption that a single bird will do for each number. New questions open up about the character of the complexity on either side of the relationship between knower and the known (see below). That improvement and these questions are one sufficient answer to the question 'What is the Dream about? What is the theory of complexes and elements for?'

It is only one answer because, of course, if the reply to the question 'What is the theory we are discussing?' is 'Make it and see' (p. 136), then the reply to the question 'What is the theory for?' ought to be 'Make it and see what you can do with it.' That the theory made by Interpretation [b] can be used for an improved understanding of false judgement is a potent mark to its credit. No doubt this is subordinate to its more far-reaching use to launch the dialogue's final assault on the question 'What is the nature of expertise?'. That, after all, was the question with which Socrates began the whole inquiry (145de, p. 3). But we can find a route back to the discussion of expertise by considering an objection to the *rapprochement* just concluded between the Aviary and Interpretation [b].

The objection is this. The Dream says that elements are perceivable (202b). The 'one hundred timbers' of a wagon are obviously perceivable, as are wheels, axle, etc. Numbers and their constituents, however, are not perceivable. And surely that puts a question mark over the making of connections between the Dream and Part II?

My reply is that there are independent reasons for preferring to put the question mark on the Dream's reluctance to look beyond the realm of the perceivable.

Perception in the Dream

Every reader of Part III wonders why the Dream insists on perceivable elements. An object which has perceivable elements must be perceivable itself.[65] The Dream maintains that 'we and *everything else'* have perceivable elements. It thereby commits itself to an ontology of sensible things and nothing else, and to the thesis that knowledge is exclusively of (complex) sensible things.

Such a view should be anathema to Plato. Yet nowhere in Part III does he attack the claim that elements are perceivable. What he targets for criticism (202de, 203c) is the thesis (the Dream theory's elucidation of AK_o) that elements are unknowable and knowledge is exclusively of complex things. We are clearly meant to conclude that elements are knowable (206b); on that point the Dream was wrong. This does not entail that the Dream was also wrong to say that elements are perceivable. But it does remove the *motivation* suggested earlier (pp. 174–5) for Socrates' statement that elements are perceivable. If elements are not unknowable, we will not fear that we have no epistemic access to them at all, and we will not need to be reassured that they are at least perceivable. We will be free to speculate that some elements—the elements of some things, perhaps even some of the elements of all complexes—are not perceivable.

But before casting off the restrictive commitment to perceivable elements, we should examine it more closely. On Interpretation [a], perceivable elements, be they parts, ingredients, or qualities, are named (the niggardly version) or implied (the more charitable version) whenever a statement is made about a complex object. They are presumably perceived when, or on some of the occasions when, the object itself is perceived, even though Interpretation [a] denies they can be picked out individually for identification and description. For Interpretation [a], therefore, to remove the restriction to perceivable elements would simply be to let the Dream theory take cognizance of the full range of everyday conversation, in which much is mentioned that is neither perceivable nor constituted out of perceivable elements (cf. p. 139). With Interpretation [b] the liberating effect goes further and requires a lengthier explanation.

Interpretation [b]'s perceivable elements, whether parts, ingredients, or qualities, are named whenever an account is given of a complex and implied whenever an intermediate analysis is given. The 'one hundred timbers' of a wagon are presumably perceived when, or on some of the occasions when, a wagon is perceived,

---

65. Cf. Frege, *The Foundations of Arithmetic* (1884), trans. J. L. Austin (Oxford: 1950), 31: 'It does not make sense that what is by nature sensible should occur in what is nonsensible'.

even if they are not picked out individually for identification and description. On the other hand, Interpretation [b], unlike Interpretation [a], does allow an element to be identified and described on its own. When we come to the model of letters and syllables, we will find that an important part of learning to read and write is learning to discriminate each letter with the aid of eye and ear (206a). There is no reason why, *mutatis mutandis*, perception should not play a similarly positive role in the process of acquiring expertise about wagons. Nevertheless, perception is not involved in asking and answering the question 'What is a wagon?' any more than it is involved in asking and answering the question 'What is five and seven?'.

'What is a wagon?' is an abstract, general question, about the essence or being (207c) of any wagon anywhere. A list of wagon elements '$e_1 \ldots e_{100}$' purports to give the makeup of any wagon anywhere; so too, at the intermediate level, does 'Wheels, axle, body, rails, yoke'. The complex thereby analyzed is not a particular wagon you can see, touch, and load up with hay. It is the type or kind of vehicle of which Farmer Giles has one example, Farmer Brown another. It is an abstract, not a wooden object: in the traditional jargon, a universal. As such, it is well suited to illustrate the ways in which Interpretation [b] can improve upon the Aviary's account of knowledgeable and unknowledgeable thinking in cases where perception is not involved.

These last remarks have revealed yet another indeterminacy in the Dream. 'We and everything else' are complexes. Interpretation [a] finds it natural to spell this out as: Theaetetus, Theodorus, Farmer Giles's wagon, this stone, and every perceivable complex object you can make statements about. Interpretation [b], it now appears, would mention man, badger, wagon, clay, and every other *type* of perceivable complex object that you might hope to analyze or define. Both are compatible with the text. 'We and everything else' can as easily refer to kinds as to particular examples of them. But if Interpretation [b] is about the analysis of kinds or types, then the shift from Interpretation [a] to Interpretation [b] is a transition from particular to general as well as from statement to analysis, from act of judgement to capacity, from mundane knowledge to expertise.

It can, however, be misleading to say that 'Wheels, axle, body, rails, yoke' is an analysis of a universal, not an analysis of a particular wagon. It can sound, absurdly, as if an abstract object has wheels going round and round on an axle. That is not what is meant at all.

What is meant is that *every* wagon has wheels and an axle, in virtue of being a wagon. An analysis of a universal is a universal analysis of its instances.

It may be helpful to illustrate this point by comparing the first major definition of the dialogue and the last, 'Clay is earth mixed with liquid' (147c) and 'Knowledge is true judgement with an account' (201cd). Being definitions, both are abstract and general. Not all definitions define by analysis (see below), but both of these do. They purport to give the makeup of clay and knowledge wherever they occur. Clay and knowledge in this context are therefore universals. But to say that earth and liquid are the essential constituents of clay, true judgement and an account the essential constituents of knowledge, is not to say that one abstract object is composed of earth and liquid and another of cognitive capacities. It is to say, abstractly and generally, that any and every piece of clay, any and every instance of knowledge, has these constituents, in virtue of being clay and being knowledge.

Some philosophers, Plato among them, wish to assert that universals exist; others do not. But this, one of the central issues in the traditional 'problem of universals', does not concern us here. I am not discussing the ultimate ontological status of the abstract general thing which is the subject of the definitional statement 'Clay is earth mixed with liquid'. I am trying to clarify what it means to say that the subject of this analysis is abstract and general. Still less need we raise the question whether there is a Platonic Form of clay, wagon, or knowledge, which would take us beyond the claim that these universals exist to the further claim that they exist apart from and independently of their instances (cf. p. 38). That question is of interest to Plato, but not here.[66] All we need to recognize for present purposes is that it is legitimate to speak of analyzing types of thing as well as particular things. Then we can distinguish the analysis of abstract objects (universals, like the types we are discussing, and numbers) from the analysis of concrete particular things such as Theaetetus or Farmer Giles's wagon. As with identification (p. 68), I shall speak of the former as abstract analysis, of the latter as

---

66. *Parmenides* 130cd is hesitant about a Form of clay (translators there write 'mud', but the Greek word is the same as at *Theaet.* 147ac). *Phaedrus* 247de describes, and *Parmenides* 133b ff. makes puzzles about, a Form of knowledge. Forms for each type of artefact, like bed or wagon, are postulated at *Republic* 596bc ff., but Aristotle, *Metaphysics* I 9, 991b 6–7 implies that artefacts are not included in the Theory of Forms he is familiar with. In sum, clay, wagon, and knowledge are as problematic a trio of Forms as you could expect to find.

concrete analysis. What came to light three paragraphs ago is that Interpretation [b] aspires to give a theory of abstract, not of concrete analysis.

Apply this to the statement at 202b that elements are perceivable. Under Interpretation [b] the Dream yields a theory of abstract analysis, but it is restricted to the abstract analysis of *perceivable* types of thing, i.e. types each and every example of which is perceivable, such as clay and wagon. They and they alone can have perceivable elements (parts, ingredients, or qualities). Officially, therefore, the theory made by Interpretation [b] does not reach to the abstract analysis of nonsensible types of thing, i.e. types no example of which is perceivable, like knowledge. The essential constituents of knowledge, according to Interpretation [b]'s reading of Def. K_0, are a twinned pair of capacities, and capacities are not the sort of thing you can perceive with the senses (cf. *Republic* 477c). The same goes for the abstract analysis of numbers: this too lies beyond the reach of the theory, so long as it is restricted to perceivable types.

Were it not that AK_0 supplies a motivation for making elements perceivable, the restriction would seem arbitrary in a dialogue which has let abstract identification and misidentification range over a variety of kinds of abstract object. Look back to the collection of impossible judgements at 190bc, where the mistaken identifications of beauty and ugliness, cow and horse, two and one, stand, or rather fall, together. More recently, in Part II's positive treatment of abstract misidentification, there was a bird in the aviary not only for each number but also for each letter I know (199a), and letters are perceivable types. The discussion dealt with numbers and an arithmetical mistake. But the model itself was designed for abstract identification and misidentification involving perceivable types as well as abstract identification and misidentification involving numbers. An improved model for the former should therefore help with the latter—as indeed it did. In short, once AK_0 is rejected, the restriction to perceivable types appears to be an unnecessary limitation which debars the theory from recognizing the extent of its own capacities.

But we are free to take an active part in the inquiry, even if it takes us beyond the confines of the written dialogue. We can question whether the restriction is necessary or wise. And it is clear that we must question it if we want a full understanding of expertise.

Remember Theaetetus' first answer to the question 'What is knowledge?': geometry and the other mathematical sciences, cobbling and other practical crafts (146cd). There is no reason to confine the Dream theory (as developed by Interpretation [b]) to everyday crafts of making and doing. The wainwright's expertise is such a craft, as are the various clay-using trades of 147ab; such skills are necessarily and properly based on perceivable elements. But the phrase 'we and everything else' points to a larger scheme of inquiry and a scientific study of natural kinds in which the question 'What is man?' would have the central place envisaged for it during the Digression in Part I (174ab). The idea of expertise about man is heavy with moral and political implications, as Plato well knew (175c); it was his most persistent dream. But however far-reaching the ambitions of the Dream as we are now viewing it, they do not extend to abstract mathematics. This is the most obvious effect of the restriction to perceivable types, and the one which the dialogue most obviously encourages us to be impatient with.

Mathematical expertise and mathematical topics are profusely illustrated in the opening scene and frequently mentioned in the subsequent discussion (154bc, 162c, 162e, 165a, 169a, 170d, 173e–174a, 185cd, 190bc, 195e ff., 204be). The restriction of the theory to perceivable types stops it taking account of the complexity of mathematical knowledge and the complexity of abstract mathematical objects. Should a budding mathematical genius like Theaetetus be content with that? Should we, who have read this dialogue from the beginning?

Lurking, moreover, in the text of the Dream itself is some of the mathematical terminology that will be used when Theaetetus grows up and moves geometry forward from the particular cases of incommensurability proved by Theodorus to a general analysis of incommensurability. In this terminology, traces of which survive in Euclid, *Elements* X Defs. 3–4, there is an important contrast between the word *rhētos* (used of lines which are commensurable either in length or in square and of commensurable areas) and the word *alogos* (used of lines and areas which are not thus commensurable). The same pair of words are in contrast at 202b, where 'expressible' translates *rhētos* and 'unaccountable' (likewise 'without an account' at 201d) translates *alogos;* the contrast is repeated at 205de. Add the fact that *logos*, the key word in the Dream, is the Greek for 'ratio', which makes it a key word in the mathematical theory of irrationals, and it begins to seem likely that at least some of Plato's readers would wonder whether an allusion to mathematical usage was intended. Implicit in the very language of the Dream is a question whether the restriction to perceivable types is necessary or wise.

But more is at stake than mathematics. Let us go back to the observation (p. 185) that the theory made by Interpretation [b] does not reach to the abstract analysis of nonsensible types of thing such as knowledge, the essential constituents of which are not perceivable. The abstract analysis 'Knowledge is true judgement with an account' is *part* of the theory to which this observation applies. In an important sense, the theory does not recognize its own account of knowledge. It has only a partial grasp of itself. More dramatically put, the theory does not know what knowledge is, nor can we know through it, not simply because we have it upon hearsay (p. 130), but for the deeper reason that it does not know itself.

We are now ready for a simple lesson in spelling.

The theory at Stage Three: letters and syllables (202c–203c)

With the introduction of the model of letters and syllables, the abstract indeterminacies of Socrates' dream give way to the limpid specificity of the first syllable of Socrates' name. 'What is SO?', asks Socrates, pursuing the thought that syllables (the complexes of language) have accounts, whereas letters (the elements of language) do not. Theaetetus replies that it is S and O, and they agree that this should stand as the account of the syllable SO. But he cannot produce an account of the letter S in the same way. 'How *can* anyone give the letters of a letter?' (203ab).

The passage bears the hallmark of Interpretation [b]. 'What is SO?' is a question of the form 'What is *o* considered in itself?'. The answer is an analysis which lists the essential constituents of the syllable, the letters which make it the syllable it is. The letters are not analyzable in the same way, so they are elementary constituents and the analysis is an account in sense (b): an enumeration of all the elements.

Statements can be made about unanalyzable letters. One such statement, that S is 'a mere sound like a hissing of the tongue', is what explains why S is unanalyzable (203b). The example of letters brings out very clearly that to be unanalyzable is not at all the same as to be indescribable.

Finally, letters are perceivable types. Here is a box of letters:

How many letters does it contain? If you answer 'Two', you are treating S and O as *types*. In this sense there are just 26 letters in the English alphabet, 24 in the Greek. If you say 'Six', you are counting the *tokens* or particular examples of S and O. In this sense innumerable letters are inscribed and uttered every day.[67] Both answers are legitimate, but it is clearly types, not tokens, that Theaetetus is referring to when he speaks of the seven vowels of ancient Greek (203b). The letters and syllables of the model are types, and the account of SO as S and O is a paradigm for abstract rather than concrete analysis. Interpretation [b] indisputably prevails.

It prevails, however, without any suggestion that this is what the Dream theorist intended all along. We are told that the theory was conceived with the model of letters and syllables in view (202e). We are not told how it was conceived that the model should be used. Socrates and Theaetetus undertake to test the theory by testing the model on and for themselves (203a). They will interrogate letters and syllables as if they were hostages (202e) for the elements and complexes of the theory. Where letters and syllables provide a satisfactory exemplification of the theses of the theory, the latter will be accepted as true. Unsatisfactory answers from the alphabet will be held against the theory. This is no longer exposition but inquiry. It is Socrates' and Theaetetus' own thoughts about letters and syllables, as formulated in the exchange at 203ab, which now give the edge to Interpretation [b].

Stage Three is in fact largely taken up with Socrates and Theaetetus declaring their own minds on the several theses of the theory. To recapitulate, there are three theses, arranged (as Socrates recognizes at 203c) in an argument:

Def. K_p Knowing o is having true judgement concerning o with an account (*logos*) of o.

AL_o There actually are some objects of which there is no account, and others that have an account.

AK_o Some objects are unknowable, others knowable,

where the deduction of 'others knowable' requires the true judgement presupposition we noticed on p. 132–3 above. At Stage Two AL_o and AK_o were elucidated by

---

67. 'Letter' is to be understood throughout the discussion as covering both written letters and the sounds (phonemes) which written letters represent. Cf. note *ad* 202e.

$AL_{e/c}$ Elements have no account; complexes do have accounts

and

$AK_{e/c}$ Elements are unknowable, complexes knowable.

(These formulations assume, as Socrates does, that both elements and complexes actually exist.) Finally, the decision to treat letters and syllables as hostages for the elements and complexes of the theory is a decision to let $AL_{e/c}$ and $AK_{e/c}$ stand or fall by the still more specific theses

$AL_{l/s}$ Letters have no account; syllables do have accounts

and

$AK_{l/s}$ Letters are unknowable, syllables knowable.

Theaetetus is pleased with the whole thing (202ce). But Socrates says that he does not like $AK_{e/c}$ (202de). He prepares to demolish it by refuting $AK_{l/s}$ (203a, 203c). Since $AK_{e/c}$ is the Dream theory's elucidation of AK_o, which follows validly (granted the true judgement presupposition) from Def. K_o and AL_o, we are naturally curious to know what he thinks of the two premises of the basic argument (cf. p. 134).

About the first premise he is surprisingly vague. His rhetorical question 'For what knowledge could there be apart from an account and correct judgement?' (202d) implies the answer 'None', but all this tells us is that an account and correct judgement are necessary conditions for knowledge. Does he think them jointly sufficient, as they need to be if Def. K is the correct definition of knowledge? What meaning of 'account' and what scope of true judgement is he accepting as essential constituents of knowledge? Does he even agree with the voices in his dream that a definition of knowledge should be couched in terms of objects rather than propositions? These questions remain open.

The second premise is approved in the exchange between Socrates and Theaetetus at 203ab. More precisely, $AL_{e/c}$ is approved by endorsement of $AL_{l/s}$. The surprise here is the explanation with which Theaetetus follows up his rhetorical question 'How *can* anyone give the letters of a letter?'. He draws on a classification of letters which makes it transparently clear how each letter could be defined by its place in the system and its specific difference from other letters in the same immediate grouping. Three such groupings are presupposed, according as a letter has (i) voice (in modern terminology these are the vowels), (ii) sound without voice (semivowels), or (iii) neither voice nor sound (mutes).[68] Thus S is one of the letters in group (ii), distinguished from its fellows (e.g. L and R) by the characteristic hiss to which Theaetetus refers. In effect, Theaetetus gives an account of the letter S in order to explain why letters have, as he puts it, 'no sort of account whatever'.

It is not, of course, the same *sort* of account as the previous account of the syllable SO as S and O. It does not define by analysis into elements, but by relating S to other letters in the classification and specifying respects of sameness and difference. It moves outwards, so to speak, not inwards. In technical language, it is a definition *per genus et differentiam*, but I shall subsume it under a vaguer and more general contrast between definition by classification and definition by analysis. The latter is what Socrates was asking for when he said 'let us have the account of S *in the same way*'. The former is what Theaetetus implicitly gave in explanation of his inability to meet the request. It is also the kind of definition that Theaetetus himself contributed in the mathematics scene at 147e–148b.

Is Plato encouraging us to be impatient with Part III's exclusive concentration on definition by analysis?[69] I hope that readers will agree that he is. But let us be clear, as with the double dialogue of Part II (p. 118), that this is a response we are making to the text, not the decypherment of its hidden meaning or the discovery of Plato's own preferred solution to the problem set by AK_0. An idea is put in front of us, the idea of definition by classification. It is not taken up and developed in the written dialogue. We can only discover what it might contribute to the inquiry by taking it up and thinking with it ourselves.

Suppose for a moment that knowledge of o was defined as true judgement concerning o with a definition by classification of o. Not only would elements then be knowable, but knowledge of any object o would involve other objects besides o. Knowledge would no longer be a one-to-one (proprietary) relation between the knowing mind and o considered in and by itself; o could only be known as part of a whole interrelated system.

A splendid result, one might think (cf. pp. 172–3). But here's the snag. AL_0 and AK_0 still hold. Only now it is ultimate genera that have no accounts and are unknowable. The parts are knowable but

---

68. For a more formal statement of this classification, see *Cratylus* 424c (where it is credited to contemporary grammarians) and *Philebus* 18bc.
69. Cf. Fine [52], 380.

not the whole. Whether definition moves inwards or outwards, it is a linear process and must eventually reach something which cannot be defined in the same way as the things it helps to define. So it is no solution to replace one sort of definition by another. Plato may have put Theaetetus' embryonic classification of letters in front of us as a suggestive pointer to another path of inquiry. He should not, if he is clearheaded, be hinting that a classification within which each letter could be located and defined by its relation to the others would avoid the regress to unknowables.

An analogous and equally serious regress threatens, of course, if Def. K is construed as Def. $K_{p(e)}$ or Def. $K_{p(j)}$ (cf. p. 133). All it takes to get the regress going is the plausible assumption that explanation or justification is a linear process like definition. Socrates' vagueness about how much, or what version, of Def. K he is approving at 202d may be a suggestive pointer to other paths we might have travelled from Stage One, but none of them escapes the difficulty. We face the regress in the version set for the Dream theory by Interpretation [b]'s understanding of 'account' as 'completed analysis into elements'. But it is important to be aware that this is a special case of a quite general problem which many other epistemologies, ancient and modern, have to confront.

Parts and wholes: (i) the dilemma (203c–205e)

To read the middle portion of Part III is to be reminded of the feelings induced by the middle portion of the whole dialogue: first seasickness, then the relief of plain sailing.

In the first and longest section (203c–205e), a dilemma is mounted to prove that $AK_{1/s}$ (and hence $AK_{e/c}$) is false. It is necessarily false because its falsity follows from each of a pair of exhaustive alternatives. Either

(I) A syllable is (the same as) its several constituent letters,

or

(II) A syllable is not (the same as) its several constituent letters, being a single form resulting from their combination.[70]

70. I insert 'the same as' because Socrates makes it very clear in the sequel, as he does not when the disjunction is first stated at 203c, that (I) and (II) are to be construed as, respectively, affirming and denying the *identity* of a syllable with its

(I) is alleged to make letters as knowable as syllables, (II) to make syllables as unknowable as letters. Either way, it is false that letters are unknowable and syllables can be known. It is necessarily false because (I) and (II) exhaust the possibilities: one or the other (but not both) of them must be true.

The pattern is neat, but the arguments are tricky. It is quite a challenge to keep them under control and not succumb to another bout of nausea. Theaetetus struggles manfully, and in his resistance to the arguments gives plenty of signs to the reader that a challenge is what Plato intends the dilemma section to be.

The second section (206ab) is as brief and straightforward as the Jury section of Part II. Socrates argues that $AK_{e/c}$ is as a matter of fact false to our experience of mastering the alphabet and other domains, where knowledge is both built up from and grounded on a secure grasp of the elements of the subject. Knowledge of elements is primary.

I emphasise the resemblance to Part II for two reasons. One is that readers were promised that the dialectic of parts and wholes in Part III would be relevant to certain issues in Part II (p. 123). The other is that, if the dilemma section is a challenge like the puzzles of Part II, it calls for a reading strategy similar to that which kept seasickness at bay before. The dilemma is not needed to prove that $AK_{e/c}$ is false. That job is done independently in the second section at 206ab, and Socrates winds up by giving it as his opinion that the falsity of $AK_{e/c}$ could be shown in other ways as well (206c). Furthermore, the dilemma arguments for the falsity of $AK_{e/c}$ are patently unsound. Let us therefore formulate the challenge: Spot the false assumption which makes them unsound. We may presume that some important moral is to be won by reflecting on these arguments, or else Plato would not have spun them out at such length.

Fortunately, the dialogue makes it very clear what the false assumption is. It is the principle

WP A whole is (the same as) all its constituent parts.

More provokingly and metaphysically: anything which has parts just is those parts and nothing more. Or to use a formulation often

---

letters. Watch for the words 'same' and 'different' at 203e, 204a, 205b, 205d. Without the insert it would be possible to distinguish an 'is' of composition from the 'is' of identity so as to be able to say, truly and without inconsistency, both that a syllable *is* (composed of) its letters and that it *is not* (identical with) the letters. See David Wiggins, *Sameness and Substance* (Oxford: 1980), 30 ff.

found in modern discussions: a thing is merely the sum of its parts (if it has any). Whichever version you look at, it is easy to sense that something is wrong but you need to formulate subtle distinctions to say exactly what it is. This is the harder and more important challenge of the dilemma arguments. Experienced readers will know that much metaphysics can hang on how successfully the challenge is faced.

In modern philosophy WP is commonly discussed as a thesis about particular physical objects like this table or that tree. Can any such object be identified with the sum of its constituent atoms? Can my boat survive the replacement (simultaneous or successive) of all its planks? These are intriguing questions, but since Interpretation [b], now prevailing, makes a theory of abstract rather than concrete analysis, we shall be concerned in the first instance with WP as a thesis about types. The syllables over which (I) and (II) divide are (perceivable) types.

At the level of types WP is a denial of structure. By way of illustration, consider the following questions. Does the first syllable of Socrates' name occur in the name 'Aristotle'? No, because S and O are not juxtaposed. Does it occur in the name 'Demosthenes'? No, because although S and O are juxtaposed, they are the wrong way round. Yet if the syllable SO was *just* the letters S and O, and nothing more, the answer to both questions would be 'Yes'. S and O are indeed all the letters of the syllable SO. But they do not make SO unless they are juxtaposed in that order.

Another example: accepting that earth and liquid are the two constituents of clay, we should not infer that the verb phrase 'mixed with' is idle in the definition 'Clay is earth mixed with liquid'. Otherwise anyone who looks at a puddle in a ploughed field could claim to have found clay. A third case came up earlier when we noticed that 'Knowledge is true judgement with an account' omits to specify a suitable relationship between true judgement and account (pp. 175–6).

These are three examples in which something essential is missed out when a question of the form 'What is *o*?' is answered by an analysis which merely enumerates elementary or nonelementary constituents. 'S and O' does not specify the *arrangement* of the letters, 'Earth and liquid' omits the *mixture* of ingredients, 'True judgement with an account' is silent about the *relationship* of one capacity to another. The extra factor which these analyses leave out is not a further constituent; *ex hypothesi* all the constituents are accounted for. The extra factor is the structure which unifies the constituents into a complex whole. For these examples and others like them, WP is false.[71]

WP is first stated, with a flourish, at 204a, in the course of the argument under (II). Theaetetus denies it, then hesitates over one version of it (204ab), and is finally overwhelmed by the elaborate and tricky 'proof' by which WP is secured (204b–205a)—though not without some qualms along the way and a flicker of resistance at 204e. Once granted WP, Socrates proceeds, reasonably enough, as follows.

The assumption of the argument is (II) that a syllable is not the same as its letters (203e, 205b). Theaetetus agrees that letters are the only natural candidates for the parts of a syllable; if you are looking for a syllable's component parts, it would be ridiculous to suggest any other items than the letters (205b).[72] So the assumption comes to this, that a syllable is not the same as its parts. By WP anything with parts is the same as those parts. A syllable, therefore, if it is not the same as its parts, has no parts. The upshot is that if a syllable is not a whole of which the letters are parts, it is not a whole of parts at all.[73] And a syllable which is partless, i.e. simple and incomposite, must be unaccountable and unknowable for the same reason as the elementary letters are (205ce). Thus WP is the crux of the argument under (II) and is signalled as such by the manoeuvring undertaken to overcome Theaetetus' resistance to it.

But at 205d Socrates implies that his argument under (I) also depended on WP, because it assumed that a syllable is a whole which has letters as its constituent parts. Socrates, in other words, takes

(I) A syllable is (the same as) its several constituent letters

to be a special case of WP. Now the argument was that from (I) it follows that a syllable like SO cannot be known without both its

---

71. Aristotle, *Topics* VI 13, 150a 15–17, goes so far as to say that *any* definition of the form 'A and B' or 'A with B' is vulnerable to all the arguments against WP. He is recommending tactics for dialectical debate, not stating metaphysical doctrine, but the chapter is extremely relevant to Part III.

72. This agreement is not so innocent as it may look. Intuitively, it does seem ridiculous to divide SO into four half-letters ᴄ & ɔ & ᴖ & ᴗ. But why? Easy as it would be to take an axe and hack a wagon into a hundred splintered pieces, it seems ridiculous to offer these as the elements of a wagon instead of Hesiod's 'one hundred timbers'. Again, why? Perhaps these and other counterintuitive divisions would not be ridiculous if WP was really true.

73. What on earth is it then? And how are we now to conceive a single form arising from the combination of letters, as described in the addendum to (II)? To complain about these obscurities is to anticipate and reinforce the next and final step in the deduction.

constituent letters S and O being known, and further, that not only *both* letters but *each* letter individually will be known by anyone who knows the syllable (203cd). To use an obvious symbolism: $K(SO) \rightarrow K(S \& O) \rightarrow K(S) \& K(O)$. You may well think the inferences scandalous, especially the second. But consider a couple of examples for which WP seems adequate.

The answer to the question 'Who are the Dioscuri?' is: Castor and Pollux. Nothing further need be said. It is true that they are twins and had various adventures together, ending up as stars in the sky. This explains why our language has a (plural) name for the two of them. But to speak of the Dioscuri is not necessarily to imply that they are together, or even that they are both alive. It is just to speak of Castor and Pollux. Conversely, it would be correct to say that I mentioned the Dioscuri several times in the Introduction to Part II, even though I used the singular names 'Castor' and 'Pollux', never the plural 'Dioscuri'.

This example is a plural particular. At the level of particulars, WP is a denial that structure (arrangement, togetherness) is essential to a thing's being the particular thing it is. (Would New Zealand still exist if North Island drifted off to South America? If not, togetherness or proximity of parts is essential to New Zealand as it is not to the Dioscuri.) The next example is a particular token of a definable type. Imagine that you have five wagons in a barn, and focus your mind on the wheels of the first, the axle of the second, the body of the third, the rails of the fourth, and the yoke of the fifth. The object composed of these five parts would be a wagon if WP was true of wagons. It is not a wagon for the same reason as S and O in 'Aristotle' or 'Demosthenes' do not make the syllable SO: the parts are not connected in the right way. We may call it a wagonsum, for the entity we are now speaking of really is a mere sum of wagon parts.[74] And we may define the (perceivable) type of which it is a token by saying that the answer to the question 'What is a wagonsum?' is, precisely, 'Wheels, axle, body, rails, yoke'.

74. Technically sophisticated readers are asked to note that I do not mean it is what logicians call a mereological sum. That would entail applying WP to wheels as well as to wagonsums, with the result that a wagonsum could survive as a heap of sawdust. Nor is it the set which has the five wagon parts for its members. Sets are abstract objects which cannot, like the Dioscuri, be responsible for a kidnapping and cannot, like a particular wagonsum, be destroyed by fire or saw. The notions of set and sum have undergone such refinement in modern logic that additional refinements would be needed to enable them to recapture the intuitive force of ancient arguments about parts and wholes. For technical guidance, see Tyler Burge, 'A Theory of Aggregates', *Noûs* 11 (1977), 97–117; Peter Simons, *Parts: A Study in Ontology* (Oxford: 1987).

I offer the Dioscuri and wagonsums as two examples to try out as substitutes for the syllable SO in the argument under (I). To me at least the argument is vastly improved. This is because objects like the Dioscuri and a wagonsum are individuated *as* pluralities, by specification of their parts: nothing more, nothing less. In their case, what Socrates says of syllables at 203d is unqualifiedly true: the parts are epistemologically prior to the whole. Whatever knowing an object amounts to (cf. p. 75), how could one know the Dioscuri otherwise than by knowing Castor and knowing Pollux?

If this is correct—and, as always, readers should think twice before agreeing with me—the argument under (I) is actually valid. It is unsound because its premise (I) is false. WP may be adequate for the Dioscuri and wagonsums but it does not hold of syllables; the syllable SO is not just the syllablesum (S & O). Still, if (I) had been true, the conclusion would be true, and a parallel conclusion will be true for any example of which WP does hold.[75] Even if this is to estimate too highly the worth and interest of the argument, WP is clearly the source of whatever plausibility it has. In their dependence on WP, the two arguments, the argument under (I) and the argument under (II), stand or fail together. Hence to question WP is to undermine the entire argumentation of the dilemma section. Both horns crumple.

Let WP have been questioned, then. What follows? What moral can we draw for the dialogue? Elsewhere Plato argues that a whole must have unity as well as parts; a whole, like the syllables of (II), is a single form resulting from all the parts (*Parmenides* 157c ff.; cf. *Sophist* 244e ff.). But this is extremely abstract and general. A wagonsum is one wagonsum, a heap of sawdust one heap: does that make them wholes as well as sums? Are they a single form resulting from all the parts? Perhaps we need an additional distinction. Perhaps Theaetetus was right to resist (204ab) Socrates' suggestion that there is no difference between whole and sum, but

---

75. Bostock [9], 212, seems to agree. Note that the suggestion does not require me to uphold the fallacious thesis that all predicates of unstructured wholes transfer without further ado to the individual parts. Some do, some do not, as Plato well knew (*Hippias Major* 300e ff.). Thus, if a whole is smaller than Socrates, every part of it is smaller than Socrates, but if a whole weighs ten pounds, it obviously does not follow that every part weighs ten pounds; this applies to any sum, aggregate, or whole, structured or not. The present argument is about the transfer of the epistemological predicate 'is known'. If, or when, WP does license the transfer of 'is known', the transfer of 'is knowable' follows at once. That and no more is what Socrates claims at 205d.

wrong to agree (204bd) that a sum (which is one) is the same as all the parts (which are many). Or perhaps the notion of a *sum* is ambiguous between the two terms, *whole* and *all*, which WP would identify. These are not just logical teasers. In the ancient context, as today, they are the prelude to quite fundamental problems of metaphysics.[76] The Dream is a case in point.

If WP is (i) sufficient to validate the dilemma arguments (as suggested just now), (ii) false, but (iii) it is a falsehood to which the Dream is committed, or (iv) it is a falsehood to which the theory made by one or another interpretation of the Dream is committed, then the dilemma arguments are after all a genuine *reductio ad absurdum* of the Dream or of the theory made by a particular interpretation of the Dream. Viewed by itself, the dilemma is unsound and proves nothing, because both horns rely on a false assumption. Viewed in the wider context supposed by (iii) or (iv), it is a compelling proof, not indeed of the falsehood of $AK_{e/c}$, but of the internal incoherence of any theory which attempts to combine $AK_{e/c}$ with the assertion that a complex is (the same as) the sum of or all its elements.

The key text is one we have glanced at many times before:

Q4 Just in the same way as the elements themselves are woven together, so their names may be woven together and become an account of something—an account being essentially a complex of names. (202b)

We noticed earlier, when discussing Wittgenstein, that the Dream is vague and indeterminate about how the elements are 'woven together' to form the complexes that analysis would unravel (p. 164). But the image of weaving does at least suggest something stronger than a claim that each complex is one single complex. It suggests, in fact, a recognition of structure both in the complexes and in their accounts. Ryle would agree. His interpretation is all about Plato's recognition of structure in statements (accounts in sense (a)) and in the complexes that statements are of. He has on his side the fact that the weaving image returns in the *Sophist* (259e, 262cd) to make the very points that Ryle would have Socrates making here.

Things look quite different, of course, to those who favour Inter-

---

76. Compare, for example, Aristotle's attempt to discriminate *whole, sum,* and *all* in *Metaphysics* V 25–26, and his analysis of unity in *Metaphysics* X; also *Metaphysics* V 6, 1016b 11–16 on shoesums.

pretation [a] and the list model of statements. The list model is precisely a denial that statements are essentially structured. The verb phrase 'woven together' will be discounted as merely a phrase, which is not put to work in a philosophically productive way.[77] It is no accident that scholars who take this view also believe that the Dream theory is committed to WP and that the dilemma is a fair *ad hominem* critique.[78] If WP is applied to the complexes that statements are about, with the result that there is no more to any object described by the theory than its various constituents, then lists of those constituents really would seem to be an appropriate and sufficient means to mirror and record the world in statements. Besides, the list model of statements is a special case of WP. In its generality WP covers both statements and the complexes they are about.

Nor is the dispute settled by going over to Interpretation [b] and the list model of analysis. Certainly, the list model of analysis is another case of WP and may be used to argue that the Dream theory is committed to WP.[79] But now the weaving image invites the question: Why accept the list model of analysis? Why not take a Rylean view of accounts, even when 'account' means 'definition' or 'analysis', and recognize that both definitions and the abstract types they analyze are essentially structured? We can still maintain, against Ryle and Wittgenstein, that in Plato's thinking the essential structuredness of accounts is consequential on the essential structuredness of the complexes they are of, not the other way round (p. 164). Whatever the order of priority as between language and the world, a theory that recognizes structure can do better justice to the three examples we were looking at a short while back: the syllable SO, clay, knowledge itself.

This innovation is not merely compatible with the text of the Dream. It clearly suits Socrates' use of the image of weaving better than either the list model of statements or the list model of analysis. As in their account of accounts, so in their account of the Dream, Interpretations [a] and [b] omit the idea of structure which is unobtrusively but, once you think about it, undeniably present in Socrates' talk of weaving. Supposition (iv) wins over (iii). It is not the

---

77. McDowell [3], 233–34. Cornford [2], 143, 300, 305, simply translates the *Theaetetus* and the *Sophist* passages in such a manner that the weaving image appears only in the latter, being replaced in the former by the neutral term 'combined'.

78. Cornford [2], 151, McDowell [3], 244.

79. Fine [52], 382–84.

Dream itself but the theories so far made from it which the dilemma reduces *ad absurdum*. You can read the Dream ungenerously, so that it conforms with WP. But it is better not to.

However, one image does not make a theory. It is easy to conclude that, while the theory made by Interpretation [b] is better than the theory made by Interpretation [a], it would be better still without the list model of analysis. Once WP is denied at the level of types or kinds, it obviously follows that a complete and adequate analysis (definition) is something more than an enumeration of elements. But what exactly is the 'something more', and how does it relate to the elements? It is very clear that there is more to a wagon than you get by 'having gone over the whole by way of the elements' (207c). A proper analysis of the being of a wagon will acknowledge the structural connections between the 'one hundred timbers' and record their contribution to the functioning of the whole. It is not so clear what sort of formula would be appropriate to knowledge, or to discriminating the different types of clay at 147ab. Do we even want to retain the idea of elements (perceivable or otherwise) as part of a revised notion of analysis? (A modern ear finds it more appropriate to clay than to knowledge.) How, if at all, should definition by analysis be combined with definition by classification? These are the hard questions that need answering if one is actually to make the better theory to which the dilemma arguments are now pointing.

Ultimately, the problem is a problem for metaphysics and the philosophy of science. Given that WP is false, what is the structure of natural kinds and other definable types of thing? Their diverse content is obvious. Less obvious is what makes each of them a unity. We still need what Theaetetus could not produce at Stage One (p. 134), an account of accountability.

One way readers can come to grips with these issues is by journeying on to the *Sophist, Statesman,* and *Philebus.* (The *Statesman,* which is the sequel-dialogue to the *Sophist* as the *Sophist* is to the *Theaetetus,* is obsessed with the idea of weaving.) The three dialogues practise and describe methods of definition which involve both classification and analysis at the same time. Generic kinds are taken as wholes and steadily divided to reach the type or kind under investigation. The type can then be defined by 'weaving together' (the image recurs at the culmination of the *Sophist*—268c) the names of the kinds forming the hierarchically structured system within which the type has been located.

Consider, for example, a definition of the art of sophistry as 'that part of the acquisitive art which exchanges, which exchanges by selling, either selling one's own productions or retailing those of others, and which in either case sells knowledge' (*Sophist* 224e). This assembles the results of an analysis which divided the art of acquisition into acquisition by hunting and acquisition by exchange, then exchange into giving and selling; selling was then divided into selling one's own productions and selling those of other people, while the items sold were divided into those for the body and those for the soul, and so on to the end. A partial analysis of the whole (e.g. the art of acquisition) yields a definition by classification of the part (e.g. sophistry), thereby revealing that the part is what it is by virtue of its place in the whole system.

Now we already know (p. 190) the advantage of definition by classification: if there is a lowest level to the hierarchy, where division cannot be carried further, the 'atoms' of the system (*infimae species*) can still be defined by the classification which has emerged from division of the whole. We also know the disadvantage: unknowability at the top. But perhaps a solution to the regress can be found in a more adventurous interpretation of the ontology underlying these new methods of definition.

One such interpretation, supported by some of Aristotle's criticisms of Plato, is that what looks to us like a definition by classification is to be thought of as a definition by analysis. The object to be defined is actually constituted—from above, so to speak—by the kinds whose names are woven together to form the account. The higher kinds are constituents of the lower, its structure is their hierarchical arrangement, and its elements are the very highest kinds in the classification.[80] In that case, surprising as it may seem, a partial analysis (division) of the whole is the same thing as an analysis (definition) of the part.[81] We are close to the thought—a

---

80. This realignment of the term 'element' explains how for Aristotle it can be a deep metaphysical *question* whether the elements of things are their genera or the internal constituents into which they divide as a syllable divides into its letters: *Metaphysics* III 1, 995b 27–29, III 3, 998a 20–25, V 3.

81. Compare, in order of difficulty, Crombie [6], 115; Cornford [2], 268–72; G.E.M. Anscombe, 'The New Theory of Forms', *Monist* 50 (1966), 403–20; Aristotle, *Metaphysics* VII 12–14, *Posterior Analytics* II 5; Rudolf Carnap, *The Logical Structure of the World* (1928), trans. Rolf A. George (London 1967), 109 ff.—this last being a remote and unlikely parallel which may alleviate the surprise for some readers. Carnap's dream (strongly influenced by his reading of the *Tractatus*) was to make empiricism rigorous by using the techniques of modern logic to construct the world from what is given in immediate experience. What he takes as his elements are full momentary cross-sections of the total stream of experience: your total experience now would be one

subtle variant on the *Theaetetus* dilemma—that the whole and all the parts are known together or not known at all; for knowledge (as opposed to true judgement) neither is epistemologically prior to the other.

An Introduction to the *Theaetetus* can do no more than point to the prospect of further developments in the *Sophist* and elsewhere. Plato's late dialogues and Aristotle's *Metaphysics* are a rich mine of theorizing on the topics now in view. Both Plato and Aristotle continue to use the model of letters and syllables. Plato even dreams of learning the alphabet of nature out of which all specific complexes are formed (*Statesman* 278cd; cf. *Sophist* 253ae, *Philebus* 16c ff.). Aristotle is more modest. He does not believe in a universal alphabet. Different types of thing have different elements. So for him the letters and structure of a syllable are no more than an important analogy for the relation of matter and form in the complex wholes which are defined and studied by natural science.[82] But he insists as strongly as any philosopher has ever done that a whole is other and more than the sum or heap of its constituents. For readers who prefer their metaphysics to have one foot on the ground, Aristotle may be a more suitable companion than Plato for reflecting on the dilemma arguments.

*   *   *   *   *   *   *   *   *   *   *   *

This process of reflection should, however, travel backwards within the written dialogue as well as forwards and beyond it. Recall the tricky argument in Part I (158e–160c) for a completely universal thesis of nonidentity over time (p. 18). Why is Socrates healthy distinct from Socrates ill? Because, it was argued, taken as wholes they are unlike (159b). Why make the question of identity turn on taking them as wholes? Well, if WP is true of the complexes that statements are about, as suggested by Interpretation [a] plus the list model of statements, the question of identity does turn on the likeness and unlikeness of wholes. Any qualitative change is the loss of one constituent and the gaining of another, and WP entails

---

such element. Being elements, they are by definition unanalyzable and therefore—so he, unlike Wittgenstein (p. 150), supposes—indescribable. How, then, to say anything about them or construct anything with them? The answer is 'quasi analysis': 'quasi analysis of an essentially unanalyzable entity into several quasi constituents means placing the entity in several kinship contexts on the basis of a kinship relation, where the unit remains undivided' (p. 116).

82. *Physics* II 3, 195a 16–21; *Metaphysics* VII 10, VII 17, and VIII 3 (the chapter containing the obscure report on Antisthenes—n. 54 above).

that nothing can survive a change of constituents. Given WP, unlike wholes are necessarily distinct.

But why suppose that WP is the operative assumption in the argument? Well, consider the alternative. If a concrete whole is not (the same as) its constituents, but a single form resulting from their combination, what is the epistemological status of the principle of unity? Is it accessible to perceptual awareness? Given Plato's view that there is no such thing as a sensory impression of unity or one (185d, p. 58), Reading A will maintain that WP is true of sensible things insofar as they are revealed to perception, Reading B that WP is one more thesis Theaetetus must embrace if his definition of knowledge is to hold good.[83] Either way, the argument goes through to its Humean conclusion. The wholes on either side of the perceptual encounter are reduced to a succession of momentary subjects' momentary perceptions of the momentarily occurring qualities of momentary objects.

An interesting analogy may be observed here between the argument in Part I and certain currents in the modern debate about identity. Given WP, my boat perishes and another, distinct boat succeeds it, the moment one plank or one atom is lost and another takes its place. Here WP is applied to physical parts; in Part I's argument about identity and likeness it was applied to qualitative constituents. Its effect in both cases is to prohibit the retaining of any stable identity through change. This is welcome, for epistemological reasons, to the Heraclitean theory of perception (p. 17), but it is not a view that anyone would defend for its own sake. The thesis which in various versions has been formidably defended in modern times is

WPT A whole is (the same as) the sum of its successive parts-at-a-time/the successive momentary stages of its history.

WPT is similar in spirit to WP but in substance entirely different, and its advocates claim to make good sense of change and identity.[84] To return to my boat, which according to WPT is a certain momentary collection of planks and features occurring at 2:00 P.M. on

83. Compare pp. 11–12 on the status of the identification of perceiving with appearing at 152b.

84. See, for example, Quine's elegant Heraclitean reflections in 'Identity, Ostension, and Hypostasis', in his *From a Logical Point of View* (Cambridge, Mass.: 1953), 65–79, or the view of persons articulated by David Lewis, 'Survival and Identity', in Amélie Oksenberg Rorty ed., *The Identities of Persons* (Berkeley, Los Angeles & London: 1976), 17–40.

Monday, followed by another momentary collection of planks and features occurring at 2:01 P.M. on Monday, and so on through the hours, days, and weeks of what we ordinarily take to be the lifespan of a single enduring boat. This boat, so defined, can survive change. For it is now defined as a *process* (flux) in which one stage succeeds another, and change is simply unlikeness between stages.

Now recall that Part I left us with the question whether, once the Humean conclusion is reached, we are allowed to construe the perceiving subject or perceived object (man or stone) as an aggregate of distinct perceptions/sensible qualities perceived. Can momentary perceptions and momentary qualities be detached from their partners in the perceptual encounter and aggregated together, or is it only foolish 'people', not the wise Heracliteans, who attempt to do this (pp. 18–19, comparing 157b and 160b)? WPT would encourage the attempt. Modern logic offers the resources to carry it through. But it is still appropriate for epistemologists to ask, like Plato in the final refutation of flux at 179c–183c, whether the momentary or time-bound elements to which everything is reduced are really intelligible on their own. Perhaps such intelligibility as they possess, real or apparent, derives from our prior understanding and acceptance of ordinary continuing wholes.[85]

This is not the place for me to reopen consideration of Part I. You may wish to do it, now that a connection between those earlier arguments and the dilemma section of Part III has come to light. Nor is it the only connection to be explored. Can it be mere coincidence, for example, that the identical phrase 'some single form' is used both in the statement of (II) (203c; cf. 204a) and in Part I's formulation of the important idea of the unity of consciousness (185d)? The only thing I would insist on here is that the more food for thought you find in such connections, the more you should appreciate that the indeterminacy of the Dream is not just a literary device. Vital philosophical benefits accrue from keeping both Interpretation [a] and Interpretation [b] in play (p. 149). There are both analogies and disanalogies between the complex wholes that statements are about and the complex wholes that definitions define, as there are between statements and definitions themselves. A philosophical reader will not be frustrated by the indeterminacy, but stimulated to explore.

85. Cf. Wiggins, *op. cit.*, 168–69; Roderick M. Chisholm, *Person and Object: A Metaphysical Study* (London: 1976), Appendix A; P. T. Geach, 'Some Problems about Time', reprinted from *Proceedings of the British Academy* 51 (1965) in his *Logic Matters* (Oxford: 1972), 302–18.

One such reader in ancient times was Aristotle. As on an earlier
occasion (p. 169), let us imagine him reading the *Theaetetus*. He is
struck by Part I's thesis that unlike wholes are necessarily distinct.
He quickly concludes that WP, from which the thesis derives, must
be false in all its applications to objects capable of change. Not
musical Socrates but Socrates must be taken as the whole (for the
example, cf. p. 168). Moreover, it is because the constituents (*matter*)
of this whole are themselves unified by structure (*form*) that a
human being like Socrates is capable of retaining a stable identity
through change.[86] So far, so good. But when Aristotle comes to the
Dream in Part III and makes the shift we imagined earlier from
Interpretation [a] to Interpretation [b], he realizes that the requirements of change cannot be the reason why WP is untrue of the
abstract objects that definitions define. They are unchangeable. For
them, as for numbers, the thesis that unlike wholes are necessarily
distinct is true:

> As, when one of the parts of which a number consists has
> been taken from or added to the number, it is no longer the
> same number, but a different one, even if it is the very
> smallest part that has been taken away or added, so the
> definition and the essence will no longer remain when
> anything has been taken away or added. (*Metaphysics* VIII
> 3, 1043b 36–1044a 2; trans. Ross)

The question is, Does this disanalogy between concrete wholes,
which can change, and abstract wholes, which cannot, rule out
other points of analogy?

Aristotle hopes not. In particular, he hopes to shed light on the
unity of definition, and the prior unity of its objects, by an analogical
extension of the matter/form apparatus which served him so well
when combatting WP for concrete wholes.[87] This hope is the pivot
on which a good deal of the *Metaphysics* turns. In the case of a
syllable, the extension is natural and easy: we define the type SO
by specifying its matter (the constituent letters S and O) and its
form or structure (juxtaposition in that order). Aristotle wants to
offer a comparable treatment for more difficult cases, among them
the biologist's definitions of man and badger. This is his alternative
to the elaborate ontological structures of Plato's late dialogues. It
does not take much imagination to see that from Aristotle's point

---

86. Cf. Aristotle, *Physics* I 7.
87. Cf. *Metaphysics* VIII 6.

of view it would be a philosophical as well as a literary disaster to demand a single-minded, univocal interpretation of the Dream.

* * * * * * * * * * *

The most difficult case, however—difficult both for Plato and Aristotle to deal with and for the modern reader to follow their reflections—is numbers. Why should anyone object to Socrates' claim at 204bc that six is the same as four and two and also the same as three and two and one? Is that not simply to say that '6 = 4 + 2' and '6 = 3 + 2 + 1' are both theorems of arithmetic? It is much easier to object when Socrates generalizes from six to 'all things made of number' (204d). If an army, for example, was identical with a certain number or plurality of men, it would become a different army each time someone died from dysentery or wounds, and it would be true to say that the Athenian army which fought in 369 was already in existence years before Theaetetus and the rest were summoned to serve. This makes it obvious that an army is not to be equated with the number of its men. By contrast, it seems perverse, even senseless, not to equate four and two with six. What could be meant by a suggestion that six is not just (the sum of) four and two but a single form arising from their combination?

Once again, the great obstacle to understanding is Frege. The problem now is not just that, when confronted with a series of expressions like 'Twice three', 'Three times two', 'Four and two', 'Three and two and one' (204c), we find it easy to agree that each expression designates the same thing—they are four expressions referring, by way of four different senses, to one and the same number, the number 6. We find the sense/ reference distinction a useful way to explain how '6 = 4 + 2', taken as asserting the identity of the number 6 with the number which is the sum of 4 and 2, can be informative and enlarge our understanding of arithmetic. But the prior problem is this: Why do we take '=' as the expression of *identity*? Far more pervasive than the sense/reference distinction, and independent of it, is the influence of Frege's earlier onslaught in *The Foundations of Arithmetic* on the ancient Greek conception of number.

Euclid's definition of number as a multitude composed of units (*Elements* VII Def. 2) was shattered forever by the destructive power of Frege's polemic.[88] The definition had had a long innings. Leibniz

---

88. *The Foundations of Arithmetic, op. cit.*, 39 ff. Euclid is merely the first of a long list of mathematicians and philosophers who are pilloried in Frege's critique.

still found it appropriate in the early eighteenth century, so long as it was restricted to whole numbers (note the nomenclature) in contrast to fractions and irrational numbers (which the Greeks treated as ratios rather than numbers). Leibniz was not departing from the traditional conception of (whole) number when he proposed,

> The simplest definitions of numbers are constructed like this: *Two* is one and one; *Three* is two and one; *Four* is three and one; and so on'.[89]

Now we are reading an ancient Greek discussion of number. It is essential that we try to feel our way back into the Euclidean perspective, which is the closest we can get to the mathematics of Plato's time. Only so can we appreciate why Plato would object to Leibniz's definition of six as five and one.

If a number is conceived in Euclid's way as a multitude composed of units, thinking about number in the abstract is a good deal more like thinking about an army than we are used to. It is thinking about a multitude of abstract units instead of thinking about a multitude of sweaty soldiers. Just as there can be more than one army of, say, 10,000 men, so there can be more than one multitude composed of 6 units—more than one abstract sextet. Instead of thinking as we do of *the* number 6, uniquely positioned in the ordered series of unique integers 1, 2, 3, 4, . . . , Greek arithmetic has no number 1 (this is excluded by the definition of number), and arithmetical operations like addition and multiplication are carried out with an indefinite multitude of abstract multitudes (pairs, trios, quartets, etc.), as many multitudes of as many units being assumed as are needed for the purpose to hand. Consequently, where Frege writes '=' and asserts identity, Euclid speaks of equality in the sense of equinumerosity:

> If as many numbers as we please be in continued proportion, and there be subtracted from the second and the last *numbers equal to the first* [not, as we would say: and the first number be subtracted from the second and the last], then,

89. Leibniz, *New Essays on Human Understanding*, trans. and edd. Peter Remnant & Jonathan Bennett (Cambridge: 1981), Bk. IV, Chap. ii, p. 366 (pagination of the Akademie-Verlag edition). Leibniz's approval of the Euclidean definition is at p. 156. Compare Aristotle, *Metaphysics* XIII 7, 1081b 12–17.

as the excess of the second is to the first, so will the excess
of the last be to all those before it.   (*Elements* IX 35)[90]

If you want to devise a simpler example, try thinking of what we
write as '6 = 6' as asserting, not that the number 6 is identical with
itself, but that a sextet has the same number of units as a sextet, i.e.
any sextet is equinumerous with any other. Then '6 = 4 + 2' comes
out as saying, not that the number 6 is identical with the number
which is the sum of 4 and 2, but that there are exactly as many units
in a sextet as in a quartet together with a pair.

Back now to the *Theaetetus*. The *difference* between a multitude of
ten thousand abstract units and an army of ten thousand soldiers is
that the former is not capable of change. Take away one unit and
you have a different number, as Aristotle observes (similarly Plato,
Cratylus 432a); take away one soldier and the army is diminished,
not destroyed. The *likeness* between Greek numbers and armies,
however, is such that Aristotle still feels able to press the question
'What makes any given number (multitude) a unity or *one* single
number?', implying that the units in a number are only its matter.[91]
WP, in other words, is as false of (Euclidean) numbers as it is of syllables and definable essences. If Aristotle is right about this—or better, if there is any sense at all in what he is saying—then it is not perverse for Socrates to ask whether six is the same as four and two.

A sextet is equinumerous with a quartet taken together with a
pair. That much is an elementary truth of arithmetic. A sextet is
also itself made up of a quartet and a pair. Is it identical with these
constituents as well as being equinumerous with them? This is no
longer a mathematical question, which young Theaetetus would be
equipped to deal with. It is a philosophical worry about the nature
of the entities which make Euclid's theorems true. In the present
context, with the spotlight on WP and a whole battery of tricky
arguments challenging us to say what is wrong with it, we are
bound to conclude that Plato agrees with Aristotle that WP is false
of numbers, even if he disagrees with him about the form of the
solution. Six is not the same as four and two or five and one; it is

90. The algebraic paraphrase given by Sir Thomas Heath, *The Thirteen Books of Euclid's
Elements* 2nd edition (Cambridge: 1926), is
$$(a_{n+1} - a_1){:}(a_1 + a_2 + \ldots + a_n) = (a_2 - a_1){:}a_1$$
where the repeated use of a single symbol 'a_1' presupposes in the modern manner
that equal numbers are identical.

91. Cf. *Metaphysics* VII 13, 1039a 11–14, VIII 3, 1044a 3–5, VIII 6, 1045a 7–12, XIII 8,
1084b 5 ff. Also relevant are *Categories* 6, 4b 20–5a 37, *Physics* IV 14, 224a 2–15.

the number they have or make. Like a syllable, a sextet is a single form resulting from the combination of its elementary or nonelementary constituents.

Readers are now invited to go back over pp. 103–4, pp. 122–3, to reach their own assessment of how far matters have improved. Notice, in particular, how the argument under (I) ties in with Socrates' behaviour at 196b, where he treats knowing five and knowing seven as no different from knowing twelve. But to go further into the complexity of abstract mathematical objects would take us far beyond the written dialogue. We know that the nature of numbers was a major subject of debate between Plato and Aristotle and their philosophical colleagues. Aristotle gives a highly partisan account of the controversy in *Metaphysics* XIII–XIV. The discussion is technical and often difficult to follow.[92] A modern reader is left wondering whether any of the philosophers involved has a coherent solution. Wondering, indeed, whether a coherent solution is possible within the limits imposed by the Euclidean conception of number.

There is some progress in philosophy, and Frege contributed a fair portion of it. The distance from *Metaphysics* XIII–XIV to the luminous clarity of *The Foundations of Arithmetic* is so vast that we should be content to say that the *Theaetetus* encourages us to take a small but important step in the right direction. To deny WP for the number of an army is at least to distinguish a number from the collective subject which has it (recall 185ce, 198c) and from the units (soldiers) of which the collection is composed. To go further and repeat the denial for abstract multitudes is to launch oneself into a set of problems which it took Frege's genius to solve. The complexity of abstract mathematical objects, and the corresponding complexity of mathematical knowledge, is even more of a challenge than Plato knew.

In a diary entry for 1924 Frege wrote,

> It is already a step forward when a number is seen not as a thing but as something belonging to a thing, where the view is that different things, in spite of their differences, can possess the same One, as different leaves can, say, all possess the colour green. Now which things possess the

92. For assistance, consult Julia Annas, *Aristotle's Metaphysics Books M and N* (Oxford: 1976); M. F. Burnyeat, 'Platonism and Mathematics. A Prelude to Discussion', in Andreas Graeser ed., *Mathematics and Metaphysics in Aristotle* (Bern & Stuttgart: 1987), 213–40.

number one? Does not the number one belong to each and every thing?[93]

No ancient Greek philosopher would suspect irony in the last two sentences.

* * * * * * * * * * * *

We have now traced connections from the dilemma section to Part I and to Part II as well as to the Dream and the ramifying concerns of Part III. The dialectic of parts and wholes runs backwards through the entire dialogue, forwards to Plato's late dialogues and to Aristotle, and onwards through Leibniz to Frege. As with the Dream, so with the *Theaetetus* as a whole: you can read it ungenerously, so that it is no more than the sum of its three Parts. But it is better not to.

Parts and wholes: (ii) progress towards knowledge (206ab, 207d–208b)

Part III is not all bafflement and challenge. Plain sailing can be enjoyed at 206ab (the shorter second section of the middle portion of Part III), which attacks $AK_{e/c}$, and then again at 207d–208b, which criticises Interpretation [b]'s understanding of Def. K_o. Taken together, these two sections complete the refutation of the theory made by Interpretation [b]. I combine them here, not only because what comes between is material we have discussed already (concerning the distinction between the two senses of 'account' on which Interpretations [a] and [b] are based), but also because, when they are read together, they can be seen to be pressing for a positive conception of knowledge which is even more demanding than that proposed by Interpretation [b].

At 206ab old Socrates and young Theaetetus reminisce about their schooldays. In learning to read and write their task was to become able to distinguish and identify each letter in itself, whatever its position in written or spoken words. (It will be important that this is identification in the context of words, not simple perceptual recognition of S and O in isolation.) Similarly in music lessons the aim was to be able to distinguish each note in a melody (notes being the elements of music) and identify it by the string it belongs

93. *Posthumous Writings*, trans. Peter Long & Roger White (Oxford: 1979), 264.

to.[94] Conclusion: knowledge of elements is (i) clearer than knowledge of complexes, (ii) more decisive for mastery of the subject. On both counts $AK_{e/c}$ is false.

The argument is straightforward, but the conclusion is carefully nuanced, with both (i) and (ii) expressed in comparative terms. Socrates implies that knowledge of any complex in a given domain presupposes knowledge of the elements, but he does not repeat his earlier claim (203d) that knowledge of letters must come first, before you can know the syllables they enter into. It is true that a child might learn the alphabet as a set of separate letter types before being taught to read and write syllables and words. But he has not embarked on the process Socrates describes at 206a until he is confronted with written complexes to read (e.g. in a book) and spoken complexes to write down (e.g. when the schoolmaster gives a dictation).[95] He masters the elements *as* the elements of those complexes, not just as bare letters on their own.

The point can be put more formally. 'Element' is a relative term. Letters and musical notes are not just shapes and sounds. They are shapes and sounds which are the termini for certain systematic processes of analysis and classification over a domain of complexes. This is what makes them elements. They are elements *for* the complexes through which they are reached. Correspondingly, knowing the elements is the basis *for* knowing the complexes they compose. This is the upshot of (ii). Literacy is a complex skill, with a structure of its own. It is not just knowing the letters *and* knowing the complexes they compose. It is knowing the latter on the basis of knowing the former.

This is not to say that knowing the letters is sufficient for knowing the syllables they compose. Once we recognize that structure is

94. Typical Greek note names are, for example, *nētē:* the 'nearest' string, *hypatē:* the 'furthest away', *mesē:* 'the string in the middle'. (Thus Fine [54], 386, is wrong to think that Socrates is describing two tasks, the first being to identify each note, a second and more advanced accomplishment being to say which string it belongs to.) But there were different tuning systems (*harmoniai*) relative to which these names would pick out different notes. Either Plato presupposes that schoolboys begin from a single standard tuning for the instrument (probably the 'Dorian' one), or, more interestingly, his silence about musical structure has the same provocative intent as his silence about the order of letters in a syllable. In music it is even more obvious than in spelling that the enumeration of elements is not enough. It is actually impossible to enumerate musical elements without reference, implicit or explicit, to structure. (For the technical information used here I owe thanks to Andrew Barker.)

95. Compare *Statesman* 277e–278c. Dictation is the subject of some amusingly fallacious dilemma arguments at *Euthydemus* 276a–277c.

essential to the being of a syllable, it follows that a fully literate person must know how letters are 'woven together' to form syllables and words. He must know the principles of combination and arrangement (the rules of spelling) as well as knowing the letters themselves. A great deal is made of this point in the *Sophist* (253a, 261d). In the *Theaetetus* it is left tacit, because Plato is challenging us to deal with the dilemma for ourselves. But we can affirm the importance of structure and arrangement without denying what (ii) asserts, that knowledge of the letters is both necessary to the art of reading and writing, and basic to it.

As for (i), Socrates does not expand on the statement that elements are more clearly known, but we may guess that the crucial factor is their simplicity. So far from simplicity being the cause of unknowability, as was argued at 205ce, the clarity of knowing becomes greater as complexity decreases. Conversely, clarity decreases as we go from simple letters to syllables to words to sentences.

Thus it is in a logical rather than a temporal sense that the knowledge of elements is primary. Socrates is not describing our ability to say 'That's S', 'That's O', when the letters appear in isolation or in a recitation of the alphabet. He is analyzing the more advanced skill which enables us to write or read S and O correctly in, for example, the names 'Socrates', 'Aristotle', and 'Demosthenes'. The names are presented as wholes to sight or hearing, and we have to spell them out correctly. Getting each letter right and in the right order is an intellectual achievement, not a simple case of perceptual recognition. Imagine a wainwright's apprentice being told to fetch the 'one hundred timbers' of a wagon and lay them out in the proper order for building to begin. He will use his eyes to pick out the right pieces of wood, but perception is not involved in his knowing which pieces to look for. Just so, when we read and write, we use eyes and ears, but perception does not and could not give us our knowledge of spelling (cf. 163bc). The knowledge of elements on which literacy is based is not just familiarity with certain shapes and sounds. It is knowing the letters *as* the elements of syllables and words.

Literacy, moreover, is serving here as a model for grown-up cases of expertise. When Socrates extrapolates from schoolboy experience to (i) and (ii), he is claiming that you have not mastered any branch of study (theoretical or practical) until you know the elements of the domain and are able on the basis of this knowledge to 'spell out' the complexes they compose. Contrast the Dream, which said that you have perfect knowledge (202c) of an object *o* when you can analyze it into its (unknowable) elements. A double shift has taken place. Instead of knowledge being conceived as a one-to-one (proprietary) relationship between the mind and a single complex considered in itself, the focus now is on an expert's mastery of a whole domain of complexes. Instead of knowledge looking inwards from a complex to its elements, it now proceeds outwards from the elements to a varied range of complexes. Under Socrates' interrogation the hostage-model of letters and syllables has turned against the Dream.

There is no doubt that (i) and (ii) offer a better appreciation of the complexity of expertise than the dialogue has achieved so far. At the same time they set extremely demanding standards for knowledge. How many of us know the 'one hundred timbers' of a wagon or the elements of the periodic table which enter into modern chemistry's analysis of clay? Even for an ancient who views earth and water as two of the fundamental elements of all material things, it would take theoretical expertise, not just everyday familiarity with earth and liquid, to become aware of their status as elements. In short, if knowledge of *o* means expertise about *o*, and expertise rests on the knowledge of elements, there is very little knowledge around. Theodorus may know a thing or two, but there is plenty he does not know (144e–145b), and the majority of people know nothing at all.

Is this too harsh a verdict to pass on ourselves and our fellow human beings? It is no surprise to be told that most of us are not experts on anything, but the statement 'Most of us know nothing at all' comes as a smack in the face. It is one thing to say that expertise is a matter of having knowledge that most people do not have (145de, p. 3, pp. 19–20), quite another to say that knowledge is a matter of expertise, which most people do not have. Nowadays we tend to think of knowledge democratically. Knowledge is a mundane possession which anyone can have and everyone does have. Modern epistemology follows suit. The focus of attention is on examples like knowing that one has a pencil in hand or knowing that the wind is cold (cf. p. 5), more advanced examples such as a chemistry professor's knowledge of the periodic table being shuffled off into a rather specialized subject called the philosophy of science. But the theory that (i) and (ii) put before us is a theory of knowledge as such. It does not say that some knowledge is like literacy and involves mastery of a domain on the basis of knowing the elements. It says that knowledge is like literacy in this respect.

We are free, of course, to reply that, while such demanding standards are appropriate to expert craftsmen and scientists, they do not apply to all knowledge worthy of the name. Up to now the *Theaetetus* has maintained an equable interest in all grades of knowledge from the most mundane to the most exalted, from Socrates' recognition of Theaetetus as he arrives with his companions (144c) to the systematic study of the nature of every whole (174a). The literacy model seems apposite to the second, but not to the first. Let us then call a spade a spade. What 206ac has delivered is an admirable theory of expertise, but it is not, unfortunately, a good answer to the question 'What is knowledge?'.

There is a sense in which a twentieth-century reader is bound to make this response. Our conception of knowledge is unequivocally democratic. But let me repeat a question I asked towards the end of Part II (p. 122): How do we decide when a philosopher is simply and straightforwardly wrong about a concept and when he is working with (or advocating) a concept different from the one we are used to? That question was prompted by K', which proclaims that active knowledge is incompatible with mistakes:

> K' It is impossible to judge *either* that something one actively knows is something else one knows *or* that something one actively knows is something one does not know.

Now it so happens that K' makes its presence felt again in the section 207d–208b, where it proves fatal to Interpretation [b]'s understanding of Def. K_o.

At 207d Socrates and Theaetetus resume their reminiscing. There is a stage in the learning of one's letters when one is liable to spell the same syllable differently or to spell different syllables the same way in the context of different words.[96] The first syllable of 'Theaetetus' is the same as the first syllable of 'Theodorus'. A learner may spell it correctly (THE) when writing 'Theaetetus' and incorrectly (TE) when writing 'Theodorus'. Or again, the first syllable of 'Theaetetus' is different from the first syllable of 'Terpsion'. A learner may spell 'Theaetetus' correctly but when asked to write 'Terpsion' think that it too begins THE. Such a person, we may agree, is not yet literate, has not yet mastered the art of reading and writing. We certainly will agree if the learner is in the same

96. Both types of mistake are mentioned by Socrates at 207d, both again (in reverse order) by Theaetetus at 207de, but the only one illustrated is spelling the same syllable differently.

position with respect to each of the four syllables of Theaetetus'
name (208a). However flawlessly he spells 'Theaetetus', he is not a
'finished pupil' (206ab) if, where other words are concerned, he is
liable to mistakes involving four different syllables.

But does it follow, if we agree that the learner under discussion is
not yet literate, that he does not know (the correct spelling of)
'Theaetetus'? There is no suggestion that he gets 'Theaetetus' right
by accident or that he is liable to get it wrong next time.[97] On the
contrary, he writes THE because he thinks, correctly, that this is how
the first syllable of Theaetetus' name ought to be written (207e). So
why not say that the learner knows (the correct spelling of) 'Theaetetus' but not 'Theodorus' and 'Terpsion'? It seems outrageous to suggest that someone who spells 'Theaetetus' correctly, and not by accident, does not know the first syllable of that name unless he also
knows the correct spelling of *other* words like 'Theodorus' and 'Terpsion'. Must one really master 'antidisestablishmentarianism' in order to satisfy the examiners that one does indeed know the correct
spelling of everyday words like 'table', 'men', and 'is'?

Socrates' answer to this last question is an emphatic 'Yes'. Whatever the outrage to twentieth-century sensibilities, he is construct-
ing a counterexample to refute Def. K$_o$ in the version put forward
by Interpretation [b]. The example is expressly designed to show
(208ab) that to know 'Theaetetus' it is not sufficient to have a command of the correct spelling of the word plus true judgement about
it (here, presumably, the ability to divide it accurately into four
syllables). Socrates' claim, therefore, is that, *because* the learner
does not know 'Theodorus' and 'Terpsion', neither does he know
'Theaetetus'. His flawless spelling of 'Theaetetus' is not the manifestation of knowledge. The implication is that only a fully literate
person counts as knowing 'Theaetetus'.

Suppose we disagree. Suppose we insist on crediting our learner
with knowledge of the first syllable of Theaetetus' name. Then we
will find ourselves at odds with K'. For when the learner writes
'Theodorus' he misidentifies something he knows: he judges that
THE, which he knows, is TE. We may plead that the learner is not
using his knowledge of THE (perhaps he is disoriented by the new
context), but this excuse is no longer available when he writes
'Terpsion'. For here he is actively exercising his supposed knowl-

97. As supposed by Cornford [2], 157–58, Crombie [6], 110, 113, Morrow [51], 309–
10. For the correct view see McDowell [3], 253–54, White [8], 178 with n. 53, Fine
[52], 387–88.

edge of THE, like the dunce who used his knowledge of eleven to judge that five and seven is eleven. That this is absurd is one of the firmest points in the dialogue. So long as it stands, Socrates' counterexample to Def. K_0 is unassailable. His refutation has the weight of K' behind it.

This is an extremely interesting position to have reached. The twentieth-century response to Socrates' counterexample is of a piece with the modern response to the initial puzzle of Part II. Both presuppose that knowledge is compatible with mistakes: not of course in the sense that one can know that p when p is false, but in the sense that one can know an object o and still make mistakes about it. This presupposition is vital if a democratic conception of knowledge is to be sustained. Indeed, the modern response in Part II was actually to require knowledge as a condition of mistakes (p. 74, p. 108). Conversely, if you do not allow knowledge to be compatible with mistakes, you must follow the alternative response to the puzzles of Part II and accept in Part III the legitimacy of a counterexample which implies that most people know nothing at all.

Even broader horizons open up when we reflect that K' is a special case of the idea that knowledge must be *unerring*, which has had a guiding role in the discussion since 152c (cf. 160d, 200e). Its effect in Part I was that the object of knowledge had to shrink within the confines of a moment. Its effect in Part III has been that knowledge must expand to take in every detail of a whole field of study. In the one case, nothing more than a fleeting glimpse was safe enough to be knowledge; in the other, nothing less than total mastery of the domain.

Recall, moreover, that in Part I it transpired that even a fleeting glimpse might not be safe enough. Under pressure from the requirement that knowledge be unerring, the object of knowledge finally turned into a nonentity with no determinate character at all. Correspondingly, K' could easily lead Part III to the conclusion that total mastery of a given domain is not enough for knowledge. Knowledge of anything requires knowledge of everything. This would follow if there exists a set of elements which are the elements of everything whatsoever.

The two sections we are considering assume a departmentalization of elements: one set of elements for the wainwright, another for the musician, yet another for reading and writing. Elements on this view are what you reach by the methods of analysis appropriate to a given field. But the Dream speaks of *the* primary elements of which 'we and everything else' are composed. Does this hint at a universal alphabet? Does it make sense to speculate that the departmentalized elements we have been dealing with are not ultimate because the really primary elements lie beyond the 'one hundred timbers' of a wagon, beyond the elementary constituents of clay, beyond even the elements of music? Outside the *Theaetetus* there is evidence that Plato thought such speculation both possible and necessary.[98] Add K' and it results that no-one knows anything unless they know everything.

So extreme a conclusion is not of course canvassed here. Yet it was a serious thesis of the *Republic* that the only knowledge worthy of the name is that enjoyed by someone who has attained a synoptic grasp of all the sciences in the light of their connection with the Good.[99] The extreme conclusion is not to be dismissed out of hand. One of the morals that could be drawn from the negative outcome of the dialogue is that in sober truth no-one knows anything unless they know everything.[100] But a twentieth-century reader is already hard put to it to swallow the interim conclusion that knowledge is expertise and that no-one knows anything in a given domain unless they have total mastery of the domain on the basis of its elements.

A concept I have found helpful in this regard is the concept of understanding. Platonic claims about knowledge often become more palatable when they are reexpressed as claims about understanding. Try these:

(1) Someone who spells 'Theaetetus' right but gets 'Theodorus' wrong does not understand the spelling of 'Theaetetus'.

(2) It is impossible to judge either that something one actively understands is something else one understands or that something one actively understands is something one does not understand.

(3) Understanding an object *o* is being able to elucidate the relationships of elements and complexes in the domain of *o*.

98. *Timaeus* 48bc, *Statesman* 278d; Aristotle, *Metaphysics* I 6, 987b 19 ff., XIII 9, 1086a 22 ff. Galen, *In Hippocratis de natura hominis* 53.27–54.12 Mewaldt, explicitly ascribes to Plato a distinction between departmentalized elements such as Hesiod's 'one hundred timbers' or the elements of harmonics and the truly primary elements of all things.

99. See *Republic* 508e–509a, 511ad, 531cd, 533b–534d.

100. Cf. Aristotle, *Posterior Analytics* II 13, 97a 6–22, discussing a thesis propounded by Speusippus, Plato's nephew and his successor as head of the Academy, to the effect that no-one can define anything without knowing everything.

(4) No-one fully understands anything unless they understand everything in the light of the Good/ the ultimate elements of the universe.

The question is not whether you accept all these claims straight off, but whether you become more sympathetic when the verb 'to understand' replaces the verb 'to know'. The simplest case is (1), which in my view changes from false to true when the substitution is made. The other claims are harder to judge, but if you agree with me on (1) you may be willing to envisage an understanding of 'understanding' whereby even (4) could strike one as the sober truth.

The essential clue here is the connection between understanding and explanation. To explain something is to help people understand it. When Aristotle describes knowledge as the ability to explain scientifically why something is so, I find it helpful to gloss this as an account of understanding rather than of knowledge as knowledge is conceived in philosophy today.[101] For modern philosophers typically connect knowledge with the justification of belief or the reliability of information, not with the explanation of some fact that a person believes or is reliably informed about. An alternative gloss is that Aristotle is giving an account of knowledge, but it is an account which identifies knowledge with understanding.[102] Either way Aristotle is an ancient reader of the dialogue whose own thought on the topics of Part III is usefully mediated into modern English through the concept of understanding. My suggestion is that the same holds for Plato himself. I have an ally in Bishop Berkeley, who conceived himself to be following Plato when he wrote, 'We know a thing when we understand it'.[103]

Why, after all, is Plato so interested in definition, analysis, and classification? They would not feature in a modern discussion of knowledge. But they might turn up in a modern discussion of explanation and understanding. Elements are not just what you reach at the limit of analysis. In both ancient and modern thought they are what you reach at the limit of an analysis undertaken in order to find a firm basis for explaining the whole in question. Likewise the point of definition by classification, as in the mathematics scene at 147e–148b, is not to make dry-as-dust catalogues of

101. M. F. Burnyeat, 'Aristotle on Understanding Knowledge', in Enrico Berti ed., *Aristotle on Science: The "Posterior Analytics"* (Padua: 1981), 97–139.

102. Barnes [50], 204–5.

103. *Siris* § 253 (see Part I, n. 15). Compare the quotation from Locke at p. 126 above.

what there is, but to understand things that are important and difficult to understand. More broadly, the issue at stake in the choice between definition by analysis and definition by classification is whether a given whole should be explained from within itself or by relating it to other items in the domain, or by some combination of both procedures in the manner suggested by Socrates' recent affirmation of (i) and (ii). All this makes good sense in the context of an expert's understanding of their field. It would sound strange in a discussion of knowledge today.

Again, when knowledge is construed in terms of justified true belief or the reliability of information, it is obviously compatible with mistakes. Partial information about a thing can still be reliable; justified true belief on some aspects does not exclude going wrong on others. But can you claim to have an expert understanding of music, for example, if you are at home with the sonata form but cannot explain the principles of a fugue? It is at least not obvious where a line can be drawn beyond which understanding need not go.

'So much the worse for Plato', you may say, 'if certain claims make better sense of understanding than of knowledge. Knowledge is what the *Theaetetus* set out to discuss and it is no defence of

Def. K$_{o(e)}$ Knowing o is having true judgement concerning o with an explanation based on the relationships of elements and complexes in the domain of o

that it would make a serviceable account of an expert's understanding of o.'

The objection assumes it is a criticism of Plato that a dialogue which in Part I was thoroughly in tune with the concerns of modern epistemology should reach a point in Part III where it can seem helpful to replace our verb 'to know' by the verb 'to understand'. That is a large assumption. Perhaps modern epistemology has lost touch with the breadth of vision to which the *Theaetetus* aspires. Perhaps it is a feature of modern life that the concepts of knowledge and understanding have become more distinct than they were. To reach a conclusion about (1)–(4) we must interrogate our own thought as well as Plato's.

In any case, the dialogue has not abandoned interest in the kind of mundane knowledge illustrated by Socrates' recognition of Theaetetus at the beginning of the inquiry (144c). That very example sets the scene for the final argument of Part III.

Telling the difference (208c–210a)

The first sign that mundane knowledge has come back into focus is that the third sense of 'account' is introduced as 'what the majority of people would say' (208c).[104] The least this can mean is that the majority of people would say that Def. K_o is a plausible definition of knowledge when 'account' is taken in sense (c): a differentiation of o from other things. In other words, when 'account' is taken in sense (c), Def. K_o is a plausible definition of the ordinary man's concept of knowing an object.

A more challenging idea is that the majority of people would say, or would accept on reflection, that sense (c) of 'account' yields a reasonable meaning for the Dream as a whole. In that case we have to develop Interpretation [c], a popular version of the Dream, before Def. K_o can be dismissed as 'only the poor man's dream of gold' (208b). Interpretation [c] will state a general theory of the nature and limits of mundane knowledge.

But first, what exactly is this third sense of 'account', a differentiation of o from other things? Socrates gives both a verbal formula and an example. The verbal formula is 'being able to tell some mark by which the object you are asked about differs from all other things' (208c). The example is 'the brightest of the bodies that move round the earth in the heavens', which Theaetetus accepts as a satisfactory answer to the question 'What is the sun?' (208d). The example shows that the question referred to in the formula ('the object you are asked about') is a question of the form 'What is o?'. The formula indicates that this question is no longer to be construed as a request for an analysis, definition, or explanation of o. 'What is o?' is now a request for a mark by which o may be identified and distinguished from all other things.

This is still not crystal clear. Glance back to the recognition at 144c. Theaetetus approaches with his companions, and Socrates says, 'I know him. He's the son of Euphronius of Sunium.' Is 'the son of Euphronius of Sunium' an account in sense (c)? It answers the question 'Who is that?'. It differentiates the boy from everyone and everything else. But it expresses the result of Socrates' recognition, not the basis for it. It does not answer the question 'How, by what distinguishing mark, did Socrates know him?'.

104. It is also what 'some people' do say (208d)—perhaps Antisthenes (cf. p. 170), perhaps a philosopher bent on explicating ordinary thought. But this is a parenthetical reference with nothing like the prominence given to 'what the majority of people would say'.

Contrast 'the brightest of the bodies that move round the earth in the heavens'. Like 'the son of Euphronius of Sunium', this is a uniquely individuating description, true of just one thing in the universe. Unlike 'the son of Euphronius of Sunium', it also gives a basis for recognition. If you need a way of telling which object is the sun, you can look for the brightest of the heavenly bodies. If you need evidence for a claim to have recognized the sun, you can adduce the fact that it is much the brightest of the various bodies that move round us up there in the sky. The example suggests that what the formula calls a *mark* of differentiation should be something that can be used as a basis for recognition, a means of identification. In which case 'the son of Euphronius of Sunium' is not an account in sense (c).

This suggestion is confirmed as we read on. At 209c Socrates invokes the Wax Block. It becomes clear that for Socrates to get the differentness of Theaetetus imprinted on his block is not merely to have a uniquely individuating answer to the question 'Who is Theaetetus?'. It is to have an answer that will make him identify Theaetetus correctly when he meets him tomorrow at the beginning of the *Sophist*. This must be an answer in terms of observable features; the differentness under discussion must be accessible to perception. For on the Wax Block model recognition takes place when a perception is fitted into the trace of itself which was stamped on the wax at an earlier meeting (193c with 191d).[105] It makes sense for previous perception to have left a record which differentiates Theaetetus' peculiar snub-nosedness from all the other snub-nosednesses that Socrates has seen (209c). It does not make sense for previous perception to have left a record of Theaetetus' parentage. The fact that Theaetetus is the son of Euphronius of Sunium is not an observable feature of the boy, hence not a mark he can be recognized by.

Even better sense is made when this conclusion is carried back to the new definition of knowledge. We should be glad to be discussing

Def. $K_{o(r)}$ Knowing o is having true judgement concerning o with the ability to say how to recognize o,

rather than

---

105. Recognition of conceptions within the mind (Part II, n. 32) would be irrelevant here. Equally irrelevant, as Cornford [2], 159 n. 1, observes, is the technical notion of a *differentia*. A *differentia* is that part of a definition by classification which differenti-

Def. K$_{o(u)}$ Knowing o is having true judgement concerning o with
the ability to cite a uniquely individuating description
of o.

Def. K$_{o(u)}$ just encourages one to think up way-off descriptions
which it would be quite unreasonable to cast as the differentiating
condition of knowledge. Perhaps, for example, Theaetetus was the
only Athenian who sat on Cape Sunium looking out over the sea
at a particular moment in the year 400 B.C. Why should the ability
to say *that* make the difference between true judgement concerning
Theaetetus and knowledge of him? Def. K$_{o(r)}$ is much the more
interesting candidate.

Let us then examine Def. K$_{o(r)}$, beginning with its first component:
true judgement. As before, we may follow Socrates' example and
narrow the scope of true judgement so that it combines appropriately with the given sense of 'account' (p. 175). Socrates' example,
the true judgement he imagines himself making, is a correct identification of Theaetetus (209b). Thought is applied to perception to
produce the judgement 'This is Theaetetus—one who is a human
being, etc.'. The exact content of the thought (how to expand 'etc.')
is a problem that will concern us later. For the moment it is enough
that we can recognize, before it is explicitly invoked at 209c, the
conceptual apparatus of the Wax Block section of Part II: a perception, minimally articulated by the demonstrative 'this' (cf. pp. 93–
4); the perceived item sitting right beside the speaker (144d); a
thought about who Theaetetus is, its content as yet unspecified (cf.
p. 92); and a connecting of the perception with the thought to
produce a judgement identifying what is perceived (cf. 195cd). The
difference from Part II is that the discussion requires an example of
true judgement instead of an example of false judgement.

With true judgement narrowed to true judgements of identification, we next reflect that knowledge is a capacity, not an event. If
Socrates knows Theaetetus today, he will know him tomorrow. As
before, we may understand Def. K$_{o(r)}$ as conjoining the capacity,
not the episode, of true judgement with the capacity to produce an
account in sense (c) (p. 179). The example we are looking at is the
manifestation of a capacity in virtue of which Socrates can be said,
in the nice phrasing of 208e, to be 'a judger of' Theaetetus: he has
a capacity for identifying him correctly when he meets him.

---

ates o from other things in the same genus. It takes the whole definition to differentiate o from all other things (e.g. *Republic* 534bc).

Finally, suppose that Socrates also has a capacity to say how, by what distinguishing mark, Theaetetus may be recognized. He not only can identify Theaetetus correctly; he can also explain how, on what basis, he does it. His account answers the question 'How do you know it is Theaetetus?' and thereby justifies a claim to have recognized him. In sum, to know Theaetetus is to have the ability to identify him together with the ability to offer proof of the recognition.

An admirable account, one might think, of what the ordinary man ordinarily means when he talks of knowing people and things.[106] It

106. This is the moment to confess to the reader that the interpretation now before you is 'all my own work'. Other scholars will give you only Def. $K_{o(u)}$ and no special role for perception. The result is such a different story from mine that I may be forgiven, at so late a stage in this Introduction, if I leave detailed comparison to you. You should know, however, that the divergence between my story and theirs is associated at two points with divergent appreciations of Plato's Greek.

(a) At 209b I translate 'This is Theaetetus—', giving the pronoun 'this' the same demonstrative force as it has in 'this snub-nosedness of yours' at 209c. In both cases 'this' points to what Socrates perceives beside him, while the rest of the exemplary sentence at 209b connects Socrates' perception with his thought about who Theaetetus is. In other current translations the sentence gives us only Socrates' thought about who Theaetetus is, e.g. 'Theaetetus is the one who is a human being, etc.' in McDowell, the same minus 'the' in Cornford. Perception plays no special role, and the pronoun 'this' has to be given the anaphoric force it would have in a formulation such as 'Whoever it is that is a human being, etc., this is Theaetetus'. Indeed, Miss Levett's own version was precisely 'anyone who is a human being, etc., is Theaetetus'.

(b) I scorned Def. $K_{o(u)}$ because it is an unconvincing analysis of knowing o. It would be more convincing as an analysis of knowing what o is. Thus it seems reasonable that you know what the sun is if you can say that it is the brightest of the bodies that move round the earth in the heavens, and that you know who Theaetetus is if you can say that he is the son of Euphronius of Sunium. (Even so, there are descriptions and descriptions: do you know who Theaetetus is if all you can say about him is that he was the only Athenian who sat on Cape Sunium looking out over the sea at a particular moment in the year 400 B.C.?) Now it has been suggested (McDowell [3], 229 with 115, Fine [52], 388 with 367) that for Plato 'knowing o' and 'knowing what o is' are interchangeable. There is not just an entailment from the former to the latter, which no-one would dispute, but the other way round as well. If this was correct for concrete objects like Theaetetus, then Def.$K_{o(u)}$, as a moderately convincing analysis of knowing what o is, would become an equally convincing analysis of knowing o. If the two notions were for Plato equivalent, then, where I insist on a basis for recognition, a uniquely individuating description would do.

But the linguistic evidence adduced for this suggestion (*Meno* 79c, *Theaet.* 147b) concerns abstract objects, not concrete things like Theaetetus. Plato's Greek appears on the surface to treat 'knowing o' and 'knowing what o is' as interchangeable when the value of o is e.g. virtue or knowledge in the abstract. The most this shows is Plato inclining towards the entirely sensible view that, in contexts where an abstract universal is under discussion as the thing to be defined, knowing it is knowing its has a lot in common with the account of knowing given by J. L. Austin in a well-known paper on 'Other Minds', which helped to inaugurate the era of 'ordinary language philosophy' at Oxford. Here, for example, is an Oxford revival of Socrates' mark of differentiation:

> If you have asked 'How do you know it's a goldfinch?' then I may reply 'From its behaviour', 'By its markings', or, in more detail, 'By its red head', 'From its eating thistles'. That is, I indicate, or to some extent set out with some degree of precision, those features of the situation which enable me to recognize it as one to be described in the way I did describe it.[107]

It is true that being able to tell *a* goldfinch when you see one in the garden is the ability to recognize instances of a perceivable type, not the ability to recognize one particular individual such as Theaetetus. But Austin includes knowing a particular person within the scope of his discussion,[108] and it seems possible that Socrates would be willing to consider

Def. $K_{t(r)}$ Knowing an object of type *t* when you meet one is having true judgement concerning *t*s (i.e. being able to identify *t*s) with the ability to say how to recognize a *t*.

For at 208d he considers an account which fails to differentiate *o*, because it grasps only some feature that *o* has in common with other things. He insists that it will not be an account of *o*—in other words, an account of *o* must be proprietary to *o*. But he adds that the nondifferentiating account will be an account of the things that share the common feature, which makes it sound like the perfect account for someone who wants to be able to say how to recognize, not *o*, but *t*s in general.

---

definition (cf. p. 38). It does not display Platonic licence for an inference from 'Every reader of this note knows who Theaetetus is' to 'Every reader of this note knows Theaetetus'.

I have kept these matters to a footnote because they involve delicate questions about the original Greek. The Greekless reader may be assured that the divergence of overall interpretations will not be resolved on linguistic grounds. On the contrary, the linguistic issues will resolve themselves when the philosophical message is clear. Read on.

107. J. L. Austin, 'Other Minds', reprinted from *Aristotelian Society Supplementary Volume* 20 (1946) in his *Philosophical Papers* (Oxford: 1961), 51.

108. *Op. cit.*, 48, 53, 58, 63.

Be that as it may, both type recognition and object recognition face a version of the familiar epistemological regress. If an object o or instances of a type t may be recognized by mark m, how is m itself to be recognized? By a differentiating mark m' of its own? Then how is m' to be recognized? Eventually we must reach a mark that is distinct and detectable in itself, not on the basis of some feature that it has. Let this be m''. Then m'' has a name, 'm'''', but no account in sense (c); it is perceivable but not, on our present definition, knowable.

Readers are now invited to develop Interpretation [c] for themselves, adjudicating once again, from a third viewpoint, the issues we raised while developing Interpretations [a] and [b] (pp. 136–45). I leave it to you to decide how successfully the Dream can be read right through with 'account' in sense (c), so that elements come out as the most basic cues for recognition. I simply call attention to a real life example where a number of the cues for recognition involve peculiarities that are either not describable at all or not describable in sufficient detail to differentiate them from similar features in other cases. The entry under 'White-backed Woodpecker (*Dendrocopos leucotos*)' in my bird-spotter's guidebook lists the following features:

> Rather uncommon in old deciduous forests and mixed woods with old, rotting trees. The largest of the *Dendrocopos* group [cf. 'the brightest of the bodies that move round the earth in the heavens' at 208d], with a distinct white upper rump and lower back, and black upper back (diagnostic) [cf. 'this snub-nosedness of yours' at 209c]. The white back of the smaller Three-toed Woodpecker extends all the way to the neck. Bill is longer than that of any of the spotted woodpeckers [cf. Theodorus saying 'these features are not quite so pronounced' in Theaetetus as in Socrates at 143e]. In flight the white lower back and upper rump are very distinctive. Female has a black instead of a red crown; immatures have only a little red on the crown. Call is similar to that of Great Spotted Woodpecker.[109]

109. Bertel Bruun, *The Hamlyn Guide to Birds of Britain and Europe* (London & New York: 1970), 190. Note the inclusion of both relational and intrinsic features and the constant reliance on comparison. We should not be disturbed by Socrates' switch from relational differentiation ('the brightest . . .') at 208d to differentiation by intrinsic features ('this snub-nosedness of yours') at 209c. Recognition works from whatever bases it can find. Two further seeming discrepancies between 208d and 209c are dealt with below at pp. 230–1.

It is a similar set of recognitional cues, I suggest, that Socrates has in mind for the particular case of Theaetetus when he refers to the distinctive snubness of Theaetetus' nose, the distinctive way his eyes protrude, and the other details of his makeup (209c).

Some comments to clarify the status of this suggestion. First, I acknowledge that Socrates does not apply the term 'element' to the distinctive features by which Theaetetus may be recognized. He speaks of Theaetetus being made up of them, but you would not think this sufficient reason to recall 'the primary elements, as it were, of which we and everything else are composed' (201e) unless you came to the passage with the expectation that sense (c) of 'account' should yield a third interpretation of the Dream. I shall not try to add to the reasons I have already given to encourage precisely that expectation. Besides, the artist who was to be consulted on facial resemblances at 144e–145a might be able to name more ultimate, more basic visual cues than Socrates can.

Second, Socrates does not consider the mode or modes of composition whereby so complex a thing as Theaetetus is made up of his limbs and features. He does not discourse on concrete analysis. The question of parts and wholes has been thoroughly aired already, and there is no need here either to affirm or to deny that Theaetetus is identical with the sum of his limbs and features.[110]

Nor, thirdly, does Socrates renew the problem of unknowability. AK_o has been sufficiently discredited for this to be unnecessary, and readers can work on the problem for themselves. What has not yet been discussed is whether the discrediting of AK_o should lead to a rejection or modification of Def. K_o, or to a rejection or modification of AL_o. But this, the central conundrum of Part III (p. 134), remains unsettled for Interpretations [a] and [b] as well as for Interpretation [c].

That said, I return to Def. $K_{o(r)}$, the refutation of which can be discussed independently of my controversial proposals about Interpretation [c]. The key premise for the refutation is established at 209cd, where we have already noticed the recurrence of Wax Block imagery and its connection with Theaetetus' peculiar snub-nosedness. We need to see how and why this connection comes to be the pivot on which the final argument turns.

---

110. The idea that 209c reduces Theaetetus to a bundle or collection of qualities is favoured by McDowell [3], 255, and by Richard Sorabji, *Matter, Space, and Motion: Theories in Antiquity and Their Sequel* (London: 1988), 45. But the text does not say that Theaetetus is no more than the things he is composed of. It says no more than that he is composed of them.

We start at 209a, where Socrates takes a closer look at true judge-ment by itself, the first component of the new definition of knowl-edge. He tries to imagine what it would be like to have true judge-ment which is not yet knowledge, e.g. to have true judgement concerning Theaetetus without the ability to say how he may be identified and distinguished from other things. Would this mean that his thought failed to grasp any point of difference between Theaetetus and others? Apparently it would. (Why? 206d suggests the reason that otherwise he could surely put his thought into words like anyone else who is not deaf and dumb to begin with.) But *ex hypothesi* Socrates is 'a judger of' Theaetetus: he can identify him correctly, at least on occasion. So what is the content of his thought when he judges 'This is Theaetetus'? What is his answer to the question 'Who is Theaetetus?' or, to put it in Wax Block terms, what imprint can he bring to bear on his perception of Theaetetus?

Three possibilities are reviewed: (i) A thought of one who is a human being and has a nose and eyes and mouth, etc., will not bring Theaetetus, as distinct from any other person, before the mind to be the object of Socrates' judgement (209b). This parallels for inner thought the agreement reached earlier (208d) about ac-counts: an account or thought which fails to differentiate *o* because it grasps only some feature that *o* has in common with other things, will be an account/thought of the things that share the feature, not an account/thought of *o*.[111] (ii) The same objection applies if the thought is, more specifically, of the human being with a nose that is snub and eyes that are prominent. For this does not differentiate Theaetetus from Socrates himself (209bc).

So we reach, by elimination, the conclusion (iii) that it will not be *Theaetetus* whom Socrates judges to be the person he sees coming towards him until his wax block represents the distinctive way the boy's nose is snub, the distinctive way his eyes protrude, and so on (209c). In the terminology used earlier (p. 97), perception brings Theaetetus before the mind to be the X-item of Socrates' judgement,

111. Since the argument claims that such a thought fails to produce true judgement concerning Theaetetus (because the thought fails to concern Theaetetus), not that it merely fails to produce knowledge of him, it cannot be right to suggest, with Fine [52], 388, that for the purposes of this last section of the dialogue true judgement concern-ing *o* may be illustrated by the application of a nonindividuating description, as in 'The sun is a bright star'. The argument is in fact further support for narrowing the scope of true judgement to true judgements of identification like 'This is Theaetetus'.

but only a record of Theaetetus' differentness will bring Theaetetus rather than someone else before the mind to be the Y-item.[112] A capacity to identify Theaetetus must already include a memory imprint that differentiates Theaetetus from other things (209cd). Which is to say that the possession of true judgement concerning Theaetetus already enables anyone who is not deaf and dumb to begin with to tell how—so far as it can be told in words—Theaetetus may be recognized. It appears that the second component of Def. $K_{o(r)}$ adds nothing to the first.

Neither Socrates nor Theaetetus deduces from this that true judgement is after all sufficient for knowledge. Neither comments on the fact that the return of the Wax Block has brought a dramatic change of status for the imprints, which have been demoted from knowledge to capacities for correct judgements of identification. Readers will take note of this for their final assessment of Part II. But it is also crucial for the final steps of Part III, where Socrates looks in vain for something that the second component of Def. $K_{o(r)}$ can add to differentiate knowing from having true judgement.

The second component was first presented in the formula 'being able to tell some mark by which the object you are asked about differs from all other things'. Then, after discussion, I adopted 'the ability to say how to recognize o' as a brief resumé of the intended meaning. In either version the reference is to a cognitive ability. It is not the linguistic ability to say the words that matters, but the

---

112. The X-Y terminology should help to make it clear why McDowell [3], 255–56, Fine [52], 389–90, and Bostock [9], 226 ff., are wrong to report the conclusion as saying that *any* judgement about Theaetetus presupposes a grasp of his different-ness. Anyone who knows someone and sees Theaetetus in the distance can mistak-enly judge him to be their friend. This would be a false judgement about Theaetetus. 'That is not my friend' would be a true judgement about him, though a negative one (cf. Part II n. 5). 'The person over there is sitting' could be a true judgement about him also, though not a true judgement of identification. What the argument establishes and the conclusion asserts is that a quite narrow subclass of judgements about Theaetetus presuppose a grasp of his differentness, namely, the true judge-ments of identification for which I have done battle in ns 106 and 111. The conclusion will extend further only if a true judgement of identification is in turn presupposed by other judgements, e.g. one expressed by a descriptive statement in which Theaetetus is named as subject. Now when Plato comes to discuss such statements as 'Theaetetus is sitting' in the *Sophist* (262e–263a), the presupposition holds because Theaetetus is on the scene for everyone to perceive. But Plato does not make an issue of the point, and it would be foolish to propound it as a general rule. For what then of statements about long-dead persons like Homer (152e) and Thales (174a), whom Socrates never had a chance to meet?

cognitive grasp of that which the words express. That which the words express, in the current example, is Theaetetus' differentness. What, then, is the cognitive grasp?

The difficulty is that there are only two categories of cognitive grasp available, the capacity for true judgement and knowledge, and Socrates has just shown that an imprint holding true judgement concerning Theaetetus' differentness is already involved in the *first* component of Def. $K_{o(r)}$. If the capacity for true judgement concerning Theaetetus did not involve true judgement concerning Theaetetus' differentness, the latter could be added to the former to make knowledge. But with (iii) in hand, Socrates can produce a flurry of proverbs from everyday speech to scoff at the idea that something which already involves true judgement concerning Theaetetus' differentness could be turned into knowledge by adding true judgement concerning Theaetetus' differentness (209de).

The only alternative is that the ability, capacity, or grasp to be added is a *knowledge* of Theaetetus' differentness. To which Socrates retorts that it is circular to define knowledge by reference to knowledge, whether of differentness or of anything else (209e–210a; cf. 147b).

So ends the attempt to define knowledge as true judgement with an account in sense (c). So ends the attempt to define knowledge as true judgement with an account. So ends the attempt to define knowledge. Is it a conclusive end? Is there a let-out in that final phrase 'or of anything else'? Socrates himself argued earlier that knowledge of a complex must be based on knowledge of its constituent elements and supported by a like knowledge of other complexes in the domain. Is Def. $K_{o(e)}$ open to the same dilemma as Def. $K_{o(r)}$? Can the circularity of defining knowledge by reference to knowledge be made virtuous and unobjectionable?[113]

These are just a few of the questions that readers are left to grapple with at the end of the inquiry. But before facing the problem of how to sum up Part III as a whole, we do well to consider the broader implications of the failure of the attempt to define knowledge as true judgement with an account in sense (c). For if it is true, or Plato thinks it true, that Def. $K_{o(r)}$ is a plausible definition of the ordinary man's concept of knowing an object, then the question arises

---

113. An affirmative answer to this last question is urged by Fine [52], 393 ff., referring to Armstrong, *Belief, Truth and Knowledge, op. cit.*, 153–55. For an ancient debate about whether circularity can be virtuous, see Jonathan Barnes, 'Aristotle, Menaechmus and Circular Proof', *Classical Quarterly* N.S. 26 (1976), 278–92.

whether knowing an object, as ordinarily conceived, can ever be sharply differentiated from true judgement. Is the failure of the definition simply that—a proof that Def. $K_{o(r)}$, though plausible, is incorrect? Or does it point a more Platonic moral to the effect that mundane recognitional knowledge, so called, never amounts to more than a capacity to make correct judgements of identification?[114]

The text does not answer our question. It offers the image of a shadow-painting in which objects lose their appearance of form and solidity when looked at close to (208e).[115] This prefaces the argument to 209d, where the distinction between having true judgement and having an account in sense (c) dissolves, and with it Def. $K_{o(r)}$'s contrast between true judgement and knowledge. If the image tempts us to go further, to argue that not just Def. $K_{o(r)}$ but any distinction between true judgement and mundane recognitional knowledge will prove illusory when examined close to, we must find the reasons for ourselves. The written refutation is over. From here we travel on our own.

I have already remarked that when the Wax Block returns in Part III the imprints are no longer knowledge. Knowledge requires an account, and the imprints have been demoted to capacities for correct judgements of identification. All the same, we have more reason than we had in Part II to call them knowledge. For we now have what we felt the lack of in Part II (p. 92), some guidance on what happens when a 'signature' is stamped on one's block. Socrates acquires Theaetetus' 'signature' on his block by memorizing his differentness,[116] a process that will certainly involve cooperation between thought and perception and a mind capable of comparing Theaetetus with other people (cf. 186a). And Theaetetus' differentness, to judge by Socrates' most detailed reference to it (209cd), is the whole physical appearance that distinguishes him from others. It is a Gestalt of numerous distinctive features in relation to each

114. Runciman [5], 51–52, 57, believes that this is the correct conclusion to draw from the argument but doubts that Plato was able to draw it.

115. See note *ad loc. Parmenides* 165cd is another passage to make metaphorical use of the point that the illusion created by shadow painting depends on viewing the picture from a distance.

116. It is in fact one and the same Greek word, *sēmeion*, that gets translated 'signature' at 192b (also 'sign' at 194a, 194d, 'imprint' at 191d, 193c), and 'mark' of differentiation at 208c. The commonest of the words for 'imprint' in Part II is brought back to introduce the third sense of 'account': aptly so, because it is standardly used in Greek both for the device, mark, or sign on a ring, stamp, etc., and for the mark left behind in the wax. This verbal link between imprint and mark of differentiation prefigures the epistemic connection established in the argument.

other, which would illustrate rather well the thesis broached earlier (p. 201) that the whole and all the parts are known together or not known at all. Neither is epistemologically prior to the other, we could say, because Theaetetus is known only if his peculiar snub-nosedness is known, and, conversely, it seems that 'this snub-nosedness of yours' (209c) can only be picked out and recognized in the total context of Theaetetus.[117] In short, Socrates' imprint of Theaetetus equips him with as complete and accurate a basis for recognizing the boy as one could have. How could he, how could anyone, do better than this to satisfy us that he knows Theaetetus?

It is true that the question 'How well do you know Theaetetus?' would typically invite an account of the distinctive qualities of his mind (cf. 144ab). But this is not relevant to recognitional knowledge. What is relevant is that noses are not seen in isolation and that their distinctiveness shows in the setting of a whole face or more. You may have wondered why, if each detail of Theaetetus' makeup is peculiar to him, Socrates at 209c should require more than one to differentiate him by, when a single differentiating feature sufficed for the sun at 208d. A fair question if Def. $K_{o(u)}$ is the thesis under discussion.[118] Given that it is Def. $K_{o(r)}$ instead, a touch of realism is in order. What you can see and memorize of the sun is a bright orb in the sky, little else. What you can see and memorize of Theaetetus is a mass of interconnected detail. Like a bird-spotter, you may not use all that you have memorized on every occasion of recognition—in the midst of battle, a glimpse of one detail may be enough to send you running to the rescue. Nevertheless, Theaetetus' acquaintances (not just his close friends) can be expected to be familiar with at least the main peculiarities of his appearance.

But realism has its price. Even on the most favourable view of Socrates' imprint of Theaetetus—and readers may feel that I have taken a more favourable view than the text really warrants—we must admit that it is compatible with mistakes. The Wax Block model was expressly designed to make room for the judgement 'This is Theaetetus' to be false, and it is obvious that no amount of clarity and distinctness on the block will overcome a mist outside or make Theaetetus look distinctly himself when seen far off with Theodorus. Accordingly, if we want to call an imprint knowledge,

117. Cf. Austin, *op. cit.*, 52–53.

118. The question is pursued by McDowell [3], 255–57, Fine [52], 392–93 n. 28—both with Def. $K_{o(u)}$ in mind.

on the ground that it is such a good grasp of its object, we must allow knowledge to be compatible with mistakes.

We also have to reckon with the necessarily limited experience of each wax block owner. Once again the sun is no problem: in the geocentric universe assumed here one can survey all the bodies that move round the earth in the heavens and be certain which is the brightest. But no-one can survey all the people in the world as far as the 'remotest Mysian' of 209b. Socrates is merely being realistic when he speaks of differentiating Theaetetus' snub-nosedness from 'the other snub-nosednesses I have seen' (209c), not from all the snub-nosednesses in existence. But such realism is in order only if we can rely, as before, on the fact that Theaetetus' snub-nosedness is just one element in a total Gestalt that no snub-nosed stranger is likely to replicate in full.[119]

There is a further price to pay. However realistically we treat the record of Theaetetus' differentness, the argument of 209ac has it that, apart from perception, only this record will bring Theaetetus rather than someone else before the mind to be the object of Socra-

---

119. What about identical twins and Doppelgänger? If some god were to make an exact duplicate of Theaetetus far off in Mysia (cf. *Cratylus* 432bc), would that mean that Socrates could no longer judge that this is Theaetetus coming towards him? The only sensible answer is that Plato does not give us enough philosophical apparatus to deal with a possibility so remote from the assumptions of normal social intercourse in Athens. Such worries bulk large in modern discussions of reference, where causal solutions are often favoured. Thus Fine [52], 390–91, whose attachment to Def. $K_{o(u)}$ makes any snub-nosed stranger a threat because differentiation by a single feature should suffice, suggests as one way out that what enables Socrates to make his judgement about Theaetetus might be that the causal origin of his memory trace of the characteristic snub-nosedness was Theaetetus himself, no-one else. In principle a parallel solution could be offered to our much less pressing problem of twins and duplicates. However, it is not to be taken for granted that Plato would be unduly worried by a certain amount of 'slack' in thought's relation to objects in the sensible world. Readers may find it instructive to compare the closing pages of the *Theaetetus* with an energetic debate that took place in Hellenistic times between Plato's successors in the Academy and the rival Stoic school. The Stoics propounded an empiricist theory of knowledge based on the postulate that every healthy human can attain certainty through a special kind of sensory impression which reproduces all the peculiar features of, e.g., Theaetetus with such artistic exactitude that it *could* not derive from anyone or anything but Theaetetus himself. Against this the Academics contend that it can perfectly well happen that there is simply no telling the difference between twins like Castor and Pollux, or between two eggs, two bees, two seals stamped by the same signet ring, and a host of other indiscernibles. See Cicero, *Academica* II 54, 85–86, Sextus Empiricus, *Adversus Mathematicos* VII 408–10 with 250–52; Michael Frede, 'Stoics and Skeptics on Clear and Distinct Impressions', in Myles Burnyeat ed., *The Skeptical Tradition* (Berkeley, Los Angeles & London: 1983), 65–93.

tes' judgement. Accordingly, if we want to call the differentiating imprint knowledge, we must reaffirm J2 and say that knowledge of Theaetetus is necessarily involved in identity judgements (true *or* false) about him.[120]

But then of course it will be knowledge that is activated when the judgement 'This is Theaetetus' is false. In this respect, as I hinted earlier (p. 116), the case will be just like the dunce's mistake about eleven at 199d. So if, as Socrates there insists, it is intolerable to have knowledge active in error, the imprint of Theaetetus cannot be knowledge. Like the eleven-bird in the dunce's aviary, it must be a 'piece of ignorance' or 'ignorant true judgement' instead. Otherwise it would breach K'.

We have been down this road before. The further lesson we can learn in Part III is that Socrates is as well equipped as he can be to recognize Theaetetus tomorrow. If he gets it right, he can offer an account to explain how he did it or to prove that he got it right—no extra accomplishment this, but the verbal expression of the means of identification he has already grasped. If he gets it wrong, the fault will not lie with him but with the mists and spaces of this world in which we live and meet our friends; no added account, in whatever sense, could help him do better. The moral is close to hand: either a differentiating imprint of Theaetetus is enough for knowledge of him, or nothing is.

To adopt the first alternative is to accept a concept of mundane recognitional knowledge which is not governed by K'. The modern reader should welcome this. The dunce judges 'Five and seven is eleven' from a deficiency in his knowledge of eleven. But when Socrates sees Theodorus in the distance and mistakes him for Theaetetus, this reveals a deficiency in the circumstances of viewing, not a deficient knowledge of Theaetetus. K' is more appropriate to the knowledge of abstract objects in the Aviary than to the recognitional capacities of the Wax Block.

To adopt the second alternative is to acknowledge that within the constraints of K' knowledge of Theaetetus is impossible. That sounds like a sudden lurch into scepticism, but it need not be. 'There is no knowledge of the individual' is a thesis made famous by Aristotle.[121] He was not doubting our ability to recognize our

---

120. As before (p. 227 with n. 112), it is only the Y-item for which an imprint is required. We should not be prompted, with McDowell [3], 257, to reaffirm J1.

121. Cf. e.g. *Posterior Analytics* I 31, *Metaphysics* VII 15, 1039b 27–1040a 7, XIII 10, 1086b 32 ff.

friends when we meet them. He meant that scientific knowledge (understanding) is of the universal and is expressed in universal propositions: what the scientist seeks to understand is man, or living things in general. He can of course *apply* this understanding to the individual who is one man or one living thing among many, but a 'science of Theaetetus' would be an absurdity. The second alternative is not scepticism but dedication to the ambitions that emerged when the Dream was read with 'account' in sense (b) (p. 186).

A third choice is to go for both alternatives by distinguishing two concepts of what it is to know an object o. On one side, a concept of mundane recognitional knowledge with no aspiration to be in all circumstances unerring. On the other side, a concept of the ideal understanding of o that belongs to Aristotle's scientist or, on Plato's model, to the expert who is completely 'literate' in the field. Only the second concept gives scope for K'. Common sense can be satisfied with the first.

This distinction of two concepts has much to recommend it, not least when we turn to the knowledge of perceivable types like the White-backed Woodpecker, which is accountable in two senses: it has an account in sense (c) telling how it may be recognized, as quoted above, and it has '*Dendrocopos leukotos*', the scientist's definition by classification. By assigning each sense of 'account' to a different concept of knowledge, we can do justice both to the recognitional capacities of the bird-spotter and to the ornithologist's expertise. Both can be knowledge, in different senses of the word. Def. $K_{t(r)}$ and Def. $K_{o(e)}$ may coexist in peace, even if the Platonic philosopher is not interested in knowing whether his next-door neighbour is a man or some other kind of creature (174b).

Yet it is not just lack of interest that prevents the dialogue giving explicit consideration to Def. $K_{t(r)}$. A discussion of type recognition would raise tricky problems about the relation of the Wax Block to the Aviary, where perceivable types have hitherto belonged (p. 185). Would generic imprints be derived from perception by some process of abstraction? What is the logical structure of a statement like 'That is a goldfinch' which assigns a perceived item to a general type? It is taken for granted that recognizing Theaetetus as the particular man he is includes recognizing him as a man (209b; cf. p. 92), but the dialogue does not have the logical and epistemological resources for a proper philosophical treatment of the latter. Neither the Wax Block nor the Aviary is equipped to deal with anything more complex than judgements of identification with concrete or abstract terms.[122] It is time to go on to the later dialogues, the *Sophist*, *Statesman*, and, most pertinently for the topic of type-recognition, the *Philebus* (esp. 38b–39a with 33c–34c).

Accordingly, having sketched three answers to the question we began from (pp. 228–9), I shall hand them over for readers to use as they see fit and move on to the concluding section of this Introduction. Let me simply remind you of a question that came up at the end of Part II (p. 127): Does Plato mean that the eyewitness *can* know mundane empirical facts, or is the contrast between eyewitness and jury only an analogy to get us to appreciate that knowledge must be firsthand? The eyewitness can hardly be said to know who did what to whom unless recognitional knowledge is genuinely knowledge. Recognition and true judgements of identification do not make the whole of empirical knowledge, but they are a basic essential. Once again it turns out that no final assessment of Part II is possible until we have thought through the issues raised in Part III.

Finale (210ad) and conclusions

> Socrates . . . in the *Theaetetus* . . . proceeds as far as the cleansing away of the false opinions of Theaetetus, but thereafter lets him go as now being capable of discovering the truth by himself.

> I think every practicing philosopher feels profoundly delighted with the discussion as it is.[123]

We have now discovered *in detail* why three tempting but wrong answers are wrong. Even if we do not know what knowledge is, we have learned a lot about perception, true judgement, and accounts. What Socrates says about Theaetetus at 210bc should apply to us: any further ideas we may have about knowledge will be the better for the testing we have undergone.[124] And this should

---

122. Admittedly, some scholars have suggested that a judgement like 'That is a goldfinch' is catered for by the conception imprints of 191d (see Part II, n. 40). But no-one has explained what the epistemological relation between conception and perception would be in such a case.

123. The first quotation is from the fifth century A.D., the second from the twentieth, viz. Proclus, *Commentary on the First Alcibiades of Plato* (trans. William O'Neill [Hague 1965]), 28.4–7, and Robinson [39], 13, respectively.

124. In the text Socrates' remark is not explicitly restricted to future theories *about* knowledge, and might even extend to the mathematical discoveries for which, rather than for any contribution to philosophy, Theaetetus will become famous.

be so even if the question that lingers in the mind at the end of the dialogue is not, as Plato would desire, 'What is knowledge?' but the historical question 'What does Plato think knowledge is?'.

It is not to be taken for granted that there is a definite answer to the question 'What does Plato think knowledge is?'. Many readers of the *Theaetetus* have felt that the dialogue ends on a note of bafflement, defeat, or scepticism. Three such interpretations may be distinguished, the first characteristically modern, the other two ancient: (i) Plato finds himself unable (at the time of writing) to answer the question 'What is knowledge?' in a manner that escapes the objections raised in the dialogue.[125] (ii) Plato has no answer to the question 'What is knowledge?' because he has no fixed doctrines about anything: philosophy for him being the practice of Socratic midwifery, he scrutinizes the suggestions of others and takes up no position of his own.[126] (iii) Plato has no answer to the question 'What is knowledge?' because he is actually arguing that no answer is possible: he does not believe that knowledge exists.[127]

The first and second of these interpretations, and perhaps also the third, mean to compliment Plato on his honesty and his refusal to settle for easy answers. Plato is the model philosopher for those who value integrity above solutions. But equally common is the opposite conviction that a great philosopher like Plato must have an answer to the question 'What is knowledge?'. Many readers of the *Theaetetus* have felt that the dialogue takes us to the very brink of the truth. A short step and we will reach the answer for ourselves. We have only to recall a fourth sense of 'account', one so familiar from other Platonic dialogues that we are bound to notice its omission from the survey in Part III. This, it is claimed, is the sense by which knowledge ought to be defined.

Already in antiquity it was suggested that the fourth sense is to be found in a famous passage of Plato's *Meno* (97c–98a; cf. 85cd)

125. So Crombie [6], 106, White [8], 176–83, Robinson [39], 16, Morrow [51], Annas [53], 112, Hicken [60].

126. This interpretation was designed to enlist Plato in the sceptical Academy of Hellenistic times, as we learn from the surviving portion of a rather schoolmasterly commentary on the *Theaetetus*, composed by an unknown author as early perhaps as the second half of the first century b.c., and republished from papyrus remains by H. Diels & W. Schubart, *Anonymer Kommentar zu Platons Theaetet* (Berlin: 1905), 54.38–55.13.

127. We learn of this more extreme sceptical interpretation from an anonymous *Prolegomena to Platonic Philosophy*, ed. and trans. L. G. Westerink (Amsterdam: 1962), 21–25.

where correct opinions are compared to the statues of the legendary sculptor Daedalus, which run away if you do not tie them down. Even though a correct opinion is true, it will 'run away' (i.e. you are liable to change your mind) unless you have it 'bound down' by 'reasoning out an explanation'. That 'binding' is what makes the difference between knowledge and true judgement or opinion: true judgements become knowledge when they are tied down by an explanation (*sc.* an explanation of the truth believed, not an explanation of your believing it). Accordingly, it was suggested that to perfect the definition 'Knowledge is true judgement with an account' we need only take 'with an account' to mean 'bound down by an explanation'.[128]

This is actually a suggestion that we go back to Stage One and embrace the Aristotelian thesis Def. $K_{p(e)}$.[129] Maybe we should, but then we do not need and have not been given a fourth sense for the phrase 'an account of o', still less a fourth sense we can carry right through the Dream. We can of course formulate the notion of an explanation of o, but that is something we have already discussed, without assistance from the *Meno*, as an aspect or function of definition, both definition by analysis (accounts in sense (b)) and definition by classification (pp. 217–8); if a fourth sense is to rescue Def. K_o, it ought to be as clearly distinct from (a), (b), and (c) as they are from each other.

In any case, the concept of explanation is less a cure for the problems of Part III than a contributory cause. Even if we jettison Def. K_o for Def. $K_{p(e)}$, the regress of explanation remains as worrying as the regress of definition, and readers should have little difficulty devising a counterpart to the spelling argument of 207d–208b so as to show that the explanation of an isolated truth in the domain of, say, geometry or physics is not enough for knowledge.[130]

Similar comments apply when other Platonic dialogues are mined for the missing fourth sense of 'account'. Despite the *Meno*, it is not clear that Plato himself ever proposed to *define* knowledge as true

---

128. This is the view of the anonymous commentator (n. 126 above), 2.52–3.25. The suggestion is echoed by Cornford [2], 141–42, 158.

129. At 15.19–26 the commentary duly adds 'Knowledge is judgement with demonstration' as Aristotle's version of the definition which the commentator claims to find in the *Meno*.

130. The anonymous commentator, 14.45–15.26, explicitly restricts Def. $K_{p(e)}$ to single theorems, the knowledge of which he claims is prior to systematic science. Unfortunately, the papyrus breaks off at *Theaet.* 158a, so that we do not know his response to the spelling argument of 207d–208b.

judgement with an account. Nowhere outside the *Theaetetus* does he even formulate an explicit definition of knowledge.[131] But there is no doubt that he regards being able to give an account as the characteristic expression of knowledge and understanding, in both theoretical and practical domains. A doctor, for example, can explain why a certain diet is good for his patient by giving an account of the nature of the foods prescribed. According to the *Gorgias* (464d–465a, 501ac), this sort of account distinguishes a genuine art, a body of practical *knowledge*, from a mere knack picked up by experience. Or take a mathematician like Euclid, whose *Elements* open with a long list of definitions ('A point is that which has no part', 'A line is breadthless length', etc.) and axioms ('Things which are equal to the same thing are equal to one another', etc.) and not a word of explanation or justification to back them up. According to the *Republic* (510c, 533c), mathematics is not strictly knowledge because it can give no account (explanation? justification? elucidation?) of the hypotheses on which its theorems depend. By contrast, the philosopher practised in dialectic can give and defend an account (definition) of the essence of each thing. Most importantly, he is able to defend a definition of the Form of Good and thereby distinguish it from all other things, which is a necessary condition not only for knowing the Good itself but also for knowledge of any good thing (*Rep.* 531e, 534bc). Again, in the *Phaedo* (95d) we meet the idea that the best remedy for the fear of death would be to know that the soul is immortal and to be able to give an account (proof) of the fact. And many other passages say or imply that an account is essential to knowledge without indicating a more specific meaning for the term.[132]

But nowhere in all this is there a fourth sense of 'account' capable of solving the problems of Part III. Proof, definition, elucidation, justification, explanation—each of these notions, once incorporated into a definition of knowledge, will threaten a vertical regress to unknowables (AK_o or AK_p), and each will be subject to horizontal pressure from some analogue of the spelling argument of 207d–208b. That is the beauty of Part III. The very indeterminacy of 'account' makes us concentrate on the general form of a problem

131. The closest he gets to it is at *Meno* 97c–98a and *Symposium* 202a, but neither passage makes it clear that a definition is intended, and neither need be read as presenting one.

132. E.g. *Phaedo* 73a, 76b, *Symposium* 202a, *Timaeus* 28a, 51e, *Theaetetus* 175c, *Sophist* 265c, *Philebus* 62a.

that nearly all epistemologies must face. Plato's own thoughts about knowledge are no more immune to the difficulty than anyone else's.

Another time-honoured way to have the *Theaetetus* bring us to the verge of the truth is to say that the whole dialogue (and not just Part I under Reading A) is designed to offer indirect support to the two-world epistemology of the *Phaedo* and *Republic*, where knowledge and opinion (*doxa*) are separate capacities and are assigned to different realms, knowledge being essentially of the Forms and opinion of the changing world of sensible things. Part III's contribution to this project is to prove that there is no accounting for, and hence no knowledge of, the perceivable things (types or particulars) which the *Republic* casts as the objects of opinion. If there is no knowledge of the objects of opinion, we must repudiate the first component in Theaetetus' third definition, true judgement. Our three epistemic routes will not be properly separate (cf. pp. 173–4) until knowledge has been freed from all connection with *doxa* and restricted to the Forms.[133]

But this is no solution either. The objections to Def. K_o are not to be met by taking a Form as the value of *o*. For accounts of Forms are as vulnerable to the epistemological regress as accounts of anything else, and the *Republic* accepts that Forms cannot be known singly, one by one (p. 216). Rather than relate the *Theaetetus* to the *Republic* through the objects of knowledge and opinion, it would be better to concentrate on the more formal point that, according to the *Republic*, knowledge and opinion are distinguished in the first instance as two capacities, one of which is unerring, the other not (477de). We could well read the *Theaetetus* as a long meditation on that brief passage of the *Republic*. The *Theaetetus* is the work in which Plato explores the difficulties of accommodating together, on the one hand, the idea that knowledge is unerring, on the other, the idea that a capacity which is not unerring and allows mistakes must nevertheless contain a partial grasp of the truth.

133. So Cherniss [59], Yoh [61]; cf. Paul Shorey, *The Unity of Plato's Thought* (Chicago: 1903), 34. In the same spirit Sir David Ross, *Plato's Theory of Ideas* (Oxford: 1951), 103, describes the dialogue as 'the strongest argument Plato gives anywhere for the foundation of his metaphysical theory'. Cornford [2], 162–63 (cf. 12–13) with 141–42, 158, combines the two-world conclusion with a fourth sense taken from the *Meno*. In Sayre [7], 133, 179–80, true judgement is retained and the two-world conclusion combined with a fourth sense taken from the *Sophist*'s method of division. The anonymous commentary, 2.32–39, reveals that already in antiquity some people had given to the *Theaetetus* the negative task of showing what knowledge is not of or about, to the *Sophist* the positive task of showing what it is of or about.

A meditation of such length and complexity does not leave its topic unchanged. It is no use going back to the *Republic* now. Once the spectre of AK_o has come into view, even the most ardent Platonist must confront the central conundrum of Part III: whether to stop the regress by rejecting or revising Def. K_o, or by rejecting or revising AL_o.

There is more scope for choice than may appear. The alternatives to AL_o, for example, are that everything is accountable or that nothing is (p. 132), but this trio of possibilities can be multiplied by as many senses of 'account' as we care to consider, subject to the qualification that some senses of 'account' presuppose a restricted range of objects. Thus, even if every object admits of at least one account in sense (a): a statement about it, only a perceivable object (particular or type) will have an account in sense (c), and only a type or universal can be defined. Again, if elements have no analysis, they may still have a definition by classification; conversely, if ultimate genera have no definition by classification, they may still be divided into their several species. So it is possible to maintain that everything is accountable provided this is not taken to mean that everything is accountable in exactly the same sense.

With Def. K_o we have a similar breadth of choice. One obvious possibility is that Def. K_o does not hold for the primary things, which are known without an account. This in turn may mean either (i) without any account at all or (ii) without an account *of* the object known. Thus (i) some readers of the dialogue have found it necessary or congenial to postulate a special intuitive knowing (acquaintance) for elements.[134] Alternatively (ii) the point could simply be that, although elements have no account of their own, they are knowable through and as the termini of the accounts of complexes. Just as through experience we become familiar with basic recognitional cues for people and other sensible things, so

134. Different versions of this idea may be found in Taylor [4], 344–48, Runciman [5], 40, Paul Friedländer, *Plato* Vol. 3: *The Dialogues, Second and Third Periods* (Princeton: 1969), 186–88, J. A. Lesher, '*Gnosis* and *Episteme* in Socrates' Dream in the *Theaetetus*', *Journal of Hellenic Studies* 89 (1969), 72–78. Their kind of solution would not be admissible if Fine [52], 384–85, was right to argue that, once AK_o is rejected, AL_o goes with it. Her evidence is 205de, where Socrates concludes that either elements and complexes are equally knowable *and* accountable, or they are equally unknowable *and* unaccountable. But he has no warrant in the preceding argument for this addition, and we should not be bullied by anything he says in the dilemma section. The positive plain-sailing sequel 206ab insists that elements are knowable but remains neutral as to whether or not elements have an account of their own.

through practice in analysis we learn the elements of which abstract complexes are composed and the principles of their composition. Composition is the other face of analysis. We can know the basic elements of a science in much the same way as we know our letters: not by analysis (knowing how the letters are spelled) but by mastering the principles of composition (knowing what syllables they help to spell).[135]

If, on the other hand, we prefer to hold on to Def. K_o, we can do so by allowing different senses of 'account' to define different kinds of knowing for different objects. The options multiply again. Some are options we looked at as we journeyed through Part III. Others remain to be explored. The important thing is that the only way to choose among them is to construct the best theory of knowledge we can from the materials provided in the dialogue. The same applies to the contrasting true-judgement component of Def. K_o: whether to retain it and, if so, in what role is a decision to be made in conjunction with the choice of this or that sense of 'account' for this or that kind of knowing.

Why assume, after all, that a single sense of 'account' is enough to do justice to the complexity of knowledge? Indeed, in a dialogue so concerned with parts and wholes, why assume there is no more to the meaning of 'account' than a plurality of disconnected senses? The Greek word *logos* also signifies reason, the faculty by which the mature human being is distinguished from children and animals which have only the power of perception (186bc). So why not suggest that each sense of 'account' picks out one function or group of functions that reason can perform? Articulate statement; definition, analysis, and classification; differentiation; justification, proof, and explanation—most of these can in suitable contexts be counted *a reason* for something, all of them can help us gain knowledge and understanding both of objects and of true propositions about them. But they can do this only because (to echo the suggestive phrasing of 184d) there is some single form—soul, mind, reason, or whatever one ought to call it—to which they converge and which combines their several contributions into a structured whole.[136] One might put it this way: only reason can find and appreciate the reasons that

---

135. Cf. Runciman [5], 48, Owen, 'Notes on Ryle's Plato', *op. cit.*, 365, referring not to the *Theaetetus* but to *Sophist* 253a, 261d, *Statesman* 277e–278c, *Philebus* 18cd.

136. We could even envisage an account of 'account' which related all the senses of the word to the faculty of reason in somewhat the same style as 'justice' and 'just', 'health' and 'healthy', are analyzed at *Republic* 443c–444e.

make the difference between knowledge and mere true judgement. The subsequent history of philosophy confirms that the problem of knowledge is ultimately a problem about determining the powers and limits of human reason.

This final suggestion—my last attempt to open up a line of inquiry that readers may find it rewarding to follow on their own—is motivated by a belief that epistemology becomes superficial when the securing of an objection-free definition of knowledge is made an end in itself. The defining of knowledge is important when, and only when, as with each of the three definitions in the *Theaetetus*, it leads into a detailed investigation of the powers and prospects of the human mind. From this point of view the dialogue is not only a classic treatment of the problem of knowledge. It remains an exemplary model for us to emulate today.

Twentieth-century readers of the *Theaetetus* are bound to ask the historical question 'What does Plato think knowledge is?'. My aim in this Introduction has been to share my conviction that the question should be answered in the imperative rather than the indicative mood. The dialogue's final message is: Let us try to formulate, in detail, a better answer to the question 'What is knowledge?'

SELECT BIBLIOGRAPHY OF FURTHER READING

General

The major commentaries on the *Theaetetus* are all in English. [1] is a commentary on the Greek text, [2] and [3] on English translations which readers may sometimes find it useful to compare with Miss Levett's.

[1] Lewis Campbell, *The Theaetetus of Plato* with a revised text and English notes, 2nd edition (Oxford: 1883).

[2] Francis Macdonald Cornford, *Plato's Theory of Knowledge*. The *Theaetetus* and the *Sophist* of Plato translated with a commentary (London: 1935).

[3] John McDowell, *Plato: Theaetetus*. Translated with notes (Oxford: 1973).

Almost any general book on Plato's philosophy will have a fair amount to say about the *Theaetetus*. Those which contain substantial discussions of the dialogue include

[4] A. E. Taylor, *Plato—the Man and His Work* (London: 1926).

[5] W. G. Runciman, *Plato's Later Epistemology* (Cambridge: 1962).

[6] I. M. Crombie, *An Examination of Plato's Doctrines*, Vol. II: *Plato on Knowledge and Reality* (London & New York: 1963).

[7] Kenneth M. Sayre, *Plato's Analytic Method* (Chicago & London: 1969).

[8] Nicholas P. White, *Plato on Knowledge and Reality* (Indianapolis: 1976).

A book-length study of the dialogue is contributed by
[9] David Bostock, *Plato's Theaetetus* (Oxford: 1988).

Prologue and Introductory Conversation

146d–147c: The role of examples in Socratic dialectic is debated by
[10] P. T. Geach, 'Plato's *Euthyphro*: An Analysis and Commentary', *Monist* 50 (1966), 369–82; repr. in his *Logic Matters* (Oxford: 1972), 31–44.

243

[11] Gerasimos Santas, 'The Socratic Fallacy', *Journal of the History of Philosophy* 10 (1972), 127–41.

[12] M. F. Burnyeat, 'Examples in Epistemology: Socrates, Theaetetus and G. E. Moore', *Philosophy* 52 (1977), 381–96.

147c–148d: Readers who would like to know more about Theaetetus' mathematical achievements, so far as they can be reconstructed from Plato's testimony and other evidence, may like to consult [13] M. F. Burnyeat, 'The Philosophical Sense of Theaetetus' Mathematics', *Isis* 69 (1978), 489–513.

148e–151d: Socrates' comparison of himself to a midwife is the subject of a special study in [14] M. F. Burnyeat, 'Socratic Midwifery, Platonic Inspiration', *Bulletin of the Institute of Classical Studies* 24 (1977), 7–16.

Part I

151d–184a: Interpretations of the overall strategy are given by [2], [3], [7], and by [15] Konrad Marc-Wogau, 'On Protagoras' *homomensura*-thesis in Plato's *Theaetetus*', in his *Philosophical Essays* (Copenhagen: 1967), 3–20.

[16] M. F. Burnyeat, 'Idealism and Greek Philosophy: What Descartes Saw and Berkeley Missed', *Philosophical Review* 90 (1982), 3–40; also in Godfrey Vesey ed., *Idealism Past and Present* (Royal Institute of Philosophy Lecture Series 13, Cambridge: 1982), 19–50.

A subtle reconstruction of the theory of perception, with a critique of [16], [21] and [28], is given by [17] Mohan Matthen, 'Perception, Relativism, and Truth: Reflections on Plato's *Theaetetus* 152–160', *Dialogue* 24 (1985), 33–58.

For a classic debate on the place of the *Theaetetus* in the development of Plato's philosophy, especially his views about flux in the sensible world, see [18] G.E.L. Owen, 'The Place of the *Timaeus* in Plato's Dialogues', *Classical Quarterly* N.S. 3 (1953), 79–95; repr. in his *Logic, Science and Dialectic: Collected Papers in Greek Philosophy*, ed. Martha Nussbaum (London: 1986), 65–84.

[19] H. F. Cherniss, 'The Relation of the *Timaeus* to Plato's Later Dialogues', *American Journal of Philology* 78 (1957), 225–66; repr. in his *Selected Papers*, ed. Leonardo Tarán (Leiden: 1977), 298–339.

Both these papers are reprinted in R. E. Allen, *Studies in Plato's Metaphysics* (London & New York: 1965), 313–38 and 339–78.

153d–154b: For historical and philosophical material which may shed light on the perennial appeal of the argument from conflicting appearances, see
[20] Anthony Kenny, 'The Argument from Illusion in Aristotle's Metaphysics (Γ, 1009–10)', *Mind* 76 (1967), 184–97.
[21] M. F. Burnyeat, 'Conflicting Appearances', *Proceedings of the British Academy* 65 (1979), 69–111.
[22] Julia Annas & Jonathan Barnes, *The Modes of Scepticism: Ancient Texts and Modern Interpretations* (Cambridge: 1985).

166a–168c: Conflicting interpretations of the Defence of Protagoras have played a large part in determining accounts of Protagorean relativism. See especially
[23] G. B. Kerferd, 'Plato's Account of the Relativism of Protagoras', *Durham University Journal* 42 (1949), 20–26.
[24] Gregory Vlastos, Introduction to: *Plato's Protagoras*, B. Jowett's translation extensively revised by Martin Ostwald; edited, with an Introduction by Gregory Vlastos (Indianapolis & New York: 1956).
[25] A. T. Cole, 'The Apology of Protagoras', *Yale Classical Studies* 19 (1966), 101–18.

170a–171d: Attempts to analyze and assess the argument that Protagoras' relativism is self-refuting include
[26] John Passmore, *Philosophical Reasoning* (London: 1961), chap. 4.
[27] Edward N. Lee, '"Hoist with His Own Petard": Ironic and Comic Elements in Plato's Critique of Protagoras (*Tht.* 161–171)', in E. N. Lee, A.P.D. Mourelatos, R. M. Rorty edd., *Exegesis and Argument: Studies in Greek Philosophy Presented to Gregory Vlastos* (Assen: 1973), 225–61.
[28] M. F. Burnyeat, 'Protagoras and Self-Refutation in Plato's *Theaetetus*', *Philosophical Review* 85 (1976), 172–95.
[29] Sarah Waterlow, 'Protagoras and Inconsistency', *Archiv für Geschichte der Philosophie* 59 (1977), 19–36.

171d–177c: The sense and purpose of the Digression is discussed by
[30] A. Barker, 'The Digression in the "Theaetetus"', *Journal of the History of Philosophy* 14 (1976), 457–62.
Valuable material relating to its historical context and subsequent influence may be found in
[31] Werner Jaeger, 'On the Origin and Cycle of the Philosophic Ideal of Life', Appendix 2 in W. Jaeger, *Aristotle: Fundamentals of the History of his Development*, trans. by Richard Robinson, 2nd edition (Oxford: 1948), 426–61.

[32] John Passmore, *The Perfectibility of Man* (London: 1970).

177c–179b: I know of no sustained philosophical analysis of the extremely important argument about the future (though see [35]). In view of this gap, the adventurous reader may like to find out something about the way in which, in later antiquity, arguments from the necessities of action were used to combat, not relativism, but its close rival, scepticism:

[33] Gisela Striker, 'Sceptical Strategies', in Malcolm Schofield, Myles Burnyeat, & Jonathan Barnes edd., *Doubt and Dogmatism: Studies in Hellenistic Epistemology* (Oxford: 1980), 54–83.

179c–183c: The final refutation of Heraclitean flux is discussed in [9], [18], [19], and in

[34] Robert Bolton, 'Plato's Distinction between Being and Becoming', *Review of Metaphysics* 29 (1975/6), 66–95.

184a–186e: the relation of perception and judgement, and other issues in the interpretation of this section, are discussed in [9] and in

[35] J. M. Cooper, 'Plato on Sense Perception and Knowledge: *Theaetetus* 184 to 186', *Phronesis* 15 (1970), 123–46.

[36] A. J. Holland, 'An Argument in Plato's Theaetetus: 184–6', *Philosophical Quarterly* 23 (1973), 110–16.

[37] M. F. Burnyeat, 'Plato on the Grammar of Perceiving', *Classical Quarterly* N.S. 26 (1976), 29–51.

[38] D. K. Modrak, 'Perception and Judgement in the *Theaetetus*', *Phronesis* 26 (1981), 35–54.

Part II

187d–200d: The whole discussion of false judgement is surveyed and analyzed by [8] and by

[39] Richard Robinson, 'Forms and Error in Plato's *Theaetetus*', *Philosophical Review* 59 (1950), 3–30; repr. in his *Essays in Greek Philosophy* (Oxford: 1969), 39–73.

[40] John Ackrill, 'Plato on False Belief: *Theaetetus* 187–200', *Monist* 50 (1966), 383–402.

[41] G. Rudebusch, 'Plato on Sense and Reference', *Mind* 104 (1985), 526–37.

On the puzzle of 188ac, see

[42] J. H. McDowell, 'Identity Mistakes: Plato and the Logical Atomists', *Proceedings of the Aristotelian Society* N. S. 70 (1969/70), 181–95.

Studies which treat together the puzzle of 188ac and the discussion of 'other-judging' (189b–190e) are

[43] C.F.J. Williams, 'Referential Opacity and False Belief in the *Theaetetus'*, *Philosophical Quarterly* 22 (1972), 289–302.
[44] F. A. Lewis, 'Two Paradoxes in the *Theaetetus'*, in J. M. E. Moravcsik ed., *Patterns in Plato's Thought* (Dordrecht: 1973), 123–49.
[45] Gail Fine, 'False Belief in the *Theaetetus'*, *Phronesis* 24 (1979), 70–80. [N.B.: page 77, line 34 of this paper should read: 'Theaetetus' definition follows. The discussion of false belief thus explores'.]

188d–189b: An important discussion of the puzzle about saying what is not, and of Plato's eventual solution to it in the *Sophist*, is
[46] G.E.L. Owen, 'Plato on Not-Being', in Gregory Vlastos ed., *Plato I: Metaphysics and Epistemology*, Modern Studies in Philosophy (New York: 1970), 223–67; repr. in his *Logic, Science and Dialectic: Collected Papers in Greek Philosophy*, ed. Martha Nussbaum (London: 1986), 104–37.

189b–190e: The various possibilities for making sense of the section on 'other-judging' are best approached by comparing the treatment in [9] with that in
[47] Gareth B. Matthews, 'A Puzzle in Plato: *Theaetetus* 189b–190e', in David F. Austin ed., *Philosophical Analysis: A Defense by Example* (Dordrecht: 1988), 3–15.

196d–200c: The problems of the Aviary are discussed by
[48] Frank A. Lewis, 'Foul Play in Plato's Aviary: *Theaetetus* 195B ff.', in E. N. Lee, A.P.D. Mourelatos, & R. M. Rorty edd., *Exegesis and Argument: Studies in Greek Philosophy Presented to Gregory Vlastos* (Assen: 1973), 262–84.

200d–201c: The Jury passage is debated by
[49] M. F. Burnyeat and [50] Jonathan Barnes, 'Socrates and the Jury: Paradoxes in Plato's Distinction between Knowledge and True Belief', *Aristotelian Society Supplementary Volume* 54 (1980), 173–91 and 193–206 respectively. [N.B.: the word 'not' should be deleted from page 197, line 7.]

Part III

201c–210d: Interpretations of the Dream are often conjoined with an assessment of the overall achievement of Part III. Such are
[51] Glenn R. Morrow, 'Plato and the Mathematicians: An Interpretation of Socrates' Dream in the *Theaetetus'*, *Philosophical Review* 79 (1970), 309–33.

[52] Gail J. Fine, 'Knowledge and *Logos* in the *Theaetetus*', *Philosophical Review* (1979), 366–97.

[53] Julia Annas, 'Knowledge and Language: The *Theaetetus* and the *Cratylus*', in Malcolm Schofield & Martha Craven Nussbaum edd., *Language and Logos: Studies in ancient Greek philosophy presented to G.E.L. Owen* (Cambridge: 1982), 95–114.

201c–203b: More narrowly and textually focussed on the Dream is [54] M. F. Burnyeat, 'The Material and Sources of Plato's Dream', *Phronesis* 15 (1970), 101–22.

201c–205e: For Ryle's epoch-making treatment of the Dream, see first [55] Gilbert Ryle, 'Plato's Parmenides', *Mind* 48 (1939), 129–51 and 302–25; repr. in R. E. Allen ed., *Studies in Plato's Metaphysics* (London & New York: 1965), 97–147, esp. 136–41.

Next in the order of writing is the famous, and for a long time unpublished, paper which Ryle read to the Oxford Philological Society in 1952: [56] Gilbert Ryle, 'Logical Atomism in Plato's *Theaetetus*', *Phronesis* 35 (1990); 21–46.

Certain special themes of [56] are developed, in connection with the *Sophist* and *Philebus* as well as the *Theaetetus*, in [57] Gilbert Ryle, 'Letters and Syllables in Plato', *Philosophical Review* 69 (1960), 431–51.

Some of the details in [57] are criticized by [58] D. Gallop, 'Plato and the Alphabet', *Philosophical Review* 72 (1963), 364–76.

Conclusions

The conclusions proposed in [2]–[9] may be compared with four further attempts to sum up the results of the dialogue as a whole:

[59] H. F. Cherniss, 'The Philosophical Economy of the Theory of Ideas', *American Journal of Philology* 57 (1936), 445–56; repr. in his *Selected Papers*, ed. Leonardo Tarán (Leiden: 1977), 121–32.

[60] Winifred F. Hicken, 'Knowledge and Forms in Plato's *Theaetetus*', *Journal of Hellenic Studies* 77, Part I (1957), 48–53.

These two papers are reprinted in R. E. Allen ed., *Studies in Plato's Metaphysics* (London & New York: 1965), 1–12 and 185–98.

[61] May Yoh, 'On the Third Attempted Definition of Knowledge, *Theaetetus* 201c–210b', *Dialogue* 14 (1975), 420–42.

[62] Alexander Nehamas, '*Episteme* and *Logos* in Plato's Later Thought', *Archiv für Geschichte der Philosophie* 66 (1984), 11–36.

The Theaetetus
of Plato

translated by

M. J. LEVETT

revised by
Myles Burnyeat

THE THEAETETUS
OF PLATO:
ANALYSIS

by M. J. Levett

[*Note*: The dialogue is a discussion of the question 'What is knowledge?' As in most of Plato's dialogues, the chief speaker is Socrates, who proceeds by eliciting from his companion a number of suggested definitions of knowledge. These are carefully examined, and in every case shown to be ultimately untenable. The conclusion of the dialogue is negative, and the whole effect may seem to be merely destructive. There is no doubt, however, that the discussion has not merely cleared the way for a more successful attempt, by ruling out a number of apparent possibilities, but has also pointed out the lines upon which further attempts may proceed. A considerable amount of positive teaching is concealed under the negative and destructive form.

References are to the pages and columns of the standard edition, given in the margin of most translations.]

of all things; of the things which are, that they are, and of the things which are not, that they are not.'

(ii) 152c–153d. Corresponding metaphysical theory of Heraclitus; nothing ever is, but everything is coming-to-be.

(iii) 153d–157d. Application of the theory of Heraclitus to the explanation of sense-perception.

(iv) 157e–160e. Application of these theories in explanation of delusions, dreams and the relativity of sense-perception.

(b) 160e–168c. *Superficial objections stated and answered.*

(i) 161c–161e. The theory seems to deny that there are differences of wisdom; why then was Protagoras himself thought to be specially wise? ANSWER (162d–163a): This proves nothing, and is a mere appeal to popular prejudice.

(ii) 163a–165e. The theory leads to the conclusion that we sometimes know and don't know at the same time, which is self-contradictory. ANSWER (166a–168c): All these contradictions disappear if we take seriously the infinite diversity and changeability of the world and of men's perceptions of it. Moreover (166d), when we take this seriously, we see that the theory need not deny that one man is wiser than another: it explains this by saying that one man is able to change the appearances and make them (not *true* instead of false, but) better instead of worse, while another has not this ability.

(c) 170a–172c, 177c–179b. *Serious refutation of Protagoras.*

(i) 170a–171d. The theory contradicts itself; for, since it holds that all opinions are equally true, it must admit the truth of the opinion that it (the theory itself) is false.

(ii) 171d–172c, 177c–179b. Grant that there are some cases, viz. matters of direct experience and of value, where, as the theory maintains, things are for the individual as they seem to him to be: *nevertheless* in certain other cases, viz. those involving judgements about the future, a man has not necessarily got the criterion in himself; one judgement may be true and another false, and one man wiser than another in the sense of 'better able to predict what is going to happen'.

(172c–177c. INTERLUDE: Character of the philosopher compared with that of the practical man.)

(d) 179c–183c. *Serious refutation of Heraclitus.*

(i) 179c–181b. General account of the Heracliteans, contrasted with the followers of Parmenides—the Monists.

(ii) 181b–183c. If it were true that everything is always changing in every way, it would be impossible to say or think anything at all. (And so the theory itself would be impossible.)

(e) 183c–186e. *Final refutation of the theory that knowledge is sense-perception* ('the Theory of Theaetetus').

(i) 184b–185a. Sense-perception depends on the bodily sense-organs—for example, the perception of colour on the eyes, of sounds on the ears; and the eye does not hear nor the ear see, i.e. each sense is confined to its proper objects.

(ii) 185a–e. But there are some properties, for example, being and not-being, likeness and unlikeness, same and different, which are common to the objects of all the senses. These must be considered by the soul functioning through itself without the aid of any special instrument.

(iii) 186a–e. These properties, including being and truth, are what we have to know if we are to have knowledge. Therefore, since these properties are not perceived through the senses, KNOWLEDGE IS NOT SENSE-PERCEPTION.

187a–201c. THIRD ATTEMPT TO DEFINE KNOWLEDGE: KNOWLEDGE IS TRUE JUDGMENT.

187a–c. Judgement, 'the activity of the soul when it is busy by itself about the things which are', may be either true or false. True judgement is to be knowledge. But what is false judgement?

(a) 187e–200d. *False judgement.*

(i) 188a–191a. The problem: It seems impossible to understand how there can be false judgements if

(1) (188a–c) everything is either something that we know or something that we do not know; or if

(2) (188c–189b) judging falsely is affirming the things which are not; or if

(3) (189b–191a) false judgement is judging that one thing is another.

(ii) 191a–200d. Attempts to explain false judgement by distinguishing different senses of the word 'know'.

(1) 191c–196c. *Simile of the Wax Block:* Memory distinguished from perception. False judgement can occur when you think (a) that other things you know and are perceiving are things you know, (b) that things you don't know but are perceiving are things you know, (c) that things you both know and are perceiving are other things you both know and are perceiving; and not otherwise. BUT (195b) mistakes *can* also occur in cases where perception is not concerned.

(196d–197a. *Note:* In order to carry on the discussion at all we have to make use of the very term, 'knowledge', which we are trying to define.)

(2) 197b–200d. *Simile of the Aviary:* the 'possession' of knowledge distinguished from the 'having' (application) of knowledge. False judgement is possible when you fail to 'have' (apply) knowledge which you possess. But (199c) this still does not account for our mistaking for knowledge something which is not knowledge.

(b) 200d–201c. *True judgement* is not the same thing as knowledge. For a good orator may persuade a jury to judge correctly about things which only an eye-witness could *know.*

201c–210a. FOURTH ATTEMPT TO DEFINE KNOWLEDGE. KNOWLEDGE IS TRUE JUDGEMENT ACCOMPANIED BY AN 'ACCOUNT'.

(a) 201d–202d. *Exposition:* There are elements, which cannot be known but only named; and compounds, which can be known if the names of the elements of which they are compounded are woven together into an account.

(b) 202d–206b. *Criticism:* Does the theory mean that a syllable, for example, can be known, but not its letters? Then

(i) (203c) if the syllable *is* the letters, the letters must be known if the syllable is. But

(ii) (203e) if the syllable is not the letters but some single form resulting from the combination of the letters, the syllable itself must be just as unknowable as the letters.

(iii) Further (206a), as a matter of common experience elements are more easily learnt, more 'knowable', than compounds.

(c) 206c–210a. *What then can be meant by 'account'?*

(i) 206d–e. Not the expression of thought in words, for then everyone who can express a judgement in words would have knowledge.

(ii) 206e–208b. Not a list of the elements of which the thing we are judging about is composed, for a man might be able to give such a list in one case although in another he might make mistakes about the very same elements; such a man could not be said to have knowledge even in the case where his judgement is correct.

(iii) 208c–210a. Not a grasp of the *difference* between one thing and another; for (209a–d) without such a grasp of the difference there would not even be correct judgement (so that it is not something which could be *added* to true judgement to make it into knowledge); and (209d–210a) to say we *know* the difference is to assume we understand the thing we are trying to define.

210b–d. *Conclusion:* None of the attempts to define knowledge succeeds.

The Theaetetus
of Plato

THEAETETUS

PERSONS OF THE DIALOGUE:
EUCLEIDES, TERPSION, SOCRATES, THEODORUS, AND THEAETETUS.

The prologue is supposed to take place in a street in Megara, and afterwards at the house of Eucleides, in the year 369 B.C. Eucleides and Terpsion are mentioned in Plato's Phaedo *(59c) as having come from Megara to keep company with Socrates on the day of his death. Little is known about them beyond the fact that Eucleides adhered to a strong version of the Socratic thesis that all the virtues are one thing, knowledge. He is thus a likely person to be interested in a Socratic discussion about knowledge.*

EUCLEIDES. TERPSION.

Eu. Are you only just in from the country, Terpsion? Or have you been here some time?

142

TER. I've been here a good while. In fact, I have been looking for you in the market-place and wondering that I couldn't find you.

Eu. Well, you couldn't, because I was not in the city.

TER. Where have you been, then?

Eu. I went down to the harbour; and as I was going, I met Theaetetus, being taken to Athens from the camp at Corinth.

TER. Alive or dead?

Eu. Alive; but that's about all one could say. Badly wounded for one thing; but the real trouble is this sickness that has broken out in the army.

b

TER. Dysentery?

Eu. Yes.

TER. What a man to lose!

Eu. Yes. A fine man, Terpsion. Only just now I was listening to some people singing his praises for the way he behaved in the battle.

TER. Well, there's nothing extraordinary about that. Much more to be wondered at if he hadn't distinguished himself. But why didn't he put up here at Megara?

c

Eu. He was in a hurry to get home. I kept asking him myself, and advising him; but he wouldn't. So I saw him on his way. And

259

as I was coming back, I thought of Socrates and what a remarkably good prophet he was—as usual—about Theaetetus. It was not long before his death, if I remember rightly, that he came across Theaetetus, who was a boy at the time. Socrates met him and had a talk with him, and was very much struck with his natural ability; and when I went to Athens, he repeated to me the discussion they
d   had had, which was well worth listening to. And he said to me then that we should inevitably hear more of Theaetetus, if he lived to grow up.

TER. Well, he appears to have been right enough.—But what was this discussion? Could you tell it to me?

EU. Good Lord, no. Not from memory, anyway. But I made
143   some notes of it at the time, as soon as I got home; then afterwards I recalled it at my leisure and wrote it out, and whenever I went to Athens, I used to ask Socrates about the points I couldn't remember, and correct my version when I got home. The result is that I have got pretty well the whole discussion in writing.

TER. Yes, of course. I have heard you say that before, and I have always been meaning to ask you to show it to me, though I have been so long about it. But is there any reason why we shouldn't go through it now? I want a rest, in any case, after my journey in from the country.

b   EU. Well, I shouldn't mind sitting down either. I saw Theaetetus as far as Erineum. Come along. We will get the slave to read it to us while we rest.

TER. Right.

EU. This is the book, Terpsion. You see, I have written it out like this: I have not made Socrates relate the conversation as he related it to me, but I represent him as speaking directly to the persons with whom he said he had this conversation. (These were, he told me, Theodorus the geometer and Theaetetus.) I wanted, in the
c   written version, to avoid the bother of having the bits of narrative in between the speeches—I mean, when Socrates, whenever he mentions his own part in the discussion, says 'And I maintained' or 'I said,' or, of the person answering, 'He agreed' or 'He would not admit this.' That is why I have made him talk directly to them and have left out these formulae.

TER. Well, that's quite in order, Eucleides.

EU. Now, boy, let us have it.

The scene of the dialogue itself is a gymnasium or wrestling-school in Athens and the date shortly before the death of Socrates in 399 B.C. Theodorus is a distinguished mathematician from Cyrene in Libya. Theaetetus, his pupil and a future mathematician of even greater distinction, is about 16 years old.

SOCRATES.   THEODORUS.   THEAETETUS.

Soc. If Cyrene were first in my affections, Theodorus, I should *d* be asking you how things are there, and whether any of your young people are taking up geometry or any other branch of philosophy. But, as it is, I love Athens better than Cyrene, and so I'm more anxious to know which of our young men show signs of turning out well. That, of course, is what I am always trying to find out myself, as best I can; and I keep asking other people too—anyone round whom I see the young men are inclined to gather. Now you, of course, are very much sought after, and with good reason; your geometry alone entitles you to it, and that is not your only claim. *e* So if you have come across anyone worth mentioning, I should be glad to hear.

THEOD. Well, Socrates, I think you ought to be told, and I think I ought to tell you, about a remarkable boy I have met here, one of your fellow-countrymen. And if he were beautiful, I should be extremely nervous of speaking of him with enthusiasm, for fear I might be suspected of being in love with him. But as a matter of fact—if you'll excuse my saying such a thing—he is not beautiful at all, but is rather like you, snub-nosed, with eyes that stick out; though these features are not quite so pronounced in him. I speak without any qualms; and I assure you that among all the people I *144* have ever met—and I have got to know a good many in my time— I have never yet seen anyone so amazingly gifted. Along with a quickness beyond the capacity of most people, he has an unusually gentle temper; and, to crown it all, he is as manly a boy as any of his fellows. I never thought such a combination could exist; I don't see it arising elsewhere. People as acute and keen and retentive as he is are apt to be very unbalanced. They get swept along with a rush, like ships without ballast; what stands for courage in their *b* make-up is a kind of mad excitement; while, on the other hand, the steadier sort of people are apt to come to their studies with minds that are sluggish, somehow—freighted with a bad memory. But this boy approaches his studies in a smooth, sure, effective way, and with great good-temper; it reminds one of the quiet flow of a stream of oil. The result is that it is astonishing to see how he gets through his work, at his age.

SOC. That is good news. And he is an Athenian—whose son is he?

THEOD. I have heard the name, but I don't remember it. But he is the middle one of this group coming towards us. He and his companions were greasing themselves outside just now; it looks as if they have finished and are coming in here. But look and see if you recognise him.

SOC. Yes, I know him. He's the son of Euphronius of Sunium—very much the kind of person, my friend, that you tell me his son is. A distinguished man in many ways; he left a considerable property too. But I don't know the boy's name.

THEOD. His name, Socrates, is Theaetetus. As for the property, that, I think, has been made away with by trustees. All the same, he is wonderfully open-handed about money, Socrates.

SOC. A thorough-bred, evidently. I wish you would ask him to come and sit with us over here.

THEOD. All right. Theaetetus, come here beside Socrates.

SOC. Yes, come along, Theaetetus. I want to see for myself what sort of a face I have. Theodorus says I am like you. But look. If you and I had each had a lyre, and Theodorus had told us that they were both similarly tuned, should we have taken his word for it straight away? Or should we have tried to find out if he was speaking with any expert knowledge of music?

THEAET. Oh, we should have enquired into that.

SOC. And if we had found that he was a musician, we should have believed what he said; but if we found he had no such qualification, we should have put no faith in him.

THEAET. Yes, that's true.

SOC. And now, I suppose, if we are interested in this question of our faces being alike, we ought to consider whether he is speaking with any knowledge of drawing or not?

THEAET. Yes, I should think so.

SOC. Then is Theodorus an artist?

THEAET. No, not so far as I know.

SOC. Nor a geometer, either?

THEAET. Oh, there's no doubt about his being that, Socrates.

SOC. And isn't he also a master of astronomy and arithmetic and music—of all that an educated man should know?

THEAET. Well, he seems to me to be.

SOC. Then if he asserts that there is some physical resemblance between us—whether complimenting us or the reverse—one ought not to pay much attention to him?

THEAET. No, perhaps not.

Soc. But supposing it were the soul of one of us that he was praising? Suppose he said one of us was good and wise? Oughtn't the one who heard that to be very anxious to examine the object of such praise? And oughtn't the other to be very willing to show himself off?

THEAET. Yes, certainly, Socrates.

Soc. Then, my dear Theaetetus, now is the time for you to show yourself and for me to examine you. For although Theodorus often gives me flattering testimonials for people, both Athenians and foreigners, I assure you I have never before heard him praise anybody in the way he has just praised you.

THEAET. That's all very well, Socrates; but take care he wasn't saying that for a joke.

Soc. That is not Theodorus' way. Now don't you try to get out of what we have agreed upon with the pretence that our friend is joking, or you may make it necessary for him to give his evidence—since no charge of perjury is ever likely to be brought against him. So have the pluck to stand by your agreement.

THEAET. All right, I must, then, if that's what you've decided.

Soc. Tell me now. You are learning some geometry from Theodorus, I expect?

THEAET. Yes, I am.

Soc. And some astronomy and music and arithmetic?

THEAET. Well, I'm very anxious to, anyway.

Soc. And so am I, my son—from Theodorus or from anyone who seems to me to know about these things. But although I get on with them pretty well in most ways, I have a small difficulty, which I think ought to be investigated, with your help and that of the rest of the company.—Now isn't it true that to learn is to become wiser[1] about the thing one is learning?

THEAET. Yes, of course.

Soc. And what makes men wise, I take it, is wisdom?

THEAET. Yes.

---

1. The words 'wise' and 'wisdom' in the argument which begins here represent the Greek *sophos* and *sophia*. While there are good reasons for retaining the conventional rendering of these terms, it is something of a strain to say that learning geometry is becoming wiser about it. The point of the argument will come across more naturally in English if readers substitute in their mind the words 'expert' and 'expertise'. Cf. Introduction, p. 3, pp. 19–20.

e   SOC. And is this in any way different from knowledge?

THEAET. What?

SOC. Wisdom. Isn't it the things which they know that men are wise about?

THEAET. Well, yes.

SOC. So knowledge and wisdom will be the same thing?

THEAET. Yes.

SOC. Now this is just where my difficulty comes in. I can't get a proper grasp of what on earth knowledge really is. Could we man-

146   age to put it into words? What do all of you say? Who'll speak first? Anyone who makes a mistake shall sit down and be Donkey, as the children say when they are playing ball; and anyone who comes through without a miss shall be King and make us answer any question he likes.—Well, why this silence? Theodorus, I hope my love of argument is not making me forget my manners—just be-cause I'm so anxious to start a discussion and get us all friendly and talkative together?

b   THEOD. No, no, Socrates—that's the last thing one could call forgetting your manners. But do make one of the young people answer you. I am not used to this kind of discussion, and I'm too old to get into the way of it. But it would be suitable enough for them and they would profit more by it. For youth can always profit, that's true enough. So do go on; don't let Theaetetus off but ask him some more questions.

SOC. Well, Theaetetus, you hear what Theodorus says. You won't want to disobey him, I'm sure; and certainly a wise man

c   shouldn't be disobeyed by his juniors in matters of this kind—it wouldn't be at all the proper thing. Now give me a good frank answer. What do you think knowledge is?

THEAET. Well, I ought to answer, Socrates, as you and Theodorus tell me to. In any case, you and he will put me right, if I make a mistake.

SOC. We certainly will, if we can.

THEAET. Then I think that the things Theodorus teaches are knowledge—I mean geometry and the subjects you enumerated

d   just now. Then again there are the crafts such as cobbling, whether you take them together or separately. They must be knowledge, surely.

SOC. That is certainly a frank and indeed a generous answer, my dear lad. I asked you for one thing and you have given me many; I wanted something simple, and I have got a variety.

THEAET. And what does that mean, Socrates?

Soc. Nothing, I dare say. But I'll tell you what I think. When you talk about cobbling, you mean just knowledge of the making of shoes?

THEAET. Yes, that's all I mean by it.

Soc. And when you talk about carpentering, you mean simply   *e*
the knowledge of the making of wooden furniture?

THEAET. Yes, that's all I mean, again.

Soc. And in both cases what you are doing is to define what the knowledge is of?

THEAET. Yes.

Soc. But that is not what you were asked, Theaetetus. You were not asked to say what one may have knowledge of, or how many branches of knowledge there are. It was not with any idea of counting these up that the question was asked; we wanted to know what knowledge itself is.—Or am I talking nonsense?

THEAET. No, you are perfectly right.

Soc. Now you think about this. Supposing we were asked about   147
some commonplace, every-day thing; for example, what is clay? And supposing we were to answer, 'clay of the potters' and 'clay of the stovemakers' and 'clay of the brickmakers', wouldn't that be absurd of us?

THEAET. Well, perhaps it would.

Soc. Absurd to begin with, I suppose, to imagine that the person who asked the question would understand anything from our answer when we say 'clay', whether we add that it is dollmakers'   *b*
clay or any other craftsman's. Or do you think that anyone can understand the name of a thing when he doesn't know what the thing is?

THEAET. No, certainly not.

Soc. And so a man who does not know what knowledge is will not understand 'knowledge of shoes' either?

THEAET. No, he won't.

Soc. Then a man who is ignorant of what knowledge is will not understand what cobbling is, or any other craft?

THEAET. That is so.

Soc. So when the question raised is 'What is knowledge?', to reply by naming one of the crafts is an absurd answer; because it points out something that knowledge is of when this is not what   *c*
the question was about.

THEAET. So it seems.

Soc. Again, it goes no end of a long way round, in a case where, I take it, a short and commonplace answer is possible. In the question about clay, for example, it would presumably be possible to make the simple, commonplace statement that it is earth mixed with liquid, and let the question of whose clay it is take care of itself.

THEAET. That seems easier, Socrates, now you put it like that. But I believe you're asking just the sort of question that occurred to your namesake Socrates here[2] and myself, when we were having a discussion a little while ago.

Soc. And what was that, Theaetetus?

THEAET. Theodorus here was demonstrating to us with the aid of diagrams a point about powers.[3] He was showing us that the power of 3 square feet and the power of 5 square feet are not commensurable in length with the power of 1 square foot; and he went on in this way, taking each case in turn till he came to the power of 17 square feet; there for some reason he stopped. So the idea occurred to us that, since the powers were turning out to be unlimited in number, we might try to collect the powers in question under one term, which would apply to them all.

Soc. And did you find the kind of thing you wanted?

THEAET. I think we did. But I'd like you to see if it's all right.

Soc. Go on, then.

THEAET. We divided all numbers into two classes. Any number which can be produced by the multiplication of equal numbers, we

---

2. Socrates the Younger, one of the group of friends with whom Theaetetus entered at the beginning. In later life he was a member of Plato's Academy.

3. A mathematical term for squares. By contrast, at 148ab 'power' is given a new, specially defined use to denominate a species of line, viz. the incommensurable lines for which the boys wanted a general account. It may be useful to give a brief explanation of the mathematics of the passage.

Two lines are incommensurable if and only if they have no common measure; that is, no unit of length will measure both without remainder. Two squares are incommensurable *in length* if and only if their sides are incommensurable lines; the areas themselves may still be commensurable, i.e. both measurable by some unit of area, as is mentioned at 148b. When Theodorus showed for a series of powers (squares) that each is incommensurable in length with the one foot (unit) square, we can think of him as proving case by case the irrationality of $\sqrt{3}$, $\sqrt{5}$, . . . $\sqrt{17}$. But this was not how he thought of it himself. Greek mathematicians did not recognize irrational *numbers* but treated of irrational quantities as geometrical entities: in this instance, lines identified by the areas of the squares that can be constructed on them. Similarly, we can think of the boys' formula for power or square lines at 148ab as making the point that, for any positive integer n, $\sqrt{n}$ is irrational if and only if there is no positive integer m such that $n = m \times m$. But, once again, a Greek mathematician would think of this generalization in the geometrical terms in which Theaetetus expounds it.

compared to a square in shape, and we called this a square or equilateral number.

Soc. Good, so far.

Theaet. Then we took the intermediate numbers, such as three and five and any number which can't be produced by multiplication of equals but only by multiplying together a greater and a less; a number such that it is always contained by a greater and a less side. A number of this kind we compared to an oblong figure, and called it an oblong number.   *148*

Soc. That's excellent. But how did you go on?

Theaet. We defined under the term 'length' any line which produces in square an equilateral plane number; while any line which produces in square an oblong number we defined under the term 'power', for the reason that, although it is incommensurable with the former in length, the plane figures which they respectively have the power to produce are commensurable. And there is another distinction of the same sort with regard to solids.   *b*

Soc. Excellent, my boys. I don't think Theodorus is likely to be had up for false witness.

Theaet. And yet, Socrates, I shouldn't be able to answer your question about knowledge in the same way that I answered the one about lengths and powers—though you seem to me to be looking for something of the same sort. So Theodorus turns out a false witness after all.

Soc. Well, but suppose now it was your running he had praised;   *c*
suppose he had said that he had never met anyone among the young people who was such a runner as you. And then suppose you were beaten by the champion runner in his prime— would you think Theodorus' praise had lost any of its truth?

Theaet. No, I shouldn't.

Soc. But do you think the discovery of what knowledge is is really what I was saying just now—a small thing? Don't you think that's a problem for the people at the top?

Theaet. Yes, rather, I do; and the very topmost of them.

Soc. Then do have confidence in yourself and try to believe that Theodorus knew what he was talking about. You must put your whole heart into what we are doing—in particular into this matter   *d*
of getting a statement of what knowledge really is.

Theaet. If putting one's heart into it is all that is required, Socrates, the answer will come to light.

Soc. Go on, then. You gave us a good lead just now. Try to imitate your answer about the powers. There you brought together the many powers within a single form; now I want you in the same way to give one single account of the many branches of knowledge.

e   THEAET. But I assure you, Socrates, I have often tried to think this out, when I have heard reports of the questions you ask. But I can never persuade myself that anything I say will really do; and I never hear anyone else state the matter in the way that you require. And yet, again, you know, I can't even stop worrying about it.

Soc. Yes; those are the pains of labour, dear Theaetetus. It is because you are not barren but pregnant.

THEAET. I don't know about that, Socrates. I'm only telling you what's happened to me.

149   Soc. Then do you mean to say you've never heard about my being the son of a good hefty midwife, Phaenarete?[4]

THEAET. Oh, yes, I've heard that before.

Soc. And haven't you ever been told that I practise the same art myself?

THEAET. No, I certainly haven't.

Soc. But I do, believe me. Only don't give me away to the rest of the world, will you? You see, my friend, it is a secret that I have this art. That is not one of the things you hear people saying about me, because they don't know; but they do say that I am a very odd sort of person, always causing people to get into difficulties. You must have heard that, surely?

b   THEAET. Yes, I have.

Soc. And shall I tell you what is the explanation of that?

THEAET. Yes, please do.

Soc. Well, if you will just think of the general facts about the business of midwifery, you will see more easily what I mean. You know, I suppose, that women never practise as midwives while they are still conceiving and bearing children themselves. It is only those who are past child-bearing who take this up.

THEAET. Oh, yes.

Soc. They say it was Artemis who was responsible for this custom; it was because she, who undertook the patronage of child-
c   birth, was herself childless. She didn't, it's true, entrust the duties of midwifery to barren women, because human nature is too weak to acquire skill where it has no experience. But she assigned the task to those who have become incapable of child-bearing through age—honouring their likeness to herself.

THEAET. Yes, naturally.

4. The name means 'She who brings virtue to light'.

Soc. And this too is very natural, isn't it?—or perhaps necessary? I mean that it is the midwives who can tell better than anyone else whether women are pregnant or not.

THEAET. Yes, of course.

Soc. And then it is the midwives who have the power to bring on the pains, and also, if they think fit, to relieve them; they do it *d* by the use of simple drugs, and by singing incantations. In difficult cases, too, they can bring about the birth; or, if they consider it advisable, they can promote a miscarriage.

THEAET. Yes, that is so.

Soc. There's another thing too. Have you noticed this about them, that they are the cleverest of match-makers, because they are marvellously knowing about the kind of couples whose marriage will produce the best children?

THEAET. No, that is not at all familiar to me.

Soc. But they are far prouder of this, believe me, than of cutting the umbilical cord. Think now. There's an art which is concerned *e* with the cultivation and harvesting of the crops. Now is it the same art which prescribes the best soil for planting or sowing a given crop? Or is it a different one?

THEAET. No, it is all the same art.

Soc. Then applying this to midwifery, will there be one art of the sowing and another of the harvesting?

THEAET. That doesn't seem likely, certainly.

Soc. No, it doesn't. But there is also an unlawful and unscientific *150* practice of bringing men and women together, which we call procuring; and because of that the midwives—a most august body of women—are very reluctant to undertake even lawful matchmaking. They are afraid that if they practise this, they may be suspected of the other. And yet, I suppose, reliable matchmaking is a matter for no one but the true midwife.

THEAET. Apparently.

Soc. So the work of the midwives is a highly important one; but it is not so important as my own performance. And for this reason, that there is not in midwifery the further complication, that the patients are sometimes delivered of phantoms and sometimes of *b* realities, and that the two are hard to distinguish. If there were, then the midwife's greatest and noblest function would be to distinguish the true from the false offspring—don't you agree?

THEAET. Yes, I do.

Soc. Now my art of midwifery is just like theirs in most respects. The difference is that I attend men and not women, and that I watch over the labour of their souls, not of their bodies. And the most

c important thing about my art is the ability to apply all possible tests to the offspring, to determine whether the young mind is being delivered of a phantom, that is, an error, or a fertile truth. For one thing which I have in common with the ordinary midwives is that I myself am barren of wisdom. The common reproach against me is that I am always asking questions of other people but never express my own views about anything, because there is no wisdom in me; and that is true enough. And the reason of it is this, that God compels me to attend the travail of others, but has forbidden me to procreate. So that I am not in any sense a wise man; I cannot

d claim as the child of my own soul any discovery worth the name of wisdom. But with those who associate with me it is different. At first some of them may give the impression of being ignorant and stupid; but as time goes on and our association continues, all whom God permits are seen to make progress—a progress which is amazing both to other people and to themselves. And yet it is clear that this is not due to anything they have learnt from me; it is that they discover within themselves a multitude of beautiful things, which they bring forth into the light. But it is I, with God's help, who deliver them of this offspring. And a proof of this may be seen in

e the many cases where people who did not realise this fact took all the credit to themselves and thought that I was no good. They have then proceeded to leave me sooner than they should, either of their own accord or through the influence of others. And after they have gone away from me they have resorted to harmful company, with the result that what remained within them has miscarried; while they have neglected the children I helped them to bring forth, and lost them, because they set more value upon lies and phantoms than upon the truth; finally they have been set down for ignorant fools, both by themselves and by everybody else. One of these

151 people was Aristeides the son of Lysimachus;[5] and there have been very many others. Sometimes they come back, wanting my company again, and ready to move heaven and earth to get it. When that happens, in some cases the divine sign that visits me forbids me to associate with them; in others, it permits me, and then they begin again to make progress.

---

5. Grandson of a famous Athenian statesman; his education is under discussion in Plato's *Laches*, where his father Lysimachus is anxious that his son should make more of a name for himself than Lysimachus has managed to do. Evidently this did not happen.

There is another point also in which those who associate with me are like women in child-birth. They suffer the pains of labour, and are filled day and night with distress; indeed they suffer far more than women. And this pain my art is able to bring on, and also to allay.

Well, that's what happens to them; but at times, Theaetetus, I *b* come across people who do not seem to me somehow to be pregnant. Then I realise that they have no need of me, and with the best will in the world I undertake the business of match-making; and I think I am good enough—God willing—at guessing with whom they might profitably keep company. Many of them I have given away to Prodicus;[6] and a great number also to other wise and inspired persons.

Well, my dear lad, this has been a long yarn; but the reason was that I have a suspicion that you (as you think yourself) are pregnant and in labour. So I want you to come to me as to one who is both the son of a midwife and himself skilled in the art; and try to answer *c* the questions I shall ask you as well as you can. And when I examine what you say, I may perhaps think it is a phantom and not truth, and proceed to take it quietly from you and abandon it. Now if this happens, you mustn't get savage with me, like a mother over her first-born child. Do you know, people have often before now got into such a state with me as to be literally ready to bite when I take away some nonsense or other from them. They never believe that I am doing this in all good-will; they are so far from realising that no God can wish evil to man, and that even I don't do this kind of *d* thing out of malice, but because it is not permitted to me to accept a lie and put away truth.

So begin again, Theaetetus, and try to say what knowledge is. And don't on any account tell me that you can't. For if God is willing, and you play the man, you can.

THEAET. Well, Socrates, after such encouragement from *you*, it would hardly be decent for anyone not to try his hardest to say what he has in him. Very well then. It seems to me that a man who *e* knows something perceives what he knows, and the way it appears at present, at any rate, is that knowledge is simply perception.

SOC. There's a good straight answer, my son. That's the way to speak one's mind. But come now, let us look at this thing together, and see whether what we have here is really fertile or a mere wind-egg. You hold that knowledge is perception?

6. A famous Sophist who specialized in fine distinctions of meaning between closely related words. Plato usually refers to him with dismissive irony.

THEAET. Yes.

Soc. But look here, this is no ordinary account of knowledge you've come out with: it's what Protagoras used to maintain. He said the very same thing, only he put it in rather a different way. For he says, you know, that 'Man is the measure of all things: of the things which are, that they are, and of the things which are not, that they are not.' You have read this, of course?

152

THEAET. Yes, often.

Soc. Then you know that he puts it something like this, that as each thing appears to me, so it is for me, and as it appears to you, so it is for you—you and I each being a man?

THEAET. Yes, that is what he says.

b

Soc. Well, it is not likely that a wise man would talk nonsense. So let us follow him up. Now doesn't it sometimes happen that when the same wind is blowing, one of us feels cold and the other not? Or that one of us feels rather cold and the other very cold?

THEAET. That certainly does happen.

Soc. Well then, in that case are we going to say that the wind itself, by itself, is cold or not cold? Or shall we listen to Protagoras, and say it is cold for the one who feels cold, and for the other, not cold?

THEAET. It looks as if we must say that.

Soc. And this is how it appears to each of us?

THEAET. Yes.

Soc. But this expression 'it appears' means 'he perceives it'?

THEAET. Yes, it does.

c

Soc. The appearing of things, then, is the same as perception, in the case of hot and things like that. So it results, apparently, that things are for the individual such as he perceives them.

THEAET. Yes, that seems all right.

Soc. Perception, then, is always of what is, and unerring—as befits knowledge.

THEAET. So it appears.

Soc. But, I say, look here. Was Protagoras one of those omniscient people? Did he perhaps put this out as a riddle for the common crowd of us, while he revealed the *Truth*[7] as a secret doctrine to his own pupils?

d

THEAET. What do you mean by that, Socrates?

Soc. I'll tell you; and this, now, is certainly no ordinary theory— I mean the theory that there is nothing which in itself is just one

---

7. This appears to have been the title of Protagoras' book. See 161c.

thing: nothing which you could rightly call anything or any kind of thing. If you call a thing large, it will reveal itself as small, and if you call it heavy, it is liable to appear as light, and so on with everything, because nothing is anything or any kind of thing. What is really true, is this: the things of which we naturally say that they 'are', are in process of coming to be, as the result of movement and   e change and blending with one another. We are wrong when we say they 'are', since nothing ever is, but everything is coming to be.

And as regards this point of view, let us take it as a fact that all the wise men of the past, with the exception of Parmenides, stand together. Let us take it that we find on this side Protagoras and Heraclitus and Empedocles; and also the masters of the two kinds of poetry, Epicharmus in comedy and Homer in tragedy.[8] For when Homer talked about 'Ocean, begetter of gods, and Tethys their mother', he made all things the offspring of flux and motion.—Or don't you think he meant that?

THEAET. Oh, I think he did.

Soc. And if anyone proceeded to dispute the field with an army   153 like that—an army led by Homer—he could hardly help making a fool of himself, could he?

THEAET. It would not be an easy matter, Socrates.

Soc. It would not, Theaetetus. You see, there is good enough evidence for this theory that being (what passes for such) and becoming are a product of motion, while not-being and passing-away result from a state of rest. There is evidence for it in the fact that heat and fire, which presumably generates and controls everything else, is itself generated out of movement and friction— these being motions.—Or am I wrong in saying these are the original sources of fire?

THEAET. Oh no, they certainly are.   b

Soc. Moreover, the growth of living creatures depends upon these same sources?

THEAET. Yes, certainly.

Soc. And isn't it also true that bodily condition deteriorates with

8. For Protagoras and Heraclitus, see Introduction. Empedocles described a cosmic cycle in which things are constituted and dissolved by the coming together and separating of the four elements earth, air, fire, and water. Epicharmus made humorous use of the idea that everything is always changing by having a debtor claim he is not the same person as incurred the debt. Parmenides remains outside the chorus of agreement because he held that the only reality is one single, completely changeless thing (cf. 183e).

rest and idleness? While by exertion and motion it can be preserved for a long time?

THEAET. Yes.

Soc. And what about the condition of the soul? Isn't it by learning and study, which are motions, that the soul gains knowledge and is preserved[9] and becomes a better thing? Whereas in a state

c of rest, that is, when it will not study or learn, it not only fails to acquire knowledge but forgets what it has already learnt?

THEAET. That certainly is so.

Soc. And so we may say that the one thing, that is, motion, is beneficial to both body and soul, while the other has the opposite effect?

THEAET. Yes, that's what it looks like.

Soc. Yes, and I might go on to point out to you the effect of such conditions as still weather on land and calms on the sea. I might show you how these conditions rot and destroy things, while the opposite conditions make for preservation. And finally, to put the crown on my argument, I might bring in Homer's golden cord,[10] and maintain that he means by this simply the sun; and is here explain-

d ing that so long as the revolution continues and the sun is in motion, all things are and are preserved, both in heaven and earth, but that if all this should be 'bound fast', as it were, and come to a standstill, all things would be destroyed and, as the saying goes, the world would be turned upside down. Do you agree with this?

THEAET. Yes, Socrates, I think that is the meaning of the passage.

Soc. Then, my friend, you must understand our theory in this way. In the sphere of vision, to begin with, what you would naturally call a white colour is not itself a distinct entity, either outside

e your eyes or in your eyes. You must not assign it any particular place; for then, of course it would be standing at its post; it wouldn't be in process of becoming.

THEAET. But what do you mean?

Soc. Let us follow what we stated a moment ago, and posit that

9. There seems to be a pun intended in the Greek. The word here translated as passive, 'is preserved', might equally well be taken as middle, meaning 'preserves in memory' (for which it is the regular word), with 'knowledge' as its object. The former interpretation is suggested by the use of the same word above, of preserving physical fitness; the latter by the mention of 'forgetting' below. But for the soul, to 'remember' is to 'be preserved'.

10. *Iliad* VIII 17–27. Zeus boasts that if he pulled on a golden cord let down from heaven, he could haul up earth, sea and all, bind the cord fast round the peak of Mt. Olympus, and leave the lot dangling in mid-air.

there is nothing which is, in itself, one thing. According to this theory, black or white or any other colour will turn out to have come into being through the impact of the eye upon the appropriate motion; and what we naturally call a particular colour is neither that which impinges nor that which is impinged upon, but something which has come into being between the two, and which is private to the individual percipient.—Or would you be prepared to insist that every colour appears to a dog, or to any other animal, the same as it appears to you?

THEAET. No, I most certainly shouldn't.

Soc. Well, and do you even feel sure that anything appears to another human being the same as it appears to you? Wouldn't you be much more disposed to hold that it doesn't always appear the same even to yourself because you never remain the same as yourself?

THEAET. Yes, that seems to me nearer the truth than the other.

Soc. Well now, supposing such things as size or warmth or whiteness really belonged to the object we measure ourselves against or touch, it would never be found that this object had become different simply by coming into contact with another thing and without any change in itself. On the other hand, if you suppose them to belong to what is measuring or touching, this again could never become different simply because something else had come into its neighborhood, or because something had happened to the first thing—nothing having happened to itself. As it is, you see, we may easily find ourselves forced into saying the most astonishing and ridiculous things, as Protagoras would point out or anyone who undertook to expound his views.

THEAET. What do you mean? What sort of ridiculous things?

Soc. Let me give you a simple example of what I mean, and you will see the rest for yourself. Here are six dice. Put four beside them, and they are more, we say, than the four, that is, half as many again; but put twelve beside them, and we say they are less, that is, half the number. And there is no getting out of that—or do you think there is?

THEAET. No, I don't.

Soc. Well now, supposing Protagoras or anyone else were to ask you this question: 'Is it possible, Theaetetus, to become bigger or more in number in any other way than by being increased?' What is your answer to that?

THEAET. Well, Socrates, if I answer what seems true in relation to the present question, I shall say 'No, it is not possible'; but if I

154

b

c

d

consider it in relation to the question that went before, then in order to avoid contradicting myself, I say 'Yes, it is.'

Soc. That's a good answer, my friend, by Jove it is; you are inspired. But, I think, if you answer 'Yes', it will be like that episode in Euripides—the tongue will be safe from refutation but the mind will not.[11]

Theaet. That's true.

Soc. Now if you and I were professional savants, who had already analysed all the contents of our minds, we should now spend our superfluous time trying each other out; we should start a regular Sophists' set-to, with a great clashing of argument on argument. But, as it is, we are only plain men; and so our first aim will be to look at our thoughts themselves in relation to themselves, and see what they are—whether, in our opinion, they agree with one another or are entirely at variance.

Theaet. That would certainly be my aim, anyway.

Soc. And mine. That being so, as we are not in any way pressed for time, don't you think the thing to do is to reconsider this matter quietly and patiently, in all seriousness 'analysing' ourselves, and asking what are these apparitions within us?—And when we come to review them, I suppose we may begin with the statement that nothing can possibly become either greater or less, in bulk or in number, so long as it is equal to itself. Isn't that so?

Theaet. Yes.

Soc. Secondly, we should say that a thing to which nothing is added and from which nothing is taken away neither increases nor diminishes but remains equal.

Theaet. Yes, certainly.

Soc. Thirdly, that it is impossible that a thing should ever be what it was not before without having become and without any process of becoming?

Theaet. Yes, I think so.

Soc. Now it seems to me that these three statements that we have admitted are fighting one another in our souls when we speak of the example of the dice; or when we say that, within the space of a year, I (a full-grown man) without having been either increased or diminished, am now bigger than you (who are only a boy) and, later on, smaller—though I have lost nothing and it is only that you

11. The allusion is presumably to *Hippolytus* 1. 612, where Hippolytus excuses himself from keeping an oath by saying 'The tongue has sworn but the mind is unsworn.'

have grown. For this means that I am, at a later stage, what I was   *c*
not before, and that, too, without having become—for without
becoming it is not possible to have become, and without suffering
any loss in size I could never become less. And there are innumerable other examples of the same thing if once we admit these. You
follow me, I take it, Theaetetus—I think you must be familiar with
this kind of puzzle.

THEAET. Oh yes, indeed, Socrates, I often wonder like mad what
these things can mean; sometimes when I'm looking at them I begin
to feel quite giddy.

Soc. I dare say you do, my dear boy. It seems that Theodorus   *d*
was not far from the truth when he guessed what kind of person
you are. For this is an experience which is characteristic of a philosopher, this wondering: this is where philosophy begins and nowhere
else. And the man who made Iris the child of Thaumas was perhaps
no bad genealogist[12]—But aren't you beginning to see now what is
the explanation of these puzzles, according to the theory which we
are attributing to Protagoras?

THEAET. I don't think I am, yet.

Soc. Then I dare say you will be grateful to me if I help you to   *e*
discover the veiled truth in the thought of a great man—or perhaps
I should say, of great men?

THEAET. Of course I shall be, Socrates, very grateful.

Soc. Then you have a look round, and see that none of the
uninitiated are listening to us—I mean the people who think that
nothing exists but what they can grasp with both hands; people
who refuse to admit that actions and processes and the invisible
world in general have any place in reality.

THEAET. They must be tough, hard fellows, Socrates.   *156*

Soc. They are, my son—very crude people. But these others,
whose mysteries I am going to tell you, are a much more subtle
type. These mysteries begin from the principle on which all that
we have just been saying also depends, namely, that everything is
really motion, and there is nothing but motion. Motion has two
forms, each an infinite multitude, but distinguished by their powers, the one being active and the other passive. And through the

---

12. Hesiod, *Theogony* 265. 'Thaumas' means wonder, while Iris, the messenger of
the gods, is the rainbow which passes between earth and heaven. As a purely visual
phenomenon (nothing more to it than you see at a given moment), the rainbow is
nicely chosen as the divinity to represent the philosophic impulse on behalf of the
theory that knowledge is perception; contrast the role of Eros in Plato's *Symposium*
(201e–204b).

intercourse and mutual friction of these two there comes to be an
b   offspring infinite in multitude but always twin births, on the one
hand what is perceived, on the other, the perception of it, the
perception in every case being generated together with what is
perceived and emerging along with it. For the perceptions we have
such names as sight, hearing, smelling, feeling cold and feeling
hot; also what are called pleasures and pains, desires and fears; and
there are others besides, a great number which have names, an
infinite number which have not. And on the other side there is the
race of things perceived, for each of these perceptions perceived
c   things born of the same parentage, for all kinds of visions all kinds
of colours, for all kinds of hearings all kinds of sounds; and so on,
for the other perceptions the other things perceived, that come to
be in kinship with them.

Now what does this tale really mean, from our point of view,
Theaetetus? How does it bear on what we were saying before? Do
you see?

THEAET. Not really, Socrates.

SOC. Look here, then, let us see if we can somehow round it off.
What it is trying to express, presumably, is this. All these things
are in motion, just as we say; and their motion is distinguished by
its swiftness or slowness. What is slow has its motion in one and
the same place, and in relation to the things in the immediate
d   neighbourhood; in this way it generates and the offspring are
swifter, as they move through space, and their motion takes the
form of spatial movement.

Thus the eye and some other thing—one of the things commensu-
rate with the eye—which has come into its neighbourhood, generate both whiteness and the perception which is by nature united
with it (things which would never have come to be if it had been
anything else that eye or object approached). In this event, motions
e   arise in the intervening space, sight from the side of the eye and
whiteness from the side of that which cooperates in the production
of the colour. The eye is filled with sight; at that moment it sees,
and there comes into being, not indeed sight, but a seeing eye;
while its partner in the process of producing colour is filled with
whiteness, and there comes into being not whiteness, but white, a
white stick or stone or whatever it is that happens to be coloured
this sort of colour.

This account of course may be generally applied; it applies to all
that we perceive, hard or hot or anything else. Of these we must

understand in the same way—as indeed we were saying before—
that no one of them *is* anything in itself; all things, of all kinds   *157*
whatsoever, are coming to be through association with one another,
as the result of motion. For even in the case of the active and passive
motions it is impossible, as they say, for thought, taking them
singly, to pin them down to being anything. There is no passive till
it meets the active, no active except in conjunction with the passive;
and what, in conjunction with one thing, is active, reveals itself as
passive when it falls in with something else.

And so, wherever you turn, there is nothing, as we said at the
outset, which in itself is just one thing; all things are coming into
being relatively to something. The verb 'to be' must be totally   *b*
abolished—though indeed we have been led by habit and ignorance into using it ourselves more than once, even in what we
have just been saying. That is wrong, these wise men tell us,
nor should we allow the use of such words as 'something', 'of
something', or 'mine', 'this' or 'that', or any other name that makes
things stand still. We ought, rather, to speak according to nature
and refer to things as 'becoming', 'being produced', 'passing
away', 'changing'; for if you speak in such a way as to make things
stand still, you will easily be refuted. And this applies in speaking
both of the individual case and of many aggregated together—
such an aggregate, I mean, as people call 'man' or 'stone', or to   *c*
which they give the names of the different animals and sorts of
thing.

—Well, Theaetetus, does this look to you a tempting meal and
could you take a bite of the delicious stuff?

THEAET. I really don't know, Socrates. I can't even quite see what
you're getting at—whether the things you are saying are what you
think yourself, or whether you are just trying me out.

Soc. You are forgetting, my friend. I don't know anything about
this kind of thing myself, and I don't claim any of it as my own. I
am barren of theories; my business is to attend you in your labour.
So I chant incantations over you and offer you little tit-bits from
each of the wise till I succeed in assisting you to bring your own   *d*
belief forth into the light. When it has been born, I shall consider
whether it is fertile or a wind-egg. But you must have courage and
patience; answer like a man whatever appears to you to be true
about the things I ask you.

THEAET. All right, go on with the questions.

Soc. Tell me again, then, whether you like the suggestion that good and beautiful and all the things we were just speaking of cannot be said to 'be' anything, but are always 'coming to be'.[13]

THEAET. Well, as far as I'm concerned, while I'm listening to your exposition of it, it seems to me an extraordinarily reasonable view; and I feel that the way you have set out the matter has got to be accepted.

e   Soc. In that case, we had better not pass over any point where our theory is still incomplete. What we have not yet discussed is the question of dreams, and of insanity and other diseases; also what is called mishearing or misseeing or other cases of misperceiving. You realise, I suppose, that it would be generally agreed that all these cases appear to provide a refutation of the theory we *158* have just expounded. For in these conditions, we surely have false perceptions. Here it is far from being true that all things which appear to the individual also are. On the contrary, no one of the things which appear to him really is.

THEAET. That is perfectly true, Socrates.

Soc. Well then, my lad, what argument is left for the person who maintains that knowledge is perception and that what appears to any individual also is, for him to whom it appears to be?

THEAET. Well, Socrates, I hardly like to tell you that I don't know what to say, seeing I've just got into trouble with you for that. *b*   But I really shouldn't know how to dispute the suggestion that a madman believes what is false when he thinks he is God; or a dreamer when he imagines he has wings and is flying in his sleep.

Soc. But there's a point here which *is* a matter of dispute, especially as regards dreams and real life—don't you see?

THEAET. What do you mean?

Soc. There's a question you must often have heard people ask— the question what evidence we could offer if we were asked whether in the present instance, at this moment, we are asleep and dreaming *c*   all our thoughts, or awake and talking to each other in real life.

THEAET. Yes, Socrates, it certainly is difficult to find the proof we want here. The two states seem to correspond in all their characteristics. There is nothing to prevent us from thinking when we are asleep that we are having the very same discussion that we have

---

13. An alternative translation would be: 'the suggestion that nothing is, but rather becomes, good, beautiful or any of the things we were speaking of just now'. The point is the same either way, for it is clear from 153d–154b that 'Nothing is in itself white' and 'White is nothing in itself' are to be treated as two sides of the same coin. The same will apply when 'is' is replaced, as here, by 'comes to be'.

just had. And when we dream that we are telling the story of a dream, there is an extraordinary likeness between the two experiences.

Soc. You see, then, it is not difficult to find matter for dispute, when it is disputed even whether this is real life or a dream. Indeed   *d* we may say that, as our periods of sleeping and waking are of equal length, and as in each period the soul contends that the beliefs of the moment are pre-eminently true, the result is that for half our lives we assert the reality of the one set of objects, and for half that of the other set. And we make our assertions with equal conviction in both cases.

THEAET. That certainly is so.

Soc. And doesn't the same argument apply in the cases of disease and madness, except that the periods of time are not equal?

THEAET. Yes, that is so.

Soc. Well now, are we going to fix the limits of truth by the clock?

THEAET. That would be a very funny thing to do.   *e*

Soc. But can you produce some other clear indication to show which of these beliefs are true?

THEAET. I don't think I can.

Soc. Then you listen to me and I'll tell you the kind of thing that might be said by those people who propose it as a rule that whatever a man thinks at any time is the truth for him. I can imagine them putting their position by asking you this question: 'Now, Theaetetus, suppose you have something which is an entirely different thing from something else. Can it have in any respect the same powers as the other thing?' And observe, we are not to understand the question to refer to something which is the same in some respects while it is different in others, but to that which is wholly different.

THEAET. In that case, then, it is impossible that it should have   *159* anything the same, either as regards its powers or in any other respect, if it is a completely different thing.

Soc. And aren't we obliged to admit that such a thing is also unlike the other?

THEAET. Yes, I think so.

Soc. Now supposing a thing is coming to be like or unlike to something, whether to itself or to something else; are we to say that when it is growing like it is coming to be the same, and when it is growing unlike it is coming to be a different thing?

THEAET. Yes, that must be so.

SOC. Now weren't we saying, at an earlier stage, that there is a number—indeed an infinite number—of both active and passive factors?

THEAET. Yes.

SOC. Also this, that when a thing mixes now with one thing and now with another, it will not generate the same things each time but different things?

b   THEAET. Yes, certainly.

SOC. Well, now let us apply this same statement to you and me and things in general. Take, for example, Socrates ill and Socrates well. Shall we say Socrates in health is like or unlike Socrates in sickness?

THEAET. You mean the ill Socrates as a whole compared with the well Socrates as a whole?

SOC. You get my point excellently; that is just what I mean.

THEAET. Unlike, then, I suppose.

SOC. And different also, in so far as he is unlike?

THEAET. Yes, that follows.

c   SOC. Similarly, you would say, when he is asleep or in any of the conditions we enumerated just now?

THEAET. Yes, I should.

SOC. Then it must surely be true that, when any one of the naturally active factors finds Socrates well, it will be dealing with one me, and when it finds Socrates ill, with a different me?

THEAET. Yes, surely.

SOC. Then in these two events the combination of myself as passive and it as the active factor will generate different things?

THEAET. Of course.

SOC. Now if I drink wine when I am well, it appears to me pleasant and sweet?

d   THEAET. Yes.

SOC. Going by what we earlier agreed, that is so because the active and passive factors, moving simultaneously, generate both sweetness and a perception; on the passive side, the perception makes the tongue percipient, while on the side of the wine, sweetness moving about it makes it both be and appear sweet to the healthy tongue.

THEAET. That's certainly the sense of what we agreed to before.

SOC. But when the active factor finds Socrates ill, then, to begin with, it is not in strict truth the same man that it gets hold of, is it? Because here, as we saw, it has come upon an unlike.

THEAET. Yes.

Soc. Then this pair, Socrates ill and the draught of wine, gener- *e*
ates, presumably, different things again: a perception of bitterness
in the region of the tongue, and bitterness coming to be and moving
in the region of the wine. And then the wine becomes, not bitterness, but bitter; and I become, not perception, but percipient.

THEAET. Yes, quite.

Soc. And I shall never again become *thus* percipient of anything
else. A perception of something else is another perception, and
makes another and a changed percipient. Nor again, in the case of *160*
that which acts on me, will it ever, in conjunction with something
else, generate the same thing and itself become such as it now is.
From something else it will generate something else, and itself
become a changed thing.

THEAET. That is so.

Soc. Nor will I become such for myself or it such for itself.

THEAET. No.

Soc. But I must necessarily become percipient of something
when I become percipient; it is impossible to become percipient,
yet percipient of nothing. And it again, when it becomes sweet or *b*
bitter or anything of that kind, must become so for somebody,
because it is impossible to become sweet and yet sweet for no one.

THEAET. Quite impossible.

Soc. It remains, then, that I and it, whether we are or whether
we become, are or become for each other. For our being is, by
Necessity's decree, tied to a partner; yet we are tied neither to any
other thing in the world nor to our respective selves. It remains,
then, that we are tied to each other. Hence, whether you apply the
term 'being' to a thing or the term 'becoming', you must always
use the words 'for somebody' or 'of something' or 'relatively to
something'. You must not speak of anything as in itself either being
or becoming, nor let anyone else use such expressions. That is the *c*
meaning of the theory we have been expounding.

THEAET. Yes, that's certainly true, Socrates.

Soc. Then since that which acts on me is for me, and not for
anyone else, it is I who perceive it too, and nobody else?

THEAET. Undoubtedly.

Soc. Then my perception is true for me—because it is always a
perception of that being which is peculiarly mine; and I am judge,
as Protagoras said, of things that are, that they are, for me; and of
things that are not, that they are not.

THEAET. So it seems.

Soc. How then, if I am thus unerring and never stumble in my *d* thought about what is—or what is coming to be—how can I fail to be a knower of the things of which I am perceiver?

THEAET. There is no way you could fail.

Soc. Then that was a grand idea of yours when you told us that knowledge is nothing more or less than perception. So we find the various theories coincide:[14] that of Homer and Heracleitus and all their tribe, that all things flow like streams; of Protagoras, wisest of men, that man is the measure of all things; and of

e Theaetetus that, these things being so, knowledge proves to be perception. What about it, Theaetetus? Shall we say we have here your first-born child, the result of my midwifery? Or what would you say?

THEAET. Oh, there's no denying it, Socrates.

Soc. This, then, it appears, is what our efforts have at last brought forth—whatever it really is. And now that it has been born, we must perform the rite of running round the hearth[15] with it; we must make it in good earnest go the round of discussion. For we must take care that we don't overlook some defect in this thing that is entering into life; it may be something not worth bringing up, a

161 wind-egg, a falsehood. What do you say? Is it your opinion that your child ought in any case to be brought up and not exposed to die? Can you bear to see it found fault with, and not get into a rage if your first-born is stolen away from you?

THEOD. Theaetetus will put up with it, Socrates. He is not at all one to lose his temper. But tell me, in Heaven's name, in what way is it not as it should be?

Soc. You are the complete lover of discussion, Theodorus, and it is too good of you to think that I am a sort of bag of arguments, and can easily pick one out which will show you that this theory is

b wrong. But you don't realise what is happening. The arguments never come from me; they always come from the person I am talking to. All that I know, such as it is, is how to take an argument from someone else—someone who *is* wise—and give it a fair reception. So, now, I propose to try to get our answer out of Theaetetus, not to make any contribution of my own.

14. Literally, 'have converged to the same thing'.

15. We have not much information about the ceremony here alluded to. The authorities agree (1) that it was distinct from the formal adoption by the father, (2) that it was connected with the naming of the child, (3) that the friends and relatives sent presents of shell-fish. The above passage suggests that the ceremony was some sort of symbolic test of the child's fitness to take its place in the life of the family.

THEOD. That's a better way of putting it, Socrates; do as you say.

Soc. Well then, Theodorus, do you know what astonishes me about your friend Protagoras?

THEOD. No—what is it?   *c*

Soc. Well, I was delighted with his general statement of the theory that a thing is for any individual what it seems to him to be; but I was astonished at the way he began. I was astonished that he did not state at the beginning of the *Truth* that 'Pig is the measure of all things' or 'Baboon' or some yet more out-of-the-way creature with the power of perception. That would have made a most imposing and disdainful opening. It would have made it clear to us at once that, while we were standing astounded at his wisdom as though he were God, he was in reality no better authority than a   *d* tadpole—let alone any other man.

Or what are we to say, Theodorus? If whatever the individual judges by means of perception is true for him; if no man can assess another's experience better than he, or can claim authority to examine another man's judgement and see if it be right or wrong; if, as we have repeatedly said, only the individual himself can judge of his own world, and what he judges is always true and correct: how could it ever be, my friend, that Protagoras was a wise man, so wise as to think himself fit to be the teacher of other men and worth   *e* large fees; while we, in comparison with him the ignorant ones, needed to go and sit at his feet—we who are ourselves each the measure of his own wisdom? Can we avoid the conclusion that Protagoras was just playing to the crowd when he said this? I say nothing about my own case and my art of midwifery and how silly we look. So too, I think, does the whole business of philosophical discussion. To examine and try to refute each other's appearances and judgements, when each person's are correct—this is surely an extremely tiresome piece of nonsense, if the *Truth* of Protagoras is   162 true, and not merely an oracle speaking in jest from the impenetrable sanctuary of the book.

THEOD. Protagoras was my friend, Socrates, as you have just remarked. I could not consent to have him refuted through my admissions; and yet I should not be prepared to resist you against my own judgement. So take on Theaetetus again. He seemed to be following you very sympathetically just now.

Soc. Now, Theodorus, supposing you went to Sparta and were   *b* visiting the wrestling-schools. Would you think it right to sit and watch other men exercising naked—some of them not much to look at—and refuse to strip yourself alongside of them, and take your turn of letting people see what you look like?

THEOD. Why not, if I could persuade them to leave the choice to me? Similarly I am hoping to persuade you to allow me to be a spectator and not drag me into the arena now that I am grown stiff; but to take on someone who is younger and more supple.

Soc. Well, Theodorus, what you like I'll not dislike, as the saying
c   goes. So we must again resort to our wise Theaetetus. Come, Theaetetus. Think, to begin with, of what we have just been saying, and tell me if you are not yourself astonished at suddenly finding that you are the equal in wisdom of any man or even a god?—Or do you think the Protagorean measure isn't meant to be applied to gods as much as to men?

THEAET. I most certainly don't. And, to answer your question, yes, I am very much astonished. When we were working out the
d   meaning of the principle that a thing is for each man what it seems to him to be, it appeared to me a very sound one. But now, all in a minute, it is quite the other way round.

Soc. Yes, because you are young, dear lad; and so you lend a ready ear to mob-oratory and let it convince you. For Protagoras, or anyone speaking on his behalf, will answer us like this: 'My good people, young and old,' he will say, 'you sit here orating; you
e   drag in gods, whose existence or nonexistence I exclude from all discussion, written or spoken;[16] you keep on saying whatever is likely to be acceptable to the mob, telling them that it would be a shocking thing if no man were wiser than any cow in a field; but of proof or necessity not a word. You just rely on plausibility; though if Theodorus or any other geometer were to do that in his branch of science, it's a good-for-nothing geometer he would be. So you and Theodorus had better consider whether, in matters of such importance, you are going to accept arguments which are merely
163   persuasive or plausible.'

THEAET. You wouldn't say we had any business to do that, Socrates; and neither should we.

Soc. Then, it seems, you and Theodorus say our criticism should take a different line?

THEAET. Yes, it certainly should.

---

16. A reference to a notorious declaration by Protagoras: 'Concerning gods I am unable to know whether they exist or do not exist, or what they are like in form [or: appearance]; for there are many hindrances to knowledge, the obscurity of the subject and the brevity of human life'.

Soc. Here, then, is another way in which we might consider whether knowledge and perception are the same or different things—for that is the question which our argument has held in view throughout, isn't it? And it was for its sake that we have unearthed all this extraordinary stuff?

THEAET. Undoubtedly.

Soc. Well, now, are we going to agree that when we perceive *b* things by seeing or hearing them, we always at the same time *know* them? Take, for example, the case of hearing people speaking a foreign language which we have not yet learned. Are we going to say that we do not hear the sound of their voices when they speak? Or that we both hear it and know what they are saying? Again, supposing we do not know our letters, are we going to insist that we do not see them when we look at them? Or shall we maintain that, if we see them, we know them?

THEAET. We shall say, Socrates, that we know just that in them which we see and hear. We both see and know the shape and the colour of the letters; and with the spoken words we both hear and know the rise and fall of the voice. But what schoolmasters and *c* interpreters tell us about them, we don't perceive by seeing or hearing, and we don't know, either.

Soc. Very good indeed, Theaetetus; and it would not be right for me to stand in the way of your progress by raising objections to what you say. But look, there is another difficulty coming upon us. You must think now how we are going to fend it off.

THEAET. What kind of difficulty?

Soc. I mean something like this. Supposing you were asked, 'If *d* a man has once come to know a certain thing, and continues to preserve the memory of it, is it possible that, at the moment when he remembers it, he doesn't know this thing that he is remembering?' But I am being long-winded, I'm afraid. What I am trying to ask is, 'Can a man who has learnt something not know it when he is remembering it?'

THEAET. How could that happen, Socrates? That would be a most extraordinary thing.

Soc. Then am I perhaps talking nonsense? But think now. You say that seeing is perceiving and sight is perception?

THEAET. Yes.

Soc. Then a man who has seen something has come to know *e* that which he saw, according to the statement you made just now?

THEAET. Yes.

Soc. But you do say—don't you?— that there is such a thing as memory?

THEAET. Yes.

Soc. Memory of nothing? Or of something?

THEAET. Of something, surely.

Soc. That is to say, of things which one has learnt, that is, perceived—that kind of 'something'?

THEAET. Of course.

Soc. And what a man has once seen, he recalls, I take it, from time to time?

THEAET. He does.

Soc. Even if he shuts his eyes? Or does he forget it if he does this?

THEAET. That would be a strange thing to say, Socrates.

164   Soc. Yet it is what we must say, if we are to save our previous statement. Otherwise, it's all up with it.

THEAET. Yes, by Jove, I begin to have my suspicions too; but I don't quite see it yet. You explain.

Soc. This is why. According to us, the man who sees has acquired knowledge of what he sees, as sight, perception and knowledge are agreed to be the same thing.

THEAET. Yes, certainly.

Soc. But the man who sees and has acquired knowledge of the thing he saw, if he shuts his eyes remembers but does not see it. Isn't that so?

THEAET. Yes.

b   Soc. But to say 'He doesn't see' is to say 'He doesn't know', if 'sees' is 'knows'?

THEAET. True.

Soc. Then we have this result, that a man who has come to know something and still remembers it doesn't know it because he doesn't see it? And that's what we said would be a most extraordinary thing to happen.

THEAET. That's perfectly true.

Soc. Then apparently we get an impossible result when knowledge and perception are identified?

THEAET. It looks like it.

Soc. Then we have got to say that perception is one thing and knowledge another?

THEAET. Yes, I'm afraid so.

c   Soc. Then what *is* knowledge? We shall have to begin again at the beginning, it seems. And yet—whatever are we thinking about, Theaetetus?

THEAET. What do you mean?

Soc. We appear to be behaving like a base-born fighting-cock, jumping away off the theory, and crowing before we have the victory over it.

THEAET. How are we doing that?

Soc. We seem to have been adopting the methods of professional controversialists: we've made an agreement aimed at getting words to agree consistently; and we feel complacent now that we have defeated the theory by the use of a method of this kind. We profess to be philosophers, not champion controversialists; and we don't realise that we are doing just what those clever fellows do.   *d*

THEAET. I still don't quite see what you mean.

Soc. Well, I will try to explain what I have in mind here. We were enquiring into the possibility that a man should not know something that he has learnt and remembers. And we showed that a man who has seen something, and then shuts his eyes, remembers but does not see it; and that showed that he does not know the thing at the very time that he remembers it. We said that this was impossible. And so the tale of Protagoras comes to an untimely end; yours too, your tale about the identity of knowledge and perception.

THEAET. So it appears.   *e*

Soc. But I don't think this would have happened, my friend, if the father of the other tale were alive. He would find plenty of means of defending it. As things are, it is an orphan we are trampling in the mud. Not even the people Protagoras appointed its guardians are prepared to come to its rescue; for instance, Theodorus here. In the interests of justice, it seems that we shall have to come to the rescue ourselves.

THEOD. I think you must. It is not I, you know, Socrates, but Callias, the son of Hipponicus,[17] who is the guardian of Protagoras'   *165* relicts. As it happened, I very soon inclined away from abstract discussion to geometry. But I shall be very grateful if you can rescue the orphan.

---

17. A wealthy Athenian famous for his patronage of the Sophists: 'a man who has spent more money on Sophists than everyone else put together' (*Apology* 20a). The discussion of Plato's *Protagoras* is set in his house, where Protagoras and other visiting Sophists are staying.

Soc. Good, Theodorus. Now will you give your mind to this rescue work of mine—what little I can do? Because one might be driven into making even more alarming admissions than we have just made, if one paid as little attention to the words in which we express our assertions and denials as we are for the most part accustomed to doing. Shall I tell you how this might happen? Or shall I tell Theaetetus?

THEOD. Tell us both, Socrates; but the younger had better answer. It will not be so undignified for him to get tripped up.

Soc. Well, then, here is the most alarming poser of all. It goes something like this, I think: 'Is it possible for a man who knows something not to know this thing which he knows?'

THEOD. What are we going to answer now, Theaetetus?

THEAET. That it is impossible, I should think.

Soc. But it is not, if you are going to premise that seeing is knowing. For what are you going to do when some intrepid fellow has you 'trapped in the well-shaft', as they say, with a question that leaves you no way out: clapping his hand over one of your eyes, he asks you whether you see his cloak with the eye that is covered—how will you cope with that?

THEAET. I shall say that I don't see it with this one, but I do with the other.

Soc. So you both see and do not see the same thing at the same time?

THEAET. Well, yes, in that sort of way I do.

Soc. 'That's not the question I'm setting you,' he will say, 'I was not asking you in what way it happened. I was asking you "Does it happen that you don't know what you know?" You now appear to be seeing what you don't see; and you have actually admitted that seeing is knowing, and not to see is not to know. I leave you to draw your conclusion.'

THEAET. Well, I draw a conclusion that contradicts my original suppositions.

Soc. And that is the kind of thing that might have happened to you more than once, you wonderful fellow. It might have happened if someone had gone on asking you whether it was possible to know sometimes clearly and sometimes dimly; or to know near at hand and not from a distance; or to know the same thing both intensely and slightly. And there are a million other questions with which one of the mercenary skirmishers of debate might ambush you, once you had proposed that knowledge and perception are the same thing. He would lay into hearing and smelling and other

perceptions of that kind; and would keep on refuting you and not
let you go till you had been struck with wonder at his wisdom—   *e*
that 'answer to many prayers'—and had got yourself thoroughly
tied up by him. Then, when he had you tamed and bound, he would
set you free for a ransom—whatever price seemed appropriate to
the two of you.[18]

But perhaps you'll ask, what argument would Protagoras himself
bring to the help of his offspring. Shall we try to state it?

THEAET. Yes, surely.

SOC. Well, he will say all the things that we are saying in our
attempt to defend him; and then, I imagine, he will come to grips   *166*
with us, and in no respectful spirit either. I imagine him saying:
'This good Socrates here—what he did was to frighten a small boy
by asking him if it were possible that the same man should at once
remember and not know the same thing; and when the boy in his
fright answered "No," because he couldn't see what was coming,
then, according to Socrates, the laugh was against *me* in the argument. You are too easy-going, Socrates. The true position is this.
When you are examining any doctrine of mine by the method of
question and answer, if the person being questioned answers as I
myself would answer, and gets caught, then it is I who am refuted;
but if his answers are other than I should give, then it is he who is   *b*
put in the wrong.

'Now, to begin with, do you expect someone to grant you that a
man's present memory of something which he has experienced in
the past but is no longer experiencing is the same sort of experience
as he then had? That is very far from being true. Again, do you
suppose he will hesitate to admit that it is possible for the same
man to know and not know the same thing? Or—if he has misgiv-
ings about this—do you expect him to concede to you that the man,

---

18. At this point the mercenary skirmisher is revealed as Protagoras himself. To
begin with, the skirmisher was made to sound like the Sophists Euthydemus and
Dionysodorus who are satirized in Plato's *Euthydemus:* a pair of elderly rogues who
are described as fiendishly clever combatants in argumentative warfare (*Euthyd.*
272a), keen to demonstrate their skills and to teach them to all comers—for a price
(274ab, 304c). They specialize in 'questions which leave no way out' (276e) and are
shown wielding a battery of teasers about knowing and not knowing (275d ff., 293b
ff.). But a ransom which is fixed by agreement between captor and captive can only
be a reference to a well-known practice of Protagoras' own: 'Anyone who comes to
learn from me may either pay the fee I ask for or, if he prefers, go to a temple, state
on oath what he believes to be the worth of my instruction, and deposit that amount'
(*Protagoras* 328bc, giving Protagoras' answer to a question closely related to that of
Theaetetus 161de, about his entitlement to set himself up to teach others for a fee).

who is in process of becoming unlike, is the same as he was before the process began? Do you expect him even to speak of "the man" rather than of "the men", indeed of an infinite number of these men coming to be in succession, assuming this process of becoming
c   unlike? Not if we really must take every precaution against each other's verbal traps. Show a little more spirit, my good man,' he will say, 'and attack my actual statement itself, and refute it, if you can, by showing that each man's perceptions are not his own private events; or that, if they are his own private events, it does not follow that the thing which appears "becomes" or, if we may speak of being, "is" only for the man to whom it appears. You keep talking about pigs and baboons; you show the mentality of a pig[19] yourself, in the way you deal with my writings, and you persuade your
d   audience to follow your example. That is not the way to behave.

'I take my stand on the truth[20] being as I have written it. Each one of us is the measure both of what is and of what is not; but there are countless differences between men for just this very reason, that different things both are and appear to be to different subjects. I certainly do not deny the existence of both wisdom and wise men: far from it. But the man whom I call wise is the man who can change the appearances—the man who in any case where bad things both appear and are for one of us, works a change and makes good things appear and be for him.

'And I must beg you, this time, not to confine your attack to the
e   letter of my doctrine. I am now going to make its meaning clearer to you. For instance, I would remind you of what we were saying before, namely, that to the sick man the things he eats both appear and are bitter, while to the healthy man they both appear and are the opposite. Now what we have to do is not to make one of these
167   two wiser than the other—that is not even a possibility—nor is it our business to make accusations, calling the sick man ignorant for judging as he does, and the healthy man wise, because he judges differently. What we have to do is to make a change from the one to the other, because the other state is *better*. In education, too, what we have to do is to change a worse state into a better state; only whereas the doctor brings about the change by the use of

19. The Greek pig appears often to be the type not so much of greed or uncleanliness, as of general lack of culture and of the finer perceptions. One spoke proverbially of things which 'not every pig would realise'. His shortcomings are intellectual as much as social or moral.

20. One of several puns on the title of Protagoras' book *Truth*.

drugs, the professional teacher[21] does it by the use of words. What never happens is that a man who judges what is false is made to judge what is true. For it is impossible to judge what is not, or to judge anything other than what one is immediately experiencing; and what one is immediately experiencing is always true. This, in my opinion, is what really happens: when a man's soul is in a pernicious state, he judges things akin to it, but giving him a sound state of the soul causes him to think different things, things that are good. In the latter event, the things which appear to him are what some people, who are still at a primitive stage, call "true"; my position, however, is that the one kind are *better* than the others, but in no way *truer*.

'Nor, my dear Socrates, should I dream of suggesting that we might look for wisdom among frogs. I look for wisdom, as regards animal bodies, in doctors; as regards plant-life, in gardeners— for I am quite prepared to maintain that gardeners too, when they find a plant sickly, proceed by causing it to have good and healthy, that is, "true" perceptions, instead of bad ones. Similarly, the wise and efficient politician is the man who makes wholesome things seem just to a city instead of pernicious ones. Whatever in any city is regarded as just and admirable *is* just and admirable, in that city and for so long as that convention maintains itself; but the wise man replaces each pernicious convention by a wholesome one, making this both be and seem just. Similarly the professional teacher who is able to educate his pupils on these lines is a wise man, and is worth his large fees to them.

'In this way we are enabled to hold both that some men are wiser than others, and also that no man judges what is false. And you, too, whether you like it or not, must put up with being a "measure". For this is the line we must take if we are to save the theory.

'If you feel prepared to go back to the beginning, and make a case against this theory, let us hear your objections set out in a connected argument. Or, if you prefer the method of question and answer, do it that way; there is no reason to try to evade that method either, indeed an intelligent person might well prefer it to any other. Only I beg that you will observe this condition: do not be unjust in your questions. It is the height of unreasonableness that a person who professes to care for moral goodness should be consistently unjust in discussion. I mean by injustice, in this connection, the behavior of a man who does not take care to keep

21. Literally, 'the Sophist'.

controversy distinct from discussion; a man who forgets that in controversy he may play about and trip up his opponent as often as he can, but that in discussion he must be serious, he must keep on helping his opponent to his feet again, and point out to him
168 only those of his slips which are due to himself or to the intellectual society which he has previously frequented. If you observe this distinction, those who associate with you will blame themselves for their confusion and their difficulties, not you. They will seek your company, and think of you as their friend; but they will loathe themselves, and seek refuge from themselves in philosophy, in the hope that they may thereby become different people and be rid for ever of the men that they once were. But if you follow the common practice and do the opposite, you will get the opposite results.
b Instead of philosophers, you will make your companions grow up to be the enemies of philosophy.

'So, if you take my advice, as I said before, you will sit down with us without ill will or hostility, in a kindly spirit. You will genuinely try to find out what our meaning is when we maintain (a) that all things are in motion and (b) that for each person and each city, things are what they seem to them to be. And upon this basis you will enquire whether knowledge and perception are the same thing or different things. But you will not proceed as you did just now. You will not base your argument upon the use and wont of language; you will not follow the practice of most men, who
c drag words this way and that at their pleasure, so making every imaginable difficulty for one another.'

Well, Theodorus, here is my contribution to the rescue of your friend—the best I can do, with my resources, and little enough that is. If he were alive himself, he would have come to the rescue of his offspring in a grander style.

THEOD. That must be a joke, Socrates. It was a very spirited rescue.

Soc. You are kind, my friend. Tell me now, did you notice that Protagoras was complaining of us, in the speech that we have
d just heard, for addressing our arguments to a small boy and making the child's nervousness a weapon against his ideas? And how he disparaged our method of argument as merely an amusing game, and how solemnly he upheld his 'measure of all things' and commanded us to be serious when we dealt with his theory?

THEOD. Yes, of course I noticed that, Socrates.

Soc. Then do you think we should obey his commands?

THEOD. Most certainly I do.

Soc. Look at the company then. They are all children but you. So if we are to obey Protagoras, it is you and I who have got to be serious about his theory. It is you and I who must question and answer one another. Then he will not have *this* against us, at any rate, that we turned the criticism of his philosophy into sport with boys.

THEOD. Well, isn't our Theaetetus better able to follow the investigation of a theory than many an old fellow with a long beard?

Soc. But not better than *you*, Theodorus. Do not go on imagining that it is my business to be straining every nerve to defend your dead friend while you do nothing. Come now, my very good Theodorus, come a little way with me. Come with me at any rate until we see whether in questions of geometrical proofs it is really you who should be the measure or whether all men are as sufficient to themselves as you are in astronomy and the other sciences in which you have made your name.

THEOD. Socrates, it is not easy for a man who has sat down beside you to refuse to talk. That was all nonsense just now when I was pretending that you were going to allow me to keep my coat on, and not use compulsion like the Spartans. So far from that, you seem to me to have leanings towards the methods of Sciron.[22] The Spartans tell one either to strip or to go away; but you seem rather to be playing the part of Antaeus.[23] You don't let any comer go till you have stripped him and made him wrestle with you in an argument.

Soc. That, Theodorus, is an excellent simile to describe what is the matter with me. But I am more of a fiend for exercise than Sciron and Antaeus. I have met with many and many a Heracles and Theseus in my time, mighty men of words; and they have well battered me. But for all that I don't retire from the field, so terrible a lust has come upon me for these exercises. *You* must not grudge me this, either; try a fall with me and we shall both be the better.

THEOD. All right. I resign myself; take me with you where you

e

169

b

c

22. A legendary highwayman who attacked travellers on the coast between Megara and Corinth. His most famous 'method' was to compel them to wash his feet, and kick them over the cliff into the sea while they were so doing. He was said to have been himself disposed of in a similar manner by Theseus.

23. Antaeus belongs to a tradition current among the Greek colonists of North Africa, and primarily connected with the neighbourhood of Cyrene. He was said to have lived in a cave and compelled all passers-by to wrestle with him, with results invariably fatal to them. He was finally put out of action by Heracles.

like. In any case, I see, I have got to put up with the fate you spin
for me, and submit to your inquisition. But not further than the
limits you have laid down; beyond that I shall not be able to offer
myself.

SOC. It will do if you will go with me so far. Now there is one
kind of mistake I want you to be specially on your guard against,
namely, that we do not unconsciously slip into some childish form

d of argument. We don't want to get into disgrace for this again.

THEOD. I will do my best, I promise you.

SOC. The first thing, then, is to tackle the same point that we
were dealing with before. We were making a complaint. Now let
us see whether we were right or wrong in holding it to be a defect
in this theory that it made every man self-sufficient in wisdom; and
whether we were right or wrong when we made Protagoras concede
that some men are superior to others in questions of better and
worse, these being 'the wise'. Do you agree?

THEOD. Yes.

SOC. It would be a different matter if Protagoras were here in
person and agreed with us, instead of our having made this conces-

e sion on his behalf in our attempt to help him. In that case, there
would be no need to take this question up again and make sure
about it. In the circumstances, however, it might be decided that
we had no authority on his behalf, and so it is desirable that we
should come to a clearer agreement on this point; for it makes no
small difference whether this is so or not.

THEOD. True.

SOC. Then don't let us obtain this concession through anybody

170 else. Let us take the shortest way, an appeal to his own statement.

THEOD. How?

SOC. In this way. He says, does he not, that things are for every
man what they seem to him to be?

THEOD. Yes, that is what he says.

SOC. Well, then, Protagoras, we too are expressing the judgements of a man—I might say, of all men—when we say that there
is no one in the world who doesn't believe that in some matters he
is wiser than other men; while in other matters, they are wiser than
he. In emergencies—if at no other time—you see this belief. When
they are in distress, on the battlefield, or in sickness or in a storm
at sea, all men turn to their leaders in each sphere as to God, and

b look to them for salvation because they are superior in precisely
this one thing—knowledge. And wherever human life and work
goes on, you find everywhere men seeking teachers and masters,

for themselves and for other living creatures and for the direction of all human works. You find also men who believe that they are able to teach[24] and to take the lead. In all these cases, what else can we say but that men do believe in the existence of both wisdom and ignorance among themselves?

THEOD. There can be no other conclusion.

Soc. And they believe that wisdom is true thinking? While ignorance is a matter of false judgement?

THEOD. Yes, of course.   c

Soc. What then, Protagoras, are we to make of your argument? Are we to say that all men, on every occasion, judge what is true? Or that they judge sometimes truly and sometimes falsely? Whichever we say, it comes to the same thing, namely, that men do not always judge what is true; that human judgements are both true and false. For think, Theodorus. Would you, would anyone of the school of Protagoras be prepared to contend that no one ever thinks his neighbour is ignorant or judging falsely?

THEOD. No, that's not a thing one could believe, Socrates.

Soc. And yet it is to this that our theory has been driven—this   d
theory that man is the measure of all things.

THEOD. How is that?

Soc. Well, suppose you come to a decision in your own mind and then express a judgement about something to me. Let us assume with Protagoras that your judgement is true for *you*. But isn't it possible that the rest of us may criticise your verdict? Do we always agree that your judgement is true? Or does there rise up against you, every time, a vast army of persons who think the opposite, who hold that your decisions and your thoughts are false?

THEOD. Heaven knows they do, Socrates, in their 'thousands   e
and tens of thousands', as Homer says, and give me all the trouble that is humanly possible.

Soc. Then do you want us to say that you are then judging what is true for yourself, but false for the tens of thousands?

THEOD. It looks as if that is what we must say, according to the theory, at any rate.

Soc. And what of Protagoras himself? Must he not say this, that supposing he himself did not believe that man is the measure, any more than the majority of people (who indeed do not believe it), then this *Truth* which he wrote is true for no one? On the other hand, suppose he believed it himself, but the majority of men do   *171*

24. Protagoras himself professed to teach 'virtue'.

not agree with him; then you see—to begin with—the more those to whom it does not seem to be the truth outnumber those to whom it does, so much the more it isn't than it is?

THEOD. That must be so, if it is going to be or not be according to the individual judgement.

Soc. Secondly, it has this most exquisite feature: Protagoras admits, I presume, that the contrary opinion about his own opinion (namely, that it is false) must be true, seeing he agrees that all men judge what is.

THEOD. Undoubtedly.

b Soc. And in conceding the truth of the opinion of those who think him wrong, he is really admitting the falsity of his own opinion?

THEOD. Yes, inevitably.

Soc. But for their part the others do not admit that they are wrong?

THEOD. No.

Soc. But Protagoras again admits *this* judgement to be true, according to his written doctrine?

THEOD. So it appears.

Soc. It will be disputed, then, by everyone, beginning with Protagoras—or rather, it will be admitted by him, when he grants to the person who contradicts him that he judges truly—when he

c does that, even Protagoras himself will be granting that neither a dog nor the 'man in the street' is the measure of anything at all which he has not learned. Isn't that so?

THEOD. It is so.

Soc. Then since it is disputed by everyone, the *Truth* of Protagoras is not true for anyone at all, not even for himself?

THEOD. Socrates, we are running my friend too hard.

Soc. But it is not at all clear, my dear Theodorus, that we are running off the right track. Hence it is likely that Protagoras, being older than we are, really is wiser as well;[25] and if he were to stick

d up his head from below as far as the neck just here where we are, he would in all likelihood convict me twenty times over of talking nonsense, and show you up too for agreeing with me, before he ducked down to rush off again. But we have got to take ourselves as we are, I suppose, and go on saying the things which seem to

25. Because the refutation of the thesis that everyone is equally wise establishes that some are wiser than others— and who should this be (Socrates suggests with savage irony) but Protagoras himself?

us to be. At the moment, then, mustn't we maintain that any man would admit at least this, that some men are wiser than their fellows and others more ignorant?

THEOD. So it seems to me, at any rate.

Soc. We may also suggest that the theory would stand firm most successfully in the position which we sketched out for it in our   *e* attempt to bring help to Protagoras. I mean the position that most things are for the individual what they seem to him to be; for instance, warm, dry, sweet and all this type of thing. But if the theory is going to admit that there is any sphere in which one man is superior to another, it might perhaps be prepared to grant it in questions of what is good or bad for one's health. Here it might well be admitted that it is not true that every creature—woman or child or even animal—is competent to recognise what is good for it and to heal its own sickness; that here, if anywhere, one person is better than another. Do you agree?

THEOD. Yes, that seems so to me.

Soc. Then consider political questions. Some of these are ques-   *172* tions of what may or may not fittingly be done, of just and unjust, of what is sanctioned by religion and what is not; and here the theory may be prepared to maintain that whatever view a city takes on these matters and establishes as its law or convention, is truth and fact for that city. In such matters neither any individual nor any city can claim superior wisdom. But when it is a question of laying down what is to the interest of the state and what is not, the matter is different. The theory will again admit that here, if anywhere, one counsellor is better than another; here the decision of one city may be more in conformity with the truth than that of another. It would certainly not have the hardihood to affirm that   *b* when a city decides that a certain thing is to its own interest, that thing will undoubtedly turn out to be to its interest. It is in those other questions I am talking about—just and unjust, religious and irreligious—that men are ready to insist that no one of these things has by nature any being of its own; in respect of these, they say, what seems to people collectively to be so is true, at the time when it seems that way and for just as long as it so seems. And even those who are not prepared to go all the way with Protagoras take some such view of wisdom.[26] But I see, Theodorus, that we are becoming involved in a greater discussion emerging from the lesser one.   *c*

26. On the translation of this and the preceding sentence, see Introduction, Part I, n. 41.

THEOD. Well, we have plenty of time, haven't we, Socrates?

Soc. We appear to . . . That remark of yours, my friend, reminds me of an idea that has often occurred to me before—how natural it is that men who have spent a great part of their lives in philosophical studies make such fools of themselves when they appear as speakers in the law-courts.

THEOD. How do you mean now?

Soc. Well, look at the man who has been knocking about in law-courts and such places ever since he was a boy; and compare him with the man brought up in philosophy, in the life of a student. It *d* is surely like comparing the up-bringing of a slave with that of a free man.

THEOD. How is that, now?

Soc. Because the one man always has what you mentioned just now—plenty of time. When he talks, he talks in peace and quiet, and his time is his own. It is so with us now: here we are beginning on our third new discussion;[27] and he can do the same, if he is like us, and prefers the new-comer to the question in hand. It does not matter to such men whether they talk for a day or a year, if only they may hit upon that which is. But the other—the man of the *e* law-courts—is always in a hurry when he is talking; he has to speak with one eye on the clock. Besides, he can't make his speeches on any subject he likes; he has his adversary standing over him, armed with compulsory powers and with the sworn statement, which is read out point by point as he proceeds, and must be kept to by the speaker. The talk is always about a fellow-slave, and is addressed to a master,[28] who sits there holding some suit or other in his hand. And the struggle is never a matter of indifference; it always directly concerns the speaker, and sometimes life itself is at stake.

173 Such conditions make him keen and highly-strung, skilled in flattering the master and working his way into favour; but cause his soul to be small and warped. His early servitude prevents him from making a free, straight growth; it forces him into doing crooked things by imposing dangers and alarms upon a soul that is still tender. He cannot meet these by just and honest practice, and so resorts to lies and to the policy of repaying one wrong with another;

27. If the 'greater discussion' emerging at 172c is the 'third', the other two are probably the two attempts to come to grips with Protagoras beginning respectively at 161b and 169d.

28. The master is the *dēmos*, the people, embodied in the jury of several hundred persons who decide the suit.

thus he is constantly being bent and distorted, and in the end grows   *b*
up to manhood with a mind that has no health in it, having now
become—in his own eyes—a man of ability and wisdom.

There is your practical man, Theodorus. What about our own
set? Would you like us to have a review of them, or shall we let
them be, and return to the argument? We don't want to abuse this
freedom to change our subject of which we were speaking just now.

THEOD. No, no, Socrates. Let us review the philosophers. What
you said just now was quite right; we who move in such circles are   *c*
not the servants but the masters of our discussions. Our arguments
are our own, like slaves; each one must wait about for us, to be
finished whenever we think fit. We have no jury, and no audience
(as the dramatic poets have), sitting in control over us, ready to
criticise and give orders.

Soc. Very well, then; we must review them, it seems, since you
have made up your mind. But let us confine ourselves to the leaders;
why bother about the second-rate specimens? To begin with, then,
the philosopher grows up without knowing the way to the market-
place, or the whereabouts of the law-courts or the council-chambers   *d*
or any other place of public assembly. Laws and decrees, published
orally or in writing, are things he never sees or hears. The scram-
bling of political cliques for office; social functions, dinners, parties
with flute-girls—such doings never enter his head even in a dream.
So with questions of birth—he has no more idea whether a fellow-
citizen is high-born or humble, or whether he has inherited some
taint from his forbears, male or female, than he has of the number
of pints in the sea, as they say. And in all these matters, he knows   *e*
not even that he knows not; for he does not hold himself aloof from
them in order to get a reputation, but because it is in reality only
his body that lives and sleeps in the city. His mind, having come
to the conclusion that all these things are of little or no account,
spurns them and pursues its wingéd way, as Pindar says, throughout the universe, 'in the deeps below the earth' and 'in the heights
above the heaven'; geometrising upon earth, measuring its surfaces, astronomising in the heavens; tracking down by every path
the entire nature of each whole among the things that are, and   *174*
never condescending to what lies near at hand.

THEOD. What do you mean by that, Socrates?

Soc. Well, here's an instance: they say Thales[29] was studying the

29. The first founder of Greek natural philosophy (sixth century B.C.), about whom
we have anecdotes but little solid information. Plato's anecdote of Thales falling into

stars, Theodorus, and gazing aloft, when he fell into a well; and a witty and amusing Thracian servant-girl made fun of him because, she said, he was wild to know about what was up in the sky but failed to see what was in front of him and under his feet. The same joke applies to all who spend their lives in philosophy. It really is

b   true that the philosopher fails to see his next-door neighbour; he not only doesn't notice what he is doing; he scarcely knows whether he is a man or some other kind of creature. The question he asks is, What is Man? What actions and passions properly belong to human nature and distinguish it from all other beings? This is what he wants to know and concerns himself to investigate. You see what I mean, Theodorus, don't you?

THEOD. Yes; and what you say is true.

SOC. This accounts, my friend, for the behaviour of such a man when he comes into contact with his fellows, either privately with

c   individuals or in public life, as I was saying at the beginning. Whenever he is obliged, in a law-court or elsewhere, to discuss the things that lie at his feet and before his eyes, he causes entertainment not only to Thracian servant-girls but to all the common herd, by tumbling into wells and every sort of difficulty through his lack of experience. His clumsiness is awful and gets him a reputation for fatuousness. On occasions when personal scandal is the topic of conversation, he never has anything at all of his own to contribute; he knows nothing to the detriment of anyone, never having paid any attention to this subject—a lack of resource which makes

d   him look very comic. And again, when compliments are in order, and self-laudation, his evident amusement—which is by no means a pose but perfectly genuine—is regarded as idiotic. When he hears the praises of a despot or a king being sung, it sounds to his ears as if some stock-breeder were being congratulated—some keeper of pigs or sheep, or cows that are giving him plenty of milk; only he thinks that the rulers have a more difficult and treacherous animal to rear and milk, and that such a man, having no spare time,

e   is bound to become quite as coarse and uncultivated as the stock-farmer; for the castle of the one is as much a prison as the mountain

---

a well is complemented or counterbalanced by one in Aristotle, *Politics* I 4, 1259a 6–19, which tells of Thales using his astronomical knowledge to predict a large olive crop, hiring all the available olive-presses while it was still winter, and then, when the season brought a great demand for presses, leasing them out at a large profit. The moral: it is easy for philosophers to be rich if they wish, but that is not what they are interested in. Anecdotes like these featured frequently in philosophical debates about the ideal form of life.

fold of the other. When he hears talk of land—that so-and-so has a property of ten thousand acres or more, and what a vast property that is, it sounds to him like a tiny plot, used as he is to envisage the whole earth. When his companions become lyric on the subject of great families, and exclaim at the noble blood of one who can point to seven wealthy ancestors, he thinks that such praise comes of a dim and limited vision, an inability, through lack of education, to take a steady view of the whole, and to calculate that every single man has countless hosts of ancestors, near and remote, amongst whom are to be found, in every instance, rich men and beggars, kings and slaves, Greeks and foreigners, by the thousand. When men pride themselves upon a pedigree of twenty-five ancestors, and trace their descent back to Heracles the son of Amphitryon, they seem to him to be taking a curious interest in trifles. As for the twenty-fifth ancestor of Amphitryon, what *he* may have been is merely a matter of luck, and similarly with the fiftieth before him again. How ridiculous, he thinks, not to be able to work that out, and get rid of the gaping vanity of a silly mind.

175

b

On all these occasions, you see, the philosopher is the object of general derision, partly for what men take to be his superior manner, and partly for his constant ignorance and lack of resource in dealing with the obvious.

THEOD. What you say exactly describes what does happen, Socrates.

SOC. But consider what happens, my friend, when he in his turn draws someone to a higher level, and induces him to abandon questions of 'My injustice towards you, or yours towards me' for an examination of justice and injustice themselves—what they are, and how they differ from everything else and from each other; or again, when he gets him to leave such questions as 'Is a king happy?' or 'a man of property?' for an enquiry into kingship, and into human happiness and misery in general—what these two things are, and what, for a human being, is the proper method by which the one can be obtained and the other avoided. When it is an account of matters like all these that is demanded of our friend with the small, sharp, legal mind, the situation is reversed; his head swims as, suspended at such a height, he gazes down from his place among the clouds; disconcerted by the unusual experience, he knows not what to do next, and can only stammer when he speaks. And that causes great entertainment, not to Thracian servant-girls or any other uneducated persons—they do not see what is going on—but to all men who have not been brought up like slaves.

c

d

[margin note: Alienation from society caused by understanding]

e These are the two types, Theodorus. There is the one who has been brought up in true freedom and leisure, the man you call a philosopher; a man to whom it is no disgrace to appear simple and good-for-nothing when he is confronted with menial tasks, when, for instance, he doesn't know how to make a bed, or how to sweeten a sauce or a flattering speech. Then you have the other, the man who is keen and smart at doing all these jobs, but does not know how to strike up a song in his turn like a free man, or how to tune

176 the strings of common speech to the fitting praise of the life of gods and of the happy among men.

THEOD. Socrates, if your words convinced everyone as they do me, there would be more peace and less evil on earth.

Soc. But it is not possible, Theodorus, that evil should be destroyed—for there must always be something opposed to the good; nor is it possible that it should have its seat in heaven. But it must inevitably haunt human life, and prowl about this earth. That is why a man should make all haste to escape from earth to heaven;

b and escape means becoming as like God as possible; and a man becomes like God when he becomes just and pure, with understanding. But it is not at all an easy matter, my good friend, to persuade men that it is not for the reasons commonly alleged that one should try to escape from wickedness and pursue virtue. It is not in order to avoid a bad reputation and obtain a good one that virtue should be practised and not vice; that, it seems to me, is only

c what men call 'old wives' talk'.

Let us try to put the truth in this way. In God there is no sort of wrong whatsoever; he is supremely just, and the thing most like him is the man who has become as just as it lies in human nature to be. And it is here that we see whether a man is truly able, or truly a weakling and a nonentity; for it is the realisation of this that is genuine wisdom and goodness, while the failure to realise it is manifest folly and wickedness. Everything else that passes for ability and wisdom has a sort of commonness—in those who wield political power a poor cheap show, in the manual workers a matter

d of mechanical routine. If, therefore, one meets a man who practises injustice and is blasphemous in his talk or in his life, the best thing for him by far is that one should never grant that there is any sort of ability about his unscrupulousness; such men are ready enough to glory in the reproach, and think that it means not that they are mere rubbish, cumbering the ground to no purpose, but that they have the kind of qualities that are necessary for survival in the community. We must therefore tell them the truth—that their very ignorance of their true state fixes them the more firmly therein. For they do not know what is the penalty of injustice, which is the last thing of which a man should be ignorant. It is not what they suppose—scourging and death—things which they may entirely evade in spite of their wrong-doing. It is a penalty from which there is no escape.   *e*

THEOD. And what is that?

Soc. My friend, there are two patterns set up in the world. One is divine and supremely happy; the other has nothing of God in it, and is the pattern of the deepest unhappiness. This truth the evil-doer does not see; blinded by folly and utter lack of understanding, he fails to perceive that the effect of his unjust practices is to make *177* him grow more and more like the one, and less and less like the other. For this he pays the penalty of living the life that corresponds to the pattern he is coming to resemble. And if we tell him that, unless he is delivered from this 'ability' of his, when he dies the place that is pure of all evil will not receive him; that he will for ever go on living in this world a life after his own likeness[30]—a bad man tied to bad company: he will but think, 'This is the way fools talk to a clever rascal like me.'

THEOD. Oh, yes, Socrates, sure enough.

Soc. I know it, my friend. But there is one accident to which the *b* unjust man is liable. When it comes to giving and taking an account in a private discussion of the things he disparages; when he is willing to stand his ground like a man for long enough, instead of running away like a coward, then, my friend, an odd thing happens. In the end the things he says do not satisfy even himself; that famous eloquence of his somehow dries up, and he is left looking nothing more than a child.

But we had better leave it there; all this is really a digression; and if we go on, a flood of new subjects will pour in and overwhelm *c* our original argument. So, if you don't mind, we will go back to what we were saying before.

THEOD. As a matter of fact, Socrates, *I* like listening to this kind of talk; it is easier for a man of my years to follow. Still, if you like, let us go back to the argument.

Soc. Well, then, we were at somewhere about this point in the argument, weren't we? We were speaking of the people who assert

---

30. I.e. after death he will be condemned to further earthly lives. For the belief that the philosopher, thanks to a life spent in pursuit of knowledge and virtue, can escape this cycle of reincarnation, see *Phaedrus* 243e–257a.

a being that is in motion, and who hold that for every individual things always are whatever they seem to him to be; and we said that they were prepared to stand upon their principle in almost every case—not least in questions of what is just and right. Here they are perfectly ready to maintain that whatever any community

d   decides to be just and right, and establishes as such, actually is what is just and right for that community and for as long as it remains so established. On the other hand, when it is a question of what things are good, we no longer find anyone so heroic that he will venture to contend that whatever a community thinks useful, and establishes, really is useful, so long as it is the established order—unless, of course, he means that it is *called* 'useful'; but that would be making a game of our argument, wouldn't it?

THEOD. It would indeed.

e   SOC. Let us suppose, then, that he is not talking about the name 'useful' but has in view the thing to which it is applied.

THEOD. Agreed.

SOC. It is surely this that a government aims at when it legislates, whatever name it calls it. A community always makes such laws as are most useful to it—so far as the limits of its judgement and capacity permit.—Or do you think legislation may have some other object in view?

178   THEOD. Oh no, not at all.

SOC. And does a community always achieve this object? Or are there always a number of failures?

THEOD. It seems to me that there are failures.

SOC. Now we might put this matter in a rather different way and be still more likely to get people generally to agree with our conclusions. I mean, one might put a question about the whole class of things to which 'what is useful' belongs. These things are concerned, I take it, with future time; thus when we legislate, we make laws that are going to be useful in the time to come. This kind of thing we may properly call 'future'.

b   THEOD. Yes, certainly.

SOC. Come then, let's put a question to Protagoras (or to anyone who professes the same views): 'Now, Protagoras, "Man is the measure of all things" as you people say—of white and heavy and light and all that kind of thing without exception. He has the criterion of these things within himself; so when he thinks that they are as he experiences them, he thinks what is true and what really is for him.' Isn't that so?

THEOD. It is.

SOC. 'Then, Protagoras,' we shall say, 'what about things that are

going to be in the future? Has a man the criterion of these within   *c*
himself? When he thinks certain things *will be*, do they actually happen, for him, as he thought they would? Take heat, for example.
Suppose the ordinary man thinks he is going to take a fever, and that
his temperature will go up to fever point; while another man, this
time a doctor, thinks the opposite. Do we hold that the future will
confirm either the one judgement or the other? Or are we to say that
it will confirm both; that is, that for the doctor the man will not have
a temperature or be suffering from fever, while for himself he will?'

THEOD. That would be absurd.

SOC. But, when there is a question of the sweetness and dryness
of the next vintage, I presume it would always be the grower's judge-   *d*
ment that would carry authority, rather than that of a musician?

THEOD. Of course.

SOC. Nor again, in any question of what will be in tune or out of
tune, would the judgement of a teacher of gymnastic be superior
to that of a musician—even about what is going to seem to be in
tune to the gymnastic master himself?

THEOD. No, never.

SOC. Or suppose a dinner is being prepared. Even the guest who
is going to eat it, if he has no knowledge of cooking, will not be
able to pronounce so authoritative a verdict as the professional cook
on how nice it is going to be. I say 'going to be', because we had
better not at this stage press our point as regards what is *now*   *e*
pleasant to any individual, or what has been in the past. Our
question for the moment is, whether the individual himself is the
best judge, for himself, of what is going to seem and be for him in
the future. 'Or,' we will ask, 'would not you, Protagoras, predict
better than any layman about the persuasive effect that speeches
in a law-court will have upon any one of us?'

THEOD. And in fact, Socrates, this at any rate is a point on which
Protagoras used to make strong claims to superiority over other
people.

SOC. Of course he did, my dear good fellow. No one would have
paid large fees for the privilege of talking with him if he had not   *179*
been in the habit of persuading his pupils that he was a better judge
than any fortune-teller—or anyone else— about what was going to
be and seem to be in the future.[31]

THEOD. That's true enough.

---

31. An alternative text yields: 'if he really was in the habit of persuading his pupils
that, even about the future, neither a fortune-teller nor anyone else can judge better
than one can for oneself'.

Soc. Legislation also and 'what is useful' is concerned with the future; and it would be generally admitted to be inevitable that a city when it legislates often fails to achieve what is the most useful.

THEOD. Yes, surely.

Soc. Then we shall be giving your master fair measure if we tell
b   him that he has now got to admit that one man is wiser than another, and that it is such a man who is 'the measure'; but that I, the man with no special knowledge, have not by any means got to be a measure—a part which the recent speech in his defence was trying to force upon me, whether I liked it or not.

THEOD. Now that, Socrates, seems to me to be the chief point on which the theory is convicted of error—though it stands convicted also when it makes other men's judgements carry authority and these turn out to involve thinking that Protagoras' statements are completely untrue.

c   Soc. There is more than one point besides these, Theodorus, on which a conviction might be secured—at least so far as it is a matter of proving that not every man's judgement is true. But so long as we keep within the limits of that immediate present experience of the individual which gives rise to perceptions and to perceptual judgements, it is more difficult to convict these latter of being untrue—but perhaps I'm talking nonsense. Perhaps it is not possible to convict them at all; perhaps those who profess that they are perfectly evident and are always knowledge may be saying what really is. And it may be that our Theaetetus was not far from the
d   mark with his proposition that knowledge and perception are the same thing. We shall have to come to closer grips with the theory, as the speech on behalf of Protagoras required us to do. We shall have to consider and test this moving Being, and find whether it rings true or sounds as if it had some flaw in it. There is no small fight going on about it, anyway—and no shortage of fighting men.

THEOD. No, indeed; but in Ionia[32] it seems to be even growing, and assuming vast dimensions. On the side of this theory, the Heracleitean party is conducting a most vigorous campaign.

Soc. The more reason, then, my dear Theodorus, why we should examine it by going back to its first principle,[33] which is the way
e   they present it themselves.

THEOD. I quite agree. You know, Socrates, these Heraclitean

---

32. The central part of the west coast of Asia Minor (now Turkey). The Greek cities in this area included Ephesus, where Heraclitus was born in the sixth century B.C.
33. I.e. the principle that everything is really motion (156a).

doctrines (or, as you say, Homeric or still more ancient)—you can't discuss them in person with any of the people at Ephesus who profess to be adepts, any more than you could with a maniac. They are just like the things they say in their books—always on the move. As for abiding by what is said, or sticking to a question, or quietly answering and asking questions in turn, there is less than nothing *180* of that in their capacity. That's an exaggeration, no doubt. I mean there isn't so much as a tiny bit of repose in these people. If you ask any one of them a question, he will pull out some little enigmatic phrase from his quiver and shoot it off at you; and if you try to make him give an account of what he has said, you will only get hit by another, full of strange turns of language. You will never reach any conclusion with any of them, ever; indeed they never reach any conclusion with each other, they are so very careful not to allow anything to be stable, either in an argument or in their own *b* souls. I suppose they think that if they did it would be something that stands still—this being what they are totally at war with, and what they are determined to banish from the universe, if they can.

Soc. I dare say, Theodorus, you have seen these men only on the field of battle, and never been with them in times of peace—as you don't belong to their set. I expect they keep such matters to be explained at leisure to their pupils whom they want to make like themselves.

THEOD. *Pupils*, my good man? There are no pupils and teachers among these people. They just spring up on their own, one here, *c* one there, wherever they happen to catch their inspiration; and no one of them will credit another with knowing anything. As I was just going to say, you will never get these men to give an account of themselves, willingly or unwillingly. What we must do is to take their doctrine out of their hands and consider it for ourselves, as we should a problem in geometry.

Soc. What you say is very reasonable. This problem now, we have inherited it, have we not, from the ancients? They used poeti- cal forms which concealed from the majority of men their real *d* meaning, namely, that Ocean and Tethys, the origin of all things, are actually flowing streams, and nothing stands still. In more modern times, the problem is presented to us by men who, being more accomplished in these matters, plainly demonstrate their meaning so that even shoe-makers may hear and assimilate their wisdom, and give up the silly idea that some things in this world stand still while others move, learn that all things are in motion, and recognise the greatness of their instructors.

But I was almost forgetting, Theodorus, that there are other
thinkers who have announced the opposite view; who tell us that

e 'Unmoved is the Universe',[34] and other similar statements which
we hear from a Melissus[35] or a Parmenides as against the whole
party of Heracleiteans. These philosophers insist that all things are
One, and that this One stands still, itself within itself, having no
place in which to move.

What are we to do with all these people, my friend? We have
been gradually advancing till, without realising it, we have got
ourselves in between the two parties; and if we don't in some way

181 manage to put up a fight and make our escape, we shall pay for it,
like the people who play that game on the line in the wrestling
schools, and get caught by both parties and pulled in opposite
directions.

Now I think we ought to begin by examining the other party, the
fluent fellows we started to pursue. If they appear to us to be talking
sense, we will help them to drag us over to their side, and try to
escape the others. But if those who make their stand for the whole
appear to be nearer the truth, we will take refuge with them from

b the men who 'move what should not be moved'. And if it appears
that neither party has a reasonable theory, then we shall be very
absurd if we think that insignificant people like ourselves can have
anything to say, after we have rejected the views of men who lived
so long ago and possessed all wisdom. Think now, Theodorus, is
it of any use for us to go forward upon such a dangerous venture?

THEOD. We can't refuse to examine the doctrines of these two
schools, Socrates; that couldn't be allowed.

SOC. Then we must examine them, if *you* feel so strongly about

c it. Now it seems to me that the proper starting-point of our criticism
is the nature of motion; what is this thing that they are talking about
when they say that all things are in motion? I mean, for example,
are they referring to one form of motion only, or, as I think, to
two—but don't let this be only what *I* think. You commit yourself
as well, so that we may come to grief together, if need be. Tell me,
do you call it 'motion' when a thing changes from one place to
another or turns round in the same place?

THEOD. I do, yes.

SOC. Here then is one form of motion. Then supposing a thing

d remains in the same place, but grows old, or becomes black instead

34. Both the text and the sense of this quotation are uncertain.
35. Melissus of Samos was a fifth-century follower of Parmenides.

of white, or hard instead of soft, or undergoes any other alteration; isn't it right to say that here we have motion in another form?

THEOD. Unquestionably.

Soc. Then I now have two forms of motion, alteration and spatial movement.[36]

THEOD. Yes; and that's quite correct.

Soc. Then now that we have made this distinction, let us have a talk with the people who allege that all things are in motion. Let us ask them, 'Do you hold that everything is in motion in both ways, that is, that it both moves through space and undergoes alteration? Or do you suggest that some things are in motion in both ways, and some only in one or the other?'

THEOD. Heaven knows, I can't answer that. I suppose they would say, in both ways.

Soc. Yes; otherwise, my friend, it will turn out that, in their view, things are both moving and standing still; and it will be no more correct to say that all things are in motion than to say that all things stand still.

THEOD. That's perfectly true.

Soc. Then since they must be in motion, and there is no such thing anywhere as absence of motion, it follows that all things are always in every kind of motion.

THEOD. Yes, that must be so.

Soc. Then I want you to consider this point in their theory. As we were saying, they hold that the genesis of things such as warmth and whiteness occurs when each of them is moving, together with a perception, in the space between the active and passive factors: the passive factor thereby becoming percipient, but not a perception, while the active factor becomes such or such, but not a quality—isn't that so? But perhaps 'quality' seems a strange word to you; perhaps you don't quite understand it as a general expression.[37] So I will talk about particular cases. What I mean is that the

36. In the above passage the words *kinēsis, kineisthai,* translated 'motion', 'be in motion', take on a wider sense than they would normally have. Normally they would signify some kind of movement, especially spatial movement, but the Heraclitean philosophy makes the flowing movement of a river the symbol of change in general and change in general is what 'motion' becomes when alteration is subsumed under it. For alteration too is taken widely, to include growing old as well as change of quality or character. The translations 'motion' and 'alteration' reproduce quite well the sense of language being stretched.

37. Socrates apologizes for the strangeness of the expression because this is the first occurrence in Greek of the word *poiotēs,* 'quality' or 'what-sort-ness', coined by Plato from the interrogative adjective *poios,* 'of what sort?'. Cicero, *Academica* I 24–6, was

b   active factor becomes not warmth or whiteness, but warm and white; and so on. You will remember, perhaps, that we said in the earlier stages of the argument that there is nothing which in itself is just one thing; and that this applies also to the active and passive factors. It is by the association of the two with one another that they generate perceptions and the things perceived; and in so doing, the active factor becomes such and such, while the passive factor becomes percipient.

THEOD. Yes, I remember that, of course.

c   Soc. Then we need not concern ourselves about other points in their doctrine, whether they mean what we say or something else. We must keep our eyes simply upon the object of our discussion. We must ask them this question: 'According to you, all things move and flow; isn't that so?'

THEOD. Yes.

Soc. And they have both the motions that we distinguished, that is to say, they both move and alter?

THEOD. That must be so, if they are to be wholly and completely in motion.

Soc. Now if they were only moving through space and not altering, we should presumably be able to say *what* the moving things flow?[38] Or how do we express it?

THEOD. That's all right.

d   Soc. But since not even this abides, that what flows flows white; but rather it is in process of change, so that there is flux of this very thing also, the whiteness, and it is passing over into another colour, lest it be convicted of standing still in this respect—since that is so, is it possible to give any name to a colour which will properly apply to it?

THEOD. I don't see how one could, Socrates; nor yet surely to anything else of that kind, if, being in flux, it is always quietly slipping away as you speak?

Soc. And what about any particular kind of perception; for exam-
e   ple, seeing or hearing? Does it ever abide, and remain seeing or hearing?

THEOD. It ought not to, certainly, if all things are in motion.

---

imitating this passage when he coined *qualitas* from *qualis*, the Latin equivalent of *poios*. Ultimately, therefore, the *Theaetetus* is responsible for our word 'quality'.

38. I.e. 'what they *are*', as we should say. A specially conscientious attempt to speak the language proper to the theory of flux. The words which follow apologise for the oddness of the result.

Soc. Then we may not call anything seeing rather than not-seeing; nor indeed may we call it any other perception rather than not—if it be admitted that all things are in motion in every way?

Theod. No, we may not.

Soc. Yet Theaetetus and I said that knowledge was perception?

Theod. You did.

Soc. And so our answer to the question, 'What is knowledge?' gave something which is no more knowledge than not.

Theod. It seems as if it did.   *183*

Soc. A fine way this turns out to be of making our answer right. We were most anxious to prove that all things are in motion, in order to make that answer come out correct; but what has really emerged is that, if all things are in motion, every answer, on whatever subject, is equally correct, both 'it is thus' and 'it is not thus'—or if you like 'becomes', as we don't want to use any expressions which will bring our friends to a stand-still.

Theod. You are quite right.

Soc. Well, yes, Theodorus, except that I said 'thus' and 'not thus'. One must not use even the word 'thus'; for this 'thus' would no longer be in motion; nor yet 'not thus' for here again there is no motion. The exponents of this theory need to establish some other language; as it is, they have no words that are consistent with their hypothesis—unless it would perhaps suit them best to use 'not at all thus' in a quite indefinite sense.[39]   *b*

Theod. That would at least be an idiom most appropriate to them.

Soc. Then we are set free from your friend, Theodorus. We do not yet concede to him that every man is the measure of all things,   *c* if he be not a man of understanding. And we are not going to grant that knowledge is perception, not at any rate on the line of inquiry which supposes that all things are in motion; we are not going to grant it unless Theaetetus here has some other way of stating it.

Theod. That's very good hearing, Socrates, for when these matters were concluded I was to be set free from my task of answering you, according to our agreement, which specified the end of the discussion of Protagoras' theory.

---

39. I.e. presumably, a pure contradictory: it denies one 'thus' without implying any other 'thus'. There is some textual uncertainty about the form of phrasing left open to the Heracliteans, but what is required to block any implication from e.g. 'not white' to 'not white but another colour' is something that simply denies the presence of white.

THEAET. Oh, no, indeed, Theodorus! Not till you and Socrates
d have done what you proposed just now, and dealt with the other
side, the people who say that the Universe stands still.

THEOD. What's this, Theaetetus? You at your age teaching your
elders to be unjust and break their agreements? What you have got
to do is to prepare to render account to Socrates yourself for the
rest of the discussion.

THEAET. All right, if he likes. But I would rather have listened to
a discussion of these views.

THEOD. Well, challenging Socrates to an argument is like inviting
'cavalry into the plain'. So ask your questions and you shall hear.

SOC. But I don't think, Theodorus, that I am going to be per-
e suaded by Theaetetus to do what he demands.

THEOD. But what is it makes you unwilling?

SOC. Shame. I am afraid our criticism might be a very cheap
affair. And if I feel like this before the many who have made the
universe one and unmoved, Melissus and the rest of them, I feel it
still more in the face of the One—Parmenides. Parmenides seems
to me, in the words of Homer, to be 'reverend' and 'awful'. I met
him when I was very young and he was a very old man; and he
184   seemed to me to have a wholly noble depth.[40] So I am afraid we
might not understand even what he says; still less should we attain
to his real thought. Above all, I am afraid that the very object of
our discussion, the nature of knowledge, might be left unexamined
amid the crowd of theories that will rush in upon us if we admit
them; especially as the theory we have now brought up is one
which involves unmanageably vast issues. To treat it as a side-
show, would be insult and injury; while if it is adequately discussed,
it is likely to spread out until it completely eclipses the problem of
knowledge. We must not do either. What we must do is to make
b use of our midwife's art to deliver Theaetetus of the thoughts which
he has conceived about the nature of knowledge.

THEOD. Well, if that is what you think proper, it must be done.

SOC. Now, Theaetetus, I want you to think about one point in
what has been said. Your answer was that knowledge is perception,
wasn't it?

---

40. The reference is probably not to an actual historical meeting but to the discussion
between Socrates and Parmenides in Plato's *Parmenides*. 'Depth' in Greek usage
alludes not only to profundity of thought but also to the unruffled composure
which is the proper bearing of a philosopher. In contrast to the unsteadiness of
the Heracliteans (179e–180c), Parmenides' mind is one to which it is difficult for
understanding or critical questioning to penetrate.

THEAET. Yes.

Soc. Now supposing you were asked: 'With what does a man see white and black, and with what does he hear high and low notes?' You would reply, I imagine, 'With his eyes and ears.'

THEAET. I should, yes.

Soc. Now as a rule it is no sign of ill-breeding to be easy in the *c* use of language and take no particular care in one's choice of words; it is rather the opposite that gives a man away. But such exactness is sometimes necessary; and it is necessary here, for example, to fasten upon something in your answer that is not correct. Think now. Is it more correct to say that the eyes are that *with* which we see, or that *through* which we see? Do we hear *with* the ears or *through* the ears?

THEAET. Well, I should think, Socrates, that it is '*through* which' we perceive in each case, rather than '*with* which.'

Soc. Yes, my son. It would be a very strange thing, I must say, *d* if there were a number of senses sitting inside us as if we were Wooden Horses, and there were not some single form, soul or whatever one ought to call it, to which all these converge—something *with* which, *through* the senses, as if they were instruments, we perceive all that is perceptible.

THEAET. That sounds to me better than the other way of putting it.

Soc. Now the reason why I am being so precise with you is this. I want to know if it is with one and the same part of ourselves that we reach, through our eyes to white and black, and through the other means to yet further things; and whether, if asked, you will *e* be able to refer all these to the body. But perhaps it would be better if you stated the answers yourself, rather than that I should busy myself on your behalf. Tell me: the instruments through which you perceive hot, hard, light, sweet—do you consider that they all belong to the body? Or can they be referred elsewhere?

THEAET. No, they all belong to the body.

Soc. And are you also willing to admit that what you perceive through one power, you can't perceive through another? For in- *185* stance, what you perceive through hearing, you couldn't perceive through sight, and similarly what you perceive through sight you couldn't perceive through hearing?

THEAET. I could hardly refuse to grant that.

Soc. Then suppose you think something about both; you can't possibly be having a perception about both, either through one of these instruments or through the other?

THEAET. No.

SOC. Now take a sound and a colour. First of all, don't you think this same thing about both of them, namely, that they both are?

THEAET. I do.

SOC. Also that each of them is different from the other and the same as itself?

b   THEAET. Of course.

SOC. And that both together are two, and each of them is one?

THEAET. Yes, I think that too.

SOC. Are you also able to consider whether they are like or unlike each other?

THEAET. Yes, I may be.

SOC. Now what is it through which you think all these things about them? It is not possible, you see, to grasp what is common to both either through sight or through hearing. Let us consider another thing which will show the truth of what we are saying. Suppose it were possible to enquire whether both are salty or not. You can tell me, of course, with what you would examine them. It would clearly be neither sight nor hearing, but something else.

c   THEAET. Yes, of course; the power which functions through the tongue.

SOC. Good. Now through what does that power function which reveals to you what is common in the case both of all things and of these two—I mean that which you express by the words 'is' and 'is not' and the other terms used in our questions about them just now? What kind of instruments will you assign for all these? Through what does that which is percipient in us perceive all of them?

THEAET. You mean being and not-being, likeness and unlike-

d   ness, same and different; also one, and any other number applied to them. And obviously too your question is about odd and even, and all that is involved with these attributes; and you want to know through what bodily instruments we perceive all these with the soul.

SOC. You follow me exceedingly well, Theaetetus. These are just the things I am asking about.

THEAET. But *I* couldn't possibly say. All I can tell you is that it doesn't seem to me that for these things there is any special instrument at all, as there is for the others. It seems to me that in inves-

e   tigating the common features of everything the soul functions through itself.

SOC. Yes, Theaetetus, you would say that, because you are handsome and not ugly as Theodorus would have it.[41] For handsome is as handsome says. And besides being handsome, you have done me a good turn; you have saved me a vast amount of talk if it seems to you that, while the soul considers some things through the bodily powers, there are others which it considers alone and through itself. This was what I thought myself, but I wanted you to think it too.

THEAET. Well, it does seem to me to be so.   *186*

Soc. Now in which class do you put being? For that, above all, is something that accompanies everything.

THEAET. I should put it among the things which the soul itself reaches out after by itself.

Soc. Also like and unlike, same and different?

THEAET. Yes.

Soc. What about beautiful and ugly, good and bad?

THEAET. Yes, these too; in these, above all, I think the soul examines the being they have as compared with one another. Here it seems to be making a calculation within itself of past and present   *b* in relation to future.

Soc. Not so fast, now. Wouldn't you say that it is through touch that the soul perceives the hardness of what is hard, and similarly the softness of what is soft?

THEAET. Yes.

Soc. But as regards their being—the fact that they are—their opposition to one another, and the being, again, of this opposition, the matter is different. Here the soul itself attempts to reach a decision for us by rising to compare them with one another.

THEAET. Yes, undoubtedly.

Soc. And thus there are some things which all creatures, men and animals alike, are naturally able to perceive as soon as they are   *c* born; I mean, the experiences which reach the soul through the body. But calculations regarding their being and their advantageousness come, when they do, only as the result of a long and arduous development, involving a good deal of trouble and education.

THEAET. Yes, that certainly is so.

Soc. Now is it possible for someone who does not even get at being to get at truth?

THEAET. No; it's impossible.

Soc. And if a man fails to get at the truth of a thing, will he ever be a person who knows that thing?

41. Cf. 143e.

d THEAET. I don't see how, Socrates.

Soc. Then knowledge is to be found not in the experiences but in the process of reasoning about them; it is here, seemingly, not in the experiences, that it is possible to grasp being and truth.

THEAET. So it appears.

Soc. Then in the face of such differences, would you call both by the same name?

THEAET. One would certainly have no right to.

Soc. Now what name do you give to the former—seeing, hearing, smelling, feeling cold or warm?

e THEAET. I call that perceiving—what else could I call it?

Soc. So the whole lot taken together you call perception?

THEAET. Necessarily.

Soc. Which, we say, has no share in the grasping of truth, since it has none in the grasping of being.

THEAET. No, it has none.

Soc. So it has no share in knowledge either.

THEAET. No.

Soc. Then, Theaetetus, perception and knowledge could never be the same thing.

THEAET. No, apparently not, Socrates; we have now got the clearest possible proof that knowledge is something different from perception.

187 Soc. But our object in beginning this discussion was not to find out what knowledge is not, but to find out what it is. However, we have made a little progress. We shall not now look for knowledge in sense-perception at all, but in whatever we call that activity of the soul when it is busy by itself about the things which are.

THEAET. Well, the name, Socrates, I suppose is judgement.

Soc. Your opinion, my dear lad, is correct. Now look back to the
b beginning. Wipe out all that we have said hitherto, and see if you can see any better from where you have now progressed to. Tell me again, what is knowledge?

THEAET. Well, Socrates, one can't say that it is judgement in general, because there is also false judgement— but true judgement may well be knowledge. So let that be my answer. If the same thing happens again, and we find, as we go on, that it turns out not to be so, we'll try something else.

Soc. And even so, Theaetetus, you have answered me in the way one ought—with a good will, and not reluctantly, as you did
c at first. If we continue like this, one of two things will happen.

Either we shall find what we are going out after; or we shall be less inclined to think we know things which we don't know at all—and even that would be a reward we could not fairly be dissatisfied with. Now what is this that you say? There are two forms of judgement, true and false; and your definition is that true judgement is knowledge?

THEAET. Yes. That is how it looks to me now.

Soc. Now I wonder if it's worth while, at this stage, to go back to an old point about judgement—

THEAET. What point do you mean?

Soc. I have something on my mind which has often bothered   *d*
me before, and got me into great difficulty, both in my own thought and in discussion with other people—I mean, I can't say what it is, this experience we have, and how it arises in us.

THEAET. What experience?

Soc. Judging what is false. Even now, you know, I'm still considering; I'm in two minds whether to let it go or whether to look into it in a different manner from a short while ago.

THEAET. Why not, Socrates, if this appears for any reason to be the right thing to do? As you and Theodorus were saying just now, and quite rightly, when you were talking about leisure, we are not pressed for time in talk of this kind.

Soc. A very proper reminder. Perhaps it would not be a bad   *e*
moment to go back upon our tracks. It is better to accomplish a little well than a great deal unsatisfactorily.

THEAET. Yes, it certainly is.

Soc. Now how are we to proceed? And actually what is it that we are saying? We claim, don't we, that false judgement repeatedly occurs and one of us judges falsely, the other truly, as if it was in the nature of things for this to happen?

THEAET. That is what we claim.

Soc. Now isn't it true about all things, together or individually,   *188*
that we must either know them or not know them? I am ignoring for the moment the intermediate conditions of learning and forgetting, as they don't affect the argument here.

THEAET. Of course, Socrates, in that case there is no alternative. With each thing we either know it or we do not.

Soc. Then when a man judges, the objects of his judgement are necessarily either things which he knows or things which he doesn't know?

THEAET. Yes, that must be so.

Soc. Yet if he knows a thing, it is impossible that he should not
b know it; or if he does not know it, he cannot know it.

THEAET. Yes, of course.

Soc. Now take the man who judges what is false. Is he thinking
that things which he knows are not these things but some other
things which he knows—so that knowing both he is ignorant of
both?

THEAET. But that would be impossible, Socrates.

Soc. Then is he imagining that things which he doesn't know
are other things which he doesn't know? Is it possible that a man
who knows neither Theaetetus nor Socrates should take it into his
head that Socrates is Theaetetus or Theaetetus Socrates?

c THEAET. I don't see how that could happen.

Soc. But a man certainly doesn't think that things he knows are
things he does not know, or again that things he doesn't know are
things he knows.

THEAET. No, that would be a very odd thing.

Soc. Then in what way is false judgement still possible? There
is evidently no possibility of judgement outside the cases we have
mentioned, since everything is either what we know or what we
don't know; and within these limits there appears to be no place
for false judgement to be possible.

THEAET. That's perfectly true.

Soc. Then perhaps we had better take up a different line of
enquiry; perhaps we should proceed not by way of knowing and
d not-knowing, but by way of being and not-being?

THEAET. How do you mean?

Soc. Perhaps the simple fact is this: it is when a man judges
about anything things which are not, that he is inevitably judging
falsely, no matter what may be the nature of his thought in other
respects.

THEAET. That again is very plausible, Socrates.

Soc. Now how will that be? What are we going to say, Theaetetus, if somebody sets about examining us, and we are asked, 'Is
what these words express possible for anyone? Can a man judge
what is not, either about one of the things which are, or just by
e itself?' I suppose we shall reply, 'Yes, when he is thinking, but
thinking what is not true.' Or how shall we answer?

THEAET. That's our answer.

Soc. Now does this kind of thing happen elsewhere?

THEAET. What kind of thing?

Soc. Well, for instance, that a man sees something, yet sees nothing.

THEAET. How could he?

Soc. On the contrary, in fact, if he is seeing any one thing, he must be seeing a thing which is. Or do you think that a 'one' can be found among the things which are not?

THEAET. I certainly don't.

Soc. Then a man who is seeing any one thing is seeing something which is?

THEAET. Apparently.

Soc. It also follows that a man who is hearing anything is hearing   *189*
some one thing and something which is.

THEAET. Yes.

Soc. And a man who is touching anything is touching some one thing, and a thing which is, if it is one?

THEAET. Yes, that also follows.

Soc. And a man who is judging is judging some one thing, is he not?

THEAET. Necessarily.

Soc. And a man who is judging some one thing is judging something which is?

THEAET. I grant that.

Soc. Then that means that a man who is judging something which is not is judging nothing?

THEAET. So it appears.

Soc. But a man who is judging nothing is not judging at all.

THEAET. That seems clear.

Soc. And so it is not possible to judge what is not, either about   *b*
the things which are or just by itself.

THEAET. Apparently not.

Soc. False judgement, then, is something different from judging things which are not?

THEAET. It looks as if it were.

Soc. Then neither on this approach nor on the one we followed just now does false judgement exist in us.

THEAET. No, indeed.

Soc. Then is it in this way that the thing we call by that name arises?

THEAET. How?

Soc. We say that there is false judgement, a kind of 'other-judging', when a man, in place of one of the things that are, has   *c* substituted in his thought another of the things that are and asserts that it is.[42] In this way, he is always judging something which is, but judges one thing in place of another; and having missed the thing which was the object of his consideration, he might fairly be called one who judges falsely.

THEAET. Now you seem to me to have got it quite right. When a man judges 'ugly' instead of 'beautiful', or 'beautiful' instead of 'ugly', then he is truly judging what is false.

Soc. Evidently, Theaetetus, you have not much opinion of me; you don't find me at all alarming.

THEAET. What in particular makes you say that?

Soc. Well, I suppose you don't think me capable of taking up
d   your 'truly false', and asking you whether it is possible that a thing should be slowly swift, or heavily light, or whether anything else can possibly occur in a way not in accordance with its own nature but in accordance with that of its opposite and contrary to itself. But let that pass; I don't want your boldness to go unrewarded. You like the suggestion, you say, that false judgement is 'other-judging'?

THEAET. Yes, I do.

Soc. Then, according to your judgement, it is possible to set down a thing in one's thought as another thing and not itself?

THEAET. Surely it is.

e   Soc. Now when a man's thought is accomplishing this, isn't it

---

42. In the manuscripts on which we rely for the *Theaetetus*, this sentence does not make grammatical sense; we have to supply by conjecture a word or phrase which an earlier copyist inadvertently left out. With the standard supplement (*ti*) the sentence is standardly translated 'when a man asserts that one of the things which are is another of the things which are, having substituted one for the other in his thought'. The objection to this conjecture is that it builds into the initial description of 'other-judging' the very feature which, when exposed in the sequel, will be its downfall. For the criticism which follows is designed to show that one cannot judge *F* to be the case in place of *G* without judging, absurdly, that *F* is *G*. Moreover, the standard translation does not fit Socrates' next sentence or the examples in Theaetetus' reply. The version given above fits both, but it supposes a nonstandard supplement of my own (*anti tinos*). Some scholars think it possible to accept the standard conjecture and give it a nonstandard translation, tantamount to mine and so fitting the requirements of the context. If this third option is viable, it might be appropriate to conclude that Plato designed the sentence to be ambiguous between the nonstandard and the standard understanding of it, so that, when you read the whole passage 189b–190e in the original Greek, the criticism of the definition of false judgement as 'other-judging' makes you experience the process of substituting one meaning for the other in your thought.

essential that he should be thinking of either one or both of these two things?

THEAET. It is essential; either both together, or each in turn.

Soc. Very good. Now by 'thinking' do you mean the same as I do?

THEAET. What do you mean by it?

Soc. A talk which the soul has with itself about the objects under its consideration. Of course, I'm only telling you my idea in all ignorance; but this is the kind of picture I have of it. It seems to me that the soul when it thinks is simply carrying on a discussion in which it asks itself questions and answers them itself, affirms and *190* denies. And when it arrives at something definite, either by a gradual process or a sudden leap, when it affirms one thing consistently and without divided counsel, we call this its judgement. So, in my view, to judge is to make a statement, and a judgement is a statement which is not addressed to another person or spoken aloud, but silently addressed to oneself. And what do you think?

THEAET. I agree with that.

Soc. So that when a man judges one thing to be another, what he is doing, apparently, is to say to himself that the one thing is the other.

THEAET. Yes, of course.   *b*

Soc. Now try to think if you have ever said to yourself 'Surely the beautiful is ugly',[43] or 'The unjust is certainly just'. Or—to put it in the most general terms—have you ever tried to persuade yourself that 'Surely one thing is another'? Wouldn't the very opposite of this be the truth? Wouldn't the truth be that not even in your sleep have you ever gone so far as to say to yourself 'No doubt the odd is even', or anything of that kind?

THEAET. Yes, that's so.

---

43. 'The beautiful is ugly' may mean that some particular beautiful thing is ugly, but it can also, in Greek idiom, be a way of saying that beauty is ugliness. Correspondingly with examples like 'A cow is a horse' below: this may mean that some particular cow is a horse, but it can also, as in English idiom, be a general statement equivalent to 'Cows are horses'. In favour of the second construal in each case is the fact that 'beautiful' and 'ugly' came into the discussion at 189c as the predicate term in a mistaken judgement. Moreover, the first construal fails to illustrate Socrates' contention that the man says of two distinct things that the one is the other. Accordingly, it is the second construal which is followed in the Introduction, p. 83 ff. 'Beauty is ugliness' could also be put into English as 'A beautiful thing is an ugly thing' provided that is read in the same way as 'A cow is a horse', i.e. as equivalent to the general statement 'Beautiful things are ugly'.

c   Soc. And do you think that anyone else, in his right mind or out
of it, ever ventured seriously to tell himself, with the hope of
winning his own assent, that 'A cow must be a horse' or 'Two must
be one'?

         THEAET. No, indeed I don't.

         Soc. Well, then, if to make a statement to oneself is to judge, no
one who makes a statement, that is, a judgement, about both
things, getting hold of both with his soul, can state, or judge, that
one is the other. And you, in your turn, must pass this form of
words.[44] What I mean by it is this: no one judges 'The ugly is
d   beautiful' or makes any other such judgement.

         THEAET. All right, Socrates, I pass it; and I think you're right.

         Soc. Thus a man who has both things before his mind when he
judges cannot possibly judge that one is the other.

         THEAET. So it seems.

         Soc. But if he has only one of them before his mind in judging,
and the other is not present to him at all, he will never judge that
one is the other.

         THEAET. That's true. For he would have to have hold also of the
one that is not present to his judgement.

         Soc. Then 'other-judging' is not possible for anyone either when
e   he has both things present to him in judgement or when he has
one only. So, if anyone is going to define false judgement as 'heterodoxy',[45] he will be saying nothing. The existence of false judgement
in us cannot be shown in this way any more than by our previous
approaches.

         THEAET. It seems not.

         Soc. And yet, Theaetetus, if it is not shown to exist, we shall be
driven into admitting a number of absurdities.

         THEAET. And what would they be?

         Soc. I am not going to tell you until I have tried every possible
way of looking at this matter. I should be ashamed to see us forced
191 into making the kind of admissions I mean while we are still in
difficulties. If we find what we're after, and become free men, then
we will turn round and talk about how these things happen to other

44. In Greek the opposition between 'the one' and 'the other' is expressed by the
repetition of the word meaning 'other', so that the phrase can also be understood
as the unparadoxical tautology 'the other is other'. As Socrates refrained at 189cd
from taking up the paradoxical construal of Theaetetus' 'truly false', so Theaetetus
must refrain from taking up the unparadoxical construal of Socrates' 'one is the
other'.

45. A transliteration of a variant Greek expression for 'other-judging'.

people—having secured our own persons against ridicule. While if we can't find any way of extricating ourselves, then I suppose we shall be laid low, like sea-sick passengers, and give ourselves into the hands of the argument and let it trample all over us and do what it likes with us. And now let me tell you where I see a way still open to this enquiry.

THEAET. Yes, do tell me.

Soc. I am going to maintain that we were wrong to agree that it is impossible for a man to be in error through judging that things he knows are things he doesn't know. In a way, it is possible.   *b*

THEAET. Now I wonder if you mean the same thing as I too suspected at the time when we suggested it was like that—I mean, that sometimes I, who know Socrates, have seen someone else in the distance whom I don't know and thought it to be Socrates whom I do know. In a case like that, the sort of thing you are referring to does happen.

Soc. But didn't we recoil from this suggestion because it made us not know, when we do know, things which we know?

THEAET. Yes, we certainly did.

Soc. Then don't let us put the case in that way; let's try another way. It may prove amenable or it may be obstinate; but the fact is   *c* we are in such an extremity that we need to turn every argument over and over and test it from all sides. Now see if there is anything in this. Is it possible to learn something you didn't know before?

THEAET. Surely it is.

Soc. And again another and yet another thing?

THEAET. Well, why not?

Soc. Now I want you to suppose, for the sake of the argument, that we have in our souls a block of wax, larger in one person, smaller in another, and of purer wax in one case, dirtier in another; in some men rather hard, in others rather soft, while in some it is   *d* of the proper consistency.

THEAET. All right, I'm supposing that.

Soc. We may look upon it, then, as a gift of Memory, the mother of the Muses. We make impressions upon this of everything we wish to remember among the things we have seen or heard or thought of ourselves; we hold the wax under our perceptions and thoughts and take a stamp from them, in the way in which we take the imprints of signet rings. Whatever is impressed upon the wax we remember and know so long as the image remains in the wax; whatever is obliterated or cannot be impressed, we forget and do   *e* not know.

THEAET. Let that be our supposition.

Soc. Then take the case of a man who knows these things, but is also considering something he is seeing or hearing; and see if he might judge falsely in this way.

THEAET. In what kind of way?

Soc. In thinking, of things which he knows, sometimes that they are things which he knows and sometimes that they are things which he doesn't know—these cases being what at an earlier stage we wrongly admitted to be impossible.

THEAET. And what do you say now?

192   Soc. We must begin this discussion by making certain distinctions. We must make it clear that it is impossible to think (1) that a thing you know, because you possess the record of it in your soul, but which you are not perceiving, is another thing which you know—you have its imprint too—but are not perceiving, (2) that a thing you know is something you do not know and do not have the seal of, (3) that a thing you don't know is another thing you don't know, (4) that a thing you don't know is a thing you know.

Again, it is impossible to think (1) that a thing you are perceiving is another thing that you are perceiving, (2) that a thing you are perceiving is a thing which you are not perceiving, (3) that a thing
b   you are not perceiving is another thing you are not perceiving, (4) that a thing you are not perceiving is a thing you are perceiving.

Yet again, it is impossible to think (1) that a thing you both know and are perceiving, when you are holding its signature in line with your perception of it, is another thing which you know and are perceiving, and whose signature you keep in line with the perception (this indeed is even more impossible than the former cases, if that can be), (2) that a thing which you both know and are perceiving, and the record of which you are keeping in its true line, is another thing you know, (3) that a thing you both know and are perceiving and of which you have the record correctly in line as before, is another thing you are perceiving, (4) that a thing you
c   neither know nor are perceiving is another thing you neither know nor perceive, (5) that a thing you neither know nor perceive is another thing you don't know, (6) that a thing you neither know nor perceive is another thing you are not perceiving.

In all these cases, it is a sheer impossibility that there should be false judgement. It remains that it arises, if anywhere, in the cases I am just going to tell you.

THEAET. What are they? Perhaps I may understand a little better from them; at present, I don't follow.

Soc. In these cases of things you know: when you think (1) that they are other things you know and are perceiving, (2) that they are things you don't know but are perceiving, (3) that things you both know and are perceiving are other things you both know and are perceiving.

d

THEAET. Well, now you have left me further behind than ever.

Soc. I'll go over it again in another way. I know Theodorus and remember within myself what he is like; and in the same way I know Theaetetus. But sometimes I am seeing them and sometimes not; sometimes I am touching them, and sometimes not; or I may hear them or perceive them through some other sense, while at other times I have no perception about you two at all, but remember you none the less, and know you within myself—isn't that so?

THEAET. Yes, certainly.

e

Soc. Now please take this first point that I want to make clear to you—that we sometimes perceive and sometimes do not perceive the things that we know.

THEAET. That's true.

Soc. Then as regards the things we don't know, we often don't perceive them either, but often we only perceive them.

THEAET. That is so, also.

Soc. Now see if you can follow me a little better. Supposing Socrates knows both Theodorus and Theaetetus, but is not seeing either of them, or having any other perception about them: he could never in that case judge within himself that Theaetetus was Theodorus. Is that sense or not?

193

THEAET. Yes, that's quite true.

Soc. This, then, was the first of the cases I was speaking of.

THEAET. It was.

Soc. Secondly then. Supposing I am acquainted with one of you and not with the other, and am perceiving neither of you: in that case, I could never think the one I do know to be the one I don't know.

THEAET. That is so.

Soc. Thirdly, supposing I am not acquainted with either of you, and am not perceiving either of you: I could not possibly think that one of you, whom I don't know, is another of you whom I don't know. Now will you please take it that you have heard all over again in succession the other cases described before—the cases in which I shall never judge falsely about you and Theodorus, either when I am familiar or when I am unfamiliar with both of you; or when I know one and not the other. And similarly with perceptions, if you follow me.

b

THEAET. I follow.

SOC. So there remains the possibility of false judgement in this case. I know both you and Theodorus; I have your signs upon that
c block of wax, like the imprints of rings. Then I see you both in the distance, but cannot see you well enough; but I am in a hurry to refer the proper sign to the proper visual perception, and so get this fitted into the trace of itself, that recognition may take place. This I fail to do; I get them out of line, applying the visual perception of the one to the sign of the other. It is like people putting their shoes on the wrong feet, or like what happens when we look at
d things in mirrors, when left and right change places. It is then that 'heterodoxy' or false judgement arises.

THEAET. Yes, that seems very likely, Socrates; it is an awfully good description of what happens to the judgement.

SOC. Then, again, supposing I know both of you, and am also perceiving one of you, and not the other, but am not keeping my knowledge of the former in line with my perception—that's the expression I used before and you didn't understand me then.

THEAET. No, I certainly didn't.

SOC. Well, I was saying that if you know one man and perceive
e him as well, and keep your knowledge of him in line with your perception, you will never take him for some other person whom you know and are perceiving, and the knowledge of whom you are holding straight with the perception. Wasn't that so?

THEAET. Yes.

SOC. There remained, I take it, the case we have just mentioned where false judgement arises in the following manner: you know
194 both men and you are looking at both, or having some other perception of them; and you don't hold the two signs each in line with its own perception, but like a bad archer you shoot beside the mark and miss—which is precisely what we call falsehood.

THEAET. Naturally so.

SOC. And when for one of the signs there is also a present perception but there is not for the other, and you try to fit to the present perception the sign belonging to the absent perception, in all such cases thought is in error.

We may sum up thus: it seems that in the case of things we do
b not know and have never perceived, there is no possibility of error or of false judgement, if what we are saying is at all sound; it is in cases where we both know things and are perceiving them that judgement is erratic and varies between truth and falsity. When it brings together the proper stamps and imprints directly and in

straight lines, it is true; when it does so obliquely and crosswise, it is false.

THEAET. Well, isn't that beautiful, Socrates?

Soc. Ah, when you've heard what is coming next, you will say c so all the more. For true judgement is beautiful, right enough, and error is ugly.

THEAET. No doubt about that.

Soc. Well, this, then, they say, is why the two things occur. In some men, the wax in the soul is deep and abundant, smooth and worked to the proper consistency; and when the things that come through the senses are imprinted upon this 'heart' of the soul—as Homer calls it, hinting at the likeness to the wax[46]—the signs that are made in it are lasting, because they are clear and have sufficient d depth. Men with such souls learn easily and remember what they learn; they do not get the signs out of line with the perceptions, but judge truly. As the signs are distinct and there is plenty of room for them, they quickly assign each thing to its own impress in the wax—the things in question being, of course, what we call the things that are and these people being the ones we call wise.

Or do you feel any doubts about this?

THEAET. No, I find it extraordinarily convincing.

Soc. But it is a different matter when a man's 'heart' is 'shaggy' e (the kind of heart our marvellously knowing poet praises), or when it is dirty and of impure wax; or when it is very soft or hard. Persons in whom the wax is soft are quick to learn but quick to forget; when the wax is hard, the opposite happens. Those in whom it is 'shaggy' and rugged, a stony thing with earth or filth mixed all through it, have indistinct impressions. So too if the wax is hard, for then the impressions have no depth; similarly they are indistinct if the wax is soft, because they quickly run together and are blurred. If, in 195 addition to all this, the impresses in the wax are crowded upon each other for lack of space, because it is only some little scrap of a soul, they are even more indistinct. All such people are liable to false judgement. When they see or hear or think of anything, they can't quickly allot each thing to each impress; they are slow and allot things to impresses which do not belong to them, misseeing, mishearing and misthinking most of them—and these in turn are the ones we describe as in error about the things that are and ignorant.

---

46. The word for 'heart' attributed to Homer here is *kear*, which has a superficial resemblance to the word for wax, *kēros*.

b   THEAET. That's exactly it, Socrates; no man could improve on your account.

Soc. Then are we to say that false judgements do exist in us?

THEAET. Yes, most emphatically.

Soc. And true ones, of course?

THEAET. And true ones.

Soc. And we think we have now reached a satisfactory agreement, when we say that these two kinds of judgement certainly exist?

THEAET. There's no earthly doubt about it, Socrates.

Soc. Theaetetus, I'm afraid a garrulous man is really an awful nuisance.

THEAET. Why, what are you talking about?

c   Soc. I'm annoyed at my own stupidity—my own true garrulousness.[47] What else could you call it when a man will keep dragging arguments up and down, because he is too slow-witted to reach any conviction, and will not be pulled off any of them?

THEAET. But why should *you* be annoyed?

Soc. I am not only annoyed; I am alarmed. I am afraid of what I may say if someone asks me: 'So, Socrates, you've discovered false judgement, have you? You have found that it arises not in the relation of perceptions to one another, or of thoughts to one an-

d   other, but in the connecting of perception with thought?' I believe I am very likely to say 'Yes', with an air of flattering myself upon our having made some beautiful discovery.

THEAET. Well, Socrates, what you have just shown us looks to me quite a presentable thing anyway.

Soc. 'You mean,' he goes on, 'that we would never suppose that a man we are merely thinking of but not seeing is a horse which again we are not seeing or touching, but just thinking of and not perceiving anything else about it?' I suppose I shall agree that we do mean this.

THEAET. Yes, and quite rightly.

e   Soc. 'Well then,' he goes on, 'doesn't it follow from this theory that a man couldn't possibly suppose that eleven, which he is

---

47. 'I can't stand old Socrates, either, that chattering pauper, who has thought over everything else, but neglected to find out where he could get anything to eat.' (Eupolis fr. 352). 'Garrulousness' was one of the stock gibes of the comic poets against philosophers. Cp. *Phaedo* 70 c: 'No one—not even a comic poet—could accuse me of irrelevant chattering if he were listening now.'

merely thinking about, is twelve, which again he is merely thinking about?' Come now, you answer.

THEAET. Well, my answer will be that someone who is seeing or touching them could suppose that eleven are twelve, but not with those that he has in his thought: he would never judge this in that way about them.

Soc. Well, now, take the case where a man is considering five and seven within himself—I don't mean seven men and five men, or anything of that sort, but five and seven themselves; the records, as we allege, in that waxen block, things amongst which it is not possible that there should be false judgement. Suppose he is talking to himself about them, and asking himself how many they are. Do you think that in such a case it has ever happened that one man thought they were eleven and said so, while another thought and said that they were twelve? Or do all men say and all men think that they are twelve?

196

THEAET. Oh, good Heavens, no; lots of people would make them eleven. And with larger numbers they go wrong still more often—for I suppose what you say is intended to apply to all numbers.

b

Soc. Quite right. And I want you to consider whether what happens here is not just this, that a man thinks that twelve itself, the one on the waxen block, is eleven.

THEAET. It certainly looks as if he does.

Soc. Then haven't we come back to the things we were saying at the outset? You see, anyone to whom this happens is thinking that one thing he knows is another thing he knows. And this we said was impossible; in fact, it was just this consideration which led us to exclude the possibility of false judgement, because, if admitted, it would mean that the same man must, at one and the same time, both know and not know the same objects.

c

THEAET. That's perfectly true.

Soc. Then we shall have to say that false judgement is something other than a misapplication of thought to perception; because if this were so, we could never be in error so long as we remained within our thoughts themselves. But as the matter now stands, either there is no such thing as false judgement; or a man may not know what he knows. Which do you choose?

THEAET. You are offering me an impossible choice, Socrates.

Soc. But I'm afraid the argument will not permit both. Still—we must stop at nothing; supposing now we were to set about being quite shameless?

d

THEAET. How?

Soc. By consenting to say what knowing is like.

THEAET. And why should that be shameless?

Soc. You don't seem to realise that our whole discussion from the beginning has been an enquiry about knowledge, on the assumption that we do not yet know what it is.

THEAET. Oh, but I do.

Soc. Well, then, don't you think it is a shameless thing that we, who don't know what knowledge is, should pronounce on what *e* knowing is like? But as a matter of fact, Theaetetus, for some time past our whole method of discussion has been tainted. Time and again we have said 'we are acquainted with' and 'we are not acquainted with', 'we know' and 'we do not know', as if we could to some extent understand one another while we are still ignorant of what knowledge is. Or here's another example, if you like: at this very moment, we have again used the words 'to be ignorant of', and 'to understand', as if these were quite proper expressions for us when we are deprived of knowledge.

THEAET. But how are you going to carry on the discussion at all, Socrates, if you keep off these words?

197 Soc. Quite impossible, for a man like me; but if I were one of the experts in contradiction, I might be able to. If one of those gentlemen were present, he would have commanded us to refrain from them, and would keep coming down upon us heavily for the faults I'm referring to. But since we are no good anyway, why don't I make bold to tell you what knowing is like? It seems to me that this might be of some help.

THEAET. Then do be bold, please. And if you don't keep from using these words, we'll forgive you all right.

Soc. Well, then, have you heard what people are saying nowadays that knowing is?

THEAET. I dare say I have; but I don't remember it at the moment.

b Soc. Well, they say, of course, that it is 'the having of knowledge'.

THEAET. Oh, yes, that's true.

Soc. Let us make a slight change; let us say 'the possession of knowledge'.

THEAET. And how would you say that was different from the first way of putting it?

Soc. Perhaps it isn't at all; but I will tell you what I think the difference is, and then you must help me to examine it.

THEAET. All right—if I can.

Soc. Well, then, to 'possess' doesn't seem to me to be the same as to 'have'. For instance, suppose a man has bought a coat and it is at his disposal but he is not wearing it; we would not say that he 'has' it on, but we would say he 'possesses' it.[48]

THEAET. Yes, that would be correct.

Soc. Now look here: is it possible in this way to possess knowl-   c
edge and not 'have' it? Suppose a man were to hunt wild birds, pigeons or something, and make an aviary for them at his house and look after them there; then, in a sense, I suppose, we might say he 'has' them all the time, because of course he possesses them. Isn't that so?

THEAET. Yes.

Soc. But in another sense he 'has' none of them; it is only that he has acquired a certain power in respect of them, because he has got them under his control in an enclosure of his own. That is to say, he has the power to hunt for any one he likes at any time, and   d
take and 'have' it whenever he chooses, and let it go again; and this he can do as often as he likes.

THEAET. That is so.

Soc. Well a little while ago we were equipping souls with I don't know what sort of a waxen device. Now let us make in each soul a sort of aviary of all kinds of birds; some in flocks separate from the others, some in small groups, and others flying about singly here and there among all the rest.

THEAET. All right, let us suppose it made. What then?   e

Soc. Then we must say that when we are children this receptacle is empty; and by the birds we must understand pieces of knowl-edge. When anyone takes possession of a piece of knowledge and shuts it up in the pen, we should say that he has learned or has found out the thing of which this is the knowledge; and knowing, we should say, is this.

THEAET. That's given, then.

Soc. Now think: when he hunts again for any one of the pieces   198
of knowledge that he chooses, and takes it and 'has' it, then lets it go again, what words are appropriate here? The same as before, when he took possession of the knowledge, or different ones?— You will see my point more clearly in this way. There is an art you call arithmetic, isn't there?

THEAET. Yes.

---

48. The Greek verb for 'I have' can mean not only 'I possess', but also 'I have it on' (e.g. an article of clothing) or 'I have hold of it'.

Soc. Now I want you to think of this as a hunt for pieces of knowledge concerning everything odd and even.

THEAET. All right, I will.

Soc. It is by virtue of this art, I suppose, that a man both has
b under his control pieces of knowledge concerning numbers and also hands them over to others?

THEAET. Yes.

Soc. And we call it 'teaching' when a man hands them over to others, and 'learning' when he gets them handed over to him; and when he 'has' them through possessing them in this aviary of ours, we call that 'knowing'.

THEAET. Yes, certainly.

Soc. Now you must give your attention to what is coming next. It must surely be true that a man who has completely mastered arithmetic knows all numbers? Because there are pieces of knowledge covering all numbers in his soul.

THEAET. Of course.

c Soc. And a man so trained may proceed to do some counting, either counting to himself the numbers themselves, or counting something else, one of the external things which have number?

THEAET. Yes, surely.

Soc. And counting we shall take to be simply a matter of considering how large a number actually is?

THEAET. Yes.

Soc. Then it looks as if this man were considering something which he knows as if he did not know it (for we have granted that he knows all numbers). I've no doubt you've had such puzzles put to you.

THEAET. I have, yes.

d Soc. Then using our image of possessing and hunting for the pigeons, we shall say that there are two phases of hunting: one before you have possession, in order to get possession, and another when you already possess in order to catch and have in your hands what you previously acquired. And in this way even with things you learned and got the knowledge of long ago and have known ever since, it is possible to learn them—these same things—all over again. You can take up again and 'have' that knowledge of each of them which you acquired long ago but had not ready to hand in your thought, can't you?

THEAET. True.

e Soc. Now this is what I meant by my question a moment ago. What terms ought we to use about them when we speak of what the arithmetician does when he proceeds to count, or the scholar when he proceeds to read something? Here, it seems, a man who knows something is setting out to learn again from himself things which he already knows.

THEAET. But that would be a very odd thing, Socrates.

Soc. But are we to say that it is things which he does not know that such a man is going to read and count—remembering that we *199* have granted him knowledge of all letters and all numbers?

THEAET. That wouldn't be reasonable, either.

Soc. Then would you like us to take this line? Suppose we say we do not mind at all about the names; let people drag around the terms 'knowing' and 'learning' to their heart's content. We have determined that to 'possess' knowledge is one thing and to 'have' it is another; accordingly we maintain that it is impossible for anyone not to possess that which he has possession of, and thus it never happens that he does not know something he knows. But he may yet make a false judgement about it. This is because it is possible for him to 'have', not the knowledge of this thing, but *b* another piece of knowledge instead. When he is hunting for one piece of knowledge, it may happen, as they fly about, that he makes a mistake and gets hold of one instead of another. It was this that happened when he thought eleven was twelve. He got hold of the knowledge of eleven that was in him, instead of the knowledge of twelve, as you might catch a ring-dove instead of a pigeon.

THEAET. Yes; that is reasonable, now.

Soc. But when he gets hold of the one he is trying to get hold of, then he is free from error; when he does that, he is judging what is. In this way, both true and false judgement exist; and the things that worried us before no longer stand in our way. I daresay you'll *c* agree with me? Or, if not, what line will you take?

THEAET. I agree.

Soc. Yes; we have now got rid of this 'not knowing what one knows'. For we now find that at no point does it happen that we do not possess what we possess, whether we are in error about anything or not. But it looks to me as if something else more alarming is by way of coming upon us.

THEAET. What's that?

Soc. I mean, what is involved if false judgement is going to become a matter of an interchange of pieces of knowledge.

THEAET. What do you mean?

Soc. To begin with, it follows that a man who has knowledge *d* of something is ignorant of this very thing not through want of knowledge but actually in virtue of his knowledge. Secondly, he judges that this is something else and that the other thing is it. Now surely this is utterly unreasonable; it means that the soul, when knowledge becomes present to it, knows nothing and is wholly ignorant. According to this argument, there is no reason why an accession of ignorance should not make one know something, or of blindness make one see something, if knowledge is ever going to make a man ignorant.

e   THEAET. Well, perhaps, Socrates, it wasn't a happy thought to make the birds only pieces of knowledge. Perhaps we ought to have supposed that there are pieces of ignorance also flying about in the soul along with them, and what happens is that the hunter sometimes catches a piece of knowledge and sometimes a piece of ignorance concerning the same thing; and the ignorance makes him judge falsely, while the knowledge makes him judge truly.

Soc. I can hardly refrain from expressing my admiration of you, Theaetetus; but do think again about that. Let us suppose it is as you say: then, you maintain, the man who catches a piece of igno-
200   rance will judge falsely. Is that it?

THEAET. Yes.

Soc. But presumably he will not think he is judging falsely?

THEAET. No, of course he won't.

Soc. He will think he is judging what is true; and his attitude towards the things about which he is in error will be as if he knew them.

THEAET. Of course.

Soc. He will think he has hunted down and 'has' a piece of knowledge and not a piece of ignorance.

THEAET. Yes, that's clear.

Soc. So, after going a long way round, we are back at our original difficulty. Our friend the expert in refutation will laugh. 'My very
b   good people,' he will say, 'do you mean that a man who knows both knowledge and ignorance is thinking that one of them which he knows is the other which he knows? Or is it that he knows neither, and judges the one he doesn't know to be the other which he doesn't know? Or is it that he knows one and not the other, and judges that the one he knows is the one he doesn't know? Or does he think that the one he doesn't know is the one he does? Or are you going to start all over again and tell me that there's another set of pieces of knowledge concerning pieces of knowledge and ignorance, which a man may possess shut up in some other ridicu-
c   lous aviaries or waxen devices, which he knows so long as he

possesses them though he may not have them ready to hand in his soul—and in this way end up forced to come running round to the same place over and over again and never get any further?' What are we going to say to that, Theaetetus?

THEAET. Oh, dear me, Socrates, I don't know what one ought to say.

Soc. Then don't you think, my boy, that the argument is perhaps dealing out a little proper chastisement, and showing us that we were wrong to leave the question about knowledge and proceed to enquire into false judgement first? While as a matter of fact it's   *d* impossible to know this until we have an adequate grasp of what knowledge is.

THEAET. Well, at the moment, Socrates, I feel bound to believe you.

Soc. Then, to go back to the beginning, what are we going to say knowledge is?—We are not, I suppose, going to give up yet?

THEAET. Certainly not, unless you give up yourself.

Soc. Tell me, then, how could we define it with the least risk of contradicting ourselves?

THEAET. In the way we were attempting before, Socrates; I can't   *e* think of any other.

Soc. In what way do you mean?

THEAET. By saying that knowledge is true judgement. Judging truly is at least something free of mistakes, I take it, and everything that results from it is admirable and good.

Soc. Well, Theaetetus, as the man who was leading the way across the river said, 'It will show you.'[49] If we go on and track this down, perhaps we may stumble on what we are looking for; if we   *201* stay where we are, nothing will come clear.

THEAET. You're right; let's go on and consider it.

Soc. Well, this won't take long to consider, anyway; there is a whole art indicating to you that knowledge is not what you say.

THEAET. How's that? What art do you mean?

Soc. The art of the greatest representatives of wisdom— the men called orators and lawyers. These men, I take it, use their art to produce conviction not by teaching people, but by making them judge whatever they themselves choose. Or do you think there are

---

49. According to the scholiast the story was: some travellers came to the bank of a river, which they wished to cross at the ford; one of them asked the guide, 'Is the water deep?' He said, 'It will show you', i.e. don't ask the guide, you must try it for yourself.

any teachers so clever that within the short time allowed by the
b   clock they can teach adequately the truth of what happened to
people who have been robbed or assaulted, in a case where there
were no eye-witnesses?

THEAET. No, I don't think they possibly could; but they might
be able to *persuade* them.

Soc. And by 'persuading them', you mean 'causing them to
judge', don't you?

THEAET. Of course.

Soc. Then suppose a jury has been justly persuaded of some
matter which only an eye-witness could know, and which cannot
otherwise be known; suppose they come to their decision upon
c   hearsay, forming a true judgement: then they have decided the
case without knowledge, but, granted they did their job well, being
correctly persuaded?

THEAET. Yes, certainly.

Soc. But, my dear lad, they couldn't have done that if true judgement is the same thing as knowledge; in that case the best juryman
in the world couldn't form a correct judgement without knowledge.
So it seems they must be different things.

THEAET. Oh, yes, Socrates, that's just what I once heard a man
say; I had forgotten, but now it's coming back to me. He said
d   that it is true judgement with an account[50] that is knowledge; true
judgement without an account falls outside of knowledge. And he
said that the things of which there is no account are not knowable
(yes, he actually called them that),[51] while those which have an
account are knowable.

Soc. Very good indeed. Now tell me, how did he distinguish
these knowables and unknowables? I want to see if you and I have
heard the same version.

THEAET. I don't know if I can find that out; but I think I could
follow if someone explained it.

Soc. Listen then to a dream in return for a dream. In my dream,
e   too, I thought I was listening to people saying that the primary
elements, as it were, of which we and everything else are composed, have no account. Each of them, in itself, can only be named;

---

50. 'Account' translates *logos*, on which see Introduction, p. 134.

51. The parenthesis may alternatively be translated: '(that was the word he used)'.
The translation in the text expresses surprise about the claim that some things are
not knowable at all. The alternative translation calls attention to the particular Greek
word used for 'knowable'.

it is not possible to say anything else of it, either that it is[52] or that
it is not. That would mean that we were adding being or not-being   *202*
to it; whereas we must not attach anything, if we are to speak of
that thing itself alone. Indeed we ought not to apply to it even such
words as 'itself' or 'that', 'each', 'alone', or 'this', or any other of
the many words of this kind; for these go the round and are applied
to all things alike, being other than the things to which they are
added, whereas if it were possible to express the element itself and
it had its own proprietary account, it would have to be expressed
without any other thing. As it is, however, it is impossible that any
of the primaries should be expressed in an account; it can only be   *b*
named, for a name is all that it has. But with the things composed
of these, it is another matter. Here, just in the same way as the
elements themselves are woven together, so their names may be
woven together and become an account of something—an account
being essentially a complex[53] of names. Thus the elements are unaccountable and unknowable, but they are perceivable, whereas the
complexes are both knowable and expressible and can be the objects
of true judgement.

Now when a man gets a true judgement about something without
an account, his soul is in a state of truth as regards that thing, but   *c*
he does not know it; for someone who cannot give and take an
account of a thing is ignorant about it. But when he has also got an
account of it, he is capable of all this and is made perfect in knowledge. Was the dream you heard the same as this or a different one?

THEAET. No, it was the same in every respect.

SOC. Do you like this then, and do you suggest that knowledge
is true judgement with an account?

THEAET. Yes, certainly.

SOC. Theaetetus, can it be that all in a moment, you and I have   *d*
today laid hands upon something which many a wise man has
searched for in the past—and gone grey before he found it?

---

52. The translation is intended to leave it unclear, as the original is unclear, whether
'anything else' refers here to the statement that it is, or to anything it might be said
to be. The two construals come to much the same if the first is understood, as it
probably ought to be, not as the statement that it exists, but as the incomplete initial
portion of a statement saying that it is something or other. The whole sentence could
then be printed thus: 'it is not possible to say anything else of it, either that it is . . .
or that it is not . . .'.

53. Literally, 'a weaving together'—the Greek noun *sumplokē*, like the English word
'complex' itself, is related to the verb translated 'woven together' in the previous
two lines.

THEAET. Well, it does seem to me anyway, Socrates, that what has just been said puts the matter very well.

Soc. And it seems likely enough that the matter is really so; for what knowledge could there be apart from an account and correct judgement? But there is one of the things said which I don't like.

THEAET. And what's that?

Soc. What looks like the subtlest point of all—that the elements *e* are unknowable and the complexes knowable.

THEAET. And won't that do?

Soc. We must make sure; because, you see, we do have as hostages for this theory the original models that were used when all these statements were made.

THEAET. What models?

Soc. Letters—the elements of language—and syllables.[54] It must have been these, mustn't it, that the author of our theory had in view—it couldn't have been anything else?

THEAET. No, he must have been thinking of letters and syllables.

203   Soc. Let's take and examine them then. Or rather let us examine ourselves, and ask ourselves whether we really learned our letters in this way or not. Now, to begin with, one can give an account of the syllables but not of the letters—is that it?

THEAET. Well, perhaps.

Soc. It most certainly looks like that to me. At any rate, supposing you were asked about the first syllable of 'Socrates': 'Tell me, Theaetetus, what is SO?' What would you answer to that?

THEAET. That it's S and O.[55]

Soc. And there you have an account of the syllable?

THEAET. Yes.

b   Soc. Come along then, and let us have the account of S in the same way.

THEAET. How *can* anyone give the letters of a letter? S is just one

54. The Greek words used in a general sense for 'elements' and 'complexes' are also regularly used for 'letters' and 'syllables'. Thus one word, *stoicheion*, is translated 'element' when the context is general (as above, 201e) and 'letter' when the reference is to linguistic elements; and one word, *sullabē*, is translated 'complex' when the context is general (as above, 202b) and 'syllable' when the reference is to complexes of letters. A third word, *grammata*, meaning 'letters' or language in general, is used here and at 203a, 204a, 206a, 207de, to specify when 'element' and 'complex' are to be taken linguistically and when generally.

'Letter' must be understood throughout the discussion as covering both written letters and the sounds (phonemes) which written letters represent.

55. Theaetetus actually says, 'That it's sigma and omega', using the names of the *Greek* letters in Socrates' name.

of the voiceless letters, Socrates, a mere sound like a hissing of the tongue. B again has neither voice nor sound, and that's true of most letters. So the statement that they themselves are unaccountable holds perfectly good. Even the seven clearest have only voice; no sort of account whatever can be given of them.[56]

Soc. So here, my friend, we have established a point about knowledge.

Theaet. We do appear to have done so.

Soc. Well then: we have shown that the syllable is knowable but   *c*
not the letter—is that all right?

Theaet. It seems the natural conclusion, anyway.

Soc. Look here, what do we mean by 'the syllable'? The two letters (or if there are more, all the letters)? Or do we mean some single form produced by their combination?

Theaet. I think we mean all the letters.

Soc. Then take the case of the two letters, S and O; these two are the first syllable of my name. If a man knows the syllable, he must know both the letters?

Theaet. Of course.   *d*

Soc. So he knows S and O.

Theaet. Yes.

Soc. But can it be that he is ignorant of each one, and knows the two of them without knowing either?

Theaet. That would be a strange and unaccountable thing, Socrates.

Soc. And yet, supposing it is necessary to know each in order to know both, then it is absolutely necessary that anyone who is ever to know a syllable must first get to know the letters. And in admitting this, we shall find that our beautiful theory has taken to its heels and got clean away from us.

Theaet. And very suddenly too.   *e*

Soc. Yes; we are not keeping a proper watch on it. Perhaps we ought not to have supposed the syllable to be the letters; perhaps we ought to have made it some single form produced out of them, having its own single nature—something different from the letters.

Theaet. Yes, certainly; that might be more like it.

Soc. We must look into the matter; we have no right to betray a great and imposing theory in this faint-hearted manner.

---

56. The 'seven' are the seven vowels of ancient Greek, as contrasted with two classes of consonant: mutes like B, which cannot be pronounced without a vowel, and semivowels like S, which can.

THEAET. Certainly not.

204   Soc. Then let it be as we are now suggesting. Let the complex be a single form resulting from the combination of the several elements when they fit together; and let this hold both of language and of things in general.

THEAET. Yes, certainly.

Soc. Then it must have no parts.

THEAET. Why is that, now?

Soc. Because when a thing has parts, the whole is necessarily all the parts. Or do you mean by 'the whole' also a single form arising out of the parts, yet different from all the parts?

THEAET. I do.

Soc. Now do you call 'sum'[57] and 'whole' the same thing or
b   different things?

THEAET. I don't feel at all certain; but as you keep telling me to answer up with a good will, I will take a risk and say they are different.

Soc. Your good will, Theaetetus, is all that it should be. Now we must see if your answer is too.

THEAET. We must, of course.

Soc. As the argument stands at present, the whole will be different from the sum?

THEAET. Yes.

Soc. Well now, is there any difference between all the things and the sum? For instance, when we say 'one, two, three, four,
c   five, six'; or, 'twice three', or 'three times two', 'four and two', 'three and two and one'; are we speaking of the same thing in all these cases or different things?

THEAET. The same thing.

Soc. That is, six?

THEAET. Precisely.

Soc. Then with each expression have we not spoken of all the six?

THEAET. Yes.

Soc. And when we speak of them all, aren't we speaking of a sum?

THEAET. We must be.

Soc. That is, six?

THEAET. Precisely.

---

57. The word translated 'sum' (*pan*) and the word translated 'all' (*panta*) in the phrase 'all the parts' are singular and plural forms of the same Greek word.

Soc. Then in all things made up of number, at any rate, by 'the   *d*
sum' and 'all of them' we mean the same thing?

Theaet. So it seems.

Soc. Now let us talk about them in this way. The number of an
acre is the same thing as an acre, isn't it?

Theaet. Yes.

Soc. Similarly with a mile.

Theaet. Yes.

Soc. And the number of an army is the same as the army? And
so always with things of this sort; their total number is the sum that
each of them is.

Theaet. Yes.

Soc. But is the number of each anything other than its parts?   *e*

Theaet. No.

Soc. Now things which have parts consist of parts?

Theaet. That seems true.

Soc. And it is agreed that all the parts are the sum, seeing that
the total number is to be the sum.

Theaet. That is so.

Soc. Then the whole does not consist of parts. For if it did, it
would be all the parts and so would be a sum.

Theaet. It looks as if it doesn't.

Soc. But can a part, as such, be a part of anything but the whole?

Theaet. Yes; of the sum.

Soc. You are putting up a good fight anyway, Theaetetus. But   *205*
this sum now—isn't it just when there is nothing lacking that it is
a sum?

Theaet. Yes, necessarily.

Soc. And won't this very same thing—that from which nothing
anywhere is lacking—be a whole? While a thing from which something is absent is neither a whole nor a sum—the same consequence
having followed from the same condition in both cases at once?

Theaet. Well, it doesn't seem to me now that there can be any
difference between whole and sum.

Soc. Very well. Now were we not saying[58] that in the case of a
thing that has parts, both the whole and the sum will be all the
parts?

Theaet. Yes, certainly.

Soc. Now come back to the thing I was trying to get at just now.
Supposing the syllable is not just its letters, doesn't it follow that it   *b*

58. At 204a.

cannot contain the letters as parts of itself? Alternatively, if it is the same as the letters, it must be equally knowable with them?

THEAET. That is so.

Soc. Well, wasn't it just in order to avoid this result that we supposed it different from the letters?

THEAET. Yes.

Soc. Well then, if the letters are not parts of the syllable, can you tell me of any other things, not its letters, which are?

THEAET. No, indeed. If I were to admit that it had component parts, Socrates, it would be ridiculous, of course, to set aside the letters and look for other components.

c   Soc. Then, Theaetetus, according to our present argument, a syllable is an absolutely single form, indivisible into parts.

THEAET. It looks like it.

Soc. Now, my friend, a little while ago, if you remember, we were inclined to accept a certain proposition which we thought put the matter very well—I mean the statement that no account can be given of the primaries of which other things are constituted, because each of them is in itself incomposite; and that it would be incorrect to apply even the term 'being' to it when we spoke of it or the term 'this', because these terms signify different and alien things; and that is the reason why a primary is an unaccountable and unknowable thing. Do you remember?

THEAET. I remember.

d   Soc. And is that the reason also why it is single in form and indivisible into parts or is there some other reason for that? I can see no other myself.

THEAET. No, there really doesn't seem to be any other.

Soc. And hasn't the complex now fallen into the same class as the primary, seeing it has no parts and is a single form?

THEAET. Yes, it certainly has.

Soc. Well now, if the complex is both many elements and a whole, with them as its parts, then both complexes and elements are equally capable of being known and expressed, since all the parts turned out to be the same thing as the whole.

e   THEAET. Yes, surely.

Soc. But if, on the other hand, the complex is single and without parts, then complexes and elements are equally unaccountable and unknowable—both of them for the same reason.

THEAET. I can't dispute that.

Soc. Then if anyone tries to tell us that the complex can be known and expressed, while the contrary is true of the element, we had better not listen to him.

THEAET. No, we'd better not, if we go along with the argument.

Soc. And, more than this, wouldn't you more easily believe   *206*
somebody who made the contrary statement, because of what you
know of your own experience in learning to read and write?

THEAET. What kind of thing do you mean?

Soc. I mean that when you were learning you spent your time
just precisely in trying to distinguish, by both eye and ear, each
individual letter in itself so that you might not be bewildered by
their different positions in written and spoken words.

THEAET. That's perfectly true.

Soc. And at the music-teacher's, wasn't the finished pupil the one
who could follow each note and tell to which string it belonged—the   *b*
notes being generally admitted to be the elements in music?

THEAET. Yes, that's just what it amounted to.

Soc. Then if the proper procedure is to take such elements and
complexes as we ourselves have experience of, and make an inference from them to the rest, we shall say that the elements are much
more clearly known, and the knowledge of them is more decisive
for the mastery of any branch of study than knowledge of the
complex. And if anyone maintains that the complex is by nature
knowable, and the element unknowable, we shall regard this as
tomfoolery, whether it is intended to be or not.

THEAET. Oh, quite.

Soc. I think that might be proved in other ways too. But we   *c*
mustn't let them distract us from the problem before us. We wanted
to see what can be meant by the proposition that it is in the addition
of an account to a true judgement that knowledge is perfected.

THEAET. Well yes, we must try to see that.

Soc. Come then, what are we intended to understand by an
'account'? I think it must be one of three meanings.

THEAET. What are they?

Soc. The first would be, making one's thought apparent vocally   *d*
by means of words and verbal expressions—when a man impresses
an image of his judgement upon the stream of speech, like reflections upon water or in a mirror. Don't you think this kind of thing
is an account?

THEAET. Yes, I do. At least, a man who does this is said to be
giving an account.[59]

Soc. But isn't that a thing that everyone is able to do more or

---

59. 'Giving an account' here translates *legein*, the ordinary Greek word for 'say,
speak, speak of', which corresponds to *logos* in its wider meanings 'speech, discourse, statement'.

less readily—I mean, indicate what he thinks about a thing, if he is
not deaf or dumb to begin with? And that being so, anyone at all
e   who makes a correct judgement will turn out to have it 'together
with an account'; correct judgement without knowledge will no
longer be found anywhere.

THEAET. True.

Soc. Well then, we mustn't be too ready to condemn the author
of the definition of knowledge now before us for talking nonsense.
Perhaps he didn't mean this; perhaps he meant being able, when
207   questioned about what a thing is, to give an answer by reference
to its elements.

THEAET. As for example, Socrates?

Soc. As for example, what Hesiod is doing when he says 'One
hundred are the timbers of a wagon.'[60] Now I couldn't say what
they are; and I don't suppose you could either. If you and I were
asked what a wagon is, we should be satisfied if we could answer,
'Wheels, axle, body, rails, yoke.'

THEAET. Yes, surely.

Soc. But he might think us ridiculous, just as he would if we
were asked what your name is, and replied by giving the syllables.
In that case, he would think us ridiculous because although we
b   might be correct in our judgement and our expression of it, we
should be fancying ourselves as scholars, thinking we knew and
were expressing a scholar's account of Theaetetus' name. Whereas
in fact no one gives an account of a thing with knowledge till, in
addition to his true judgement, he goes right through the thing
element by element—as I think we said before.

THEAET. We did, yes.

Soc. In the same way, in the example of the wagon, he would
say that we have indeed correct judgement; but it is the man who
c   can explore its being by going through those hundred items who
has made the addition which adds an account to his true judgement.
It is this man who has passed from mere judgement to expert
knowledge of the being of a wagon; and he has done so in virtue
of having gone over the whole by means of the elements.

THEAET. And doesn't that seem sound to you, Socrates?

Soc. Well, tell me if it seems sound to you, my friend. Tell me
if you are prepared to accept the view that an account is a matter
of going through a thing element by element, while going through
it by 'syllables' or larger divisions falls short of being an account.
d   Then we shall be able to discuss it.

60. Hesiod, *Works and Days* 456.

THEAET. I'm certainly prepared to accept that.

Soc. And do you at the same time think that a man has knowledge of anything when he believes the same thing now to be part of one thing and now part of something else? Or when he judges that now one thing and now something different belongs to one and the same object?

THEAET. No, indeed I don't.

Soc. Then have you forgotten that at first when you were learning to read and write that is just what you and the other boys used to do?

THEAET. You mean we used to think that sometimes one letter and sometimes another belonged to the same syllable, and used to put the same letter sometimes into its proper syllable and sometimes into another?   *e*

Soc. Yes, that is what I mean.

THEAET. Well, I certainly haven't forgotten; and I don't think people at that stage can be said to have knowledge yet.

Soc. Well, suppose now that someone who is at this sort of stage is writing the name 'Theaetetus'; he thinks he ought to write THE and does so.[61] Then suppose another time he is trying to write 'Theodorus', and this time he thinks he should write TE and pro-   *208* ceeds to do so. Are we going to say that he knows the first syllable of your names?

THEAET. No. We've admitted that anyone who is at that stage has not yet knowledge.

Soc. And is there anything to prevent the same person being in that situation as regards the second and third and fourth syllables?

THEAET. No, nothing.

Soc. Now at the time when he does this, he will be writing 'Theaetetus' not only with correct judgement, but with command of the way through its letters; that must be so whenever he writes them out one after another in their order.

THEAET. Yes, clearly.

Soc. And still without knowledge though with correct judge-   *b* ment—isn't that our view?

THEAET. Yes.

Soc. Yet possessing an account of it along with his correct judgement. He was writing it, you see, with command of the way through its letters; and we agreed that that is an account.

61. Socrates actually says, 'he thinks he ought to write theta and epsilon', using the names of the *Greek* letters in the first syllable of Theaetetus' name. There are only two such letters because Greek represents the sound of TH by the single letter theta.

THEAET. True.

Soc. So here, my friend, we have correct judgement together with an account, which we are not yet entitled to call knowledge.

THEAET. Yes, I'm afraid that's so.

Soc. So it was only the poor man's dream of gold that we had when we thought we had got the truest account of knowledge. Or is it early days to be harsh? Perhaps this is not the way in which
c one is to define 'account'. We said that the man who defines knowledge as correct judgement together with an account would choose one of three meanings for 'account'. Perhaps the last is the one to define it by.

THEAET. Yes, you're right to remind me; there is one possibility still left. The first was, a kind of vocal image of thought; the one we have just discussed was the way to the whole through the elements. Now what's your third suggestion?

Soc. What the majority of people would say—namely, being able to tell some mark by which the object you are asked about differs from all other things.

THEAET. Can you give me an example of such an 'account' of something?

d Soc. Well, take the sun, if you like. You would be satisfied, I imagine, with the answer that it is the brightest of the bodies that move round the earth in the heavens.

THEAET. Oh yes, quite.

Soc. Now I want you to get hold of the principle that this illustrates. It is what we were just saying—that if you get hold of the difference that distinguishes a thing from everything else, then, so some people say, you will have got an account of it. On the other hand, so long as it is some common feature that you grasp, your account will be about all those things which have this in common.

e THEAET. I see; I think it's very good to call this kind of thing an account.

Soc. Then if a man with correct judgement about any one of the things that are grasps in addition its difference from the rest, he has become a knower of the thing he was a judger of before.

THEAET. That's our present position, anyway.

Soc. Well, at this point, Theaetetus, as regards what we are saying, I'm for all the world like a man looking at a shadow-painting;[62]

Moreover, this sound was a plosive (as in English *fathead*), rather than a fricative (as in English *thin*), and so easy enough to confuse with TE.

62. The pictorial technique referred to (*skiagraphia*) seems to have been one which depended on contrasts between light and shade to create the appearance of form

when I'm close up to it I can't take it in in the least, though when I stood well back from it, it appeared to me to have some meaning.

THEAET. How's that?

Soc. I'll see if I can explain. Suppose I have formed a correct   *209* judgement about you; if I can grasp your account in addition, I know you, but if not, I am merely judging.

THEAET. Yes.

Soc. And an account was to be a matter of expounding your differentness?

THEAET. That is so.

Soc. Then when I was merely judging, my thought failed to grasp any point of difference between you and the rest of mankind?

THEAET. Apparently.

Soc. What I had in mind, it seems, was some common characteristic—something that belongs no more to you than to anybody else.

THEAET. Yes, that must be so.   *b*

Soc. Then tell me, in Heaven's name how, if that was so, did it come about that you were the object of my judgement and nobody else? Suppose my thought is that 'This is Theaetetus—one who is a human being, and has a nose and eyes and mouth', and so on through the whole list of limbs. Will this thought cause me to be thinking of Theaetetus rather than of Theodorus, or of the proverbial 'remotest Mysian'?

THEAET. No, how could it?

Soc. But suppose I think not merely of 'the one with nose and eyes', but of 'the one with a snub nose and prominent eyes'. Shall   *c* I even then be judging about you any more than about myself or anyone who is like that?

THEAET. Not at all.

Soc. It will not, I take it, be Theaetetus who is judged in my mind until this snub-nosedness of yours has left imprinted and established in me a record that is different in some way from the other snub-nosednesses I have seen; and so with the other details of your make-up. And this will remind me, if I meet you to-morrow, and make me judge correctly about you.

THEAET. That's perfectly true.

Soc. Then correct judgement also must be concerned with the   *d* differentness of what it is about?

THEAET. So it seems, anyway.

Soc. Then what more might this 'adding an account to correct

---

and volume. A more familiar comparison for modern readers would be a pointilliste painting by Seurat.

judgement' be? If, on the one hand, it means that we must make another judgement about the way in which a thing differs from the rest of things, we are being required to do something very absurd.

THEAET. How's that?

Soc. Because we already have a correct judgement about the way a thing differs from other things; and we are then directed to add a correct judgement about the way it differs from other things. At that rate, the way a roller goes round or a pestle or anything else

e　proverbial would be nothing compared with such directions; they might be more justly called a matter of 'the blind leading the blind'. To tell us to add what we already have, in order to come to know what we are judging about, bears a generous resemblance to the behaviour of a man benighted.

THEAET. Whereas if, on the other hand, . . . ? What else were you going to suggest when you started this enquiry just now?

Soc. Well, if 'adding an account' means that we are required to get to *know* the differentness, not merely judge it, this most splendid of our accounts of knowledge turns out to be a very amusing affair.

210　For getting to know of course is acquiring knowledge, isn't it?

THEAET. Yes.

Soc. So, it seems, the answer to the question 'What is knowledge?' will be 'Correct judgement accompanied by *knowledge* of the differentness'—for this is what we are asked to understand by the 'addition of an account'.

THEAET. Apparently so.

Soc. And it is surely just silly to tell us, when we are trying to discover what knowledge is, that it is correct judgement accompanied by *knowledge*, whether of differentness or of anything else? And so, Theaetetus, knowledge is neither perception nor true

b　judgement, nor an account added to true judgement.

THEAET. It seems not.

Soc. Well now, dear lad, are we still pregnant, still in labour with any thoughts about knowledge? Or have we been delivered of them all?

THEAET. As far as I'm concerned, Socrates, you've made me say far more than ever was in me, Heaven knows.

Soc. Well then, our art of midwifery tells us that all of these offspring are wind-eggs and not worth bringing up?

THEAET. Undoubtedly.

Soc. And so, Theaetetus, if ever in the future you should attempt

c　to conceive or should succeed in conceiving other theories, they will be better ones as the result of this enquiry. And if you remain barren, your companions will find you gentler and less tiresome; you will be modest and not think you know what you don't know. This is all my art can achieve—nothing more. I do not know any of the things that other men know—the great and inspired men of to-day and yesterday. But this art of midwifery my mother and I had allotted to us by God; she to deliver women, I to deliver men that are young and generous of spirit, all that have any beauty. And *d* now I must go to the King's Porch to meet the indictment that Meletus has brought against me; but let us meet here again in the morning, Theodorus.

Myles Burnyeat is Laurence Professor of Ancient Philosophy at Cambridge University and Fellow of Robinson College, Cambridge. After National Service in the Royal Navy, during which he became a Russian interpreter, he studied Classics and Philosophy at King's College, Cambridge. He taught for fourteen years in the Philosophy Department at University College London, then returned to Cambridge to teach in the Faculty of Classics. He has held visiting appointments at the Universities of California at Berkeley and Los Angeles, and at Cornell, Harvard, Princeton, and the University of Pittsburgh.